Windows® XP

Tips & Techniques

About the Authors

Walter Glenn is the author or co-author of 14 books, including *Windows 98 in a Nutshell* (O'Reilly & Associates, 1999) and *How to Use Windows XP* (Sams, 2001). He has been working in the computer industry for 15 years, starting as a computer technician and moving to network administration and engineering. He holds several industry certifications, including Microsoft Certified Systems Engineer (MCSE) and Microsoft Certified Trainer (MCT). Currently, he is president of Glenn & Associates, where he provides network administration and technical support for medium-sized enterprise organizations. Glenn lives with his family in Huntsville, Alabama.

Rowena White is a Web application developer, writer, and graphic artist. Having been a writer for more than 20 years, she has authored more than 50 technical references and 30-plus articles for numerous computer books and art magazines. When she's not writing and raising her children, White operates a successful e-commerce business and airbrushes wildlife portraits, many of which have been donated to local zoos and wildlife parks. White lives with her family of five in the outskirts of Seattle.

About the Technical Editor

Diane Poremsky is a consultant who specializes in Microsoft Windows, Outlook, and Office training and development. She is a Microsoft Outlook MVP (Most Valuable Professional), in recognition for her technical support of Microsoft Outlook. She is a technical editor for a number of computer books and is a columnist, author, and technical reviewer for *Exchange and Outlook* magazine. Poremsky currently resides in East Tennessee with her family.

Windows® XP

Tips & Techniques

Walter Glenn
Rowena White

McGraw-Hill/Osborne

New York   Chicago   San Francisco
Lisbon   London   Madrid   Mexico City
Milan   New Delhi   San Juan
Seoul   Singapore   Sydney   Toronto

McGraw-Hill/Osborne
2600 Tenth Street
Berkeley, California 94710
U.S.A.

To arrange bulk purchase discounts for sales promotions, premiums, or fund-raisers, please contact
McGraw-Hill/Osborne at the above address. For information on translations or book distributors outside the
U.S.A., please see the International Contact Information page immediately following the index of this book.

Windows® XP Tips & Techniques

1234567890 FGR FGR 0198765432

ISBN 0-07-222334-0

Publisher	Brandon A. Nordin
Vice President &	
Associate Publisher	Scott Rogers
Acquisitions Editor	Margie McAneny
Project Editor	Patty Mon
Acquisitions Coordinator	Tana Diminyatz
Technical Editor	Dana Poremsky
Copy Editors	Lisa Theobald, Lunaea Weatherstone
Proofreader	Stefany Otis
Indexer	Irv Hershman
Computer Designers	Carie Abrew, Lucie Ericksen
Illustrators	Michael Mueller, Lyssa Wald
Series Design	Roberta Steele
Cover Series Design	Greg Scott

This book was composed with Corel VENTURA™ Publisher.

Contents at a Glance

Contents

Acknowledgments

As is always the case, this book could not have happened without the help of a number of people. Foremost, thanks go to my co-author, Rowena White, for working so hard to get this book out on time. Thanks also to Margie McAneny, our acquisitions editor, for giving us the chance to work on the book in the first place, for keeping everything on track, and for understanding when it occasionally went off track.

We'd also like to thank Diane Poremsky, our technical editor, who provided a wonderful review of the material.

And as always, thanks to the folks at Studio B, particularly Neil Salkind, for helping to put this project together.

—Walter

My appreciation honors both Walter Glenn and Margie McAneny for the amount of trust they gave me when I signed on to this project. Their support and understanding are immeasurable. In all of my 20-plus years of writing, I have never worked with a more professional team of individuals. Tana Diminyatz, our acquisitions coordinator, held this project together with grace and delightful charm. Her positive attitude and uplifting personality encouraged me beyond compare. The editing team of Diane Poremsky, Patty Mon, Lisa Theobald, and Lunaea Weatherstone were patient, thorough, and extremely valuable to the quality of this book. Thank you all for your hard work and dedication to this project.

—Rowena

Introduction

Windows XP is the latest in a long line of Windows operating systems. Arguably, it the fastest and most stable version of Windows yet. Windows XP is built on the Windows NT model and shares much more with Windows NT and Windows 2000 than it does with Windows 95 or Windows 98. The designers of Windows have taken great pains to simplify the interface and keep some of the complexities of the operating system from jumping out and scaring new users. This means that a lot of untapped power lies under the surface, just waiting for you to find it.

Who Should Read This Book

This book is intended for people who already have a pretty good idea of how to use Windows, and therefore it does not spend much time explaining basic concepts. This book should be most valuable to people who are comfortable with Windows and want to take their understanding to the next level. It should also serve as a valuable reference, as it is logically broken down into specific tasks.

What This Book Covers

This book contains 27 chapters, each of which focuses on a specific aspect of using Windows XP. Within each chapter, you'll find ways to improve the way you use Windows and the way that Windows responds to you.

Part I of the book, "Installation and Setup," introduces the reader to the new features of Windows XP and describes the installation of Windows XP. In addition, this part addresses the installation and removal of Windows components, hardware, and applications that will occur following the initial Windows installation.

Part II, "Windows Basics," covers the basic aspects of using Windows XP, including using the new desktop interface, working with the file system, and printing. This part also covers logging on and off, shutting Windows down using various modes, and using the new Fast User Switching feature.

Part III, "Networking," covers Windows XP networking. It introduces the basics of Windows networking, as well as how to set up and configure connections. This part also examines various networking tasks, such as sharing resources and working when not connected to a network.

Part IV, "Internet," covers the Internet features built into Windows XP. Readers will learn how to get Windows connected to the Internet (including a discussion of sharing connections among multiple computers) and learn many tips and techniques for using Internet Explorer, Outlook Express, and the new MSN tools: MSN Explorer and MSN Messenger.

Part V, "Having Fun," covers the lighter aspects of using Windows XP, including tools for managing graphics, Windows Media Player and Movie Maker, and the many games that come with Windows XP. Readers will learn to scan, edit, print, and share photos. They will also learn to use Media Player to listen to music, watch movies, and create CDs.

Part VI, "Customizing Windows," looks at the many ways readers can customize Windows to better suit their needs. This part begins with a look at changing Desktop themes, screen savers, and display settings. This part also includes tips for configuring hardware, using hardware profiles, managing advanced Windows settings (such as startup and environmental variables), and even editing the Windows Registry.

Finally, Part VII, "Maintenance and Performance," provides tips and techniques for keeping a computer running Windows XP in top shape. This part covers backing up Windows, using the disk management and administrative tools included with Windows, and scheduling management tasks to occur automatically. This part also introduces the reader to troubleshooting concepts that target the various areas in which Windows can fail, including application problems, hardware problems, and other system failures. Finally, this part examines methods for improving the overall performance of Windows and for monitoring different aspects of system performance.

How to Read This Book

This book is designed to be read in a number of ways. Obviously, you could sit down and read the book cover to cover and learn all sorts of wonderful techniques for getting the most out of Windows XP. However, the information in any given chapter does not rely on knowing information from previous chapters. If you are interested in exploring a particular part of Windows XP, such as tuning performance or customizing the Desktop, then by all means jump straight to that chapter and start reading. If you need to accomplish a specific task, you can find it in the text, read about it, and get back to work. Hopefully, you will find that this book answers a lot of questions you may already have about Windows XP. We hope that it will serve as a good reference in the future for questions you may not yet have.

PART I

Installation and Setup

CHAPTER 1

Windows XP:
New Features and Installation

TIPS IN THIS CHAPTER

et's face it. Windows XP has some pretty big shoes to fill. It needs to offer the stability that users of Windows NT and Windows 2000 have enjoyed for years. It needs to offer the ease of use and support for a wide variety of hardware that users of Windows 98 and Windows Me are accustomed to. It also needs to offer new features, be faster than its predecessors, and preferably not require anyone to upgrade their computers to run it.

Obviously, no new version of Windows can give everyone exactly what they want. Believe it or not, though, Windows XP comes pretty close. Although Windows is a complex system, it is still fairly easy to install, configure, and start using. How far you take it is up to you.

This chapter introduces you to the new features offered by Windows XP and to the many choices you can make during the Windows XP installation process.

Introducing Windows XP

Windows XP is the answer to a long-standing goal at Microsoft: to unify the different versions of Windows under a single product line. Until the release of Windows XP, Windows has existed as two distinct series of products: the Windows 9x family and the Windows NT family.

The Windows 9x family, which includes Windows 95, Windows 98, Windows 98 Second Edition, and Windows Me, is intended primarily for home users. These versions of the Windows operating system have been designed to support maximum compatibility with available hardware and software.

The Windows NT family, which includes Windows NT, Windows 2000, and now Windows XP, was originally intended for business users. These operating systems have been designed for maximum stability and, as a result, experience fewer crashes and other problems than their Windows 9x counterparts. However, earlier Windows NT versions often sacrificed hardware and software compatibility to achieve this goal. Windows 2000 was the first member of the Windows NT family to provide both stability and wide-reaching support for existing hardware and software.

Windows XP, the latest member of the Windows NT family, is actually an upgrade to both the Windows 9x and Windows NT line of products. Windows XP is offered in three editions:

- Windows XP Home Edition, which is intended for home and small business users. This edition effectively replaces the Windows 9x product line. Users of Windows 98, Windows 98 Second Edition, and Windows Me are eligible to upgrade directly to Windows XP Home Edition. Other operating systems, including Windows 95, cannot directly upgrade to Windows XP Home Edition.

- Windows XP Professional Edition, which is intended for business users and advanced home users. This edition is a direct successor to Windows 2000 Professional. Users of Windows 98, Windows 98 Second Edition, Windows Me, Windows NT 4.0, Windows 2000 Professional, and Windows XP Home Edition are eligible to upgrade directly to Windows XP Professional.

- Windows XP 64-bit Edition, which supports the new Intel Itanium 64-bit processor. This edition is intended for users of advanced workstations and ships only with computers that include the new processor.

▶ *NOTE*

This book focuses on the Windows XP Home and Professional Editions. For the most part, you will find that the features and interface offered by these two editions is identical. However, Windows XP Professional does support a number of features that Windows XP Home Edition does not (many of which are presented later in this chapter). Throughout this book, attention is drawn to any differences in the two editions.

New and Improved Features in Windows XP

The first thing you will notice about Windows XP is that it has been given a facelift. A less-cluttered desktop, a redesigned Start menu, and a new look for windows and buttons all give Windows XP a more stylish and friendly appearance. In addition to the interface changes (which you'll learn all about in Chapter 4), a number of features have been added or improved in Windows XP. The most important of these features include the following:

- **Files and Settings Transfer Wizard** This feature provides a way to transfer designated files and system settings from one installation of Windows to a new installation of Windows XP, whether that new installation is on the same computer or not. This feature is described in the section "Using the Files and Settings Transfer Wizard" later in this chapter.

- **Better multiuser capabilities** Like Windows 2000, Windows XP lets you configure multiple user accounts on the same computer and provides ways to keep each user's system settings and personal files separate and private. A new feature to Windows XP, Fast User Switching now allows multiple users to remain logged onto Windows at the same time and even keep individual applications running. This feature is described in Chapter 12.

- **New media capabilities** Windows XP includes a host of features and tools for handling media files. Windows Media Player 8 serves as a video, DVD, and music player and even lets you create music CDs. Windows Movie Maker is an application for capturing and editing video and audio to create your own video files. These features are covered in Chapters 20 and 21.

- **CD burning** Windows XP comes with built-in CD-burning capabilities that support most modern CD-R and CD-RW drives. You can burn CDs directly from Windows Explorer and Windows Media Player.

- **Compressed folders** Windows XP includes built-in support for compressed folders in both the ZIP and Microsoft Cabinet (CAB) format. You can even work directly with files 4in compressed folders.

- **Better help and support** Windows Help contains many new features, including links to online help files, support newsgroups, better automatic troubleshooters, and a new Remote Assistance feature that lets a remote support person view your desktop and make changes. Help and support are covered in Chapter 9.

- **New Internet tools** Windows XP abounds with new Internet tools. Internet Connection Favorites lets you create favorite Internet connections that you can quickly access to accommodate different ISPs or network setups. Internet Connection Firewall is a simplified

Network Address Translation (NAT) server that helps secure your computer from unauthorized Internet access. Of course, Windows XP also includes new versions of Internet Explorer and Outlook Express, as well as the new MSN Explorer. These features are all covered in Part IV.

- **System Restore** This is a similar, but improved, version of the System Restore utility that debuted in Windows Me. System Restore automatically creates restore points whenever you make changes to your system (and also at scheduled intervals). These restore points hold many vital system configuration settings and can be used to revert your Windows settings to an earlier point should a problem occur. This feature is discussed in Chapter 26.

- **Remote Desktop** This feature lets you connect to and control a computer running Windows XP from a remote computer running any version of Windows. A remote control window displays the full desktop of the main computer. You can learn about this feature in Chapter 14.

Installing Windows XP

If you have installed some version of Windows before, nothing about the installation of Windows XP will surprise you too much. Installing Windows XP is nearly identical, in fact, to installing Windows 2000. Those familiar with installing Windows 98 or Windows Me will notice a number of differences, but the process is similar.

Here are the basic steps you will take when installing Windows XP:

1. Decide which edition you need: Windows XP Home or Professional Edition. For help on deciding, consult the previous section, "Introducing Windows XP."

2. Decide whether you need the full or upgrade version of the edition you have chosen. If you have a version of Windows (either installed on your computer or on the installation CD) that qualifies for an upgrade, you can save some money. There is no feature difference between the full and upgrade versions.

3. Make sure your computer meets the minimum hardware requirements for installing Windows XP and that the software you use is compatible with Windows XP or that updates are available from the software manufacturer.

4. Decide on the type of installation you will use: upgrade, new, or clean.

5. Prepare your computer for the upgrade. This process will vary depending on the type of installation you perform.

6. Optionally, you can use the Files and Settings Transfer Wizard to save user settings and files from your old installation of Windows so that you can transfer them to Windows XP following the installation.

7. Perform the installation, make sure that all your hardware and software works, and then activate Windows.

8. Use the Files and Settings Transfer Wizard to apply any saved user settings to the new installation.

With the exception of the first step, deciding which edition to install, all the steps in this procedure are discussed in detail in the following tips.

Meeting the Minimum Hardware Requirements

Before you install Windows XP, you must make sure that your computer meets the minimum hardware requirements for the installation. Table 1-1 lists the minimum and recommended hardware requirements published by Microsoft for both Windows XP Home and Professional Editions.

If you are unsure about your hardware, it's not difficult to figure out what you have. The following list explains how to determine the hardware configuration on your computer:

- **RAM and Processor**   If you are running Windows (any version), right-click the My Computer icon on your desktop and choose the Properties command. Near the bottom of the dialog box that opens, you'll see the type of processor you have and the amount of memory installed. If Windows is not installed, look at the information that appears on your screen just when you turn on the computer (when the memory countdown occurs). This screen should list the type of processor and amount of memory.

- **Hard Disk**   Within Windows, just right-click the hard disk (usually the C: drive) in Windows Explorer and choose Properties. The dialog box that opens shows the size of the hard disk and the available free space. If you don't have Windows installed, access the BIOS settings for your computer when the computer starts. (You can usually do this by pressing DEL or one of the function keys.) The size of the hard disk is listed somewhere in these settings. Unfortunately, the exact location depends on the type of BIOS your computer uses.

- **Video**   Within Windows, right-click the Desktop and choose Properties to open the Display Properties dialog box. The Settings tab of this dialog shows the model and capabilities of your video card. If you don't have Windows installed, you'll have to figure it out using the documentation for your video card or computer. Most modern cards meet the recommended requirements.

Hardware	Minimum	Recommended
Processor	233MHz or higher; processor must be Intel Pentium/Celeron or AMD K6/ Athlon/Duron family	300MHz or higher; processor must be Intel Pentium/Celeron or AMD K6/Athlon/Duron family
Memory	64MB supported, but may limit features available	128MB
Disk Space	1.5GB	2GB for a typical Windows installation, space for additional features and applications, and extra space for Windows swap file (see Chapter 27)
Video	Super VGA, 800x600 or higher resolution	Super VGA, 800x600 or higher resolution
Other	CD-ROM, DVD, or other access to Windows installation files; compatible keyboard and mouse	Modem or networking card for network/Internet access; sound card and speakers or headphones; 400MHz or higher processor for digital video camera capture; DVD drive, DVD decoder, and 8MB of video RAM for DVD playback

Table 1-1   Minimum and Recommended Requirements for Installing Windows XP

▶ **QUICK TIP**

In practice, you will discover that while Windows XP can be made to run on a computer that meets the minimum requirements, you won't have much fun using it. A better suggestion is to use the recommended guidelines as the minimum computer you will need for Windows XP and work up from there. If you run demanding applications or run a lot of applications at the same time, you are going to need a more powerful computer. Whether that means simply adding more RAM or going with a faster processor depends on your situation. If you create movies, save a lot of music files, or play big computer games, you will need more disk space.

Choosing an Installation Method

Once you have chosen an edition of Windows XP to install and made sure your computer meets the minimum installation requirements, you must decide on an installation method. You can install Windows XP in one of three ways:

- **Upgrade**   If a previous version of Windows that qualifies for an upgrade to Windows XP is already installed on your computer, you can perform an upgrade. During the upgrade, Windows XP is installed over the previous operating system, overwriting the old system files. Any applications you have installed and settings you have made are retained.

- **New installation**   A new installation is used for one of two purposes: The first is to replace your existing operating system altogether. This differs from an upgrade in that application and user settings are not retained. You can, however, use the Files and Settings Transfer Wizard to transfer settings to the new installation. The second purpose for performing a new installation is to install Windows XP on a different hard disk or partition than your existing Windows operating system. If you do this, you will be able to choose which operating system to boot into when you start your computer—a type of system often called *dual-booting*.

- **Clean installation**   A clean installation is used to install Windows XP onto a computer that has a blank, formatted hard disk (or a disk you want to format during the installation process). During a clean installation, you will actually boot your computer using the Windows XP CD-ROM and specify a number of options about how to configure your computer before the more familiar graphical phase of Windows XP Setup begins.

▶ **NOTE**

If you purchase the upgrade version of Windows XP, you can still perform any type of installation—not just an upgrade. The only real difference between the full and upgrade versions of the software has to do with licensing. During a new or clean installation of Windows XP, you are asked to insert the installation disk for a qualified previous version of Windows so that Setup can determine whether you are allowed to use the upgrade version of the software.

Using the Windows XP Upgrade Advisor for Windows XP Professional

Once you have established that your computer meets the general hardware requirements for running Windows XP, you need to determine whether your specific hardware and software is supported. If you are installing Windows XP Professional, you can make this determination before actually installing Windows XP using a utility named the Windows XP Upgrade Advisor.

> **QUICK TIP**
>
> *No Upgrade Advisor is included with Windows XP Home Edition. However, you can still run the Upgrade Advisor for Windows XP Professional, even if you plan to install the Home Edition. If your computer is found to be compatible with Windows XP Professional, it should also be compatible with the Home Edition.*

If you've already purchased a copy of Windows XP Professional, the Upgrade Advisor is included on the installation CD. If you have not yet purchased Windows XP, you can download a free copy of the Upgrade Advisor from *http://www.microsoft.com/ windowsxp/pro/howtobuy/upgrading/ advisor.asp*. Be aware, however, that this is a pretty big download—around 32MB, in fact.

NOTE

The Upgrade Advisor is the same tool used to scan your system for compatibility issues during the actual installation of Windows XP. For this reason, you may see references during the process that lead you to believe you are installing Windows XP. Don't worry, though. The Upgrade Advisor will not change your system in any way.

 To find out if your computer will be able to run Windows XP, run the Windows Upgrade Advisor using the following steps:

1. Insert the Windows XP Professional CD. If your computer does not run the CD automatically, use Windows Explorer to navigate to the CD and run the setup.exe program. If you downloaded a copy of the Windows Upgrade Advisor from the Internet, find the downloaded file and run that instead (and skip steps 2 and 3).

2. On the Welcome to Microsoft Windows XP window that appears, click the Check System Compatibility link.

3. Click the Check My System Automatically link.

4. If an Internet connection is available, the Windows Upgrade Advisor runs a utility named Dynamic Update to find and retrieve any new installation files Microsoft has made available. It then runs the Windows Upgrade Advisor.

5. The Windows Upgrade Advisor scans your hardware and software for compatibility issues and then displays any findings in an upgrade report like the one shown in Figure 1-1. Upgrade issues come in three flavors: blocking issues that will prevent the installation of Windows XP, hardware that may need additional files during or after the upgrade, and software that does not support Windows XP.

6. If any compatibility issues are listed, click the Full Details button to see a full report that discusses both the consequences of the incompatibility and any recommended solutions.

7. If you want to save the report as a text file that you can read later, click Save As. You can also print the report by clicking Print.

8. Click the Finish button to close the Windows Upgrade Advisor.

Once you have your upgrade report in hand, you need to decide which compatibility problems need your attention. You must take care of any blocking issues in the report before you install Windows XP. Blocking issues might include not having enough disk space or memory, for example. You will also do best to take care of any hardware incompatibilities before the installation, especially for hardware that will be used during the installation. This includes such items as disk drives, network adapters, and so on. Fixing software incompatibilities will be a judgment call, as most will not prevent a successful installation of Windows XP. You need to decide whether the software is necessary to you and, if so, find out whether updates are available from the software manufacturer.

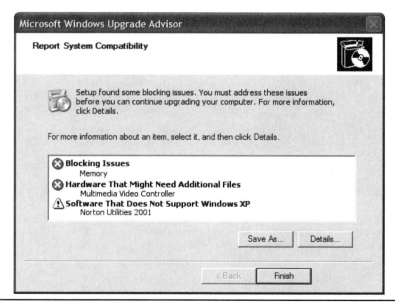

Figure 1-1   The Windows Upgrade Advisor scans your system and then displays an upgrade report with any compatibility issues.

Getting Ready for the Installation

After you determine that your computer supports Windows XP and that your software is compatible, you need to take a number of actions to prepare your computer for the installation.

- *Check for viruses.* Run a full scan of your computer. If you don't already have a virus program, get one. They aren't expensive and are lifesavers when you need them. Make sure you get one that runs with both Windows XP and your current version of Windows.

- *Back up your computer.* This should go without saying, but you would be surprised at the number of people who perform major system changes (like installing a new version of Windows) without backing up first. It is best to perform a full backup that will let you restore everything to its previous state should something go wrong with the installation.

- *If you are not upgrading and want to transfer your current system settings to the new installation of Windows XP, run the Files and Settings Transfer Wizard.* This process is covered in the next section, "Using the Files and Settings Transfer Wizard."

- *Make sure you have the installation disks for any software you need to reinstall and any software and manuals you have for your hardware.* This is particularly important if you are performing a clean installation.

- *If you are upgrading or performing a new installation, turn off any virus programs or other third-party disk utilities (like Norton Utilities) before starting the installation.* You should also close all running programs.

▶ *CAUTION*

If your computer is part of a network, make sure that you check with your network administrator before installing or upgrading to Windows XP. The administrator will let you know whether it is okay to use Windows XP on the network and, if it is, any networking or other configuration options you need to know.

Using the Files and Settings Transfer Wizard

The Files and Settings Transfer Wizard is a new and welcome feature. The wizard provides a simple interface for transferring selected files and settings from one Windows installation (running Windows XP or a previous version) to another installation running Windows XP. If you are upgrading from a previous version of Windows, you do not need to bother with transferring information; all settings are upgraded during the installation and the files on your computer are left in place. However, in several circumstances the Files and Settings Transfer Wizard is useful:

- If you purchase a new computer with Windows XP installed and want to move your documents, desktop customizations, and settings from your old computer, you can transfer this information directly using a network, direct cable connection, or removable media.

- If you plan to erase your hard drive and perform a clean installation of Windows XP, you can save your files and settings first to removable media or to another computer and then transfer the information back to your computer after the installation.

- If you perform a new installation of Windows XP on a computer that already contains a previous version of Windows (so that the computer can dual-boot between the two versions), you can use the Wizard to transfer the files and settings to the new installation.

TRY IT You will use the Files and Settings Transfer Wizard twice: the first time to save files and settings from the old operating system, and then to apply saved changes to the new installation of Windows XP.

To save information from the old operating system using the Files and Settings Transfer Wizard, use the following steps:

1. Insert the Windows XP CD. If your computer does not automatically open the splash screen, use Windows Explorer to access the CD and run the setup.exe file manually.

2. On the Windows XP splash screen, click the Perform Additional Tasks link.

3. On the next screen, click the Transfer Files and Settings link. This action starts the Files and Settings Transfer Wizard.

4. Click Next to proceed past the welcome page of the wizard.

5. If your old computer is running Windows XP, the wizard will ask you to identify which computer is currently operating. Select the Old Computer option and click Next. If your old computer is not running Windows XP, the wizard assumes it is the old computer and skips this step.

6. Next, the wizard displays the Select a Transfer Method page, as shown in Figure 1-2. Click the option that best suits your needs and click Next.

   - **Direct Cable** This option requires a serial cable connected between the two computers; it does not work with a parallel or universal serial bus (USB) connection.

   - **Home or Small Office Network** This option requires first that the two computers be connected by a local area network (LAN) and that both computers are on the same subnet (see Chapters 13 and 14). You also need to run the Files and Settings Transfer Wizard on the new computer before running it on the old computer. When you run it on the old computer, the wizard sends out a network broadcast looking for the new computer running the wizard. If it does not find it, this option is unavailable. Note also that if you use this method, files and settings are transferred directly to the new computer. You won't need to save them first and then apply them manually.

   - **Floppy Drive or Other Removable Media** Use this option to select a floppy, ZIP drive, CD-R, CD-RW, or writeable DVD drive. Unless you have a lot of time to burn, don't even bother with a regular floppy drive.

   - **Other** Use this option to specify a folder on your hard drive or a network drive to which to save the information.

7. The next page of the wizard, shown in Figure 1-3, lets you specify the information you want to transfer to the new computer. Click the appropriate option to transfer settings only, files only,

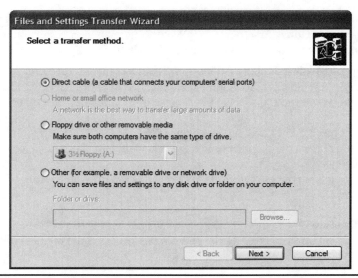

Figure 1-2 Select a transfer method for moving files and settings to the new computer.

or both settings and files. The list box to the right of the options changes to display the files affected by your selection.

8. If you want to customize the actual list of files and settings to be transferred, click the Let Me Select a Custom List of Files and Settings When I Click Next option.

9. Click Next to continue. If you chose to customize files, the Select Custom Files and Settings page appears, as shown in Figure 1-4. (If you chose not to customize files, you can skip right to

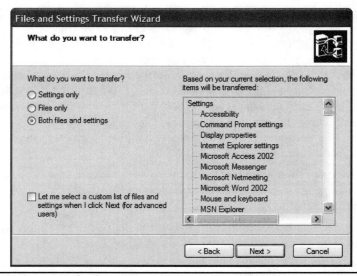

Figure 1-3 Choose the type of information you want to transfer to the new computer.

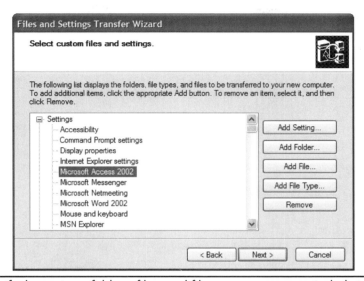

Figure 1-4   Specify the settings, folders, files, and file types you want to include in the transfer.

step 10.) By default, all available settings are chosen so the Add Setting button is useful only if you have already removed settings. Use the other buttons to add specific files and folders and general file types (by three-letter extension) to the list of information to be transferred. Click Next when you are done.

10. The wizard may next display a list of suggestions for software you may need to install on the new computer. This list is based on the types of files you chose to save. If this list is displayed, click Next to go on.

11. The wizard begins to collect the information to be saved and displays its progress as it saves the files and settings. When it is done, a summary page is displayed. Click Finish to close the wizard.

After you have collected the information from your old computer, the next step is to apply that information to the new computer. To do that, use the following steps on the new computer (assuming you already have Windows XP installed):

1. Choose Start | All Programs | Accessories | System Tools | Files and Settings Transfer Wizard.

2. Click Next to proceed past the welcome page of the wizard.

3. The wizard asks you to identify the computer. Select the New Computer option and click Next.

4. Next, the wizard offers to create a Wizard disk that you can use to run the wizard on the old computer and collect information (if you don't have the Windows XP CD). Click the I Don't Need the Wizard Disk Option and then click Next.

5. The wizard asks where it can find the information saved from the old computer. Select From Direct Cable, Floppy Drive or Other Removable Media, or Other, depending on how you saved the information. Click Next to go on.

6. The wizard begins to apply the files and settings to your new computer. When it is done, it displays a dialog asking you to log off so that it can finish applying settings. Click Yes to log off.

7. Log back in to Windows XP and the applied settings and files will be available.

▶ *CAUTION*

Before using the Files and Settings Transfer Wizard to move settings to your new computer, be sure that your old computer is working properly. Registry problems can be replicated to the new system.

Upgrading to Windows XP

When you upgrade to Windows XP, the setup program uses the settings from the existing version of Windows. This makes upgrading the simplest type of installation to perform, as it requires the least amount of input from you. There are also other advantages to upgrading:

• Your current system files are retained so that you can uninstall Windows XP later, should something go wrong or you decide you don't want it.

• You will not need to reinstall your applications, although you may need to update some of them to work with Windows XP.

• Most of your hardware settings are retained, meaning you will have less work to do following the installation.

TRY IT   Upgrading to Windows XP is a straightforward procedure. Here's how you perform an upgrade:

1. Make sure your system is ready for the upgrade. See the "Getting Ready for the Installation" section earlier in the chapter for advice on this.

2. Insert the Windows XP installation CD. A splash screen should appear automatically. If it doesn't, use Windows Explorer to find and run the setup.exe program on the CD.

3. Click the Install Windows XP link. This starts the Windows XP Setup program and displays the welcome screen shown in Figure 1-5.

4. On the Installation Type drop-down list, make sure Upgrade (Recommended) is selected and click Next.

5. Setup displays the Windows XP software licensing agreement. Once you have read it, select the I Accept This Agreement option and click Next. If you do not agree to the licensing terms, the Setup program ends.

6. Enter the 25-digit product key from the back of your Windows XP CD case. Click Next when you're done.

7. Setup displays the Upgrade Report screen, shown in Figure 1-6. An upgrade report displays any problems or incompatibilities Setup detects that might interfere with the installation. This report provides the same information as the Upgrade Advisor discussed previously. Choose

Figure 1-5 The Welcome screen of Windows Setup lets you choose whether to upgrade or perform a new installation.

whether you want to see only hardware issues, to see a full reporting of hardware and software issues, or not to see a report at all. Click Next to go on.

8. Setup offers to download any setup files that have been updated by Microsoft since your Windows XP CD was created. If you are connected to the Internet, you should go ahead and

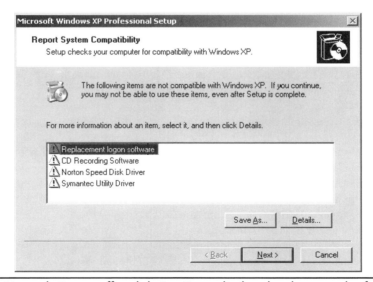

Figure 1-6 The Upgrade Report offered during Setup displays hardware and software incompatibility that can interfere with the installation.

download the updated files, since they often include new hardware and software compatibility patches. If you are not connected to the Internet, don't worry about it too much. You can always download updates later. Chapter 2 explains how. Click Next when you are ready.

9. If Setup detected any incompatible hardware or software during, it displays it now. If serious hardware issues are reported, you should exit Setup, fix the problems (which usually means removing the hardware or finding updated software), and perform your upgrade later. If minor hardware or software issues occur, you will have to decide for yourself whether you want to proceed. Click Next when you're ready.

At this point, Setup copies a host of installation files from CD, reboots your computer, and continues the installation, pretty much without requiring further input from you. Your computer may reboot once or twice during the process. After the final reboot, Windows XP starts and you'll be ready to get to work. Read the section "Activating Windows XP" for advice on what to expect when Windows starts the first time.

Performing a New Installation

As mentioned, a new installation is used for one of two purposes. The primary purpose is to install Windows XP over your existing version of Windows without retaining any of your application or system settings. However, this type of installation does retain the existing folder and file structure on your hard disk that has nothing to do with the actual Windows installation. This means that the following is preserved:

- Any folders and files created by applications you installed on your previous version of Windows. Of course, even though the files and folders are still there, the Windows Registry database is replaced, so you will have to reinstall all applications you want to continue using. For those you don't want to use anymore, simply delete the folders.

- Any documents you have created are left alone. All the documents in your My Documents folder will remain after the installation, for example.

The other purpose for using the new installation method is to configure dual-booting between your previous operating system and Windows XP. On a dual-boot system, you can choose the operating system you want to start each time you start your computer. You create a dual-boot system by installing Windows XP onto a different disk partition than the current operating system.

The easiest type of dual-boot system to create is one that has both Windows 98/Me and Windows XP installed. For this type of system, Windows 98/Me must be installed first, and a separate disk partition (or unpartitioned space where you can create a partition) must be large enough to hold Windows XP and any applications you install for it. From Windows 98/Me, install Windows XP into the separate partition using the new installation method described next.

You can also create a dual-boot system with Windows 2000 and Windows XP, but there are stricter requirements. You must install each operating system on a separate drive or disk partition. You must install Windows 2000 first and then install Windows XP. Finally, if the computer participates in a Windows 2000 domain, you must give your computer a different name under each operating system so that both operating systems can interact properly with the network.

TRY IT   The procedure for creating a new installation of Windows XP is similar to the procedure for upgrading. For that reason, the following steps are kept brief where the process is similar and the discussion is expanded where the process differs.

1. Insert the Windows XP installation CD. A splash screen should appear automatically. If it doesn't, use Windows Explorer to find and run the setup.exe program on the CD.

2. Click the Install Windows XP link. This starts the Windows XP Setup program.

3. On the Installation Type drop-down list, make sure New Installation (Advanced) is selected and click Next.

4. Read the license agreement, accept it, and click Next.

5. Enter your product key and click Next.

6. Windows Setup displays a Setup Options page, as shown in Figure 1-7. You can set up three types of options using this page:

   • **Advanced Options**   This button opens a dialog that lets you specify the path where the installation files are located (if you want to use files stored on a network, for example), the path to which Windows will be installed, and whether you will be able to choose the drive letter and partition to which Windows is installed. If you are creating a new installation that will overwrite an existing operating system, you must install it to the same partition and folder as the current system. If you want to create a dual-boot setup, you need to enable the option for choosing the drive letter and partition.

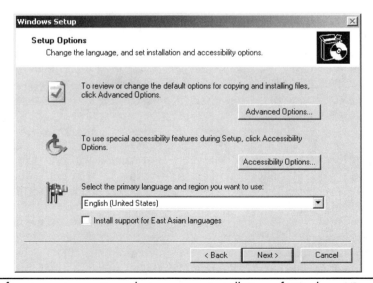

Figure 1-7   Configuring setup options during a new installation of Windows XP

- **Accessibility Options** This button lets you enable two accessibility options that will run during the Setup program: Microsoft Magnifier (which displays a window with an enlarged version of a selected part of the screen for people with visual impairments) and Microsoft Narrator (which reads the contents of the Setup dialog boxes aloud over your computer's speakers).
- **Language Settings** The drop-down list lets you select the primary language to be used during the setup process.

7. Next, Setup offers to download any Setup files that have been updated by Microsoft since your Windows XP CD was created. If you are connected to the Internet, you should go ahead and download the updated files, since they often include new hardware and software compatibility patches. If you are not connected to the Internet, remember that you can always download updates later. Chapter 2 explains how. Click Next to go on.

Setup now copies files from the CD, reboots your computer, and proceeds with the rest of the installation. From this point on, the installation is identical to the process used during a clean installation of Windows XP (with the exception of booting from the Windows CD to begin) and is discussed in the next section.

Performing a Clean Installation

A clean installation is one in which you boot your computer using the Windows XP CD and install Windows XP on a blank, formatted hard-disk partition. If your partition is not already formatted, Setup gives you the chance to format it. Setup also lets you create partitions if none exist.

▶ *NOTE*

If you do not have a CD-ROM drive or computer that supports booting from a CD, you can use a set of floppy disks to boot your computer and start the Windows XP installation. These floppies are available for download as disk images that you can use to create disks. Go to http://support.microsoft.com/directory/article.asp?ID=KB;EN-US;Q310994 *for links to downloading images for both the Home and Professional Editions (make sure you get the right ones). Follow the instructions on the download page to create the disks.*

Most people who buy Windows XP will upgrade their existing installation. After all, it is faster and you won't have to reinstall applications or reconfigure all your Windows settings. This is unfortunate, though, as any installation of Windows that has been around for a while is going to have unnecessary baggage to bring along into the upgrade. This baggage includes files and Registry entries left behind after you uninstall applications, applications that are still installed but forgotten, system settings that are less than optimal, temporary files scattered all over the place, and so on. A clean installation is a chance to wipe everything out and start over from scratch. It means a little extra work for you, reinstalling applications and reconfiguring Windows, but it also results in a more stable, better organized system.

TRY IT   To perform a clean installation of Windows XP, use the following steps:

1. Boot your computer using the Windows XP CD or floppy boot disks. Windows Setup starts automatically.

2. During its initial phase, Windows scans your system for any hard-disk drives that match its list of supported software drivers. If you need to install a third-party SCSI (Small Computer System Interface) or RAID (redundant array of independent disks) driver for Windows to recognize your drive, press F6 at this time. Follow the instructions from the manufacturer of your drive on installing the drivers.

3. When Setup has finished its initial scan, it displays a welcome screen. To continue with the installation, press ENTER. You can also press F3 to exit Setup or press R to repair an existing Windows XP installation.

4. Next, Setup displays the Windows licensing agreement. Read it and then press F8 to go on.

5. The partitioning screen is displayed next, as shown in Figure 1-8. This is the same screen you will see using the new installation type if you select the advanced option of being able to choose a partition. The partitioning screen lists the current partitions configured on each of your hard disks along with their size and partition type (NTFS, FAT32, or Raw for unformatted partitions). The screen also lists unpartitioned space in which you can create a new partition. You have three options on this screen:

   - *Set up Windows in the partition that is currently selected.* Use the arrow keys to change the selection. Choosing this option proceeds with the Windows installation.

   - *Create a new partition in unpartitioned space.* Choosing this option leads to a screen that lets you specify the size of the new partition. You can specify any size up to the amount of

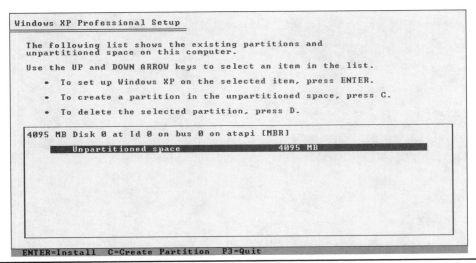

Figure 1-8   Creating and managing disk partitions during Windows XP setup

unpartitioned space you have, but you should make sure that you create a partition big enough to hold Windows XP. See the previous section, "Meeting the Minimum Hardware Requirements," for advice on disk space.

- *Delete a partition.* This option deletes the selected partition after presenting a screen asking you to confirm the deletion.

6. Setup presents several options for formatting the partition you have selected, as shown in Figure 1-9. You can format a partition using either the NT File System (NTFS) or the 32-bit File Allocation Table (FAT32) file systems. If the selected partition has already been formatted, you are also offered a quick version of each of these format options. Using the quick version saves time, but a full format includes a full disk scan during the format, so a full format is usually the better choice.

7. Windows displays a progress screen while it formats your partition. After this, Windows copies files to your hard disk and restarts the computer.

8. When the computer restarts, Setup continues. Setup next configures Regional and Language Options. The default setting is English and a standard US keyboard layout. Modify these choices if you need to and click Next to go on.

9. Enter your name and an organization name. You must enter a name, but you can leave the Organization field blank. Click Next to go on.

10. Enter the 25-digit product key from the back of your CD case and click Next.

11. Enter a name for your computer and a password for the default administrator account. Setup suggests a computer name based on your name and a string of random numbers, but you'll probably want to change this to something better. The computer name is used to identify the computer on a network. You can name computers using the names of people who use them, their locations, or what they are used for—whatever suits you up to 15 characters in length.

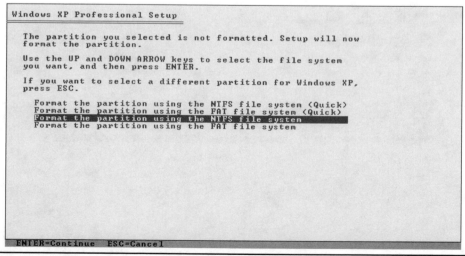

Figure 1-9   Formatting disk partitions during Windows XP setup

12. Setup asks you to check the system date and time and enter your time zone. Click Next when you are done.

13. Setup now displays the Network Settings dialog box with two options for configuring your computer on the network:

   - **Typical Settings**   This option installs standard networking services, including the Client for Microsoft Networks, the QoS (Quality of Service) Packet Scheduler, File and Print Sharing for Microsoft Networks, and the TCP/IP (Transmission Control Protocol/Internet Protocol) networking protocol. In addition, this option configures the computer so that it automatically configures its TCP/IP settings by first looking for a server that can provide them and, if that fails, assigning them to itself.

   - **Custom Settings**   This options lets you manually configure your network settings by installing additional networking services and protocols and by configuring specific TCP/IP (or other protocol) settings. You can learn more about these networking options in Chapter 11.

14. Now set up the computer to be a member of a workgroup or Windows domain. If you are on a small peer-to-peer network with no dedicated Windows servers, choose Workgroup. All computers on the network that share a common workgroup name will be able to easily share resources. If your computer is a member of a large network, it may be part of a Windows domain. Workgroups and domains are covered in more detail in Chapter 11.

Once you assign a workgroup or domain name, Setup finalizes the installation without needing any more input from you. When it's finished, Setup restarts your computer and you'll be ready to start using Windows.

Activating Windows XP

Windows XP is the first version of Windows to include the new product activation feature. Essentially, this feature is used to tie your copy of Windows to a specific computer. This is done by taking an inventory of several of the hardware components of your computer, such as your RAM, hard drive, processor, and so on. This inventory is stored anonymously in a database at Microsoft along with the product identification number for your software.

You must activate your copy of Windows within 30 days of installation or you will no longer be able to use it. You can activate your copy of Windows XP in two ways:

- **Over the Internet**   This method is easy, fast, and automatic.

- **Over the telephone**   This method usually ends up with you having to wait through a few busy signals, read a product identification number to a Microsoft employee, and then type in a confirmation code by hand. It takes a little longer, but really isn't too much of a hassle.

In theory, product activation prevents the same copy of Windows from being installed on more than one computer. Unfortunately, this new feature causes a couple of problems. Many people believe it is an invasion of their privacy and that it represents a lack of trust by Microsoft of their customers. As for privacy concerns, you can rest assured that the only personal information stored aside from your software identification number and hardware inventory is your country.

The second problem product activation causes is a little more annoying. As long as you do not change your hardware, you will be able to reinstall and reactivate Windows as much as you want. In addition, you can change your hardware and successfully reactivate Windows over the Internet as long as you don't change your hardware *too much*. Upgrading to a faster hard disk or new processor won't necessarily lock you out. However, upgrading too much hardware at once (such as a new hard disk and new processor at the same time) can prevent you from being able to reactivate Windows automatically. You will have to make the phone call, explain what you're doing, and activate Windows manually. Finally, you are allowed to reactivate Windows after big hardware changes only a certain number of times within a 120-day period. Unfortunately, Microsoft has not made public the exact number of times you can reactivate or over what period, although the company promises that most typical users will never have a problem. If you reinstall more than 120 days following your last installation, Internet activation will work and no explanation is needed.

TRY IT   When Windows XP starts the first time after you install it, an icon that looks like a set of keys appears in the system tray with a pop-up balloon asking you to activate Windows and letting you know how many days you have left before you must activate. You can click this icon to start the Activation Wizard or you can open the Start menu and choose All Programs | Accessories | Activate Windows.

1. On the first page of the Activate Windows Wizard, shown in Figure 1-10, choose the method you want to use to activate Windows: over the Internet or by telephone.

2. If you choose to activate over the Internet, the next page of the wizard offers to let you register Windows in addition to activating it. Unlike activation, registration is optional. What happens next depends on whether you register:

   • If you choose to register, after you click Next an extra page appears, where you can enter the personal information required to register, including your name, address, and so on. Registration is mostly used by Microsoft's marketing department to include you on the offering list for new products and services. You do *not* need to register in order to use Windows XP. If you do register, the wizard attempts to activate and register Windows and then displays a summary page if successful. Click Finish to return to Windows.

   • If you choose not to register, the wizard attempts to activate Windows over the Internet and displays a summary page if successful. Click Finish to return to Windows.

3. If you choose to activate by telephone or if activation over the Internet is not successful, the wizard next displays a page with a phone number you can call to get help (pick a country from the drop-down list and the appropriate phone number is shown). The wizard also generates a rather lengthy installation ID that you will need to read to the support person. In turn, that person will read back to you a confirmation ID for you to type in. Once you've done all that, click Finish to activate Windows.

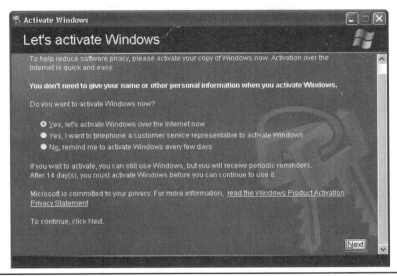

Figure 1-10   Using the Activation Wizard to activate and, optionally, to register Windows XP

Uninstalling Windows XP

If you upgrade to Windows XP from a previous version of Windows, the Setup program keeps a backup of the system files for the previous version. Should you decide you don't want Windows XP on your computer, you can uninstall it.

▶ *NOTE*

You cannot uninstall Windows XP if you upgraded from Windows NT or Windows 2000 Professional. This option is available only if you upgrade from Windows 98, Windows 98SE, or Windows Me.

TRY IT   To uninstall Windows XP after an upgrade, use the following steps:

1. Click Start and open the Control Panel.
2. Click the Add or Remove Programs link. If the Control Panel window is in Classic View, double-click the Add or Remove Programs icon.

3. The Add or Remove Programs window appears, displaying a list of programs installed on your computer. Select the Windows XP Uninstall entry and then click the Change/Remove button that appears. This opens the Uninstall Windows XP dialog box shown here:

4. Select the Uninstall Windows XP option and click Continue.

5. A dialog box appears asking you to confirm that you want to uninstall Windows XP. Click Yes.

6. Windows runs the uninstallation program and restarts using the previous operating system.

► **QUICK TIP**

The backup of your previous version of Windows takes up at least 50MB of disk space and often much more. If you are sure you want to keep Windows XP on your computer, use the Uninstall Windows XP dialog box to remove the backup of your previous operating system.

CHAPTER 2

Managing Windows Components and Applications

TIPS IN THIS CHAPTER

When you install Windows XP, a number of useful components are installed with it. These include common accessories like Internet Explorer for Web browsing, Outlook Express for e-mail, Windows Media Player for music and video playback, a calculator, some games, and a number of other items.

You can get only so much use out of Windows by itself, though. Eventually, you will want to add other applications. This chapter looks at choosing, installing, managing, and removing applications. It also shows you how to add Windows components that come with the operating system but may not have been installed during your installation, and how to remove components you do not want. Finally, this chapter shows you how to use a tool named Windows Update to download and install software patches and updated components that Microsoft has made available since the release of Windows XP.

Installing an Application

An application is a set of program files that perform some function, such as word processing or graphics editing. You'll find that many of the programs written for other versions of Windows will work just fine with Windows XP. Before you get started learning how to choose and install an application, however, be aware that you should never try to install the following types of applications on Windows XP:

- *Anti-virus programs that are not designed for Windows XP.* Running virus software that has not been updated for Windows XP is a sure way to cause problems with your system. Most major anti-virus software manufacturers had updates ready the day Windows XP was released, so getting an update should not be a problem.

- *Disk utilities that are not designed for Windows XP.* If you have disk scanning or defragmenting software, programs for removing and cleaning up after applications, or troubleshooting programs designed for other versions of Windows, do not install them on Windows XP.

How to Choose an Application

Applications are stored on a number of different forms. Most applications that you purchase through retail outlets are stored on CD-ROM, though more are starting to appear on DVD. You may still have older programs that were stored on a stack of floppy disks. When you download a program, a compressed file may open automatically and begin installing when you double-click it, or it may require that you decompress it first and then start the installation yourself.

Regardless of an application's form, you need to know the following information about choosing applications that will run on Windows XP. Microsoft has logo guidelines in place for software manufacturers that have tested their applications with Windows XP. Two levels of compatibility are available under these guidelines:

- **Designed for Windows XP**   Products that meet this level of compatibility are specifically created to take advantage of the new features of Windows XP and have been tested by

Microsoft and the software manufacturer. These products carry a special logo denoting their status, shown left.

- **Compatible with Windows XP**   Products that meet this level of compatibility may not meet all the requirements of the Designed for Windows XP testing process and may not take advantage of new features in Windows XP. However, these programs have been tested by the manufacturer or by Microsoft to ensure that no compatibility problems exist.

While these compatibility guidelines are useful when buying new software, you must keep in mind that they represent only software that has been submitted for testing and approval by the manufacturer. Many programs, especially those designed for earlier versions of Windows, will work perfectly; they just haven't been tested. You can often find out from the manufacturer's Web site whether a program has problems running on Windows XP.

Even if an older program does have compatibility problems, you may be able to use the Program Compatibility Wizard to help it along. This useful tool is covered in Chapter 6.

▶ **QUICK TIP**

Microsoft has created a Web site named Windows Catalog that is essentially a showcase for software and hardware products that have passed Windows compatibility testing. The site is fully searchable and is a good first place to look for compatible applications. You can get there by clicking the Windows Catalog shortcut in the All Programs folder on your Start menu or by going to http://www.microsoft.com/windows/catalog.

What Happens When an Application Is Installed

At its simplest, an application can be a single file that runs when you double-click it. Applications can also be quite complicated, with hundreds of files in different folders scattered across your hard drive and complex interactions with Windows and other applications.

When you install an application, a special installation program walks you through the process. Each type of software has its own look and feel and exactly what you see and what you have to do during the installation is dependent on that software's design. However, in general, the following typically occurs when a program is installed:

- Program files are copied from the installation source (usually a CD or floppy disk) to a folder on your hard drive. Most installation routines create a folder for a program inside the Program Files folder on your C: drive.

- Some program files may be copied to other locations on your hard drive. Many applications use additional folders in various places on your disk that contain pieces of the program. For example, program files that are shared with other programs are often copied to folders inside your Windows folder and to a folder named Common Files in your Program Files folder. Program files that are customized for each user of a computer may be copied to each user's folder inside the Documents and Settings folder.

- Shortcuts may be created on your Start menu, Desktop, and Quick Launch bar that make it easier to find and run the application.

- Some programs include small components that run continuously in the background. For example, most anti-virus programs keep a small program running all the time that scans files as they are transferred to your computer. For some applications, you'll see an icon in the System Tray on the Taskbar that indicates a program is running.

- The installation program may create entries in the Windows Registry that identify the application, store user settings, and govern how the program runs and how it interacts with other programs and with Windows.

Managing Windows Components

Windows *components* refers collectively to programs, services, and other software that are packaged with Windows and that you can add or remove from your system. When you install Windows XP, the majority of available components are included in the installation. However, a number of useful components are not. While a full list would probably bore you, here are a few of the more interesting components not included by default:

- **Fax Services**   Lets you send and receive faxes using your fax/modem. You can also share the fax service with other computers on a network. Fax Services are covered in detail in Chapter 7.

- **Internet Information Server**   A Web and File Transfer Protocol (FTP) server that includes support for Microsoft Front Page. Internet Information Server is included only with Windows XP Professional.

- **Advanced networking services and tools**   If you need to install Print Services for UNIX, the Simple Network Management Protocol (SNMP), or Message Queuing, they are all available.

Components are handled through the Add or Remove Programs utility, which is part of the Windows Control Panel. As the name implies, this is also the tool used for installing and removing other applications from your computer.

Updating Windows

Windows Update is a Web-based service that has been around since Windows 98 and provides a convenient location for downloading and installing updated Windows components. The types of components you will find on Windows Update include these:

- **Patches**   These are usually fixes for problems that Microsoft has discovered with Windows. The most important of these are patches that fix security problems, but many other types of problems are addressed as well.

- **Component Updates**   When Microsoft releases a new version of a Windows component, it is always made available on the Windows Update Web site. You may find the latest version of Windows Media Player or Internet Explorer, for example.

- **Driver Updates**   Microsoft often releases updated versions of hardware drivers designed for Windows XP.

- **Application Updates**   You can find updates for many applications that fix compatibility issues with Windows XP.

Windows XP also includes a feature for automatically updating critical components. This feature runs in the background, periodically checking in with the Windows Update site. If it discovers a new update, it will notify you and, if you choose, download the update for you automatically.

Adding a Program to Windows

Most programs are installed using a special installation application that copies files and makes all the necessary settings in Windows for you. However, the thousands of different applications available come in a variety of formats that can require different installation techniques.

Fortunately, a few basic techniques are used for the majority of formats:

- If your software is on CD-ROM or DVD, the installation program may start automatically when you insert the disk. This requires that the AutoRun feature on your computer is enabled (see Chapter 8 for more on this feature).

- If the AutoRun feature is turned off or if your software comes on a disk that doesn't support it, such as a floppy disk or some CD-ROMs, you must start Setup yourself. You can do this by locating the Setup program file (usually named setup.exe, install.exe, or something similar) and running it yourself or by using the Add or Remove Programs utility in Windows. To locate the file yourself, choose Start I Run, and then use the Browse button to find the file on your system.

- If you are installing a program that you downloaded, you will need to find the downloaded file using Windows Explorer. If the file is an executable (if it has an .exe extension), double-click it and follow the instructions that appear. If the file is compressed using the ZIP format, you can open the file using Windows Explorer (which now includes a built-in compression program) and find the Setup program file inside.

No matter what the format of your application, you can always consult the documentation or the manufacturer of the software if you have problems installing it.

▶ | **QUICK TIP**

Many manufacturers (especially those that provide software for download) include a text file with instructions for installing the application. This file is usually named readme.txt, readme.1st, setup.txt, install.txt, or something similar.

To install a program that comes on CD, DVD, or floppy disk using the Add or Remove Programs utility, use the following steps:

1. From the Start menu, open the Control Panel.

2. Click the Add or Remove Programs link. If the Control Panel window is in classic view, double-click the Add or Remove Programs icon. This opens the Add or Remove Programs window.

3. Click the Add New Programs icon at the left of the window to switch to the Add Programs page, shown in Figure 2-1.

4. If you are installing an application from CD or floppy disk, insert the disk into the appropriate drive.

5. Click CD or Floppy. Windows begins searching on any CD, DVD, or floppy disks in your drive for a valid setup program file (files named setup.exe or install.exe).

6. If Windows finds a setup program file, it displays a dialog with the path to the file it found. Verify that this file is on the disk you want to install from and click Finish.

7. If Windows does not find a valid setup program file (which will definitely be the case if you are installing from a folder you downloaded), it presents a dialog box that lets you browse for the file manually. Once you find the file and select it, click Open and Windows displays another dialog with a path to the file. Click Finish.

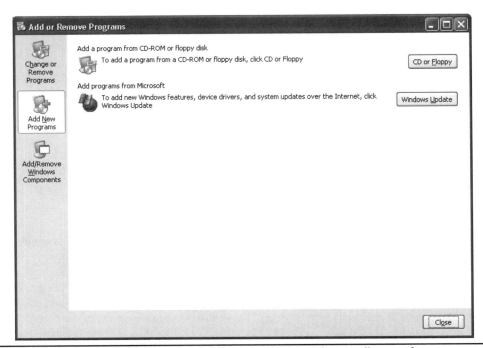

Figure 2-1   Using the Add or Remove Programs utility to start the installation of a program

At this point, the setup program chosen by the software manufacturer takes over. The vast majority of these programs use a wizard that takes you through the installation. Although each installation is unique you can usually expect to supply a similar set of information, such as the following:

- The folder on your computer into which you want to install the application
- Your name and organization name
- Specific components of the application you want to install
- Where you would like shortcuts to the program created

▶ | **QUICK TIP**

Before you install any application, you should use System Restore to create a new restore point. If something goes wrong during the installation, you can return Windows to the state it was in before you started the installation. For details on System Restore, refer to Chapter 26.

Changing and Removing Programs

After an application is installed, you can use the Add or Remove Programs tool to remove the program and to change details concerning its installation. Each application offers particular management capabilities. Many applications provide only the ability to uninstall, and some provide more management features. For example, in a full-featured set of applications like Microsoft Office, you can do the following:

- *Remove the program.* This action typically uses an automated uninstall routine that comes with the application and takes care of removing program files, shortcuts, and Registry entries.

- *Repair the program.* This action reinstalls the program using the same settings as the previous installation, restoring corrupt or missing program files and shortcuts.

- *Change the program.* This action usually lets you run the setup program again to add or remove application features for the installation. With Microsoft Office, for example, you might remove a feature you don't use or add a program you left out during the first installation.

▶ **NOTE**

While Windows tracks the installation of all 32-bit applications and some older 16-bit applications, it cannot track many older applications, which won't be accessible using the Add or Remove Programs tool. You will have to remove these manually. Many of these applications come with their own uninstall routines that you can launch from the application's folder. If no uninstall routine is apparent, you can delete the programs folder yourself. However, you should also check for any references to this program that Windows may have created; these are usually found in the configuration files still used for older applications—autoexec.bat, config.sys, and win.ini. Of course, you should exercise caution whenever modifying any system files; make a backup copy so that you can easily reverse any changes you make.

To remove a program with the Add or Remove Programs tool, use the following steps:

1. Click Start, and then click Control Panel.

2. Click the Add or Remove Programs link. If the Control Panel window is in classic view, double-click the Add or Remove Programs icon.

3. The Add or Remove Programs window opens, showing a list of programs currently installed on your computer, as shown in Figure 2-2.

4. Click the entry for the program that you want to change or remove. When you select a program, its entry expands to show the amount of disk space it takes up, how often it is used, the last time it was used, and often a link to support information for the program.

5. All programs have a Remove button associated with them. If you want to remove the program from your computer, click Remove to have Windows start the uninstall program that came with the application. This program will walk you through the program's removal.

6. Many programs also have a Change button. This button usually runs the original setup program that you used to install the application and lets you make changes to the installation, such as changing which specific components are installed.

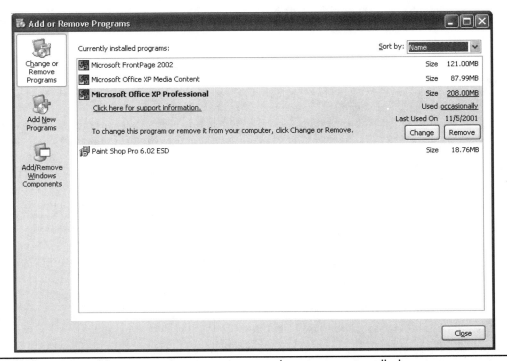

Figure 2-2   Using Add or Remove Programs to view the programs installed on your computer

▶ *NOTE*

In step 5, if other users are logged on to the computer, Windows will warn you that uninstalling an application in use by other users may cause them to lose data. You are given the chance to switch to active users (assuming you have permissions) and log out. For more on managing users, see Chapter 12.

▶ ***QUICK TIP***

If you have installed a lot of programs, use the Sort By drop-down list in the Add or Remove Programs window to sort the program list by name, size, the frequency of use, or the last time the programs were used.

Adding and Removing Windows Components

Most of the components available within Windows XP are installed by default during a typical installation. However, a number of additional components are available and you may want to explore these. Your installation of Windows XP may also include components that you do not use and would like to remove. Adding and removing Windows components is accomplished using the Add or Remove Programs tool in the Control Panel.

▶ ***QUICK TIP***

You may notice that many Windows components do not show up in the list of components you can change using Add or Remove Programs. You can change this. Components are listed in a special file named sysoc.inf, which is found in the \Windows\inf folder. Open this file with Notepad and you will see a list of components. The list looks a bit cryptic, but you'll notice that many of the entries have the word hide *listed toward the end. Simply remove this text throughout the sysoc.inf file and you'll see many more choices the next time you open the Add or Remove Programs tool. Make a backup copy of the file before you make changes just in case something goes wrong.*

 To add or remove a component using the Add or Remove Programs tool, follow these steps:

1. Click Start, and then click Control Panel.

2. Click the Add or Remove Programs link. If the Control Panel windows is in classic view, double-click the Add or Remove Programs icon,

3. Click Add/Remove Windows Components. This opens the Windows Components Wizard shown in Figure 2-3.

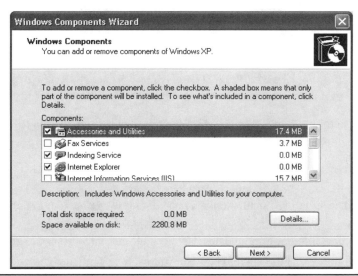

Figure 2-3   Check additional components from the list to install, or clear the check box to remove components.

4. Check the box next to a component to add that component to Windows. Clear the check box to remove the component (don't worry if you make a mistake, as no changes are committed until you click Next).

5. Some components on the list, such as Accessories and Utilities, are really categories that contain a number of subcomponents. Select one and click Details to select the individual components in the category or check the box next to the category to install all its components.

6. Once you have selected the components you want to add and remove, click Next. Windows begins adding and removing components. During this process, you may be prompted for the location of your Windows XP installation files. If you installed Windows XP from CD, you will need to have your disk handy.

7. The wizard displays a summary page when it has finished adding and removing components. Click Finish.

Using the Windows Update Web Site

Windows Update is an online source for free patches and component updates from Microsoft. When you enter the site, a small ActiveX program is downloaded that scans your computer for currently installed components (don't worry—no personal information is sent to Microsoft during this process). After the Windows Update site knows the components on your system, it presents a list of updates tailored to your situation—updates that are for your version of Windows and only those updates that you have not yet installed.

▶ **NOTE**

Just in case you're wondering, the information that is scanned on your computer by the Windows Update site includes the version numbers of Windows, Internet Explorer, and other programs you have installed, as well as the Plug and Play ID numbers of your hardware devices.

TRY IT To find and install updates using the Windows Update site, use the following steps:

1. From the Start menu, point to Programs, and then click Windows Update.

2. If you have not visited the Windows Update site before, you are prompted to install and run Windows Update Control, a small ActiveX program used to scan your system. Click Yes.

3. On the Welcome to Windows Update page, click the Scan for updates link. Windows Update scans your computer looking for updates. Updates fall into three basic categories:

   • **Critical Updates** These are updates that Microsoft strongly recommends that you install. They include mostly security patches and "bug" fixes. Windows Update automatically selects all critical updates to be installed, but you'll be able to review and deselect them if you want.

   • **Windows XP** These are updates to Windows components and additional components that Microsoft makes available from time to time.

   • **Driver Updates** These are updates to drivers for hardware that Windows Update found on your computer during the scan.

4. The navigation pane at the left of the Windows Update Window, shown in Figure 2-4, lists the number of updates in each category that are available. Click a category (Critical Updates, for example) to view a list of updates in that category.

5. Selecting updates on the Windows Update site works much like using the shopping cart found on most online shopping sites. You can read a description of the update (many have a Read More link for a detailed explanation) and then click Add to add the update to the list of updates you want to install. The total number of items you have selected to install appears at the top of the page (see Figure 2-4). Once an update is added to the list, you can remove it by clicking Remove.

6. After you have selected the updates you want to install, click the Review and Install Updates link. This opens the Total Selected Updates page shown in Figure 2-5. Review the list of updates and Remove any that you may not want. The total size of the download for all updates is shown at the top of the page.

7. When you have determined the updates you want to install, click Install Now.

8. Windows Update displays a dialog box with the software licensing agreement for the selected updates. Click Accept to continue. If you click Don't Accept, the process ends and nothing is installed.

9. Windows downloads and installs the selected updates. When it is done, you are informed whether the installation was successful or whether problems were encountered. If an update

fails because of a problem downloading, you can always try again later. If an update fails during installation, Windows will give you more details regarding the problem so that you can try to solve it.

10. If you are prompted to restart your computer, click Yes. Otherwise, you are returned to Windows following the installation of the updates.

▶ **NOTE**

Some updates can be installed only by themselves, independent of other updates. Windows Update will let you know when you try to select an update of this type.

Configuring Automatic Updates

The first time that Windows XP starts after being installed, an icon for the automatic updating feature appears in your notification area (the space on the Taskbar next to the clock). You can configure automatic updating by clicking the icon or by using the System Properties dialog box (right-click the

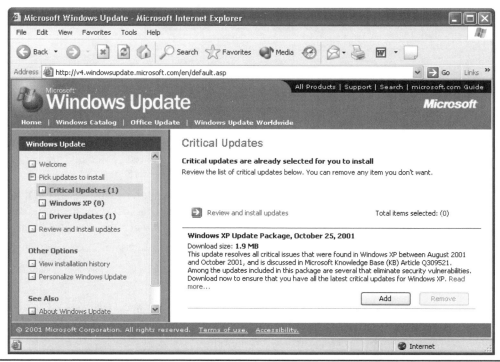

Figure 2-4   Select the updates you want to install using Windows Update.

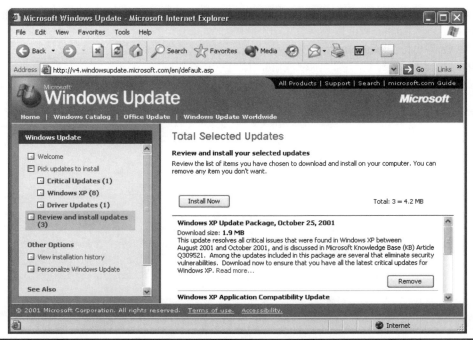

Figure 2-5   Review the selected updates and decide which you want to install.

My Computer icon and choose Properties from the shortcut menu). You can use three settings for automatic updating:

- Download updates automatically when they are detected and notify you when they are ready to install. An icon appears in the notification area and includes a message that updates are ready to be installed. Clicking the icon lets you review and install the updates.

- Notify you when an update has been detected and ask whether you want to download it. Once it is downloaded, you'll be asked again whether you want to install it. An icon appears in the notification area when the update is detected and appears again when the download is finished.

- Turn off automatic updating. If you do this, you'll be able to update Windows only using the Windows Update Web site, which is covered in the earlier section, "Using the Windows Update Web Site."

Unless you are connected to the Internet using a persistent connection—one that is always on, such as cable modem, DSL, or your company's network—you will do best to turn off automatic updating. There are two reasons for this. First, Windows must check periodically to determine whether updates are available. If you use a dial-up connection, Windows will dial the connection once in a while and you don't get to control the schedule. The second reason not to use automatic updating with a dial-up connection is that the downloads can be pretty big. You certainly don't want

Windows deciding for itself when it will download large files, so if you do use automatic updating with a dial-up connection, at least make sure you configure it to notify you before performing the actual download.

Using automatic updating after it is configured is straightforward. Once an update is downloaded, the icon in the notification area pops up a text balloon letting you know it's ready to be installed. Click the balloon or the icon and Windows opens a dialog box with a brief description of the update. You can install the update or view additional details about it; the details screen is shown in Figure 2-6. If you do not want to install a particular update, remove the check mark next to it. When you have decided which updates you want to install, click Install to proceed. Once the update is installed, you are either returned to Windows or asked to restart your computer. You can also click Remind Me Later to have Windows notify you again at a later time.

> ## QUICK TIP
>
> *If you choose not to install a specific update that you have downloaded, Windows deletes its files from your computer. If you change your mind later, you can download it again by clicking Restore Declined Updates on the Automatic Updates tab of the System Properties dialog box. If any of the updates that you previously declined still apply to your computer, they are displayed the next time Windows notifies you of available updates.*

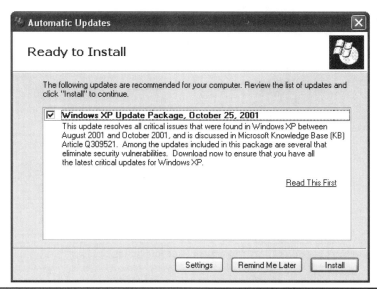

Figure 2-6   Reviewing a downloaded update before installing it

TRY IT In Windows XP Home Edition, you must be logged on using a computer administrator account to install components or to modify Automatic Update settings. In Windows XP Professional, you must be logged on with an account that is a member of the Administrators group. To configure Automatic Updating, use the following steps:

1. Click Start, and then click Control Panel.
2. Click the Performance and Maintenance link. If your Control Panel window is in classic view instead of category view, double-click the System icon and skip the next step.
3. Click the System icon.
4. Click the Automatic Updates tab.
5. On the Automatic Updates tab, shown in Figure 2-7, choose how you want to be notified of updates or whether you want to use Automatic Updates at all.

Figure 2-7   Configuring a notification setting for Automatic Updates

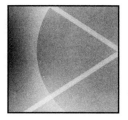

CHAPTER 3

Adding, Removing, and Configuring Hardware

TIPS IN THIS CHAPTER

Since the IBM PC was first created and shortly followed by a host of clones from other companies, the hardware used in computers has changed a lot. While you may occasionally still see legacy hardware around today, most modern hardware is faster and easier to install, and it can be managed automatically by Windows.

This chapter starts by providing a basic understanding of hardware—types of hardware available, hardware resources on a computer, and software drivers Windows uses to interface with hardware. From there, it goes on to cover the installation and configuration of hardware in Windows XP.

Understanding Hardware

Before you buy and install hardware onto your computer, it is important that you have a good understanding of what types of hardware are available and how that hardware works with Windows XP.

Types of Hardware

You can connect hardware to your computer in a lot of ways, from opening the case and installing a new card to plugging a cable into one of many kinds of external ports. A few port types will let you connect hardware while Windows XP is running (these are called *hot-pluggable* devices); for some port types and for all internal cards, you must power down the PC to connect a device. Table 3-1 lists the various types of connectors used by modern computers, whether they support hot-pluggable devices, and the hardware commonly used on the connector.

Connector	Hot-Pluggable	Common Hardware
Serial Port	No	Serial mouse, modem, computer-to-computer cabling, and many Personal Digital Assistants (PDAs)
Parallel Port	No	Printers and computer-to-computer connections
USB Port	Often	Modems, printers, external hard drives, and networking
PS/2 Port	Often	Mouse and keyboard
Display Port	No	Monitor
FireWire Port	Yes	High-speed port typically used for digital video cameras, hard drives, and printers
Other Ports	Sometimes	Audio ports, video ports for TVs or cameras, and other specialized ports
PC Card Slot	Yes	Usually found on notebooks, and supports many types of hardware, most commonly networking and modem
PCI Adapter Card	No	Plug and Play hardware of all types, including modem, sound card, video adapter card, network adapter card, etc.

Table 3-1   Types of Hardware Used on Modern PCs

Connector	Hot-Pluggable	Common Hardware
AGP Adapter Card	No	Video adapter card
ISA Adapter Card	No	Legacy hardware of all types, including modem, sound card, network adapter card, etc.

Table 3-1   Types of Hardware Used on Modern PCs *(continued)*

▶ *CAUTION*

Although a connector type may support hot-pluggable devices, not all devices that use that connector type will be hot-pluggable. You should always consult your hardware's documentation for the final word on whether you can connect it while your computer is running. Also, plugging in other types of devices can cause problems. For instance, plugging in an audio cable while your computer is on won't hurt your computer, but feedback could damage your speakers at high volume levels.

Hardware Resources

Every device connected to your computer uses resources that let the device communicate smoothly with the rest of the computer. For most modern devices (such as those using universal serial bus [USB], Firewire ports, or a Peripheral Component Interconnect [PCI] slot), Windows configures the resources used by the device automatically using its Plug and Play technology. On legacy hardware, such as Industry Standard Architecture (ISA) cards and some serial and parallel port devices, you may need to configure the resource settings on the hardware manually (often using *jumpers* or *DIP switches* [dual in-line package]) and even tell Windows what resources are being used by the device after you've configured it.

The following resources are used by most hardware:

- **Input/Output (I/O) Address**   A hexadecimal number that identifies the device for communications with the processor, or CPU. All I/O addresses assigned on a computer must be unique.

- **Interrupt (IRQ)**   Channels used by devices to signal the processor that they need its attention. PCs have 15 interrupt settings, numbered 0, 1, and 3–15. Many Plug and Play–compatible devices can share an interrupt, and Windows will set up these devices for you. Most legacy devices will not share an interrupt, so you must configure an interrupt that does not conflict with another device. See the "Determining How Resources Are Allocated on Your Computer" section later in this chapter for more on this.

- **DMA (Direct Memory Access) Channel**   Six channels used by a limited number of devices that need to have direct access to a computer's memory. Your floppy drive always takes DMA 2. Other devices may need to be configured manually.

- **Memory Addresses**   Some devices use specific addresses in your computer's memory to transfer information to the processor.

Drivers

Most hardware that you install on your computer also requires a software component to help translate between the hardware and Windows; this software component is called a *driver*. Windows comes with a huge number of drivers for common hardware built into the operating system, which is why Windows usually doesn't have much trouble configuring your hardware during installation. Nonetheless, some devices, especially those manufactured after the release of Windows XP, require that you supply the driver software.

> ▶ **QUICK TIP**
>
> *If you can't find drivers written specifically for Windows XP, you can try drivers written for Windows 2000. Fully test the hardware following the installation of the drivers and if it doesn't work as expected use the System Restore utility (covered in Chapter 22) to restore your system to its previous state.*

For the most part, the installation of a driver is pretty straightforward; the tricky part is making sure you have the right driver to install. New hardware should come with a driver disk. For older hardware or hardware that doesn't include Windows XP drivers, you can always check the manufacturer's Web site; most manufacturers post new drivers regularly.

Microsoft offers a driver testing program to all manufacturers. After a driver is fully tested by Microsoft, it is digitally signed. This signature lets you know that the driver has been tested and that it has not been modified since testing. If you attempt to install a driver that has not been signed, Windows presents a warning to that effect, although you can continue the installation. You'll find that many drivers are written for Windows XP and tested by the manufacturer but are not signed. The reason for this is that the testing process is expensive. If you trust the manufacturer, don't worry too much about it.

> ▶ **QUICK TIP**
>
> *You can change the way Windows notifies you when it detects an unsigned driver. From the System Properties dialog box (Start | Control Panel | System), select the Hardware tab. Then click Driver Signing. You'll have three options: install unsigned drivers without notifying you, prompt you when unsigned drivers are detected, and never install unsigned drivers.*

Installing Hardware

Installing hardware with Windows XP is not difficult. After following the manufacturer's directions for physically installing the hardware, one of three things will happen:

- If you connected a hot-pluggable device, Windows XP should notice automatically and open a wizard that steps you through the process of installing the driver and configuring the hardware.

- If you connected a device that was not hot-pluggable, but is Plug and Play–compatible, Windows XP detects the device when you start your computer and opens the same wizard used for hot-pluggable devices.

- If you installed a device that is neither hot-pluggable nor Plug and Play–compatible, Windows XP may not detect it. You will need to use the Add/Remove Hardware utility to configure the device. This is discussed in the section "Installing a Device Manually with the Add Hardware Wizard."

Configuring Hardware

In Windows XP, all the tools for configuring hardware are found in one convenient location: the Hardware tab of the System Properties dialog (Start | Control Panel | System), shown in Figure 3-1. From this tab, you can do the following, which are discussed in the tips section of the chapter.

- Launch the Add Hardware Wizard, which scans your computer for hardware not automatically detected and helps you configure any hardware it finds.

- Set Driver Signing options for the computer, which govern the notifications you receive when installing unsigned drivers.

- Open the Device Manager, the central tool used for viewing and configuring hardware in Windows XP.

- Manage hardware profiles, which are collections of hardware configurations that you can choose when booting your computer.

Figure 3-1   Start hardware-related utilities from the Hardware tab of the System Properties dialog box.

▶ *NOTE*

Most of the procedures described in this chapter require that you be logged on with an administrator type account (or as a member of the Administrators group in Windows XP Professional). This particularly applies to installing and working with device drivers.

Determining Hardware Compatibility with Windows XP

Before you install a device (before you even buy it, for that matter), you can determine whether that device has been tested by Microsoft for compatibility. The easiest way to do this is to look for the "Designed for Windows XP" logo on the device packaging. If this logo is not present, or if you don't have the packaging, you can consult Microsoft's Hardware Compatibility List at *http://www.microsoft .com/hcl/*.

Enter the name of the product and/or the hardware category to search. The resulting list contains all the hardware that matches and shows whether each device is compatible with or designed for various Windows operating systems, including Windows XP.

Determining How Resources Are Allocated on Your Computer

Hopefully, you won't need to manage your own hardware resources. If you are using older devices, however, you may find yourself moving jumpers or setting switches on the device to get it to work with other devices on the computer. Your device documentation should have details on what resources the device needs to have configured, the acceptable settings for each resource, and how to perform the configuration. Before you can configure the device, however, you need to know what resources are free on your computer for the device to use. The Device Manager tool answers this need.

TRY IT   To view resources assigned on your computer with Device Manager, do the following:

1. Click Start, and then click Control Panel.
2. Click the Performance and Maintenance link and then click the System icon. If the Control Panel window is in classic view, just double-click the System icon instead.
3. Switch to the Hardware tab and click Device Manager.
4. Select View | Resources By Type. This view, with the interrupt request (IRQ) resource type expanded, is shown in Figure 3-2.

Device Manager displays all the resources used along with the devices using them. Usually, you can choose an open setting (such as IRQ 9 in Figure 3-2) to use for your device. If your device doesn't support any of the open settings, you may have to configure another device to use a different setting.

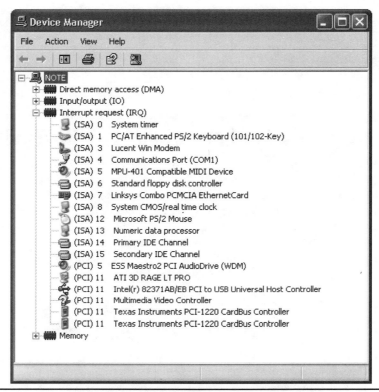

Figure 3-2   Viewing IRQ resources used by Windows in Device Manager

> ### QUICK TIP
>
> *You can use Device Manager to print a report by clicking the Print button on the toolbar. On the Print dialog that opens, make sure you select the option to print a system summary rather than a report of all devices. The system summary includes basic system information and resource usage in a few pages. The report of all devices is okay for a real system inventory, but it can be as long as few dozen pages.*

Installing a Device That Windows Detects Automatically

Windows XP will try its best to do all the driver installation work for you when you connect a new device. If you connect a hot-pluggable device, Windows pops up a balloon in the notification area informing you that it detects the device. If Windows already has a driver for the device, it installs it automatically and pops up another balloon informing you that the device is ready to use.

If Windows does not have a driver, or if the device is not hot-pluggable, you are presented with the Found New Hardware Wizard, which walks you through the steps for installing a driver and configuring the device.

▶ *NOTE*

Some devices, such as CD-ROM drives and hard drives, may not need drivers or any configuration. When you first start Windows after installing the device, it just becomes available.

TRY IT   To configure a device using the Found New Hardware Wizard, use the following steps:

1. The Found New Hardware Wizard starts automatically when Windows detects a new device. The first screen of the wizard, shown in Figure 3-3, presents two options:

   • **Install the Software Automatically**   This is the best option to try first. When you click Next, Windows searches any CDs, DVDs, and floppy disks in the computer and searches the Windows Update site for drivers compatible with the device. If it finds drivers, Windows notifies you and lets you select one to install. It's usually best to install the driver with the latest date. If Windows can't find drivers, you can cancel the installation or click the Back button to go back and select the option to install drivers from a specific location.

   • **Install from a List or Specific Location**   This option lets you specify a location for the driver or choose a driver from a list maintained by Windows. This option is covered throughout the remainder of these steps.

2. If you choose to install from a list or specific location, the next screen asks you to select from among two options:

   • **Search for a Driver**   This option lets you specify where Windows should search for the driver. If you downloaded a driver, for example, you might select the Include This Location in Search option and enter the path to the downloaded files. When you click Next, Windows searches for a driver and installs it if one is found. If a driver is not found, you can cancel the installation or back up in the wizard (click Back). If you back up, you can specify an alternative location and try the search again or select the option to choose a driver.

   • **Choose a Driver**   This option lets you choose from a list of drivers that come with Windows XP or choose a specific driver from another location to install. Since Windows will already have searched its own list for compatible drivers, you should choose this option only if you want to install a driver for another device that you are sure will work with your device. This option is covered throughout the remainder of these steps.

3. If you elected to choose a driver yourself, Windows presents a list of hardware categories, such as disk drives, network adapters, and so on. Select the category for your device and click Next.

4. Select a manufacturer from the list of manufacturers and models. Then select the device model for the driver you want to install. If you have a disk with an alternative driver, click Have Disk and specify the location and the driver file.

5. Windows displays a list of drivers that match the model you specified or that were found on the disk. Select the model whose driver you want to use and click Next. Windows may display a dialog box warning you that the device and driver don't match. If it does this, click Yes to use the driver anyway.

6. At this point, one of two things will happen:

   • Windows displays a dialog informing you that the location you specified contains no information about your hardware. If this happens, you'll have to go back and try another model or specify another location.

   • Windows displays a dialog informing you that the driver it found has not passed compatibility testing. Click Continue Anyway to use the driver or click Stop Installation to cancel.

7. Windows installs the driver and displays the final page of the wizard. Click Finish to return to Windows. If you are prompted to restart your computer, do so.

▶ *CAUTION*

It should probably go without saying, but be very careful when installing drivers not specifically built for your hardware and designed for Windows XP. In fact, you should probably avoid this procedure unless you're instructed to do so by the manufacturer of your hardware. The driver may work fine, but if it does not, the effects range from the device not working to Windows not being able to start.

Figure 3-3   You can have Windows search for a driver automatically or specify a driver yourself.

Installing a Device Manually with the Add Hardware Wizard

If Windows does not detect your device when you install it, you must use the Add Hardware Wizard. During the first stages, the wizard scans your system for new Plug and Play–compatible hardware. Since this type of hardware is usually detected automatically, the wizard rarely finds anything at this point. After this, the wizard can also search your computer for other types of hardware and often finds legacy devices that are not Plug and Play–compatible, but for which Windows does come with drivers. If the wizard does not detect your device, you'll have to set it up yourself.

▶ *NOTE*

If you have an installation disk for your device, try using it to install the hardware before using the Add Hardware Wizard. Often, the installation program provided by the manufacturer is quicker and more reliable.

TRY IT   Use the following steps to configure a device using the Add Hardware Wizard:

1. Click Start, and then click Control Panel.

2. Click the Printers and Other Hardware link and then click the Add Hardware link to start the Add Hardware Wizard. Note that you can also start this wizard from the Hardware tab of the System Properties dialog.

3. On the initial page of the wizard, click Next. Windows starts a scan of your computer to detect any new hardware that it recognizes. If it recognizes new hardware and has drivers for it, the wizard installs those drivers and finishes.

4. If it does not detect any new hardware, the wizard displays a dialog asking whether the hardware is connected to the computer yet. If you answer No, the wizard exits. If you answer Yes, the wizard continues.

5. Next, the wizard displays a list of hardware installed on your computer, as shown in Figure 3-4. Hardware that has been detected, but has some kind of problem (a driver has not been installed or there is a resource conflict, for example) is listed at the top followed by the working hardware on your computer. You have two options here:

   • You can select an installed device with a problem and click Next to see a description of the problem and where to go to fix it. The wizard ends at this point. You can also select an installed device without a problem and the wizard will end.

   • You can scroll to the bottom of the list, select the Add a New Hardware Device entry, and click Next to set up a legacy device not already detected by Windows. The remainder of this procedure assumes you select this option.

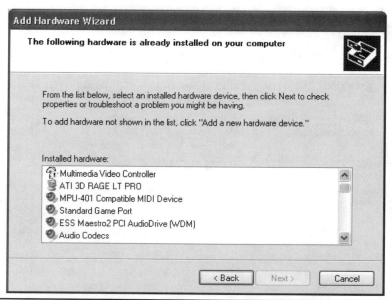

Figure 3-4   The Add Hardware Wizard can show you what's wrong with an installed device or let you add a new device.

6. When you select the Add a New Hardware Device entry and click Next, the Add Hardware Wizard presents you with two options:

- **Let the Wizard Search for and Install the Device Automatically**   If you select this option, the wizard starts a scan of your computer that may take a few minutes. Also, the scan has been known to cause problems—like crashing a computer. For the most part, though, it's pretty safe. At the end of the scan, you are shown a list of any hardware found. As you finish the wizard, Windows will search for drivers and install them. If it doesn't have drivers, you can select the driver yourself.

- **Install the Hardware from a List**   This option lets you select a manufacturer and model for the type of hardware and install a driver. The procedures for installing drivers for both this and the automatic search option are similar to those described in the "Installing a Device That Windows Detects Automatically" section earlier in this chapter.

Troubleshooting When a Device Isn't Working

Device Manager, shown in Figure 3-5, is the central tool used to manage hardware in Windows XP. By default, devices are grouped into categories such as disk drives, modems, and ports. Expand any category to see the devices.

Figure 3-5   Using Device Manager to configure and troubleshoot hardware devices

The icon associated with a device gives a clue to its status:

- A working device shows a normal device icon.
- A disabled device shows a red *x* over the icon.
- A device with a problem shows an exclamation point (!) over the icon. Problems can include bad or missing drivers or resource conflicts, for example.
- A device without a driver shows a yellow question mark for an icon and an exclamation point over the icon.

You can open a Properties dialog box by double-clicking any device. This dialog always includes at least three tabs (some devices include additional tabs):

- **General**   This tab, shown in Figure 3-6, displays basic device information (type, manufacturer, and location) and device status (including a description of why the device isn't working if there's a problem). Depending on the status of the device, a button for resolving problems appears; the actual button changes depending on the status.
- **Driver**   This tab is covered in the section "Working with Drivers," later in the chapter.

- **Resources**   This tab displays the current resources used by a device. Most devices are configured automatically. You can set resources manually by disabling the Use Automatic Settings option, selecting the resource you want to change, and clicking Change Setting. A window at the bottom of the tab displays any conflicts with other devices caused by the current settings.

When a device does not work, it's usually due to one of three reasons:

- *The drivers are not installed or are not compatible.*   This is discussed in the "Working with Drivers" section.

- *There is a resource conflict.*   This can happen with older hardware. You will need to use the Resources tab to find and resolve the conflict manually.

- *The hardware itself has a problem.*   Hardware can fail for a number of reasons—some of them fixable. When this happens, Device Manager may simply inform you that the device is not working properly. The General tab of a device's Properties dialog will feature a Troubleshoot button when this is the case. Click the button to open a question-based troubleshooter that will walk you through some of the problems that commonly occur with the device.

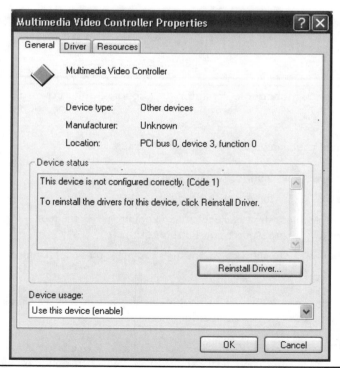

Figure 3-6   Using Device Manager to determine why a device is not working

Removing a Device

Removing a hardware device is easier than installing one: You simply remove the device in Windows (which removes references and drivers) and then unplug the device from the computer. To remove the device in Windows, open Device Manager and select the device from the list. Choose Action | Uninstall. Windows displays a dialog asking you to confirm the removal of the device. Click OK and the device is uninstalled. You should now disconnect the device from your computer.

> **QUICK TIP**
>
> *You can also uninstall a device by right-clicking the device and choosing Uninstall or by clicking the Uninstall button on the Device Manager toolbar.*

Disabling a Device

If you don't want to remove a device permanently, you can temporarily disable it. This is particularly useful in three circumstances:

- You are having a problem with Windows that you suspect the device is causing and need to disable it while you troubleshoot the problem.

- You want to install a device temporarily that will conflict with another device. You can disable the first device until you are done with the second.

- You want to create hardware profiles in which certain devices are disabled. This is discussed further in the section "Configuring Hardware Profiles" a little later in the chapter.

TRY IT To disable a device, use the following steps:

1. In Device Manager, right-click the device and choose Properties.
2. On the General tab of the device's Properties dialog, select the Do Not Use This Device (Disable) option from the Device Usage drop-down list.
3. Click OK.

Working with Drivers

Windows XP sports a number of great features not present in other versions of Windows for working with drivers. All these features are available on the Driver tab of a device's Properties dialog, shown in Figure 3-7.

Figure 3-7 The Driver tab lets you view details, update, roll back, and uninstall drivers for a device.

The Driver tab provides basic information about the driver, such as the provider, date, and version and lets you perform four actions:

- **View driver details**   Click Driver Details to view a list of actual driver files used by the device.
- **Update the driver**   Click Update Driver to launch a wizard that walks you through updating the driver. This process is almost identical to installing a driver for a new device, which is discussed previously in the section "Installing a Device That Windows Detects Automatically."
- **Roll the driver back**   When you update a driver, Windows stores a backup of the previous driver. If you experience problems with the updated driver, click Roll Back Driver to uninstall the update and revert back to a previous version of the driver.
- **Uninstall the driver**   Uninstalling the driver removes the device from your computer. This is the same effect as removing the device, which was discussed in the "Removing a Device" section.

Configuring Hardware Profiles

A hardware profile is a collection of configuration information about the hardware on your computer. Within a profile, each piece of hardware (such as networking adapters, ports, monitors, and so on) can be enabled, disabled, or given specific configuration information. You can have any number of hardware profiles on a computer and switch between different profiles when booting into Windows XP. Hardware profiles might be useful, for example, for a notebook computer on which different hardware is attached, depending on the location.

By default, one profile is created during the installation of Windows XP and is named Profile 1. You create additional profiles by copying an existing profile and renaming it. Once you have created your profiles, you can configure how the hardware behaves in that profile by booting Windows using the profile and then configuring the hardware using Device Manager. Within each profile, you can disable any devices you want or assign different resource settings.

Hardware profiles are managed using the Hardware Profiles dialog box, shown in Figure 3-8. You access this dialog from the System Properties dialog's Hardware tab, where you click Hardware Profiles. Select the profile to base a new profile on, click Copy, and provide a name for the new profile. Click Rename to give the old profiles more meaningful names.

Select a profile and click Properties to set two options regarding the profile:

- *Whether the computer is a portable computer*   If you use a docking station with your notebook computer (and if that docking station is one that Windows XP supports), you can specify whether the profile is to be used when the computer is docked or undocked. When a supported docking station is used, Windows XP can determine whether a notebook computer is docked or undocked and apply the correct profile automatically.

- *Whether the profile should be included on the Profile menu when Windows XP starts*
  If you have profiles that you would prefer to keep hidden, disable this option.

Figure 3-8   Creating and managing hardware profiles

If multiple hardware profiles are configured, Windows XP displays a menu when it starts, from which you can choose a profile. By default, Windows will automatically load the first profile on the list in 30 seconds if you don't choose one. You can modify the time Windows waits (and whether it will load a profile automatically at all) using the settings at the bottom of the Hardware Profiles dialog (see Figure 3-8). You can modify the order in which profiles appear on the list using the up and down buttons next to the profiles.

PART II
Windows Basics

CHAPTER 4
Using the Windows Desktop

TIPS IN THIS CHAPTER

The Windows Desktop, Start menu, and Taskbar work pretty much the same in Windows XP as they have since their introduction in Windows 95. The Windows XP Desktop sports a cleaner look than its predecessors, though. Desktop icons (except for the Recycle Bin) have been removed by default, the Start menu has been redesigned, buttons on the Taskbar are grouped by similarity, and the notification area (formerly called the System Tray) collapses to hide all but frequently-used icons and the clock.

While the Windows XP Desktop appearance is simpler and many features appear to have been removed, most of them have just been disabled to make things a bit easier for beginners. As usual, a lot of power lurks beneath the surface, and you can take advantage of it if you're willing to do a little exploring.

Getting Back Your Desktop Icons

For some reason, the designers of Windows decided it would be easier for people if the My Computer, My Documents, and other familiar icons were removed from the Desktop and positioned prominently on the Start menu. While having access to these icons on the Start menu is useful, many people (especially longtime users of Windows) prefer having them on the Desktop as well. Fortunately, adding them back is easy.

From the Start menu, right-click an icon you want to display on the Desktop (such as My Computer). From the shortcut menu that opens, choose Show on Desktop. This works with the My Documents, My Computer, and My Network Places icons.

You can also enable the display of these icons on the Desktop Properties dialog box (discussed in Chapter 21), by clicking Customize Desktop on the Desktop tab.

QUICK TIP

You can copy some icons on the Start menu (such as My Pictures or My Music) to the Desktop by dragging them there. This will copy the entire folder *with its contents and not simply the shortcut to the folder. If you drag the My Documents, My Computer, or My Network Places icons to the Desktop, a shortcut to those locations is created instead of a fully functional copy.*

Switching to the Classic Start Menu

While the new Start menu in Windows XP is appealing to many, you may prefer the Classic Start menu style used in previous versions of Windows. Switching to the Classic Start menu affects only how items on the Start menu are arranged; it does not affect the new Windows XP style for buttons and windows. In addition, the Classic Start menu does not contain a list of recently-used programs.

TRY IT To switch to the Classic Start menu style, use the following steps:

1. Click Start and then click Control Panel.
2. In the Control Panel window, click Appearance and Themes.
3. In the Appearance and Themes window, click the Taskbar and Start Menu icon. This opens the Taskbar and Start Menu Properties dialog box.
4. Click the Start Menu tab.
5. Select the Classic Start Menu option.
6. Click OK to apply the new settings.

QUICK TIP

You can get to the Taskbar and Start Menu Properties dialog box quickly by right-clicking the Windows Taskbar and choosing Properties.

Changing What Appears on the Start Menu

The Start menu is the centerpiece of the Windows Desktop. It includes shortcuts for running programs, getting to various locations on your computer and network, and controlling system settings.

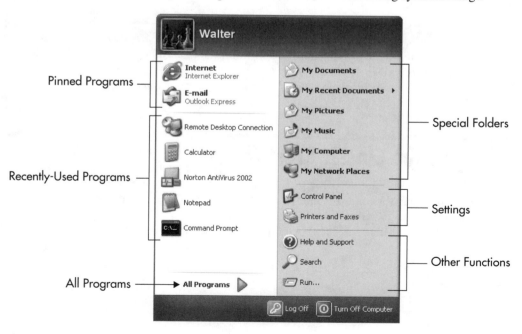

The Start menu has several distinct areas:

- **Pinned Programs**   At the top left are shortcuts for running your default Web browser and e-mail program. These shortcuts are "pinned" to the Start menu so that they always appear there. When you install Windows, these two shortcuts are configured as Internet Explorer and Outlook Express. However, when you install new Web or e-mail software, you'll have the option of setting them as the default programs. Configuring these defaults is discussed later in this section.

- **Recently-Used Programs**   Under the Internet shortcuts, you'll find links to the programs you have run most recently. By default, six links are shown. You can change the number shown, clear the entire list at any time, and even prevent the links from being shown at all. This is discussed later in this section.

QUICK TIP

You can "pin" any of the shortcuts on the recently-used programs list to your Start menu by right-clicking the shortcut and choosing the Pin to Start Menu command. This command moves the shortcut to a position under your Internet shortcuts, where it will remain until you remove it. Unpin an icon by right-clicking and choosing Unpin from Start Menu. You can also pin shortcuts from other locations on the Start menu or from Windows Explorer.

- **All Programs**   The All Programs submenu is roughly the same as the Programs submenu in previous versions of Windows; it displays shortcuts to most of the programs installed on your computer. These shortcuts are often divided into program groups, or folders that group together items related to a single piece of software. Learn more about using the All Programs submenu in the "Managing the All Programs Menu" section later in this chapter.

- **Special Folders**   At the upper right of the Start menu, you'll find shortcuts to many of the special folders on your computer. Many of these shortcuts represent icons that used to be found only on the Windows Desktop.

- **Settings**   Here you'll find shortcuts for configuring various settings on your computer, such as the Control Panel. Other items, such as Printers and Faxes, may also appear here. Configuring settings is covered in Chapter 22.

- **Other Functions**   The final section of the Start menu contains links for Help and Support (covered in Chapter 9), the Search function (Chapter 5), and the Run dialog box (Chapter 6).

TRY IT   As with most other interfaces in Windows, the Start menu is customizable. To configure your Start menu, use the following steps:

1. Right-click the Windows Taskbar and choose Properties. This opens the Taskbar and Start Menu Properties dialog box.
2. Click the Start Menu tab.

3. Click the active Customize button. The rest of this procedure assumes you are using the regular Start menu option; clicking Customize opens the Customize Start Menu dialog box. If you are using the Classic Start menu, clicking the Customize button opens a dialog box similar to the one used in previous versions of Windows.

4. Select an icon size. This option controls the size of icons displayed on the left side of the Start menu, in the Internet and recently-used programs areas.

5. Choose the number of recently-used programs to display on the Start menu. By default, this is set to six, but you can configure it for anything from zero to thirty. Setting the number to zero effectively disables the feature.

► | ## QUICK TIP

You can clear a specific program from the recently-used programs list by right-clicking it on the Start menu and choosing Remove From This List.

6. Clear the list of recently-used programs by clicking Clear List.

7. Configure your Internet and e-mail programs. Uncheck either option to remove it from the Start menu. The drop-down menu for each item holds a list of programs that you can choose to display on the Start menu. Note that selecting a different option (for example, MSN Explorer instead of Internet Explorer) does not change the default program used to open Web pages; it merely changes the shortcut on the Start menu.

8. Click the Advanced tab. The Advanced tab holds a number of additional options for configuring the Start menu:

- **Open submenus when I pause on them with my mouse**   When this option is selected, submenus are automatically opened after a brief delay. When deselected, you must click a submenu to open it.

- **Highlight newly installed programs**   When this option is selected, any programs that you have installed, but not yet run, are highlighted on the All Programs menu.

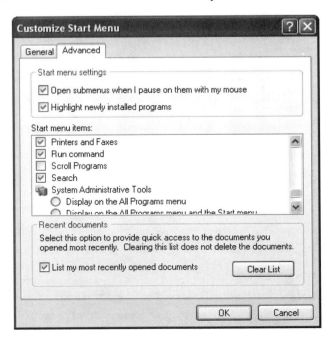

> ► **QUICK TIP**
>
> *Configure your My Computer Start menu icon to work as a menu. This gives you quick access to your drives from the Start menu. Also, configure your Control Panel as a menu to quickly access system settings instead of wading through the Control Panel window.*

- **Start menu items**   You can specify the items that appear on the Start menu and control from this list. This includes items you're already familiar with (My Computer, Control Panel, and so on), as well as your Favorites menu and System Administrative Tools. For many of these items, you can choose whether the link should be displayed as a simple shortcut or as an expandable menu. This list also contains two other features: you can toggle on and off the ability to drag and drop items on the Start menu and whether Windows scrolls submenus that are too long to fit on your screen.

- **Recent documents**   select whether you want the My Recent Documents menu to appear on the start menu. Click Clear List to reset the recently-used document list.

Managing the All Programs Menu

The All Programs menu, shown in Figure 4-1, provides shortcuts for most of the programs installed on your computer and works in pretty much the same way that the Programs menu did in previous versions of Windows. It is divided into folders called *program groups;* each application that you install normally creates its own program group and creates a shortcut for launching the application and a few other items inside.

The All Programs menu (and the rest of the Start menu) is customizable for each user who logs onto a computer and is built based on two different folders found in the Documents and Settings folder. Within the Documents and Settings folder (usually on the C: drive), you'll find a separate folder for each user of the computer and another folder named All Users. Within each of these folders is another folder named Start Menu. This folder contains all the shortcuts and subfolders that appear on the All Programs menu. Documents and Settings\All Users\Start Menu contains shortcuts for programs that are accessible by all users. The Start Menu folder in each user's individual folder contains additional shortcuts available only to that user and any custom shortcuts and folders the user has created. The

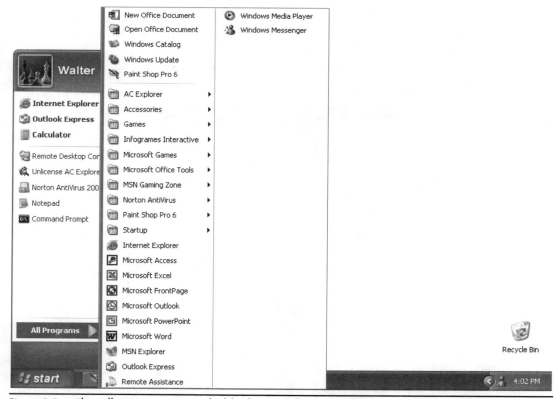

Figure 4-1   The All Programs menu holds shortcuts for most of the programs installed on your computer.

> **QUICK TIP**
>
> *You can also rearrange the All Programs submenu from the Start menu itself by dragging items around, the same way you could with previous versions of Windows. You can even drag items from Explorer directly onto the Start and All Programs menus to create new shortcuts there.*

All Programs menu that any particular user sees is based on the combined items from the All Users\Start Menu folder and that user's Start Menu folder.

You can rearrange your Start Menu by creating new folders inside your own Start Menu folder and by moving shortcuts around. Any shortcuts that you place directly in the Start Menu folder (instead of in the Programs folder or one of its subfolders) appear in a special place at the top of the All Programs menu (or directly on the Start menu if you are using the Classic Start Menu style).

Clearing the Run List

The Run command on the Start menu opens a dialog box, where you can type in the path (or browse) for a program, folder, document, or Web site to launch. Windows keeps track of items that have been typed into the Run dialog box; you can choose from a list of past commands using a drop-down list. Occasionally, you may want to clear the contents of this list, either for security reasons or because it has become too cluttered.

If you are comfortable editing the Windows Registry, you can clear items from the Run history. If you are not comfortable editing the Registry, check out Chapter 23 first for tips on using the Windows Registry, and then give this procedure a try.

TRY IT To clear the history for the Run dialog box, use the following steps:

1. Click Start and then click Run.

2. In the Run dialog box that opens, type **regedit.exe** and click OK.

3. In the Registry Editor, navigate to the following key: HKEY_CURRENT_USER\Software\ Microsoft\Windows\CurrentVersion\Explorer\RunMRU.

4. The Run history is stored as a series of values in the RunMRU subkey, ranging from *a* to *z*. Select the entry you want to remove and press DELETE.

5. Click Yes to confirm the deletion.

6. Double-click the MRUList value.

7. In the Value data field, delete the letter corresponding to the value you deleted in step 4 and click OK.

8. Close the Registry Editor.

> ▶ **QUICK TIP**
>
> *Microsoft has created a number of additional utilities named Power Toys that are available as a free download at* http://www.microsoft.com/windowsxp/pro/downloads/powertoys.asp. *One of these utilities, named Tweak UI, provides a feature that lets you wipe out your entire Run history at once and optionally clear the history every time Windows starts.*

Taming the Notification Area

The notification area (formerly known as the System Tray) is the far right portion of the Taskbar that contains the system clock and several small icons. Windows uses the notification area to display notification icons when it needs your attention on some matter. For example, if you have automatic updating enabled (see Chapter 1), Windows displays a globe icon in the notification area when a new update becomes available from Microsoft. Windows also displays icons when new hardware is added to your system. Clicking a notification icon normally opens a window that provides more information or steps for resolving a situation.

Other icons in the notification area represent programs running in the background, such as Windows Messenger or an anti-virus program. The guidelines for using these icons are up to the manufacturer, and all of them work a bit differently. Nonetheless, here are a few tips for manipulating them:

- You can usually hold your pointer over the icon to view a pop-up tip with the name of the program. Hold the pointer over the clock to view the date.
- Try clicking or right-clicking an icon to open a menu with options for manipulating the program. There will often be an option for closing the background program or for launching its associated full application. Note that not all icons provide a menu.
- Try double-clicking an icon to run a program if no menu is available.

Windows XP includes a new feature that collapses the notification area so that only frequently-used icons (and all notification icons) are displayed. When this happens, a small button with a left-pointing arrow appears that you can use to expand the notification area. When you move your mouse away, it collapses again.

TRY IT You can control how the notification area hides icons. To do this, use the following steps.

1. Right-click the Taskbar and choose Properties. This opens the Taskbar and Start Menu Properties dialog box.
2. Use the Hide Inactive Icons option to toggle the automatic hiding of icons.

3. Click the Customize button to open the Customize Notifications dialog box.

4. This dialog box displays a list of icons currently displayed in the notification area and a list of icons that have been displayed in the past. Click an item to select it.

5. Use the drop-down list in the Behavior column to have Windows always hide the icon, always show the icon, or hide the icon only when it is inactive.

QUICK TIP

You can access the Customize Notifications dialog box more quickly by right-clicking the notification area on the Taskbar and choosing Customize Notifications.

Synchronizing System Time

As always, you can quickly access the Date and Time Properties dialog box for setting your system clock by double-clicking the clock in the notification area (the long way to get there is through the Control Panel). In addition to setting the date, time, and time zone, you can now use this dialog box to configure an Internet time server. After you set the server by choosing from a list of available servers, Windows regularly contacts the time server over the Internet to synchronize your system's clock. Synchronization normally occurs about once per week, and you can't change this schedule.

You can, however, synchronize the clock manually whenever you want by clicking Update Now on the Internet Time tab, as shown here.

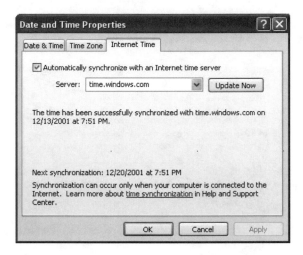

Internet time synchronization works best if you have a persistent Internet connection, such as through your company network, DSL, or cable. If you have a dial-up Internet connection, Windows will not connect automatically to synchronize your clock; you'll need to do it manually each time instead. Finally, synchronization often does not work through firewalls, especially corporate firewalls. If you are a home user with a personal firewall, you may be able to unblock the synchronization. Consult your firewall documentation about unblocking the Network Time Protocol (NTP). Internet time synchronization is available only on computers that are members of a workgroup and not members of a domain.

> ### QUICK TIP
>
> *Some time servers are more reliable than others. For example, Microsoft's own time server has been reported to be off by several minutes on more than one occasion. For the best results, use a public time server in your time zone or use the US Naval Observatory server. You can find a good list of servers at* http://www.eecis.udel.edu/~mills/ntp/servers.htm.

Managing the Taskbar

The Taskbar, that familiar compilation of buttons and icons that appears at the bottom of the Desktop, is much the same as the Taskbar from previous versions of Windows. In fact, the Windows XP Taskbar sports only three new features:

- The notification area is able to hide unused icons automatically to help reduce its size. This feature is covered in the earlier section, "Taming the Notification Area."

- The Taskbar can be locked, which prevents you from accidentally moving or resizing the Taskbar and from deleting icons on the toolbars. In addition, locking the Taskbar removes the dividers between toolbars and the toolbar names, resulting in a more streamlined appearance.

- If multiple documents are open in the same application, all documents are grouped under a single Taskbar button instead of each document having its own button.

You can also manipulate the Taskbar in other ways, such as moving it, altering its size, and adding to it a number of toolbars. Before you can do any of this, however, you must first unlock the Taskbar if it is locked by right-clicking the Taskbar and choosing Unlock Taskbar.

Once the Taskbar is unlocked, you can resize it by placing your pointer at the topmost edge and dragging it to the size you want, up to about half the display. You can also move the Taskbar to any of the four edges of your display by placing your pointer in an open space on the Taskbar and dragging it where you want to move it. Figure 4-2 shows an enlarged Taskbar on the left side of a display.

You can also set a number of other Taskbar properties by right-clicking the Taskbar and choosing Properties to open the Taskbar and Start Menu Properties dialog box. These properties include the following:

- Locking and unlocking the Taskbar.

- Toggling the auto-hide feature, which slides the Taskbar out of view when it is not being used and back into view when you place your pointer at the bottom of the display (or on whatever edge your Taskbar is placed).

- Specifying whether the Taskbar should always stay on top of other windows or whether other windows should be allowed to obscure it.

- Specifying whether similar Taskbar buttons should be grouped. This feature is covered in Chapter 5.

- Toggling the display of the Quick Launch bar, which is covered in the next section, "Using the Quick Launch Bar."

Using the Quick Launch Bar

Toolbars are a useful feature of the Taskbar, and it's interesting that none of the toolbars included with Windows XP is displayed by default. The Quick Launch bar, in particular, is a real timesaver. It contains icons for launching frequently used applications. By default, it contains only three icons: Internet Explorer, Windows Media Player, and Show Desktop. The first two launch the respective programs. The Show Desktop icon immediately displays the Desktop, no matter how many windows or dialog boxes are open on your screen. Clicking it again restores your windows. You can also add other shortcut icons to the Quick Launch bar. The easiest way to do this is to drag an existing folder, program file, document, Web page, or other shortcut to the Quick Launch bar. Once a shortcut is created, you can manipulate it (rename, delete, and so on) by right-clicking it and using its shortcut menu.

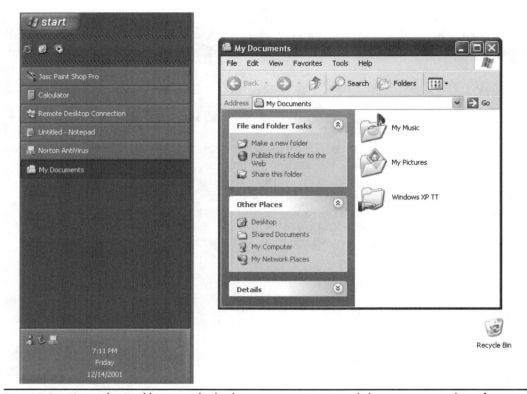

Figure 4-2   Once the Taskbar is unlocked, you can resize it and drag it to any edge of the display.

▶ │ **QUICK TIP**

You can also drag existing shortcuts from the Start menu to the Quick Launch bar. When doing this, however, it is best to drag using your right mouse button and choose Copy Here from the shortcut menu that opens. If you drag with your left mouse button, you will create a shortcut to the shortcut, which might cause a problem should the original shortcut be deleted or moved.

The Quick Launch bar is actually built based on the contents of a special Windows folder, located at C:\Documents and Settings\username\Application Data\Microsoft\Internet Explorer\Quick Launch. Each user on the computer can have his or her own customized Quick Launch bar. You can also manipulate the contents of the folder directly.

> ▶ **QUICK TIP**
>
> *You can drag the Quick Launch bar away from the Taskbar so that it is displayed as a window. First, make sure the Taskbar is unlocked. Then, position your pointer over the bar's handle (the little indented dots at the left edge of the bar) and drag the toolbar out onto your Desktop. Drag it to any other edge of the display to display it as a toolbar there. If you want to put the Quick Launch bar back in its original position, the easiest way is to close it and open it again.*

Using the Address Bar

The Address bar is such a great feature. It's easy to become addicted to it after a little use. It's designed primarily to offer a quick way of entering a Web address. Just type in an address and Windows XP opens a new browser window for you.

You can also enter other information in the Address bar, including the following:

- **Folder names**   Type **My Documents** in the Address bar, for instance, and Windows opens the folder for you.

- **A network resource**   Type ***computername*** (where *computername* is the name of a computer on your network) to open that computer or ***computername**sharename*** to open a specific shared resource on that computer.

- **A command**   Type the name of any executable file or command. For example, you could type **sol.exe** (or even just **sol**) to run the Solitaire game or the name of a command you commonly use. You should be aware, though, that when running a command from the Address bar, a command prompt window opens while the command is running and then closes immediately after. This makes it unsuitable for commands for which you need to see the output, such as *ipconfig* or *ping*. For those, it's best just to open a command prompt window. You can do this quickly by typing **cmd** into the Address bar.

- **A Web search**   Since the Address bar is designed primarily for opening Web pages, it tries to resolve any text it doesn't understand as a Web page. For example, if you type in the wrong name for a folder and no other folders or commands match the name you typed, Windows will perform a Web search based on your input. While this may sometimes yield an undesired result, it also makes the Address bar great for doing impromptu Web searches using your browser's default search engine.

The Address bar also keeps a history of commands and addresses for easy access; just click the down arrow to open a drop-down list.

Creating New Toolbars

In addition to the built-in toolbars, Windows lets you create toolbars of your own. Custom toolbars are created based on one of two items:

- **A folder**   When created based on a folder, a custom toolbar works almost exactly like the Quick Launch bar. You can fill the folder with shortcuts for quick access. You could, for example, create multiple toolbars in this manner and fill them with shortcuts relating to particular tasks.

▶ *NOTE*

After you disable a custom toolbar, you have to re-create it to get it back. You cannot simply turn it on and off.

- **A Web site**   This option creates a toolbar that actually displays the Web page you enter. While docked to the Taskbar, this type of toolbar is only marginally useful; you can't see much of a typical Web page even when you enlarge your Taskbar to maximum size. However, when you undock the Taskbar, what you get is a floating window that you can resize. This window is essentially a mini Web browser without all the menus and toolbars cluttering up the view. Clicking any link in the toolbar window opens a full browser window, as shown in Figure 4-3.

Figure 4-3   Creating a toolbar using a Web site provides a simplified browser window.

CHAPTER 5
Managing Files and Folders

TIPS IN THIS CHAPTER

Files are the basic unit of organization on your computer. Windows itself is composed of thousands of different files that interact with one another to create the desktop environment with which you are familiar. Programs are collections of files that interact with one another and with Windows files. Finally, the documents you create using those programs are also files. It is no surprise, then, that Windows includes a rich set of features for working with files. The most important of these features is the ability to organize files using folders, containers that can hold any number of files and other folders. This chapter introduces a number of techniques for working with files and folders.

Windows Explorer

Windows Explorer is the primary interface for working with files and folders in Windows; whenever you open a folder, you're using Explorer. The Explorer window boasts a number of features, not all of which are made visible by default. Figure 5-1 shows Explorer with most of its features made visible.

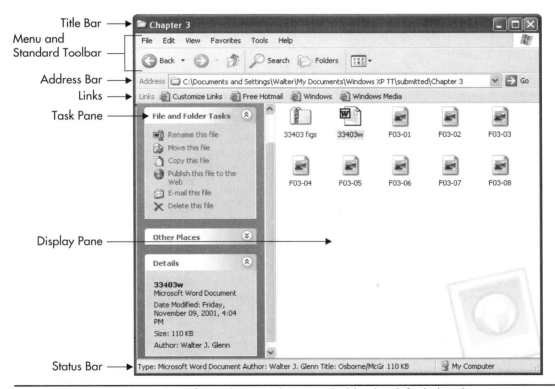

Figure 5-1 Many components of Windows Explorer are hidden by default, but they are easy to turn on.

Here are the primary features of the Windows Explorer window:

- **Title Bar**   Displays the name of the open folder. Optionally, it can also display the full working path of the folder (see "Setting Folder Options," later in this chapter, for more).

- **Menu Bar and Standard Toolbar**   Used to issue commands when you're working with files and folders. Many of these commands are also available on shortcut menus accessed by right-clicking a folder or file.

- **Links Bar**   The same toolbar present in Internet Explorer. By default, the Links bar contains shortcuts to various Microsoft Web sites, but it can be easily customized to hold links to your favorite Web sites, folders, programs, and documents. (See Chapter 16 for more on customizing the Links bar.)

- **Address Bar**   Shows the full path of the current folder. When you click the down arrow, a quick list of other locations appears, including the parent folders of the current folder and all the top-level folders on your computer (My Computer, My Documents, and so on). You can also type addresses directly into the Address bar, as you'll learn later in "Using Addresses for Folders and Files."

- **Task Pane**   Consists of three sections:
  - **Tasks**   Suggests common tasks to perform based on what type of folder or file is selected
  - **Other Places**   Shows a list of folders related to your current location
  - **Details**   Shows detailed information (such as size and modification date) of the currently selected item

- **Display Pane**   The main part of the Explorer window that shows the contents of the current folder.

- **Status Bar**   Displays information about any selected object. For example, when a file is selected, the Status bar shows the file type and size. When a drive is selected, the capacity and free space on the drive are shown. The Status bar is turned off by default (probably because much of its information is duplicated in the new task pane), but you can turn it on by choosing View | Status Bar from any open folder.

Another new feature of Windows XP Explorer is Explorer bars, which appear to the left of the normal window area, covering up the area that normally contains the task pane. A number of Explorer bars are available, including the following:

- **Folders**   Displays a hierarchical view of the folders on your computer. This view is discussed in detail in "Navigating the Folder Tree."

- **Search**   Displays the Search Companion Wizard used to search for objects on your computer. The Search Companion is covered in the section "Searching," later in this chapter.

- **Media**   Displays a number of elements from the *WindowsMedia.com* Web site and a simplified version of Windows Media Player.

- **Favorites** Displays items from a user's Favorites folder—the same folder used in Internet Explorer. This feature is covered in Chapter 16.

- **History** Displays a history of Web sites visited by the user—the same history used in Internet Explorer. This feature is covered in Chapter 15.

▶ *NOTE*

Other programs installed on your computer may create additional Explorer bars of their own.

Navigating the Folder Tree

One of the Explorer bars available in Windows Explorer is named Folders. Open it by selecting View | Explorer Bar | Folders in any open folder, or by clicking the Folders button on the Standard toolbar. The Folders Explorer bar, shown in Figure 5-2, provides a hierarchical view of all the drives and folders on your computer (sometimes called a folder *tree*), making it easy for you to jump to particular locations and drag files around. Turning on the Folders bar makes the Explorer window look and operate much like the Windows Explorer folder found in past versions of Windows.

Figure 5-2   The Folders Explorer bar provides a hierarchical view of your computer's folder structure.

Use the Folders bar to navigate through your file system. Click any folder to display its contents in the main Explorer window. A plus or minus sign next to a folder indicates that the folder contains additional folders: click the plus sign (or double-click the folder) to expand it, and click the minus sign to collapse an expanded folder.

In a large folder structure, scrolling around looking for folders can be cumbersome. Fortunately, Windows features some handy keyboard techniques to help you get around. First, make sure that the Folders bar has input focus by selecting any folder in it or by pressing TAB until a folder is highlighted. Next, use any of the following techniques:

- *Use the arrow keys to move around.* Press the up and down arrows to move up and down the folder list without expanding any folders. Press the right arrow to expand a collapsed folder, and click the left arrow to collapse an expanded folder. If a folder is already collapsed (or if a highlighted folder can't be collapsed), click the left arrow to move to the parent folder of the currently selected folder. You can also press the BACKSPACE key to move to the parent folder, but not to collapse folders.

- *Type the first few letters of a folder's name to jump to that folder.* If several folders start with the same few letters, you may not get to the exact folder you want, but you can usually come close enough to use the up and down arrows to finish the job.

- *Press a letter key to jump to the first folder that begins with that letter.* Press the same key again to go to the next folder that begins with the letter. Keep pressing the key to cycle through the entire folder list (not including folders inside collapsed folders). Press BACKSPACE to go up one level, use the left and right arrow keys to expand the branches, and press ENTER to expand a selected folder.

Moving and Copying Files

Most people move objects around by dragging them with the left mouse button. But sometimes it's difficult to tell exactly what's going to happen when you release the button. If you are dragging a file from one folder to another on the same drive, the file is moved. If you're dragging from a folder on one drive to a folder on another drive, the file is copied instead. If you move an executable file (such as one ending in *.exe*), a shortcut is usually created.

Windows does provide some subtle clues while you're dragging. When you left-drag a file (or folder), pay attention to the icon of the file as it is being dragged. The icon changes to reflect what will happen when you release the mouse button:

- A small plus sign on the icon means the object will be copied.
- A small curving arrow means a shortcut will be made.
- No change in the icon means the object will be moved.

While these visual indicators are useful, there are better ways to move and copy objects in Windows. You can exert much finer control over the process by right-dragging (dragging with your right mouse button) instead of left-dragging. When you right-drag an object to its destination, a small menu pops up (as shown next) that lets you choose whether to copy the file, move it, or create a shortcut. You can even cancel the action.

> Copy Here
> **Move Here**
> Create Shortcuts Here
>
> Cancel

> ▶ | **QUICK TIP**
> ---
> *If you insist on left-dragging objects, you can exert some control over the process. Holding down the* SHIFT *key while dragging a file that would normally be copied causes it to be moved instead. Holding down the* CTRL *key while dragging causes a file to be copied instead of moved.*

Yet another way of moving files around in Explorer is using the Cut, Copy, and Paste commands, which you may be most familiar with from their use in other programs. To move a file or folder (or even a group of items), select it and choose Edit | Cut; or press CTRL-X. Open the destination folder and choose Edit | Paste (or press CTRL-V) to paste the item. To copy an item, choose Edit | Copy (or press CTRL-C).

> ▶ | **QUICK TIP**
> ---
> *The Undo command also works in Explorer, although many people never think to use it. If you've deleted a file or sent it somewhere by mistake, choose Edit | Undo (or press* CTRL-Z*) to undo the move.*

Setting Folder Options

You can customize many of the features of Explorer, from the way folders look and work to the way files inside are displayed, from the Folder Options dialog box, which is shown in Figure 5-3. You can open this dialog from the Control Panel or by choosing Tools | Folder Options in the Explorer window.

From the General tab of the Folder Options dialog box, you can do the following:

- **Tasks**   The new task pane appears in most Explorer windows, and displays common tasks based on what you're doing at the moment. While this feature can be useful, it also takes up a lot of room in your folder, which could be used for viewing more files. Select the Use Windows Classic Folders option to turn off the task pane in Explorer.

- **Browse Folders**   The default action in Explorer when you double-click a folder is for that folder to open and display its contents in the same window you are using. Select the Open Each Folder in Its Own Window option to open a new window for every folder you open. Be careful, though, as this can lead to a lot of clutter and open windows you'll have to close eventually.

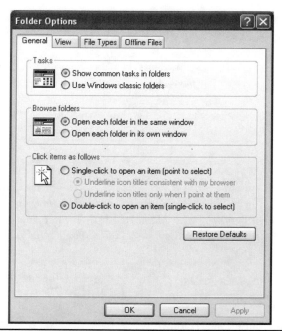

Figure 5-3   Use the Folder Options dialog box to control the way folders and files work in Windows Explorer.

- **Click Items as Follows**   Choose whether you want to open files and folders by double-clicking (the standard method) or single-clicking. Single-clicking is intended to make Explorer work something like Internet Explorer, where a single click on a link loads a new Web page. If you choose single-click, you can also choose whether the file names should be underlined (to make them look even more like links on a Web page).

▶ **QUICK TIP**

It's best to let Explorer open new folders in the same window to help save clutter on your Desktop. However, if you want to open a folder in a new window, hold down the CTRL *key while double-clicking the folder.*

The View tab of the Folder Options dialog box, shown in Figure 5-4, holds customizable features that affect not only how folders are handled, but how files are displayed. At the top of the tab, in the Folder Views section, you can control the view (list, icons, tiles, and so on) used by all folders in Explorer. Click Apply to All Folders to make all folders use the view specified in the currently open folder (the one from which you chose the Folder Options command). Click Reset All Folders to return folders to their default state.

In the Advanced Settings section of the View tab, you'll find all the interesting features that you can control. As you search through the list, you'll see that many useful features are disabled, probably in an attempt to hide some of Windows' complexities from novice users. While there are too many features to list, here are some of the more useful items:

- **Display the Contents of System Folders**   Windows does not display the contents of system folders by default. More importantly, files in these folders are usually not included when using Windows' Search function. They are hidden to protect them from being unintentionally deleted or moved.

- **Display the Full Path in the Title Bar**   Enable this option to have Windows display the full working path of the current folder in the Explorer window title bar. By default, the path is displayed only in the Address bar.

- **Show Hidden Files and Folders**   By default, files and folders whose Hidden attribute is enabled (see the section "Managing File Properties and Attributes" later in this chapter for more information on attributes) are not shown in Explorer. The idea is to protect such files from novice users, but at times you will probably want to be able to select or use hidden files. Even when it's displayed, the icon for a hidden file is transparent, letting you know that the file is supposed to be hidden.

- **Remember Each Folder's View Settings**   This option specifies that each folder's view settings are retained when the folder is closed. If this option is disabled, folders return to their default state when they are closed.

- **Hide Extensions for Known File Types**   Enabled by default, this option prevents Windows from displaying the three-letter extension on file names for file types that are registered with Windows. Disable this option to have Windows always show the extension.

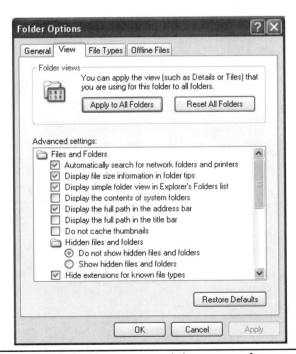

Figure 5-4   The Folder Options dialog box's View tab lets you configure many advanced Explorer features.

QUICK TIP

You can get a description of most of the advanced settings on the Folder Options dialog box View tab by right-clicking an option and choosing What's This. This technique also works for most options on other dialog boxes throughout Windows.

Customizing Folders

Windows XP includes new features for customizing folders. These features are available on the Customize tab of a folder's Properties dialog box, shown in Figure 5-5. To open the dialog box, right-click a folder and choose Properties; or you can choose View | Customize this Folder from an open folder. You can customize three settings for a folder: the type, the thumbnail view picture placed on the folder, and the icon associated with the folder when it's viewed any other way.

Windows XP includes a number of special folder types that boast special features applicable to the files placed inside. Most new folders created in Windows use the default Documents type, which is a standard folder used to place miscellaneous file types. The other available file types are

- Pictures
- Photo Album
- Music
- Music Artist
- Music Album
- Videos

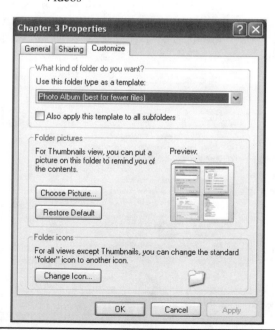

Figure 5-5   Windows XP lets you customize folders in several ways.

For the most part, specialized folder types still work like regular folders. However, they also contain special task links and viewing commands that are particular to the type of file they are meant to hold. For example, a folder of the Pictures type contains a Picture Tasks section in the Tasks pane that lets you view pictures as a slide show.

Choosing a picture for the thumbnail view of folders provides a great way to organize files. For example, you could include a picture of the album cover on folders that contain songs from a single album. Click Choose Picture to locate a picture in any of the supported image types in Windows (.bmp, .jpg, .gif, and so on).

You can also change the icon used for the folder; this affects how the folder looks in all views. Click Change Icon to view a list of icons you can use. By default, the icons shown are pulled from a file called shell32.dll in the \%SystemRoot%\system32 folder. Clicking the Browse button lets you find other icon files to use. Here are some files you can check out:

- \%SystemRoot%\system32\pifmgr.dll contains about 40 icons not often used in Windows.

- \%SystemRoot%\system32\moricons.dll contains about 100 icons, including many for non–Microsoft applications.

- \%SystemRoot%\system32\progman.exe contains about 40 action-specific icons.

- Any file on your system with an .ico extension will contain at least one icon.

- Any executable file (.exe) may contain the icon used for that file.

> **QUICK TIP**
>
> *You can use Windows' built-in Paint program to create your own icons or to edit existing icons.*

Changing Folder Toolbars

You can customize Explorer's Standard toolbar by adding or removing buttons and by changing the way those buttons are displayed. From any open Explorer window, choose View | Toolbars | Customize. The Customize Toolbar dialog box shows a list of available toolbar buttons and a list of currently used toolbar buttons. The available buttons represent all the commands found on Explorer's menus. You can add and remove any buttons you want and even change the button order. You can also use the options in this dialog box to choose whether text labels are shown for buttons and, if they are, whether they are shown to the right or under the button. Finally, you can choose whether to use large or small icons for your buttons.

Searching

The Windows XP Search Companion (which you access by choosing Start | Search) makes finding files and folders easy with its wizard-driven interface. Just tell it what kind of file you are looking for and part of the name, and Windows will most likely be able to find it for you. Nonetheless, you can make a few adjustments to maximize your searching efficiency:

- *Turn off the animated character*   Sure, the dog is cute, but the animation can waste valuable time when you already have to search for a file. On the initial page of the Search screen, click Change Preferences and then choose Without an Animated Screen Character on the Change Preferences page.

- *Use advanced searching*   Also on the Change Preferences page, you can click Change Files and Folders Search Behavior. On the next page, choose the Advanced option. Now when you search, you can immediately enter the file name and location instead of having to step through the Search Companion Wizard and tell it what kind of file you are looking for and so on.

- *Search from a particular point*   Right-click any folder in an Explorer window and choose Search to begin the Search Companion and have that folder preselected in the search criteria. When the Folders Explorer bar is enabled, you can also select a folder and click the Search button to begin a search from that folder.

- *Search for computers more quickly*   Right-click My Network Places on the Start menu or your Desktop and choose Search for Computers to open the Search Companion and quickly search for a computer on your local network.

Using Addresses for Folders and Files

Windows uses several types of addresses to locate items:

- **Uniform Resource Locator (URL)**   More commonly referred to as a Web address, a URL points your Web browser to the address of a specific document on the Internet. See Chapter 16 for more information on URLs.

- **File address**   File addresses, more commonly referred to as paths, point to locations on the local computer. C:\Windows\System32\readme.txt is an example of a file address.

- **Universal Naming Convention (UNC)**   A UNC typically refers to a location on a local area network and follows the convention *computername**sharename**filename*. For example, the address \\Walter\C\Windows\System32\readme.txt refers to a file named readme.txt in the \C\Windows\System32 path on a computer named Walter.

- **Internet e-mail address**   An e-mail address points to another person's e-mail account on the Internet. While you are probably used to seeing e-mail-addresses in the format *user@domainname.com,* the full addressing convention is actually mailto:*username@domainname.com*.

Windows features many address boxes throughout its interface, and you can enter any of these types of addresses into most of them. For example, you could type a file address into the address box in Internet Explorer to open a file or folder on your computer. You could also type an e-mail address (in its full form) into the Run dialog box to create an e-mail message to send to that address.

► **QUICK TIP**

*Shortcuts provide an interesting opportunity for you to experiment with addresses. Try this: Create a new shortcut by right-clicking your Desktop (or any folder) and choosing New | Shortcut. For the location of the item, enter **mailto:** followed by the address of someone you send a lot of e-mail to. Whenever you double-click the shortcut, a new e-mail message is created, already addressed to that person.*

TRY IT To create a new e-mail message from the Run dialog box, use the following steps:

1. From the Start menu, click Run.

2. In the Open box, type **mailto:** followed by the standard e-mail address of someone to whom you want to write a message. Click OK.

3. A new message should appear with the person's address already entered into the To field.

Customizing the Send To Menu

Send To is a submenu found on the File menu of Explorer windows and on the shortcut menu of any file or folder. The Send To menu contains a list of common locations to which you can quickly send items. For example, you can right-click a file and choose Send To | 3½ Floppy (A:) to copy the file to a floppy disk without having to locate the drive window first using Explorer.

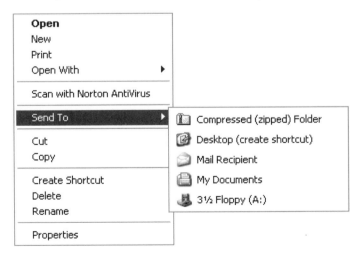

Sending an item to a location on the Send To menu works just like left-dragging the item. If you send the item to another drive, the item is copied. If you send it to another folder on the same drive, the item is moved. Holding the SHIFT key down while selecting a location moves a file instead of copying it. Holding the CTRL key down while selecting a location copies a file instead of moving it.

You can add new destinations to the Send To menu. Simply create a shortcut to the location in the C:\Documents and Settings*username*\SendTo folder to add a location for a particular user. Create the shortcut in the C:\Documents and Settings\All Users\SendTo folder to add a location for all users.

Managing File Properties and Attributes

Most items throughout Windows XP have properties associated with them, and files and folders are no exception. Right-clicking any file or folder and choosing Properties opens a Properties dialog box for that item. Figure 5-6 shows a sample Properties dialog box for a file.

The file Properties dialog box displays a number of properties:

- **File name**   The name appears in the box at the top. You can change the name right in this box.

- **Type of file**   This is the type of file, as defined by its extension. See Chapter 6 for more on this.

- **Opens with**   This shows the program associated with the file type. Click Change to choose a different program with which to open files of this type when the file is double-clicked.

- **Basic file information**   The two middle sections of the Properties dialog box show the file location, the size of the file, and the dates the file was created, last modified, and last accessed.

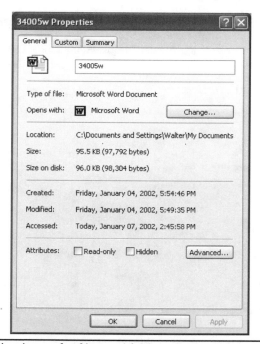

Figure 5-6   Properties dialog boxes for files and folders display information and allow you to set attributes.

- **Attributes** Both files and folders have a number of attributes. Two of these attributes (Read-only and Hidden) are available on the General tab. Four additional attributes (Archive, Indexed, Compressed, and Encrypted) are available using the Advanced button on the General tab.

  - A read-only item can be viewed and edited. When you attempt to save an edited read-only file, though, you are prompted to save a new version of the file using a different file name. You can delete a read-only file, but Windows will ask you to confirm the action first.

  - A hidden item doesn't appear in Explorer windows. You can force Windows to display hidden files (see the earlier section "Setting Folder Options" for details), and they are then displayed with transparent icons.

  - The archive attribute means that the file has been changed since the last time it was backed up. See Chapter 25 for more on this.

  - The indexed attribute determines whether the file is included in indexes built by the Windows Indexing Service.

  - The compressed attribute is turned on when a file is compressed, as described in the "Using Compressed (Zipped) Folders" section later in this chapter.

  - Turning on the encrypted attribute encrypts a file so that only the user who encrypted the file can open it. Note that encryption is available only in Windows XP Professional.

  - An additional attribute, named system, does not appear directly on the file or folder Properties dialog box. This attribute is used to denote system files used by Windows. You can tell the system attribute is turned on if the Hidden attribute is dimmed for a particular file or folder.

For the most part, a folder's Properties dialog box and the available attributes are the same as those of a file. The folder Properties dialog box does not show modified and accessed dates, but it does include information on how many files and subfolders are contained in the folder.

> ▶ **QUICK TIP**
>
> *You can select a number of folders in Explorer and then open the Properties dialog box to see the combined size of all the selected folders. This is handy when copying groups of folders to external media, where size is often a concern.*

> ▶ **QUICK TIP**
>
> *You can set the read-only, archive, system, and hidden attributes for a file or folder using the* attrib *command at the command prompt. Type **attrib /?** to get information on using this command.*

Using Compressed (Zipped) Folders

Windows XP includes built-in file compression, which allows you to reduce the size of files and folders (assuming you delete the original uncompressed files). Compression uses a standard Zip format; in fact, Windows actually uses a specialized version of WinZip 7, one of the more popular compression utilities. Files compressed in Windows XP can be unzipped by most compression utilities.

▶ *NOTE*

A second form of compression, called NTFS Compression, is also available on partitions formatted with the NT File System (NTFS). This form of compression, which you can set by clicking the Advanced button on the General tab of a file or folder's Properties dialog box, allows you to compress entire partitions at once.

To compress a file or folder, simply right-click the item and choose Send To | Compressed (Zipped) Folder. You can compress a number of files and folders at once by selecting them all and using the Send To | Compressed (Zipped) Folder command. A compressed copy of the item is placed in the same location as the original. Compressed folders are indicated by a folder 33403 figs icon with a zipper on it, as shown left, and also have the file extension .zip.

After you have created a compressed folder, you can drag files into it. Compressed folders are handled like regular folders for the most part. You can open them, move files around, and even open files right from within the compressed folder. To extract a file, simply drag it out of the folder.

You can extract an entire compressed folder at once by right-clicking it and choosing Extract All. A wizard appears to guide you through the extraction process.

Customizing the Recycle Bin

When you delete a file, it is not erased from your hard drive; instead, it is placed into a specialized folder called the Recycle Bin. You can restore the deleted file by opening the Recycle Bin, finding the file, and either dragging it out of the Recycle Bin or using a Restore command to return the file to its original location.

Each of the hard drive partitions on your computer maintains its own Recycle Bin. The actual Recycle Bin folder on each hard drive is marked as hidden, so you won't be able to see it unless you have the Show Hidden Folders option turned on, as discussed in the earlier section "Setting Folder Options." For the most part, though, you will need to interact with the Recycle Bin icon only on the Desktop. This icon represents all of the Recycle Bin folders on drives in your computer. When you drag a file on drive C: (for example) to the Recycle Bin or simply delete the file, Windows knows that the file actually belongs in the hidden Recycle Bin folder on drive C:.

You can customize the behavior of the Recycle Bin. To do so, right-click the Recycle Bin icon on the Desktop and choose Properties from the shortcut menu. The resulting Recycle Bin Properties dialog box is shown in Figure 5-7.

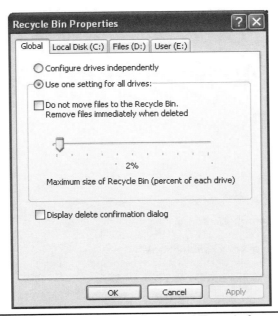

Figure 5-7   You can configure the Recycle Bin to behave differently for each drive or use one setting for all drives.

From the Global tab, you can specify whether you want to configure the Recycle Bin for each of your drives individually or use one group of settings for all the drives. If you choose to configure drives individually, the settings on the Global tab become unavailable and you must use the other tabs (named after the drives on your computer) to configure each Recycle Bin. The options on the Global tab and on each of the other tabs are identical:

- **Do Not Move Files to the Recycle Bin**   Choosing this option essentially turns off the Recycle Bin. Deleted files are immediately removed from the computer.
- **Maximum Size of Recycle Bin**   Use the slider to specify the percent of each drive's space that is used for the Recycle Bin. If you are configuring each drive independently, the drive's tab shows the actual amount of space allocated to the Recycle Bin. If you are configuring all drives at once, you'll have to figure out this information for yourself.

An additional option is available from the Global tab of the Recycle Bin Properties dialog box—the Display Delete Confirmation Dialog. This option applies to all Recycle Bins and cannot be configured for individual drives. When this option is selected, Windows opens a dialog box asking you for confirmation each time you delete an item.

> **QUICK TIP**
>
> *Select any file or folder and press* SHIFT-DEL *to bypass the Recycle Bin and permanently delete the file.*

CHAPTER 6

Running and Managing Applications

TIPS IN THIS CHAPTER

Programs are the real reason for bothering with Windows in the first place; without them, we wouldn't have much use for a computer. In Windows XP, you can run many programs at once, and more than one user can run a single program simultaneously. Of course, providing this flexibility requires a fairly sophisticated environment for running programs. Windows XP has a number of features for controlling how programs start and for managing programs after they are running.

Starting Programs Using Shortcuts

Whenever you start a program from the Start menu or from the Quick Launch bar, you are using a shortcut. You can create shortcuts just about anywhere else—on the Desktop or in any folder. You can create multiple shortcuts that run the same program in slightly different ways. For example, you might create one shortcut that runs Microsoft Word normally and another that runs it as though you were another user, or that runs it using an advanced startup switch. Customizing shortcuts is a powerful way for you to make programs run the way you want them to run.

You can create a new shortcut in a few different ways:

- Right-click in any location, and choose New Shortcut from the shortcut menu. A wizard appears that lets you specify the program for which you want to create the shortcut and name the shortcut.

- Using the right mouse button, drag any executable file (.exe) to a new location. Choose Create Shortcuts Here from the shortcut menu that appears when you release the button.

- Copy an existing shortcut by right-clicking it and choosing Copy. Right-click and choose Paste in any location to create a copy of the original shortcut.

After you have created a shortcut, you can customize it by right-clicking it and choosing Properties. In the shortcut's Properties dialog box, switch to the Shortcut tab, shown in Figure 6-1.

You can configure a number of items in this dialog box, including the following:

- **Target** The program that the shortcut will run. At the end of the target string, just after the name of the actual executable file, you can enter any startup switches supported by the program to customize the way the program runs.

QUICK TIP

For some programs, you can determine the supported startup switches by entering the name of the executable followed by /? at the command prompt. For some programs, this does not work, however; you should consult the help files or documentation for the program.

- **Start In** This field specifies the folder that Windows sets as the current directory when the shortcut is run. By default, this is set to the folder that contains the original item, but you can change this to another directory if you need to.

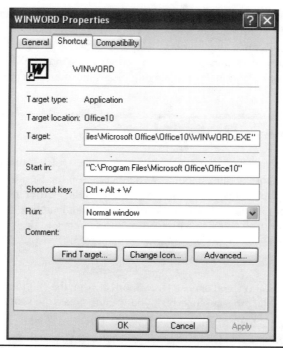

Figure 6-1 Customize the way a program runs by configuring a shortcut.

- **Shortcut Key**   Use this field to specify a key combination that runs the shortcut. See the next section, "Starting Programs Using Key Combinations," for more information.

- **Run**   Choose whether you want to run the program in a normal, maximized, or minimized window.

- **Comment**   Enter a comment that will help you remember the purpose of the shortcut.

- **Find Target**   Opens the folder in which the original target file is found.

- **Change Icon**   Changes the icon for the shortcut.

- **Advanced**   Opens a dialog box with two options. The first lets you run the program using different user credentials than the account with which you are currently logged on—useful if your account does not have the permission to run the program correctly. The second option is available only for Windows 3.1–based programs and lets you specify whether the program is run in a separate memory space. Programs are run in a separate memory space by default, but some legacy programs do not tolerate this well; you can try disabling this option if you experience problems running the program. Note that disabling this option may cause the program to interfere with Windows or with other running programs.

TRY IT   To create a shortcut and modify it to run the program always in a maximized window, use the following steps:

1. Right-click the location in which you want to create a shortcut, and choose New Shortcut from the shortcut menu.

2. Type the location for the program (or click Browse to locate the program file), and click Next.

3. Type a name for the shortcut and click Finish.

4. Right-click the new shortcut and choose Properties. In the Properties dialog box, open the Shortcut tab.

5. Use the Run drop-down list to select Maximized, and then click OK.

Starting Programs Using Key Combinations

In addition to the many built-in key combinations in Windows, you can also assign key combinations to run your programs. To do this, you must create a shortcut to the program and assign the key combination to the shortcut. Key combinations must use a character (letter, number, or symbol) and two of the following three keys: CTRL, ALT, and/or SHIFT. For example, you could assign CTRL-ALT-W, CTRL-SHIFT-W, or ALT-SHIFT-W to run a program, but you could not assign CTRL-W to run a program.

Keep in mind the following as you assign shortcuts to programs:

- If you assign the same key combination to more than one shortcut, only one of them will work. There is no way to determine which keys you have assigned to programs other than to go through all your shortcuts. Before you assign a key combination, test it to determine whether it is already used. You might also want to keep a list of assignments.

- If a key combination for a shortcut conflicts with a key combination used in an active program, the active program always wins. For example, if you set CTRL-ALT-W to run Microsoft Word and also set it to perform a function in Excel, the key combination will not run the Word shortcut as long as Excel is active.

▶ | *QUICK TIP*

Windows Help and Support has information on keyboard shortcuts implemented in Windows XP by default. In the Help and Support Center, go to the Accessibility category and then choose the help article "Windows Keyboard Shortcuts Overview."

TRY IT   To create a key combination for running a program, use the following steps:

1. Create a shortcut for the program to which you want to assign a key combination. You can also use an existing shortcut on the Start menu.

2. Right-click the shortcut and choose Properties. In the Properties dialog box, switch to the Shortcut tab.

3. Click once in the Shortcut Key box.

4. Press the keyboard combination you want to use to start the program. The default combination is a character and the CTRL and ALT keys. If you press just a character, Windows adds CTRL-ALT for you.

5. Click OK.

Starting Programs Using the Run Dialog Box

The Run dialog box (open it from the Start menu) can be used to open just about any type of resource, including programs, folders, Internet sites, and documents. Just type the exact address for the resource and Windows finds and opens it (learn more about addresses in Chapter 5). Because the Run dialog box was originally designed for running programs, though, whenever you type in an incomplete address (say, just a file name), Windows will search any paths loaded into memory looking for a match. These paths typically include \Windows, \Windows\Windows32, and many program folders. For example, you can simply type in **winword** (the name of the executable file that starts Microsoft Word) without any path information and Windows will find the file and start Word. This can often be handier than trying to find the program on the Start menu. If Windows cannot find the executable file, you may need to type in the full path to the file in the Run dialog box.

> ### QUICK TIP
>
> *If your keyboard features a Windows Logo key (usually found next to the* ALT *key), you can press* Windows Logo-R *to open the Run dialog box.*

Starting Programs Automatically at Windows Startup

You may have noticed that the All Programs menu on your Start menu contains a folder named Startup. Any shortcuts (or even full programs) that you place inside the Startup folder will run automatically each time you start Windows. The items displayed in a particular user's Startup folder actually come from two places:

- **C:\Documents and Settings\All Users\Start Menu\Programs\Startup**   Items placed in this folder start up whenever any user starts Windows.

- **C:\Documents and Settings*username*\Start Menu\Programs\Startup**   *Username* denotes a particular user account configured on the computer. Items placed in this folder start up whenever someone starts Windows and logs on using the specified account.

If you create a shortcut in the Startup folder on the Start menu, it is created in the Startup folder for whatever user account is currently logged on. To make a program start up for all users, you must create a shortcut directly in the All Users Startup folder.

▶ **NOTE**

Programs that are started with Windows, but are not included in the Startup folder, are usually started with a Registry entry. See Chapter 27 for advice on controlling these types of programs.

Starting Programs with a Particular Document

Most files in Windows have a three-letter extension appended to the file name that identifies the program associated with the file. This is how Windows knows what program to use to open a file. For example, double-clicking a file whose name ends in *.doc* tells Windows to run Microsoft Word (if it is installed) to open that file.

▶ **QUICK TIP**

If you don't see the file name extensions, you are missing an important part of Windows. Choose Tools | Folder Options in any open Explorer window, switch to the View tab of the Folder Options dialog box that opens, and remove the check mark next to the Hide Extensions for Known File Types from the Advanced list.

Often, more than one program can be used to open a particular file type. For example, you might use one program to view JPEG pictures (.jpg files) and another program to edit them. Double-clicking a file opens the file with the default program associated with that file type (see "Modifying File Types and Associations" for information on changing the defaults). To open a file with a program different than its default, right-click the file and choose the Open With option. You'll see a list of other programs associated with the file type. You can also choose Open With | Choose Program to open a dialog box that lets you choose an unlisted program with which to open the file.

Modifying File Types and Associations

Occasionally, you will need to change the default association of a program with a particular file type. This is necessary, for example, when you install a new program that changes an association without asking you (and many do this). The easiest way to change an association is to right-click a file and choose Open With | Choose Program (this was covered in detail in the previous section). In the Open With dialog box, shown in Figure 6-2, find the program you want to use to open the file and select the Always Use the Selected Program to Open This Kind of File option. When you click OK, the association is changed.

Another way to control associations is from the File Types tab on the Folder Options dialog box. Choose Tool | Folder Options in any open Explorer window, and switch to the File Types tab, shown in Figure 6-3. This tab presents a long list of all file types registered with Windows. Clicking New opens a simple dialog box that lets you type in a three-letter extension to create a new file type.

Select any file type on the list to work with it. Click the Change button to open an Open With dialog box (the same one shown in Figure 6-2) and choose another program to associate with the file type.

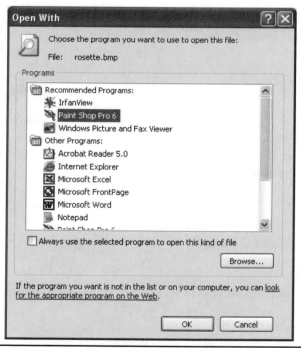

Figure 6-2   Use the Open With dialog box to change the association of a file type.

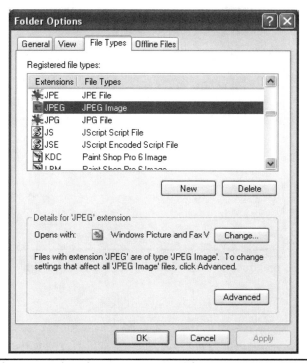

Figure 6-3 Use the File Types tab to browse registered file types and create new associations.

If you want to exert even finer control over a file association, click Advanced on the File Types tab. This opens the Edit File Type dialog box shown in Figure 6-4.

This dialog box displays all known information about the file type, including its name, icon, and all the actions that Windows can perform on the file. Options at the bottom let you specify several additional settings:

- **Confirm Open After Download**   Choose whether this type of file should be opened automatically without asking the user after it is downloaded.

- **Always Show Extension**   This option causes Windows to display the three-letter extension for files of this type even if that option is disabled in Windows.

- **Browse in Same Window**   Specify whether Windows should attempt to open a file of this type in a different program window if a program window of this type is already open.

Figure 6-4   You can also edit actions that Windows can perform on a file type.

► *CAUTION*

While you can change the way Windows performs specific actions, you will almost never need to do so unless you are testing software (or you are just really bored). Be warned that editing these actions can cause Windows to behave in unpredictable ways, and your edits can be difficult to undo.

Running Legacy Programs in Application Compatibility Mode

For the most part, your programs, including programs written for previous versions of Windows, will run just fine under Windows XP with no extra work on your part. Occasionally, though, you may run across a program that just won't run. This is especially true of older, hardware-intensive programs like games. Windows XP comes with a feature named compatibility mode, which attempts to emulate previous versions of Windows so you can run programs that expect to run under those versions.

To run a program under compatibility mode, you first create a shortcut to the program. Right-click the shortcut and choose Properties, and on the dialog box that opens, switch to the Compatibility tab, shown in Figure 6-5.

Four options are available on the Compatibility tab:

- **Run This Program Using Compatibility Mode**   Select this option and choose a particular version of Windows to emulate. Choices include Windows 95, 98/Me, NT 4.0 (with Service Pack 5), and Windows 2000. Unless you know the exact version of Windows for which your software was written, it's best to test backward. Start by trying Windows 2000 or Windows 98/Me and work back through the previous versions.

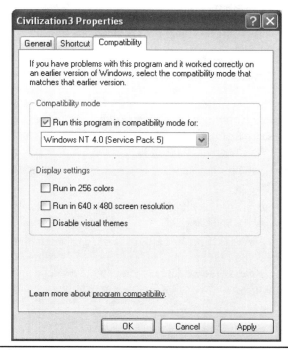

Figure 6-5   Use compatibility mode to emulate previous versions of Windows for legacy programs.

- **Run in 256 Colors**   Select this option to reduce the color depth used to run the program. Some older programs require a lower color depth, and this setting may let the program operate normally without having to emulate a previous version of Windows.

- **Run in 640×480 Screen Resolution**   Similar to the 256 colors option, this option runs the program at a resolution favored by many older programs.

- **Disable Visual Themes**   Some programs will work fine under Windows XP but experience problems when using the new Windows XP Desktop themes. Use this option to disable themes when running a particular program. In particular, many programs seem to have a problem with the feature that displays a drop shadow beneath the pointer.

> ### QUICK TIP
>
> *Although configuring compatibility manually is pretty straightforward, Windows XP also provides a Program Compatibility Wizard that steps you through the same choices available on the Compatibility tab and lets you test modes. You can access this wizard from the Help and Support utility.*

Switching Among Running Programs

Since you can run many programs at once in Windows, it makes sense that Windows lets you switch among running programs in a number of ways—some obvious and some not so obvious. To switch among running programs, you can:

- *Click another program's button on the Taskbar.* Each running program has its own Taskbar button. If multiple instances of a single program are running (for example, if you have several Web pages open), similar items are grouped under a single button.

- *Click a program's window.* If you can see a portion of the program window to which you want to switch, click it to activate that program.

- *Press ALT-TAB to switch to the next program on the Taskbar.* Press ALT-SHIFT-TAB to switch to the previous program on the taskbar.

- *Press ALT-TAB, but do not release the ALT key.* This opens a small dialog box with icons for all running programs. Press the TAB key repeatedly while still holding down the ALT key to cycle through the programs. Release the ALT key when you have selected the program you want to switch to. Press ESC at any time to exit the dialog box without switching programs.

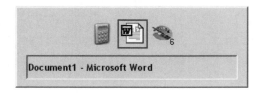

- *Press CTRL-ALT-DEL to open the Windows Task Manager.* On the Applications tab, you can choose from a list of running applications and click Switch To to go to a particular program.

▶ **QUICK TIP**

Microsoft has released a group of utilities named Powertoys for Windows XP that you can download at http://www.microsoft.com/windowsxp/pro/downloads/powertoys.asp. *Once installed, the dialog box that appears when you press* ALT-TAB *changes to an advanced version that includes a graphical preview of programs and documents as you cycle through them, as shown in Figure 6-6.*

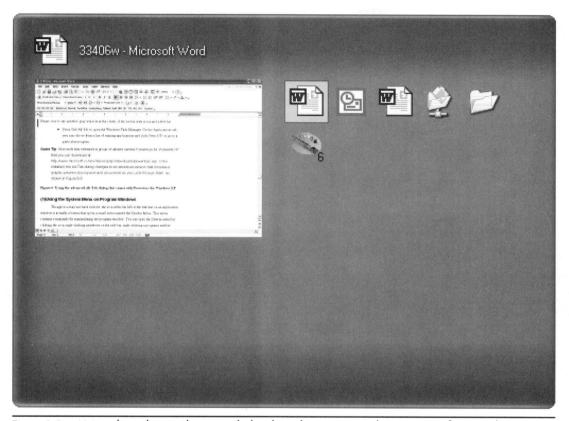

Figure 6-6   Using the advanced ALT-TAB dialog box that comes with Powertoys for Windows XP

Using the System Menu in Program Windows

Though you may not have noticed, the icon at the far left of the title bar in an application window is actually a button that opens a small menu named the System menu. This menu contains commands for manipulating the program window. You can open the System menu by clicking the icon, by right-clicking anywhere on the title bar, by right-clicking a programs Taskbar button, or by pressing ALT-SPACEBAR.

Some programs add their own commands to the System menu, but you can always find the following commands there:

- **Restore**   Works like a restore button, resizing the window to its previous state before being maximized or minimized.
- **Move**   Selects the program window so that you can move it around on your screen using the arrow keys.
- **Size**   Lets you change the size of the program window using the arrow keys.
- **Minimize and Maximize**   Works the same as the minimize and maximize buttons.
- **Close**   Closes the program window.

QUICK TIP

You can also close the active program window by pressing ALT-F4.

While the commands available on the System menu may not seem exciting (after all, they just duplicate what you can usually do more easily by clicking and dragging), they do present a way to manipulate program windows by using only your keyboard.

Ending Unresponsive Programs with Task Manager

One of the nice things about Windows XP is that running programs are protected from one another. When programs crash, they rarely affect the other programs running at the same time. When a program crashes (as opposed to when Windows itself crashes), one of three things usually happens:

- The program offers up a dialog box explaining that it has suffered a problem it can't recover from and must now close.
- Windows detects that the program has stopped responding and offers a dialog box where you can choose to end the program. Click Cancel on this dialog box to return to Windows and wait for the program a little while longer.
- The program stops accepting user input (it freezes or hangs) and you are offered no dialog box at all.

You will have to take extra measures to fix the final type of crash. First, you need to make sure that the program has actually crashed. It may be that the program has opened a dialog box in which you need to indicate some response, but the dialog box is hidden behind some other window. Try minimizing all windows (right-click the Taskbar and choose Minimize All). This may show a hidden dialog box. If this doesn't work, try pressing ALT-TAB to activate the program that isn't responding. Sometimes doing this will bring a hidden dialog box to the foreground.

If none of this works, or if you can't switch back to the program after you switch away from it, you will need to end the program yourself. Right-click any open area of the Taskbar and choose Task Manager from the shortcut menu. When the Task Manager opens, switch to the Applications tab, as shown in Figure 6-7. Select the program that is not responding (it will usually say Not Responding in the Status column) and click End Task.

▶ | **QUICK TIP**

You can also press CTRL-ALT-DEL *to open Task Manager.*

TRY IT   To use Task Manager to end a program that is not responding, use the following steps:

1. Right-click any open space on the Taskbar and click Task Manager. Or press CTRL-ALT-DEL.

2. In the Task Manager window, click the Applications tab.

Figure 6-7   Use the Applications tab of Task Manager to end a program that is not responding.

3. Select the program that is not responding, and click End Task. This opens the End Program dialog box.

4. Click End Now.

Managing Programs in a Multiple-User Environment

Like most versions of Windows, Windows XP lets you configure multiple users on a single computer. Windows XP goes previous versions one better, though, by allowing multiple users to be logged on at the same time with programs running. Of course, only one user gets to use the computer at a time, but this still provides a way for you to leave your programs running while another user logs on to take a turn. Obviously, supporting these multiuser features impacts the way that programs are installed and run.

You'll learn all the details of supporting multiple users in Chapter 12. As far as installing and running programs goes, however, you need to know that Windows XP supports three types of user accounts: Computer Administrators, Limited, and Guest. Only users that are Computer Administrators can install programs. If a user with a Limited or Guest account tries to install a program, she is given the chance to enter the account name and password of a Computer Administrator account to run the installation. Otherwise, the installation fails.

After a program is installed, any type of user account can run the program. You may need to do some tweaking with older programs that are not designed for Windows XP. For some programs, especially those that allow users to save individual preferences, you'll run into a problem trying to save configuration information when using a Limited or Guest account. This is a particular problem with some games that let you create different users inside the game. One way around this is simply to make the other users' accounts Computer Administrator accounts. Another way is to configure a shortcut for the program, and then use the advanced properties of the shortcut to let users log on as a different user when that program is running. Refer back to the section "Starting Programs Using Shortcuts," earlier in this chapter, for more information. The problem with this method, though, is that it requires that the user know the name and password for a Computer Administrator account. For this reason, the method is best used for one-time instances in which you can enter the password for a user or on computers where security is not a big concern.

The other issue you will run into when supporting multiple users is when more than one user runs the same program at the same time. For the most part, you will find that this does not cause too much of a problem, especially with programs designed for Windows XP. Even most older programs will work just fine when multiple instances are run. The programs that will cause you the most problems are those that need to access hardware resources. For example, if two users try to run a terminal program that needs to access a modem on a particular COM port, the program will most likely crash. Again, this will be a concern with older programs not designed to be used by multiple users. Unfortunately, the best course of action is simply to test programs as you install them.

Scheduling Programs to Run Automatically

Scheduled Tasks is a specialized folder that you can use to have Windows automatically run programs at specified intervals. When you schedule a task, you tell Windows what program to run, how often to run it, what time it should run, and under what user account it should run (scheduled tasks are run even when no user is logged in).

 To schedule a task, use the following steps:

1. Click Start, point to All Programs | Accessories | System Tools. Then click Scheduled Tasks. This opens the Scheduled Tasks window.

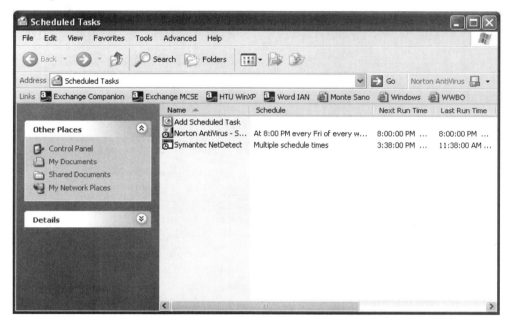

2. Double-click the Add Scheduled Task item to start the Add Scheduled Task Wizard.
3. Follow the instructions in the wizard. You will need to specify the program to be run, how often the task should be run (daily, weekly, and so on), the time of day to run the program, and the user name and password for the account under which to run the task.
4. After you have created a task, you can run it manually by right-clicking the task and choosing Run.
5. You can also modify a task at any time by double-clicking the task and using its Properties dialog box to reconfigure it. For the most part, the properties you can change are the same as those set during the creation of the task. The exception is the Settings tab, shown in Figure 6-8, which contains the following properties:

   • **Delete the Task If It Is Not Scheduled to Run Again**   Schedule a one-time-only task.
   • **Stop the Task If It Runs For**   Limit the amount of time a task runs before it is automatically ended. This option helps make sure that a task is ended if a program crashes or experiences a problem. The default setting is 72 hours.

Figure 6-8   Use the advanced task settings to provide finer control over how and when a scheduled task runs.

- **Idle Time**   Specify that the task be run only if the computer has been idle for a certain amount of time and stop the task if the computer ceases to be idle.

- **Power Management**   Prevent a task from running if the computer is running (or begins to run) on battery power and wake the computer to run the task if the computer is in standby mode.

▶ **QUICK TIP**

You can copy a task to another computer. In the Scheduled Tasks window on the computer to copy the task from, right-click the task and choose Copy. Next, open My Network Places and locate the computer to which you want to copy the task. On the remote computer, find the \Windows\Tasks folder and paste the task into it. If you don't have a network or don't have permission to access the Windows folder, you can paste the task on a floppy disk and transfer it that way. Confirm that the task works by right-clicking the task and choosing Run Now. If the task does not run, the first thing you should check is the user name and password used by the task.

CHAPTER 7
Printing and Faxing

TIPS IN THIS CHAPTER

indows XP has added some convenient features to printing and fax services that give you more control over how your printing and faxing resources are used. This chapter tells you how to configure these resources and how to use them efficiently.

If you have a printer or a fax device directly connected to your system, Windows XP detects them automatically and installs the appropriate services. If your fax device is not connected directly to your system, the fax service will not be installed; you will have to install it manually. If you are upgrading from Windows 2000 and were using the fax service prior to upgrading to Windows XP, the fax service will be installed and configured to match the settings you defined in Windows 2000.

In many environments, printers are shared among several systems through a network connection. These devices can be connected directly to a server; or if the devices have a built-in Ethernet interface, they can connect directly to the network. In a network configuration, it is recommended that you install Windows XP Professional on the system you intend to use as a device server, as more security and configuration options are available on Windows XP Professional than on Windows XP Home Edition. For example, Windows XP Home Edition supports only simple device sharing, which does not enable you to configure permission settings.

▶ **NOTE**

The Windows XP fax service does not support sharing.

Installing Additional Print Drivers

Windows XP makes it easy to add a new printer to any system. The Add Printer Wizard walks you through the process. After you add the printer, however, you may need to install additional drivers for networked systems that are not running Windows XP.

TRY IT To install additional print drivers on a print server, use the following steps:

1. From the Control Panel, click Printers and Other Hardware.

2. Click View Installed Printers or Fax Printers.

3. Right-click the printer for which you want to add a driver(s), and then select Properties from the pop-up menu.

4. Open the Sharing tab, where you can enable sharing of the printer and load additional print drivers.

5. Click the Additional Drivers button to install drivers onto the server, as shown here:

6. Insert the Support CD into the server's CD-ROM drive, or insert a disk containing the printer driver you want to install.

7. Click the check boxes for the types of drivers you want to install, and then click OK. The drivers you have selected will be installed from the Support CD.

8. Windows XP will initiate the installation and prompt you for information.

Finding Shared Printers on the Network

Finding a printer on a network is as easy as browsing for a workgroup. Double-click the My Network Places icon on the Desktop, where it is stored by default, to open the My Network Places window shown in Figure 7-1.

In a workgroup environment, in which printers and computers are assigned to particular workgroups within the network, you can click View Workgroup Computers in the Network Tasks section of this window to see a list of the computers and their associated printers and other devices. The Address text box across the top of the window displays the current workgroup, and you can use the arrow to the right of the text box to select other workgroups—or simply type the workgroup name into the text box.

TRY IT To find a network printer in a workgroup, follow these steps:

1. Double-click My Network Places on your Desktop to open the My Network Places window.

2. Under Network Tasks, select View Workgroup Computers.

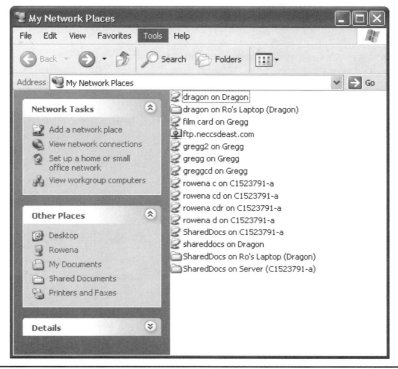

Figure 7-1   My Network Places window

3. Enter the name of the workgroup in the Address text box, or click the down arrow to the right of the text box to select a workgroup from a list.

4. Shared printers and faxes are listed under their associated workgroups.

To find a network printer on a domain, use the following steps:

1. Double-click My Network Places on your Desktop to open the My Network Places window.

2. Under Other Places, select Entire Network.

3. Double-click a domain name, and then select the desired workgroup.

4. Shared printers and faxes are listed under their associated workgroup.

Adding Network Interface Printers

If your printer has a built-in Ethernet adapter or is connected to a network interface device, all you need to do to add the printer to the network is set up a standard TCP/IP port using the handy Add

Printer Wizard. This is an attractive alternative to connecting the printer physically to a port on the print server.

 To add a network interface printer, follow these steps:

1. Connect the printer to the network and power up the printer.

2. From the Control Panel, double-click Printers and Other Hardware.

3. Click Add a Printer.

4. When the Add Printer Wizard screen displays, click Next.

5. Select the local printer option and uncheck the automatic detection option. Then click Next.

6. In the Select a Printer Port screen, click the Create a New Port option; then select Standard TCP/IP Port as the type. Click Next.

7. Read the information on the next screen that appears, and then click Next.

8. On the Add Port screen, enter the Internet Protocol (IP) address of the printer you want to add. (You can obtain this address by printing a configuration report on the printer.) Since each printer is different, you might need to refer to the operations manual that came with your device for additional installation instructions.

9. You can either accept the default name that is entered as the Port Name, or you can specify one of your own. When you are done, click Next.

10. At this time, Windows XP searches for the connected printer. If it is successful, the wizard confirms your settings and shows information about the adapter type. Click Finish to complete the task.

Setting Up Internet Printing

The Internet Information Server (IIS) supports the Internet Printing Protocol (IPP) that enables you to view and manage printers in a Web browser. Simply open your Web browser and enter **http://hostname/printers** in the Address box to see a list of shared printers on that *hostname*. The *hostname* can be a computer name, a domain name, or an IP address. Select a printer from the list to view its status, queuing, and control options.

Select View | Properties to see information regarding the selected printer, including its capabilities, estimated wait time for a print job, and other information.

 To share a printer using IPP, follow these steps:

1. From the Control Panel, choose Printers and Faxes.

2. Under Pick a Task, select Add a Printer.

3. When the Add Printer Wizard screen opens, click Next.

4. Select the second option, either A Network Printer or a Printer Attached to Another Computer. Then click Next.

5. From the Specify a Printer screen, select the third option: Connect to a Printer on the Internet or on a Home or Office Network.

6. Specify the URL where the printer can be found, using the following syntax:
   http://*hostname*/printers/*printername*/.printer
   where *hostname* is the network name of the computer running IIS. This name can be the name of a computer, a domain, or an IP address. The *printername* is the share name of the printer.

7. Click Next. You may be prompted for driver information. If so, simply follow the directions on the screen.

Fine Tuning Printer Properties

Whether your printer is part of a large network or a simple home environment, at times you might have to fine tune its properties. For example, you may have teenagers who delight in printing at odd hours of the night, and you may want to limit the hours of operation for that printer. In an office environment, where several users share the same printer, you may want the printer to create a separator page between each job. These types of adjustments are accomplished in the Advanced tab of the printer Properties window, which is shown in Figure 7-2.

On this tab are several options:

- **Always Available**   Click this option if you want users to have unlimited access to the printer.

- **Available From**   Click this option to specify the available time range for the printer. When set, users can access the printer only during these hours. Any print jobs sent outside these hours are held in the queue until the printer is available again.

- **Priority**   Documents sent with a higher priority setting are printed before other jobs in the print queue. You could create multiple printers for the same device and assign each printer a different priority. This enables you to give certain users access to the higher priority printers. If, for example, 50 jobs are in the print queue and the president of the company needs to print a proposal for a meeting, her print job can be sent to the higher priority printer and will be printed before all the other jobs in the queue.

- **Driver**   This list displays the current drivers installed on the system. If the incorrect driver is installed, click New Driver to launch the Add Printer Driver Wizard.

- **Spool settings**   Four spooling options determine how a document is *spooled,* or stored in the queue. For faster performance, add a check mark to the first and third options (Always Available and Spool Print Documents So Program Finishes Printing Faster). This causes the document to be spooled and printed as soon as the first page is spooled. If complex print jobs experience interruptions, you may want to select the first and second options (Always Available and Available From—including the times). If you print directly to the printer, the

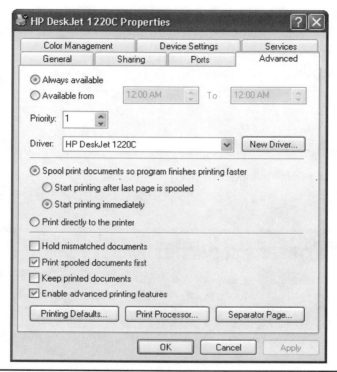

Figure 7-2   The printer Properties window's Advanced tab

application trying to print the document could be hung up until the printer becomes available. The spool file location is defined under the Print Server Properties window.

- **Hold Mismatched Documents**   This option causes the spooler to compare the properties of the document against the printer properties. If they do not match, the document is held in the queue. For example, a mismatch occurs when an application specifies a form that is not currently assigned to a printer tray. Correctly matched documents will print normally, bypassing any mismatched documents in the queue.

- **Print Spooled Documents First**   When enabled, the spooler will print documents that have completed spooling over those that are in the process of spooling, regardless of their priority settings. When this option is disabled, the spooler strictly enforces document priorities.

- **Keep Printed Documents**   When enabled, printed documents are stored in the queue. This lets them be printed directly from the queue without having to print from the original application. If file space is not an issue, this is a rather neat feature.

- **Enable Advanced Printing Features**   This option is mainly for Windows XP and Windows 2000 clients. It enables *metafile* spooling, which offers new options in the common Print dialog box for some printers and applications. If you experience printing problems, consider disabling this option.

- **Printing Defaults button**   Clicking this button opens the Print dialog box, where you can define the printer defaults for common print jobs. For example, if you create a printer that is dedicated to printing two-sided forms, you might want to set the defaults for the type of forms that are commonly used, enable two-sided printing, and so forth. This is another good application that supports the idea of creating multiple printers for the same print device. Altering the settings through Printing Defaults, however, changes the default settings as opposed to changing the settings for the current print job only.

- **Print Processor button**   A print processor tells the spooler how to alter a print job depending on the document data type. In most cases, you will not change this setting. When you click this button, it opens a Print Processor window that lists the available print processors and the default data type for the selected print processor.

- **Separator Page button**   Separator pages are useful in an office environment where several people use the same printer. When you click this button, it opens a Separator Page window that lets you select the type of separator page that best fits your needs. Separator pages print before each document to identify the owner of the document, the date and time it was printed, and other information. For more information regarding separator pages, see the next section, "Using Separator Pages and Files."

TRY IT   To set up advanced printer options, follow these steps on the print server:

1. From the Control Panel, double-click Printers and Other Hardware.
2. Double-click View Installed Printers or Fax Printers.
3. Right-click the printer you want to define, and then select Properties from the pop-up menu.
4. Click the Advanced tab and make changes there.
5. When you are finished making changes, click OK.

▶ *TIP*

You can also select Set Printer Properties from the Task pane.

Using Separator Pages and Files

Separator pages can be used to identify the print job that follows, including the name of the person who's printing, the date it was sent, and a few other facts. They also separate one print job from the next, making *your* printed copy easier to locate in a stack. Windows XP offers two separator pages that switch between PostScript and Printer Control Language (PCL), which is often used by Hewlett-Packard printers. This feature is useful with printers that don't automatically switch between languages. The type of separator page that is used is determined by the selected separator file.

Four standard separator files are installed with Windows XP:

- **Sysprint.sep**   This file switches the printer to PostScript and then prints a separator page that includes the name of the person who printed the job, job number, date, and time.
- **Pcl.sep**   This file switches the printer to PCL and then prints a separator page that includes the name of the person who printed the job, job number, date, and time.
- **Pscript.sep**   This file switches the printer to PostScript but does not print a separator page.
- **Sysprtj.sep**   This variation of sysprint.sep uses Japanese fonts, if they are available.

You can either modify the existing separator files in Windows Notepad or with some other text editor, or you can create your own separator files from scratch. These files are simple text files with the .sep file extension, and they are stored on your system at %SystemRoot%\System32.

Each separator file must begin with a single character on a line by itself. This character is the *command delimiter* that identifies commands in the file. Any character may be used as a command delimiter. In the following table, the @ is used as the command delimiter. The first line of your file must contain only a single instance of this character.

▶ *NOTE*

If you need to customize a .sep file, you should modify an existing .sep file rather than start one from scratch. Just remember to save the file with a different name so you don't overwrite the original .sep file.

Code	Description
@N	Prints the user name of the person who submitted the print job.
@I	Prints the job number.
@D	Prints the date, in the format defined by Regional Options in the Control Panel.
@T	Prints the time, in the format specified by Regional Options in the Control Panel.
@L	Prints all characters between this code and the next @ code until the page width, specified by the @W code, is reached.
@F*pathname*	Prints the contents of the file specified by *pathname*.
@H*nn*	Sends a printer-specific control code, where *nn* is a hexadecimal value—for example, @H1B sends an escape code that has a hexadecimal value of 0x1B (27 in decimal).
@W*nnn*	Sets the maximum width of the separator page to the decimal value defined by *nnn*. Characters that extend beyond this point are truncated. The default width is 80, and the maximum width is 256.
@B@S	Prints in single-width block characters.
@B@M	Prints in double-width block characters.
@U	Turns off block-character printing.

Code	Description
@*n*	Skips *n* lines. This value can be from 0 to 9.
@E	Ejects the current page from the printer.

 TRY IT — To implement a custom separator page, use the following steps:

1. In Notepad, open one of the standard separator (.sep) files, located in %SystemRoot%\System32.
2. Modify the file to meet your needs.
3. Save the file with another name and the .sep extension, and then close the file.
4. From the Control Panel, double-click Printers and Other Hardware.
5. Double-click View Printers or Fax Printers.
6. Right-click the printer you want to define and choose Properties.
7. Click the Advanced tab of the printer's Properties window.
8. Click the Separator Page button to open the Separator Page dialog box.

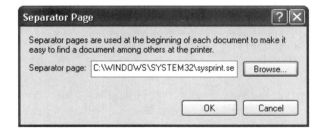

9. Click Browse, and then double-click the .sep file you want to use.
10. Click OK.

Print Server Properties

The Print Server Properties window, shown in Figure 7-3, lets you specify several properties for local printers residing on the server. This window is accessed from the Control Panel by double-clicking Printers and Other Hardware. Click View Installed Printers and Faxes, and then choose File | Server Properties.

From the Forms, Ports, and Drivers tabs in the Properties window, you can specify the list of items available for a given printer. This is important if you don't want everyone adjusting the properties of a shared printer. From the Advanced tab, you can specify a spool folder, event logs, and notification options.

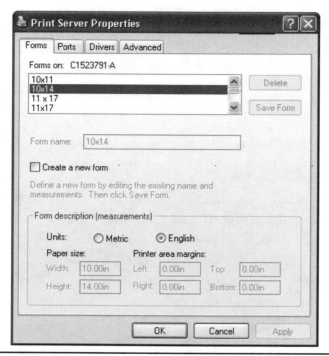

Figure 7-3   Print Server Properties window

- **Forms tab**   This tab controls the list of forms, or page sizes, you can assign to trays through the Device Settings tab in the Printer Properties window. Setting this option preserves predefined form definitions. The user can create new form definitions and delete any user-defined forms, but the predefined forms cannot be deleted.

- **Ports tab**   This tab offers the same options offered in the printer Properties window, except the options listed in this tab are server-specific.

- **Drivers tab**   This tab displays a list of installed printer drivers. You can also add, remove, or update drivers from one central location, a useful feature if the server hosts several printers.

- **Advanced tab**   This tab offers several options that pertain to the spooler. If you run out of space on the current drive where the spool folder resides, you might consider moving the spool folder to another drive. When you move this folder, it affects all of the local printers on the server.

  - **Spooler Folder options**   These options determine which events are entered in the Windows System log.

  - **Printer notifications for downlevel clients options**   Click this option if you want to be notified when remote document printing has completed.

  - **Notify computer, not user, when remote documents are printed**   The Printer notifications for downlevel clients option must be selected to enable this option. If you leave this option unchecked, the notification displays on the first workstation that the user who printed the job logged onto. If the user is logged on to more than one system, he or she may not see the notification. To prevent this from happening, it is best to check both print notification options. This will ensure that the messages are sent to the workstation where the print job was executed.

▶ *TIP*

If you want to move the spool folder to a different location for a specific printer, you must do so from the system registry. Go to the HKLM\Software\Microsoft\Windows NT\CurrentVersion\Print\Printers\ Printer key, where Printer is the name of the printer you want to modify. Set the SpoolDirectory value to the path you want to use.

TRY IT To define printer server properties, use the following steps:

1. From the Control Panel, select Printers and Other Hardware.
2. Right-click a blank portion of the screen, and then select Printer Server from the pop-up menu. Or choose File | Server Properties.
3. Select the options appropriate for your environment, and then click OK.

Auditing Printer Use

If you are using Windows XP Professional, you can audit the use of your network printers. This information can be useful in determining who uses what printer on a regular basis. If one printer shows heavy use, for example, this report can be used to determine whether another printer is required in a given area.

▶ *NOTE*

To set up auditing, you must be logged in as an administrator or a user with the rights to manage the auditing and security log.

TRY IT To set up printer auditing, use the following steps:

1. From the Control Panel, select Performance and Maintenance.
2. Choose Administrative Tools | Local Security Policy | Local Policies | Audit Policy.

3. Double-click Audit Object Access to open the Audit Object Access Properties window:

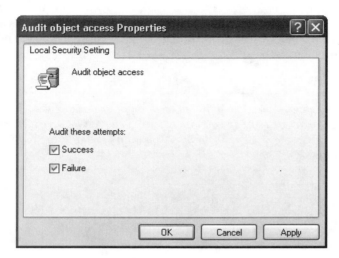

4. Add check marks to both the Success and Failure check boxes. Click OK.

5. Open Windows Explorer, and then choose Tools | Folder Options.

6. In the Folder Options window, click the View tab. Then scroll to the bottom of the Advanced Settings section.

7. Make sure that the Use Simple File Sharing (Recommended) option is unchecked, as shown in Figure 7-4. Click OK.

8. From the Start menu, select Printers and Faxes.

9. Right-click the printer you want to audit, and then select Properties from the pop-up menu.

10. In the Properties window, click the Security tab.

11. Click the Advanced button to open the Access Control Settings window.

12. Click the Auditing tab, as shown in Figure 7-5.

13. From this tab, you can add a new user or group or edit an existing user or group. Double-click the user or group you want to audit, and the Auditing Entry dialog box appears, as shown in Figure 7-6.

14. From the Auditing Entry dialog box, select the types of access you want to audit. For printers, the best information is derived from auditing failures rather than successes. If you want to monitor all events, this log can quickly grow large. When a printer event is logged, the event record is written to the System log. Security events, such as printer access attempts from an unknown user, are written to the Security log.

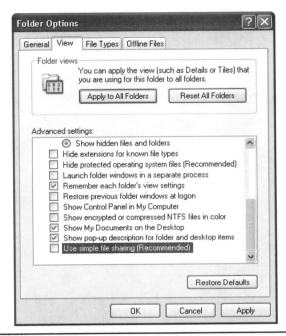

Figure 7-4   Disable Simple File Sharing

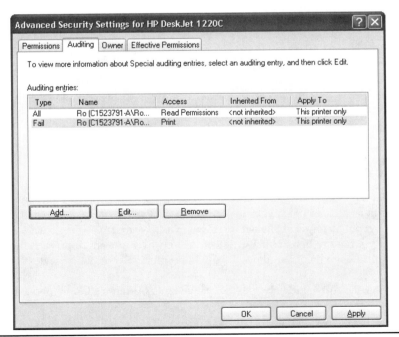

Figure 7-5   Auditing tab

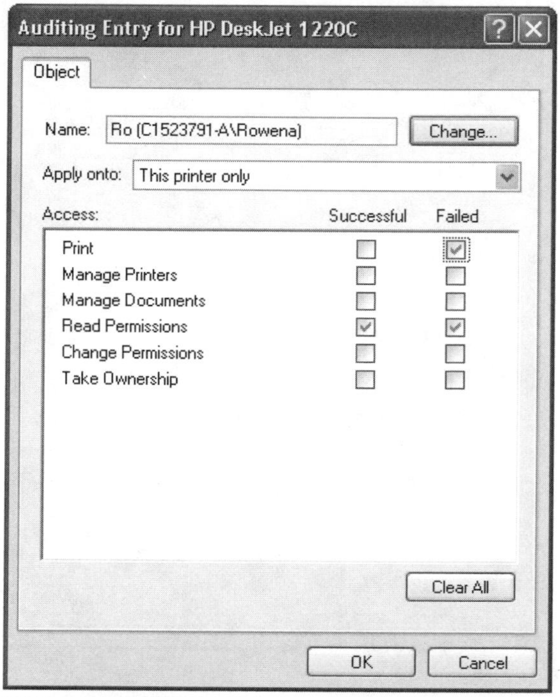

Figure 7-6   Auditing Entry dialog box

▶ *NOTE*

After you set up the audit events, you can restore Simple File Sharing in the Properties window by checking the Simple File Sharing box under Folder Options. The Security tab will no longer be visible, but the audit settings will still be active.

Printing Your Address Book

In today's day and age of electronic devices such as Palm Pilots and iPaqs, it seems ironic that anyone would want to print an address book, yet a few of us adamantly refuse to give up tangible documents. If you still enjoy keeping a physical planner up to date, this feature may be just what you need.

You can print your entire contact list or select the entries you want to print. From Outlook, choose File | Print to open the Print dialog box, which offers the following styles:

- **Card**   Prints the full name, job title, company name, business address, phone numbers, and e-mail addresses.

- **Small Book Style**   Prints a two-sided, detailed version of your contacts list. This style is meant to fit into a pocket-sized day planner.

- **Medium Book Style**   Prints a two-sided, detailed version of your contacts list. This style is meant to fit into a medium-sized day planner.
- **Memo Style**   Prints the information you have stored for the selected contacts.
- **Phone Directory Style**   Prints the full name and all the stored phone numbers. This printed list contains alphabetical separators.

TRY IT   To print a list of contacts, use the following steps:

1. Open Microsoft Outlook.
2. Click the Contacts button.
3. Either select the entire list by pressing CTRL-A, or hold down the CTRL key and click each contact you want to include in the printed document.
4. Choose File | Print to open the Print dialog box.
5. Under Print Range, you'll see an option to print the entire list of contacts or print only the contacts you have selected. By default, the entire list is printed.
6. Select the style you want to use.
   To modify a style, click the Define Styles button, and in the Define Styles dialog, click Edit to edit the selected style or click Copy to make a copy of the selected style. Click Reset to return the selected style to its original defaults.
7. When you are finished defining the style and other print options, click Print.

▶ *NOTE*

If you click Print Preview and then click Close, you will have to click the Print button again to return to the Print dialog box.

Using the Fax Feature

The Windows XP fax feature lets you send and receive facsimiles from your computer. You can choose to send and receive faxes with a local fax device attached to your computer or with a remote fax device connected to fax servers on a network. By default, the fax service is not installed with Windows XP. If you are upgrading and were using the fax service in Windows 2000, Windows XP installs the fax service automatically and retains your settings.

After the fax service is installed, you can use the provided tools to configure fax printers and fax devices, send and receive faxes, manage incoming and outgoing faxes, specify default sender information, configure notifications for fax events, and modify how that information is displayed in the Fax Console.

TRY IT   To install the fax service, use the following steps:

1. From the Control Panel, click Add or Remove Programs.
2. Select Add / Remove Windows Components.
3. In the Windows Components Wizard, check the Fax Services check box and then follow the instructions on the screen.

To use the fax service, open the Start menu and select All Programs | Accessories | Communications | Fax Console. If this is the first time you have used this service, the Fax Configuration Wizard launches. Follow the instructions on the screen to complete the process.

Fax Viewer

Fax Viewer is a new feature in Windows XP and a handy one to use. The same feature that you use to view pictures is used to view fax documents. Through this viewer, you can get a quick view of each document, rotate it, and perform basic tasks, such as annotation, without having to open an editing program.

If you store your pictures in the My Pictures folder, you can view them as a filmstrip (Figure 7-7), thumbnails, icons, or tiles. These views can be changed by selecting a different view from the View menu.

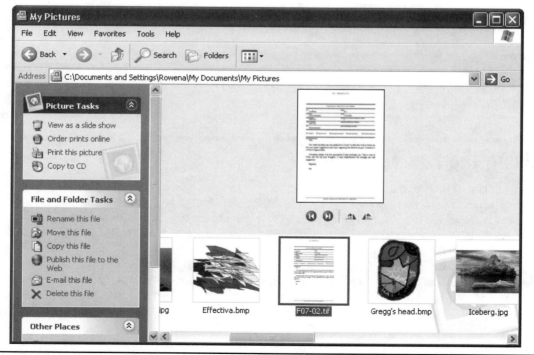

Figure 7-7   Fax Viewer in Filmstrip mode

Fax documents are stored as TIFF files. When you double-click a fax document, it automatically launches the Windows Picture and Fax Viewer application, shown in Figure 7-8.

TRY IT To access the Fax Viewer, use the following steps:

1. From the Start menu, select My Pictures.
2. By default, the View mode is filmstrip, which displays the documents in a slide-show format. Click a thumbnail image to view a larger image.
3. Double-click the image to open the Windows Picture and Fax Viewer.

Fax Configuration

With the Fax Configuration Wizard, you can configure fax printers and devices, specify default sender information, configure notifications for fax events, and modify how that information is displayed in the Fax Console.

The way you configure your fax service depends on how your environment is designed and the location of your fax resources. When a fax device is connected directly to your system, it is called

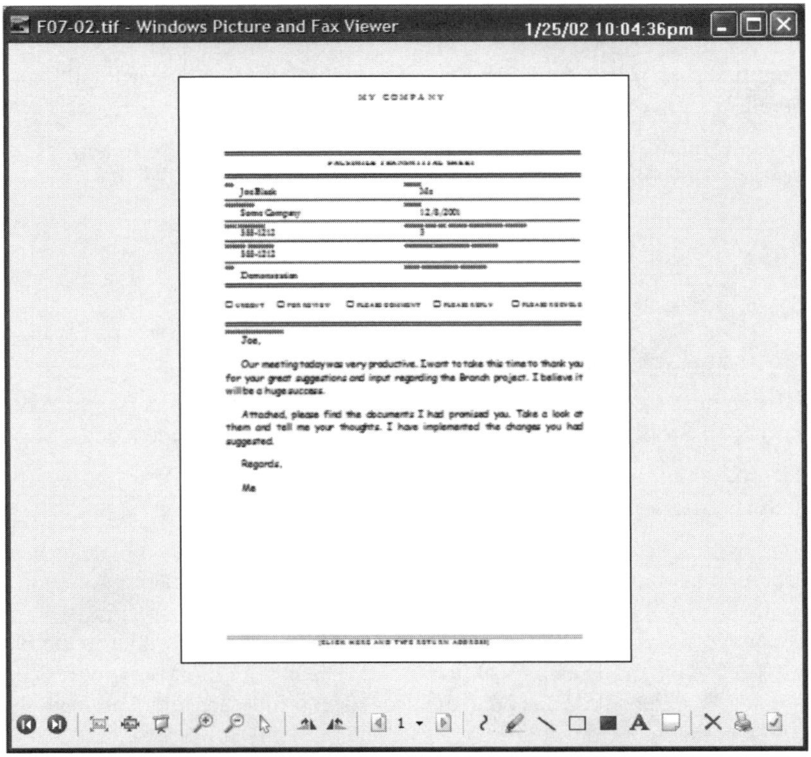

Figure 7-8 Windows Picture and Fax Viewer

a *local resource*. When such a device is connected to your system, it is detected automatically and added as a fax resource when your operating system boots up. Windows XP supports only one local fax device connected to your system. The removal of a fax device is also automatic. *Remote fax devices* are connected to your system through the network. These devices can be configured to control how users send and receive, view, and manage faxes over the network. You add a remote fax device in the same way you add a remote printer.

▶ *NOTE*

If more than one fax device is attached to your computer, the fax service will detect all of these local devices, and they will appear in the fax device list. Fax devices are listed in the same window as installed printers. However, the fax service supports only one local fax device, so you can configure only one of these devices to send and receive faxes.

As an administrator, you can add fax resources and configure them through the Fax Configuration Wizard. This wizard launches automatically the first time you open the Fax Console.

TRY IT To launch the Fax Configuration Wizard, use the following steps:

1. From the Start menu, select All Programs | Accessories | Communications | Fax Console.
2. If this is the first time you use the fax service, the Configuration Wizard will launch automatically.
3. If you have configured the fax service already and want to modify your settings, choose Tools | Fax Console | Configure Fax to launch the Fax Configuration Wizard.

Sending Faxes

You can send a fax in various ways in Windows XP:

- Send a fax cover page using the Send Fax Wizard.
- Create a document in a Windows application and then print it to a fax printer. The Send Fax Wizard opens to help you complete the task and offers to include a cover page.
- Scan a document and then print it to a fax printer. The Send Fax Wizard opens to help you complete the task and offers to include a cover page.
- Create a fax in an e-mail application that supports faxing, just as you create an e-mail message; simply specify a fax number for the recipient rather than an e-mail address.

A fax that is being sent can be monitored and managed in the Outbox folder in the Fax Console, shown in Figure 7-9. If you are using a local fax device, you can monitor the progress of your outgoing faxes in the Fax Console. Faxes that are sent successfully are removed from the Outbox folder and archived in the Sent Items folder.

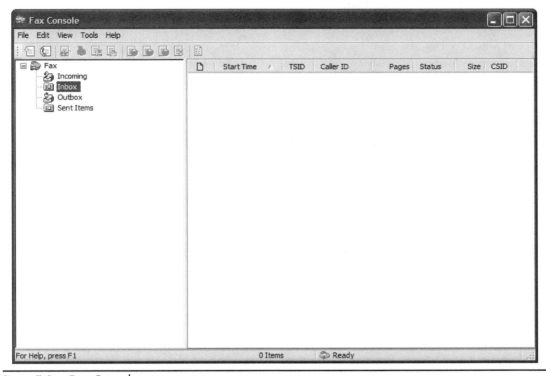

Figure 7-9   Fax Console

TRY IT   To send a fax, use the following steps:

1. From the Start menu, choose All Programs | Accessories | Communications | Fax Console.

2. If more than one fax device is installed on your system, select the one you want to use.

3. Choose File | Send a Fax.

4. In the Send Fax Wizard, follow the instructions to send the fax.

5. Click Finish when you're done.

Creating a Fax Cover Page

A fax cover page can be used to identify a fax sender and receiver, and to send a short introduction to any pages that follow. As a part of the fax service, each user has an individual folder of personal cover pages. This folder remains empty until the user creates a cover page or copies an existing cover page template into the folder.

The fax feature provides common cover page templates that can be used as is or modified to meet your specific needs. The default location for your personal cover pages is My Documents\Fax\ Personal Cover Pages.

TRY IT To create a fax cover page, use the following steps:

1. From the Start menu, choose All Programs I Accessories I Communications I Fax I Fax Console.
2. Choose Tools I Personal Cover Pages.
3. In the Personal Cover Pages dialog box, click New.

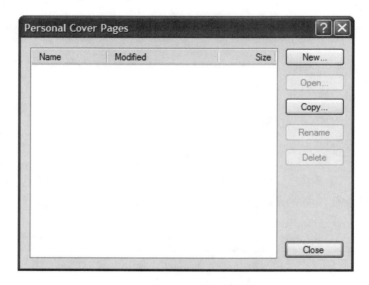

4. Create your cover page in the Fax Cover Page Editor, and then save it to the default location.

▶ *TIP*

To open the Fax Cover Page Editor without opening your Personal Cover Pages folder, open the Start menu and choose All Programs I Accessories I Communications I Fax I Fax Cover Page Editor.

After your new cover page has been saved, it appears in your Personal Cover Pages folder stored at My Documents\Fax\Personal Cover Pages. If you store your cover pages in a different location, they will not be displayed in your Personal Cover Pages folder.

Configuring XP Fax for the Outlook Address Book

Configuring the XP fax service to work with Microsoft Outlook or Outlook Express is considerably easier than it was in Windows 2000. Administrator privileges are no longer required to access your Outlook profile.

The XP fax service uses the Windows Address Book (WAB) as its default for storing fax numbers. When you install Outlook 2000 or 2002, however, the service automatically switches over to the

Outlook Address Book (OAB). Fax operations from any Office application invokes the OAB instead of the WAB, so you don't have to update two address books.

▶ *CAUTION*

In the Fax Properties window for the local computer, the Fax Service Login tab may still be present, depending on your configuration. If you change the login to something different than the local system and Outlook login, you will disable the fax service.

To send faxes from Outlook, you must include the Fax Mail Transport in your Outlook profile and enable the cover page option.

TRY IT To set up the fax service in Outlook 2002, use the following steps:

1. In Outlook 2002, choose Tools | E-mail Accounts to open the E-mail Accounts window.
2. Click Add a New E-mail Account, and then click Next.
3. From the Server Types window, click Additional Server Types, and then click Next.
4. In the Internet E-mail Settings window, select Fax Mail Transport. Then click Next.
5. Restart Outlook.

To enable and configure the cover page feature, use the following steps:

1. In Outlook 2002, choose Tools | E-mail Accounts.
2. In the E-mail Accounts window, click View or Change Existing E-mail Accounts. Then click Next.
3. In the next window, select the Fax Mail Transport account; then click Change.
4. In the Fax Configuration window, click Include a Cover Page with Faxes option and then select a cover page template.
5. If you want to change the font, click the Set Font button in the Fax Configuration window to open the Font dialog box. Make your changes, and then click OK.
6. Click OK.

CHAPTER 8
Using the Command Prompt

TIPS IN THIS CHAPTER

The Microsoft Disk Operating System (MS-DOS) is an operating system with a command-line interface that translates keyboard input into operations the computer can understand. It also governs disk input and output operations, video support, keyboard control, and several internal functions used for program execution and file maintenance.

The MS-DOS shell provides character-based interaction with Windows XP. Some MS-DOS–based programs that run in a Windows environment create Program Information Files (PIFs) that appear as shortcuts on your desktop. PIFs contain the settings required to execute the program.

If you are accustomed to performing administrative tasks at the command line, Windows XP lets you do so through multiple command-prompt sessions. Each session is protected from any failures that may occur in other sessions. In a command session, you can enter MS-DOS commands, run batch programs, and run applications.

You can access the command prompt window, shown next, by choosing Start | Run. In the text box, type **cmd**, and then press ENTER.

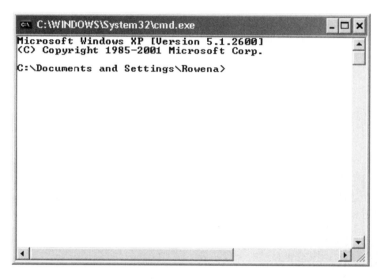

The command prompt window can be modified by right-clicking the title bar of the window and selecting Properties from the pop-up menu.

Command Window Properties

From the Properties dialog, you can modify the window to fit your needs. When you apply the changes you've made, you are given the opportunity to apply your settings to the active window or to all future command prompt windows.

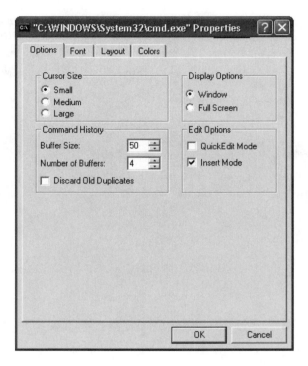

On the Options tab of the Properties dialog, you can set the following options:

- **Cursor Size**   Defines how tall the cursor in the command prompt window appears. Changing this option to Large results in a block-like cursor.
- **Display Options**   Enables you to change the command prompt window to a full-sized or adjustable-size window.
- **Edit Options**   When QuickEdit Mode is selected, you can use your mouse to cut and paste in the command prompt window. When Insert Mode is selected, you can position your cursor in the middle of a command and insert characters without typing over the rest of the command.
- **Command History**   The Buffer Size determines the number of commands a buffer can store. The Number of Buffers determines the number of processes that can have distinct history

buffers. Check the Discard Old Duplicates option if you want to eliminate old duplicate commands from the command history.

On the Properties dialog's Font tab, you can specify settings that determine how text is displayed on the screen.

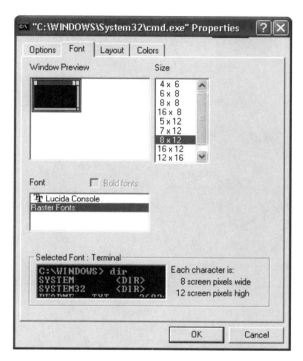

The following options are available on the Font tab:

- **Window Size**   Select how you want the characters to be sized within the command prompt window. For example, if you select 4 x 6, each character will be 4 pixels wide and 6 pixels high—a very small font size.
- **Font**   Select which font to use in the window. If, for example, you select Lucida Console, you can click the Bold fonts option. This generates a clean font that is easy to read. Or, you can keep the default Raster fonts. If you select the Lucida Console font, you can also select the font size in the form of points. A 10-point font in Lucida Console is 7 pixels wide and 10 pixels high.
- **Selected Font**   Shows how the font you select appears on the command prompt window.

The Layout tab lets you set the screen size and position.

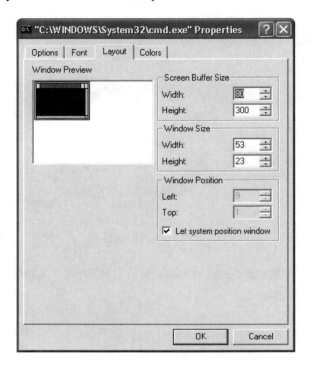

The following options are available on the Layout tab:

- **Screen Buffer Size**   Determines the width and height of the screen based on the number of characters in the buffer. If the window is smaller than the screen buffer size settings, the command prompt window will display scroll bars.
- **Window Size**   Specifies the width and height of the command prompt window.
- **Window Position**   If you check the Let System Position Window option, Windows XP will automatically position the window for you. Or, if you want the command prompt window to open in a specific location, you can enter the Left and Top coordinates.

On the Colors tab, you can set the colors for the command prompt window background and font.

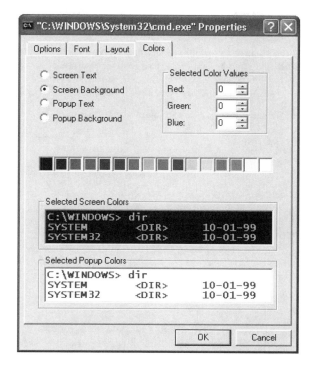

The following option is available on the Colors tab:

- **Selected Color Values** This window displays the color values that are set for the element selected on the left of the tab. Colors for selected elements can be changed by either clicking on a color swatch or adjusting the Selected Color Values.

Common Command Symbols

The following table shows common command-prompt symbols and their uses. These symbols are used in conjunction with commands to control command results. For example, if you need to input a series of properties for a given command, you may want to redirect the input to a file that contains those properties. This saves you time from having to type them each time the command is run. To do this, you would use the input redirection symbol (<) in the following manner: *sort < c:\myDirectory.txt*.

Symbol	Purpose
<	Redirects the input. Tells the system to accept input from a source other than the keyboard.
>	Redirects the output. Tells the system to send the command results to something other than the screen.
>>	Appends redirected output to an existing file.

Symbol	Purpose
| (pipe)	Used with filters in an input or output command. The filters that generally follow this symbol are *More, Find,* and *Sort.* For example, *tree c:* | *more* will display the system tree on the screen. If the output does not fit in the screen, -- *more* – displays at the bottom, indicating there is more of the tree to view. To view the next page, press ENTER.
&	Separates multiple commands in a command line (*command1 & command2*); *command2* executes after *command1* completes.
&&	Used to run one command after another, only if the preceding command completes successfully (*command1 && command2*).
|| (double pipe)	Used to run one command after another, only if the preceding command fails, meaning it completes with an error code that is greater than zero (*command1 || command2*).
^ (caret)	Used when the &, &&, ||, and ( ) symbols are passed as arguments. This symbol must precede any symbol that is passed as an argument unless the argument is embedded in quotes.
( )	Used to group or nest multiple commands: *(command1 && command2) & (command1 & command2).*

Windows XP recognizes two wildcard characters:

- **?** The question mark is used to represent any single character in a file name. For example, if you wanted to find a word whose first and third character equals *P,* you would use a wildcard to represent the second character (*P?P*). In a sense, this causes the find process to ignore the second character.

- ***** The asterisk is used to represent a series of characters. For example, if you wanted to find all files that had the extension *.exe,* you could use the asterisk to represent the file name before the extension (**.exe*).

MS-DOS Command Changes in Windows XP

Windows XP has made some changes to the way certain commands behave. To view these changes and to learn how each of these commands are used, choose Help | Support Center, and type **New ways to do familiar tasks** in the Search text box.

Launching and Exiting a Command-Prompt Session

There are no limits to the number of command-prompt sessions you can have open. If you are viewing a directory in a current command-prompt session, for example, you may want to open another command prompt window to compare that directory with another. Simply enter the *start* command. This command's results are the same as if you had typed *start cmd*. If you eliminate the program name after the *start* command, MS-DOS automatically assumes you want to launch another command session.

► **NOTE**

Command.com is the old 16-bit command processor that is still supported by Windows XP; however, unless you have an application that requires this processor, it is recommended that you use the new cmd.exe *command to initiate a command-prompt session.*

From Windows XP, you can initiate a command-prompt session in one of the following ways (a command prompt window is shown in the following illustration):

- Choose Start | All Programs | Accessories | Command Prompt.
- Choose Start | Run. In the text box, enter **cmd** and then click OK.
- Open the %SystemRoot%\System32 folder and double-click the Cmd icon.

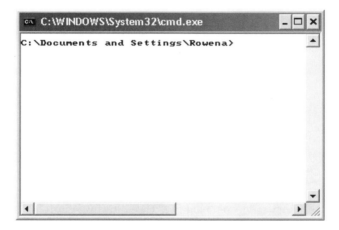

When you are done with the command-prompt session, you can close the window by typing **exit** then pressing the ENTER key.

TRY IT To initiate a command-prompt session, follow these steps:

1. Choose Start | Run.
2. In the text box, type **cmd** then click OK.
3. When you are done with the session, type **exit** and then press the ENTER key to end the session and close the command prompt window.

► **TIP**

If you are not running a character-based program or a program that does not have any unsaved files, you can close the session by clicking the close button.

Launching the Command-Prompt Session from a Folder

At times it is more convenient to launch a command-prompt session from a particular folder. For example, if you have an MS-DOS executable program located in a specific directory, it would be nice to start the command-prompt session from that directory so that you do not have to navigate to it manually once the session is open.

By setting up a shortcut menu command, you can right-click any folder in Windows Explorer to start a command-prompt session that automatically points to that folder, as shown here:

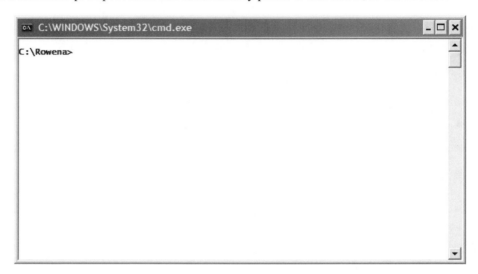

TRY IT   To set up a shortcut menu command, use the following steps:

1. In Notepad or some other text-editing application, create a text file that contains the following information:

   Windows Registry Editor Version 5.00
   [HKEY_CLASSES_ROOT\Folder\shell\Command Prompt]
   @="Command &Prompt Here"
   [HKEY_CLASSES_ROOT\Folder\shell\Command Prompt\command]
   @="cmd.exe /k pushd %L"

2. Save the file as **c:\commandPrompt.reg**. You can use any file name you want, but you must use the .reg extension.

3. Double-click the file name you just saved. When prompted, answer Yes to add the information to the system registry.

If you right-click a folder and select Command Prompt, it should open a command prompt window that points to the folder you selected. If you receive an error message, you may need to perform the following steps:

1. Open the Start menu and choose Run.

2. In the text box, type **regedit** and then click OK.

3. Navigate to HKEY_CLASSES_ROOT\Folder\shell\Command Prompt.

4. In the right pane, right-click the default entry and then select Modify from the pop-up menu.

5. In the value text box, enter **Command &Prompt Here**; then click OK.

6. Navigate to HKEY_CLASSES_ROOT\Folder\shell\Command Prompt\command.

7. In the right pane, right-click the default entry, and then select Modify from the pop-up menu.

8. In the value text box, enter **cmd.exe /k pushd %L**. Then click OK.

9. Close the system registry editor and try the command again.

These steps create a new shortcut menu command for the folders list in Windows Explorer. When you right-click a folder, you can select Command Prompt to open a command prompt in the directory of the folder you have selected.

Running a Command Automatically

Batch files let you run one or more MS-DOS commands with or without user intervention. The key to running these types of commands involves using the right command-line arguments. The /C and /K command-line arguments enable you to start a command-prompt session and run one or more commands.

▶ *NOTE*

If you enter a command string without specifying either the /C or /K argument, the command string is ignored. You must include other command-line arguments before the /C or /K arguments or they will be ignored. The /C and /K command-line arguments must be the last argument before the command string.

The /C command-line argument terminates the command-prompt session as soon as the commands complete. The /K command-line argument keeps the command-prompt session active even after the commands finish executing.

▶ *TIP*

If you want to issue other MS-DOS commands while a batch is running, use the start command. For example, to run myBatch.bat in the background, enter cmd /K start myBatch.bat.

Here's how you execute a command with the */K* argument:

1. In Notepad or some other text-editing application, create a text file that contains the following command:

   cmd /k start *commandPrompt.reg*

   If you have not created the commandPrompt.reg file, you can substitute this command string with an MS-DOS command you want to execute.

2. Save the file as **c:\commandPrompt.bat**. You can use any file name you want, but you must use the .bat extension.

3. Double-click the file name you just saved and observe what happens. If you are feeling adventurous, try exchanging the */K* argument with the */C* argument and see what happens.

Using AutoRun

In older operating systems, the autoexec.bat file was used to execute commands when the system booted. In Windows XP, a feature known as AutoRun is used to perform the same basic function. By default at startup, the command prompt executes what it finds in the following two registry values:

- The AutoRun value under HKEY_LOCAL_MACHINE\Software\Microsoft\Command Processor
- The AutoRun value under HKEY_CURRENT_USER\Software\Microsoft\Command Processor

HKEY_LOCAL_MACHINE affects all user accounts on the system, whereas HKEY_CURRENT_USER affects only the current user account. If both values are set, the HKEY_LOCAL_MACHINE value is executed before HKEY_CURRENT_USER.

Each of these values is a data type string. This type of string can contain only a single command string. If you need to execute a sequence of strings, enter them into a batch file and then execute the batch file with either the HKEY_LOCAL_MACHINE or HKEY_CURRENT_USER command-string value.

▶ **NOTE**

To disable AutoRun commands in a command-prompt session, use the /D argument when opening the session.

 To set command prompt AutoRun, use the following steps:

1. Open the Start menu and select Run.
2. In the text box, type **regedit**, and then click OK.

3. Navigate to either the HKEY_LOCAL_MACHINE or HKEY_CURRENT_USER registry entry.

4. In the right pane of the key window create a new value and name it **AutoRun**.

5. In the Value text box, enter the command exactly as you would enter it in at the command prompt, and then click OK.

Recalling and Editing a Command Line

When you enter a command at the command prompt, it is inevitable that you will recall that command or edit it at some point. Windows XP enables you to recall previous commands and edit them on the current command line. For example, if you make a mistake in a command string, rather than having to retype the entire string, you can simply fix your mistake and move on.

The following table shows the keyboard shortcuts that you can press to recall and edit commands entered at the command prompt.

Key	Function
UP	Recalls the previous command in the command history
DOWN	Recalls the next command in the command history
PGUP	Recalls the earliest command used in this session
PGDN	Recalls the last command issued
LEFT	Moves the cursor one character to the left
RIGHT	Moves the cursor one character to the right
CTRL-LEFT	Moves the cursor one word to the left
CTRL-RIGHT	Moves the cursor one word to the right
HOME	Moves the cursor to the beginning of the line
END	Moves the cursor to the end of the line
ESC	Clears the current command
F7	Displays the command history in a scrollable pop-up box
F8	Displays commands that start with the characters that are currently in the command line
ALT-F7	Clears the command history

▶ *NOTE*

The command history is stored only for the current session. Once you close the session window, the command history is cleared. However, you can copy a command and paste it into another session.

TRY IT To try the command editing keys, use the following steps:

1. Open a command prompt window.

2. Enter a few commands.

3. Press F7 to view a history of your commands.

4. Click one you want to execute.

5. Try pressing some of the other keys to see what they do.

6. When you are done, enter the **exit** command to close the command prompt window.

Redirecting Input and Output

Windows XP lets you override the default input of the keyboard and the default output of the screen. This is useful if you want to store the contents of a directory to a file for future reference, or if you want to append the output to an existing file.

To direct the output to a file, type the command, and then add a greater-than symbol (>) and the end, followed by the name of the file. For example, to send the output of a directory command to a file named myDirectory.txt, you would type **dir c:\mydirectory > c:\myDirectory.txt**.

To append information to an existing file, add two greater-than symbols to the end of the command, followed by the name of the existing file. For example, to append the output of a directory command to a file named myDirectory.txt, you would type **dir c:\mydirectory >> c:\myDirectory.txt**.

NOTE

If the specified file does not exist, Windows XP will create it for you.

If you want to use a file as input, you can use the input redirection symbol, which is the less-than symbol (<). For example, if you have created a file called c:\myDirectory.txt that lists several directories that you want to sort and display to the screen, you would enter the command **sort < c:\myDirectory.txt**.

Now, suppose you want to save the results of that sort to a file. That is simple enough to do; simply use both the input and output redirect symbols in your command. For example:

```
sort < c:\myDirectory.txt > c:\mySortedDirectory.txt
```

This command reads the myDirectory.txt file, sorts it, and saves the results to the mySortedDirectory.txt file.

TRY IT   To redirect input and output, use the following steps:

1. Open a command prompt window.

2. At the command prompt, enter **dir c:\ > c:\myDirectory.txt**.

3. To sort that list and save it to another file, enter **sort < c:\myDirectory.txt > c:\mySortedDirectory.txt**.

4. When you are done, enter **exit** to close the command prompt window.

Using Doskey Macros

Using a *doskey* macro, you can create shortcuts for common commands. These macros are available only for the current command-prompt session. Once you open a new session, the macros must be either re-created or loaded from a file that contains a list of predefined macros.

For example, if you wanted to execute the command *sort < c:\myDirectories.txt > c:\mySortedDirectories.txt* with a simple command like *sd,* you could create a macro that looks like this:

```
doskey sd=sort < c:\myDirectories.txt > c:\mySortedDirectories.txt
```

Now to execute that command, all you would need to do is enter *sd*.

Suppose you want to load several macros for each session; you could create a macro file. Using the tips described earlier in this chapter, you could have that macro file loaded each time a new command-prompt session begins. To load a macro file named c:\myMacros.txt, then, you would enter this command:

```
doskey /macrofile=c:\myMacros.txt
```

TRY IT   To use doskey macros, follow these steps:

1. Open a command prompt window.

2. Create a macro using the syntax
   doskey *macro=commandstring*
   where *macro* is the keys you want to press to execute the *commandstring*.

3. If you have created a macro file, you can load it by entering
   doskey /macrofile=*path\macrofile*
   where *path* is the path where the macro file is stored and *macrofile* is the name of the macro file.

4. Enter a macro to test the command.

5. When you are done, enter **exit** to close the command-prompt session.

Using Filters

A command filter is basically a command within a command. Its primary use is to divide, rearrange, or extract portions of information. The following filters are available in Windows XP:

- More
- Find
- Sort

The *more* filter displays the results of a command one page at a time. Subsequent pages are displayed when any key other than PAUSE is pressed. When you have seen enough, you can stop the information from displaying by pressing CTRL-C. For example, if you wanted to view the contents of a file, one display page at a time, you would enter **more < *file.txt*** (where *file.txt* is the name of the file you want to view).

The *find* filter is used to search through command output or file inputs for specified characters and display the results on the screen. By default, find searches are case sensitive. When the keyword or phrase is found, each line that contains the specified word or phrase is displayed on the screen. To use this filter, you must include the less-than (<) symbol in the command. For example, if you wanted to search for the phrase "ski resorts" in a file called SkiWashington.txt, you would enter **find "ski resorts" < c:\SkiWashington.txt**.

The *sort* filter is used to sort the specified file or command results in alphabetical order. For example, if you wanted to sort the SkiWashington file, you would enter **sort < c:\SkiWashington.txt**.

Each of these filters can also be used with commands that display their results to the screen. For example, if you wanted to sort the results of a directory listing, you would enter **dir c:\ | sort**. The pipe character (|) is used to attach a filter to the command results.

You can also combine two filters to produce desired results. For example, if you wanted to find a list of people with the last name of *Portch* and sort by their first name in a file called names.txt, you would enter **find "Portch" names.txt | sort**.

 To try out filters, follow these steps:

1. Open a command prompt window.
2. Enter **dir** to view a list of the current directory.
3. Enter **dir | sort** to view a sorted list of the current directory.
4. When you are done, enter **exit** to close the command window and end the session.

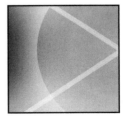

CHAPTER 9

Getting Help and Support

TIPS IN THIS CHAPTER

U nlike previous versions of Windows, Windows XP offers an awesome help and support system that can turn even the most novice user into a semi-pro. With more than 200 compiled help files and nearly 10,000 topics, you are bound to find the information you are looking for.

In the previous versions of Windows, the help files were mainly geared toward novice users. Windows XP offers an impressive collection of tutorials and reference material, including the following new features:

- Links to system tools and utilities that run within the Help and Support Center window; some of which include the Disk Defragmenter, System Configuration Utility (msconfig), Network Diagnostics, and Windows Update.

- An alphabetical list of command-line options, including their syntax and how they are used.

- An impressive variety of troubleshooters for common problems—and uncommon problems that occur on a rare basis.

- Links that actually collect information about your system, including its current configuration, installed hardware, software, and services.

- Easy access to group policy settings and advanced system information.

- External links to the Microsoft Knowledge Base and newsgroups.

- Remote Assistance; a utility that enables another user to connect to a system remotely to witness and fix problems over the Internet or a local network.

Using the Help and Support Center

To open the Help and Support Center, choose Start | Help and Support. You are greeted with the home page shown in Figure 9-1.

This page offers quick access to basic information, troubleshooting tools, and external support resources. The left pane lists common help topics, and the right pane offers links to tools and resources. The Did You Know? section is customizable. By default, this section contains headlines provided by the Microsoft support team. Some third-party vendors may alter the contents in this section to point to their product-specific support sites.

The browser-like toolbar at the top of the page provides basic navigation tools. The Home, Favorites, and History buttons act similarly to the ones in Internet Explorer, but these are focused only on the Help and Support Center.

Favorite Topics

If you find yourself frequently visiting a help topic, you can save it to your favorites list to save you the time of having to look it up each time you want to reference it. As you access your favorite topic, click the Add to Favorites button just above the topic window.

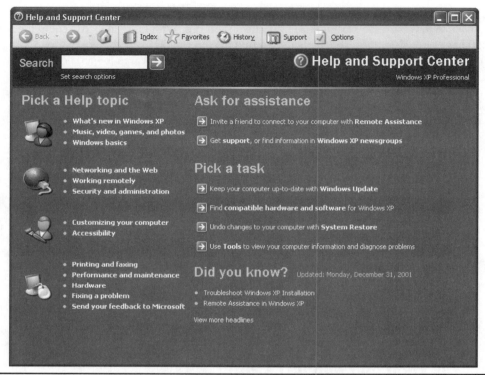

Figure 9-1   Help and Support Center home page

► *TIP*

When you add a topic to your favorites list, you might want to rename them so they mean something to you. For example, if you mark a glossary term, the default name for your favorite entry will be Glossary. This could be quite confusing if you add two or three glossary term entries to your favorites list.

► *NOTE*

Unfortunately, there is no way to reorder how your favorites appear in your list. They are listed in the order in which they are created.

When Help Stops Working

Occasionally, Windows XP becomes a bit temperamental and decides to offer a glitch or two, just to keep things interesting. If you try to bring up the Help and Support Center and nothing happens, it might be due to the following reason. The Help and Support Center uses two related modules: the Help and Support Center Service (helpsvc.exe) and the Help and Support Center executable (helpctr.exe). The problem tends to occur when multiple instances of helpctr.exe are running. To solve this problem, close the multiple instances of this executable through Windows Task Manager, as shown in Figure 9-2.

TRY IT   To end tasks, use these steps:

1. Press CTRL-ALT-DEL or CTRL-SHIFT-ESC to open the Windows Task Manager.

2. Open the Processes tab.

3. To sort the processes in alphabetic order, click the Image Name heading.

4. Click one of the helpctr.exe instances and then click End Process.

5. Repeat step 4 until no instances of this process are running, and then close Windows Task Manager.

6. From the Control Panel, select Performance and Maintenance Options | Administrative Tools | Services.

7. Right-click Help and Support; then select Restart from the pop-up menu.

8. Try starting the Help and Support Center again. It should work this time.

Figure 9-2   Windows Task Manager

Searching for Help Topics

Most of us are still used to tangible forms of references, such as books or magazines we can hold in our hands. Finding the same information in an online format can be a bit overwhelming to some people. You can get lost quite quickly when jumping from link to link. After a time, you might not even remember what it was you were looking for. Windows XP has made the process of finding what you need a simple process. From the Help and Support Center home page, you can click a subject you are inquiring about. Once that subject's window opens, type a specific word or phrase in the Search box, and then press ENTER or click the green arrow to the right of the Search box.

The results of your search are displayed in the left pane, as shown in Figure 9-3. When you pick a task from that list, the help system highlights each instance of the requested word or phrase in the right pane. If you want to view only results that contain a specific phrase, you can enclose that phrase in quotes.

The search results are grouped into the following categories:

- **Suggested Topics** Lists the help topics with an associated keyword that matches the word or phrase you entered. This list is generally small and is limited to the keywords that the help author has assigned to each topic. Because this list does not take long to load, due to limited matches, it is displayed first.

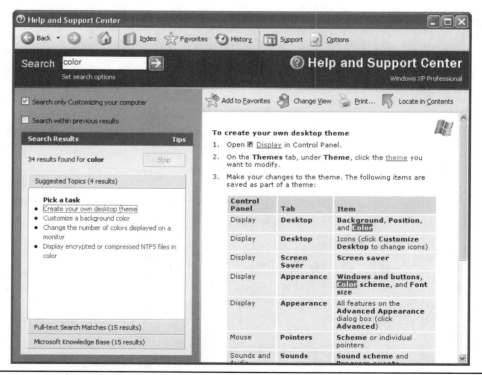

Figure 9-3 Search results

- **Full-Text Search Matches**   Displays the help topics that contain the word or phrase you entered. Because this list is not based on the keywords for each topic, your chances of finding the information you need are greater. Because this list is larger, it takes longer to load than the Suggested Topics.
- **Microsoft Knowledge Base**   Displays the matches found in the Microsoft Knowledge Base, which offers an extensive collection of articles and bug fixes that are not found in the help files.

The results of the search depend on the settings defined in the Set Search Options window, shown in Figure 9-4. You can access this dialog by clicking Set Search Options, which is under the Search text box.

From this window, you can fine-tune your search results to fit your needs. The less information the help system needs to search through, the quicker the results will be—but at the cost of providing fewer results.

In the Search text box, you can use Boolean expressions, such as *AND*, *OR*, *NOT*, and *NEAR* to narrow down your search. For example, if you want to find information on printers but not on sharing, you could enter **printing not sharing**.

▶ *NOTE*

Sometimes the Search feature does not work. Use it with discretion.

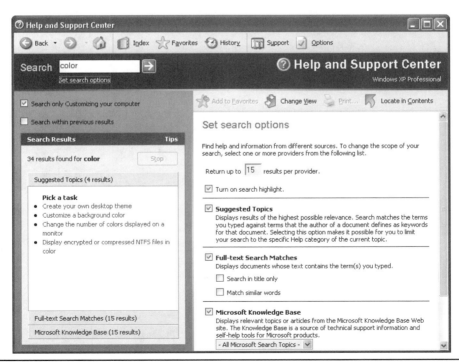

Figure 9-4   Set Search Options window

If you have no clue where to find specific information, click the Index button. The result is a list of all keywords and phrases for each help topic, as shown in Figure 9-5.

The difference between the index search and searching using the standard Search box is that as you type in the index search box, the index jumps to the first topic that matches the characters you enter. For example, if you enter *Printing,* only the keywords that begin with *Printing* are shown in the index. If you had entered the same word in the standard Search text box, you would be shown topics for Faxing and Printing and all other topics that contain the keyword Printing.

TRY IT   To perform a simple search, use the following steps:

1. From the Start menu, select Help and Support.

2. From the Help and Support Center home page, select a topic of interest.

3. In the Search text box, type a word or phrase you want to find, and then press ENTER. To narrow your search, click the Options button to define specific search criteria.

4. Double-click a topic in the left pane to view the information.

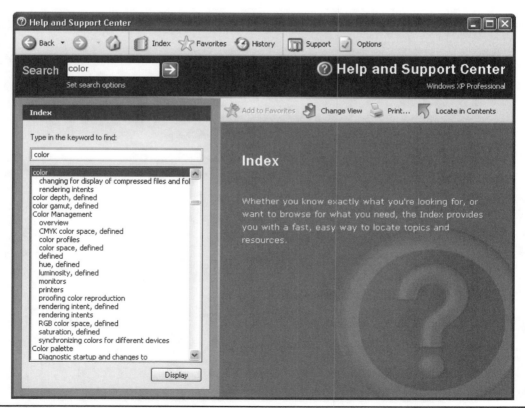

Figure 9-5   An index search

Accessing the Knowledge Base

If you know the article ID of an entry in the Knowledge Base, you can jump right to that article.

TRY IT To find a Knowledge Base article, follow these steps:

1. Open Internet Explorer.
2. In the Address text box, enter **mskb Q*articleNumber***, where *articleNumber* is the ID of the article you want to find. (The article number always starts with a *Q*.)

▶ **NOTE**

If you have customized Internet Explorer's AutoSearch settings, this technique may not work.

Accessing the Wizards

More than two dozen wizards are included in Windows XP. To find them can be a bit of a challenge unless you know where to look. The Help and Support Center offers a quick way to access each of the wizards and offers an explanation on how they are used. Figure 9-6 shows how the wizards are displayed.

TRY IT To access the Windows XP wizards, use the following steps:

1. From the Start menu, choose Help and Support.
2. Click the Index button.
3. In the index search text box, type **wizards**; then press ENTER.
4. In the search results list, double-click the wizard of interest.

Creating Help Topic Shortcuts

Each help topic in the Help and Support Center is a separate HTML file. This means you can create a shortcut to your favorite topics and place them directly onto your Desktop. Doing this is helpful for new users who are learning specific tasks. Because Windows XP does not allow you to do this directly from the Help and Support Center, you need to do it manually by copying the Universal Resource Locator (URL) address from the Properties dialog of the actual help topic. Figure 9-7 shows how you copy this information. (See the next Try It for details.)

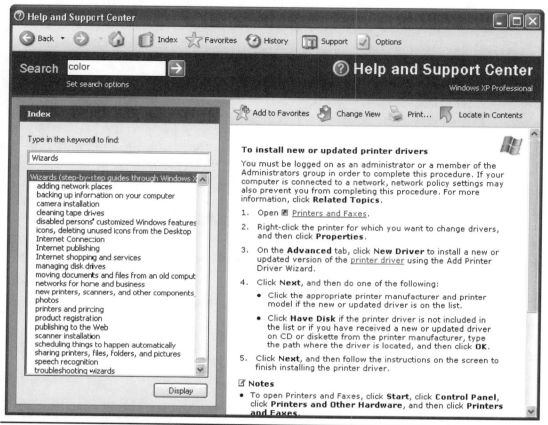

Figure 9-6   Quick access to Windows XP wizards

When you create shortcuts for help topics, you deal with URLs in one or more of the following formats:

- The Help Center Pluggable protocol, beginning with the prefix *hcp://,* is used for topics that link to external locations and applications like Remote Assistance and various newsgroups.

- The Hypertext Markup Language (HTML), beginning with the prefix *ms-its://,* is used to access compiled help files. These files can also be accessed by entering **hh** and the URL address for the topic. Using this method causes the help system to open the topic in a window that lists only topics from the same help file.

▶ *TIP*

For additional information on HTML Help URLs, access Knowledge Base article Q235226, entitled "INFO: HTML Help URL Protocols."

Figure 9-7   Copy the URL address from the Properties dialog

TRY IT   To create a shortcut to a favorite topic, use the following steps:

1. From the Start menu, choose Help and Support.
2. From the Help and Support Center home page, select a topic of interest.
3. In the right pane, right-click a blank portion of the page—do not click a link.
4. From the pop-up menu, select Properties.
5. Select the entire URL address, and then press CTRL-C to copy the address to the Clipboard.
6. Minimize all open windows so that the Desktop is visible.
7. Right-click the Desktop, but not on an icon.
8. From the pop-up menu, select New | Shortcut.
9. In the Create Shortcut dialog, type **%systemroot%\pchealth\helpctr\binaries\helpctr.exe /url** and then paste the URL address at the end of the line. For example: %systemroot%\pchealth\helpctr\binaries\helpctr.exe /url **ms-its:C:\WINDOWS\Help\howto.chm::/app_disk_logical.htm**
10. Click Next.
11. Give the shortcut a name and click Finish.

▶ *NOTE*

Make certain you copy the entire URL from the Properties dialog or the link will fail.

Customizing the Help Center

You can change the look and feel of the Help and Support Center window. You can fine-tune your searches, choose to share the Help and Support Center with other users on the network, and define other options. To access the option customization page shown in Figure 9-8, click the Options button in the Help and Support Center home page.

▶ *NOTE*

The Share option is available only in Windows XP Professional.

Unlike the earlier versions of Windows, Windows XP lets you customize the font size used in the Help and Support Center window without affecting the fonts used in Internet Explorer.

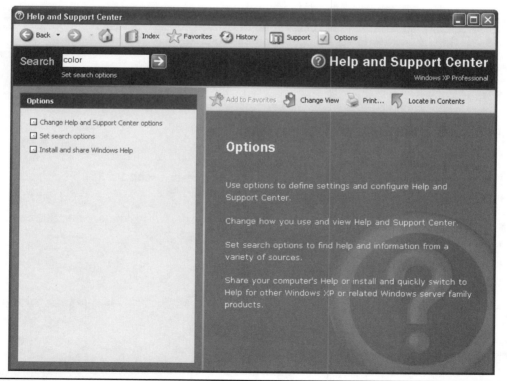

Figure 9-8   Options page

TRY IT   To customize the Help and Support Center window, use the following steps:

1. From the Start menu, select Help and Support.
2. Click the Options button to access the Options page.
3. Click Change Help and Support Center Options.
4. In the Change Help and Support Center Options page, you can choose what is displayed in the Help and Support Center window and select a font size. The following options can be defined:

   - **Show Favorites on the Navigation Bar**   If checked, the Favorites button is displayed on the upper toolbar in the Help and Support Center window. This option is checked by default.

   - **Show History on the Navigation Bar**   If checked, the History button is displayed on the upper toolbar in the Help and Support Center window. This option is checked by default.

   - **Font Size**   Enables you to change the size of the displayed font. By default, Medium is selected.

   - **Show All Text Labels**   If enabled, the icons in the upper toolbar in the Help and Support Center window will have their associated labels displayed beneath the appropriate icon.

   - **Show Only Default Text Labels**   If enabled, some of the icons in the upper toolbar in the Help and Support Center window will have their associated labels displayed beside the icons. This option is checked by default.

   - **Do Not Show Text Labels**   If enabled, only the icons appear in the upper toolbar in the Help and Support Center window, without their associated text.

5. When you are done with the Change Help and Support Center Options page, click Back to return to the Options home page.

6. Click Set Search Options to refine typical searches. Click Back to return to the Options home page. The following options are available:

   - **Return up to *nnn* Results Per Provider**   By default, this value is set to 15, which in most cases is too small for wide-range searches. You can enter any number you want, up to 999, but the recommended value is from 100 to 150.

   - **Suggested Topics**   This option, enabled by default, informs the search engine to use the index of keywords for every search. When disabled, you cannot restrict your searches to a specific topic, which could add a considerable amount of time to each search.

   - **Full-Text Search Matches**   This option is also checked by default. It instructs the search engine to look at all text within a help topic for matching words or phrases. Below this option are two refining options:

     - **Search in Title Only**   Check this option if you want the search engine to search for the word or phrase only within topic titles.

     - **Match Similar Words**   Check this option if you want the search engine to check for similar words. For example, if you enter the search word *printer,* and this option is checked, the search engine will also check for *printing* and *printers.*

- **Microsoft Knowledge Base**   Check this option if you want to search the Microsoft Knowledge Base for articles and self-help tools that contain the word or phrase you enter. To narrow your search, you can modify the following options:

  - **All Microsoft Search Topics**   Leaving this setting as is will broaden your search. To narrow it down, select a subject from the pull-down list.

  - **Search for**   Leave this value set to search for all words to include all of the words you entered. You can also choose to search for any of the words you entered, exact phrases, or a Boolean phrase.

  - **Search in Title Only**   Check this option if you want to search only the titles for the entered word or phrase.

7. If you have Windows XP Professional installed, you can click Install and Share Windows Help to share a single version of this help system with other users on the network. This feature is described in better detail in "Sharing Help Files."

Sharing Help Files

This feature is available only in Windows XP Professional. It is most useful in networks that have several systems running different versions of Windows XP. Sharing the help files offers the users of your network a central place to find information regarding a particular version of Windows XP help. This feature is commonly used by support engineers who are running a particular version of Windows XP. For example, if the members of your support team have Windows XP Professional installed and a support call for Windows XP Home Edition is received, the team can have quick access to the Windows XP Home Edition help files without having to exit from their current operating system.

▶ **NOTE**

Help files can be shared only by servers running Windows XP or Windows .NET. Earlier versions of Windows help systems cannot be installed, nor can systems running these earlier versions install Windows XP help.

After the help files are installed, the user can switch back and forth from one help version to another. The help systems can be installed on one central server and shared where other users can access them. You set up Help file sharing in the Options page of the Help and Support Center window, shown in Figure 9-9.

The Install and Share Windows Help page offers the following features:

- **Switch from one operating system's Help content to another**   This option lets you select the help file you want to view. The page lists all help systems that have been installed on your system.

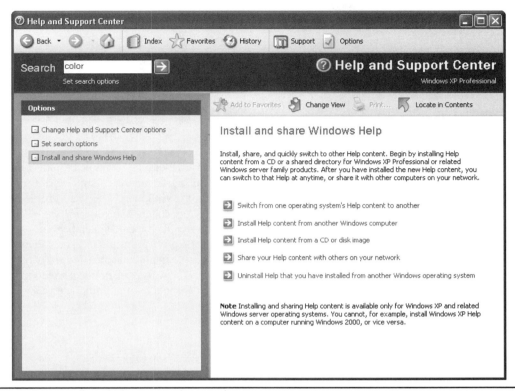

Figure 9-9   Install and Share Windows Help page

- **Install Help content from another Windows computer**   From this option, you can install help systems from other Windows systems.

- **Install Help content from a CD or disk image**   From this option, you can install other help systems onto your local system.

- **Share your Help content with others on your network**   This option lets you mark installed versions of help systems as shared or not shared.

- **Uninstall Help that you have installed from another Windows operating system** Using this option, you can remove any unwanted help systems from your hard disk.

TRY IT   To set up help sharing on a server, follow these steps:

1. From a server running Windows XP Professional, open the Help and Support Center window and then click the Options button.

2. Click Install and Share Windows Help.

3. In the Share Windows Help pane on the right, click Install Help Content from a CD or Disk Image.

4. Insert the Windows XP Home Edition CD into the CD drive, and then click the Browse button.

5. Double-click the \I386 directory on the CD; then click Find.

6. From the list of available help systems, select Windows XP Home Edition; then click Install.

7. You are ready to share that file with other users.

Using Remote Assistance

Anyone who has worked in technical support understands how challenging it can be helping a novice user over the phone. Windows XP offers a useful tool that helps eliminate the frustration of trying to help other users remotely. Remote Assistance is available in both Windows XP Home Edition and Windows XP Professional. This feature enables you to open a direct connection between two machines over the Internet or local area network (LAN). Once you're connected, you can watch the user's screen as he or she demonstrates the problem. When you know what the problem might be, you can quickly take control of the screen and fix the problem while the user sits back and watches. No lengthy or confusing explanations are required to get the user to understand how to perform the corrections.

This tool was designed for simple peer-to-peer connections without a lot of complications to understand. To use it, the following conditions must apply:

- Both users must be using Windows XP.

- Both users must have active Internet connections or reside on the same LAN.

- Both users must be able to communicate through their respective IP address.

- The two systems cannot be separated by a firewall.

The user requesting help opens his or her Help and Support Center window and then clicks Invite a Friend to Connect to Your Computer with Remote Assistance under the Ask for Assistance section. The Remote Assistance window will open, as shown in Figure 9-10.

From here, the user can choose from the following options:

- **Ask a Friend to Help**   The default option that enables the user to request help in one of the following ways:

  - **Invite Someone to Help You**   Opens a window than enables the user to send a request using Windows Messaging or e-mail.

  - **View Invitation Status (*n*)**   Displays the number of pending invitation requests.

- **Get Help from Microsoft**   Enables the user to request help directly from Microsoft Support.

- **Go to a Windows Web Site Forum**   Enables the user to ask for help in a forum environment.

Once a request is made, the receiver can click the associated link in Windows Messenger or click on the attached Remote Assistance (RA) ticket file in e-mail. The RA ticket file has the *.msrcincident*

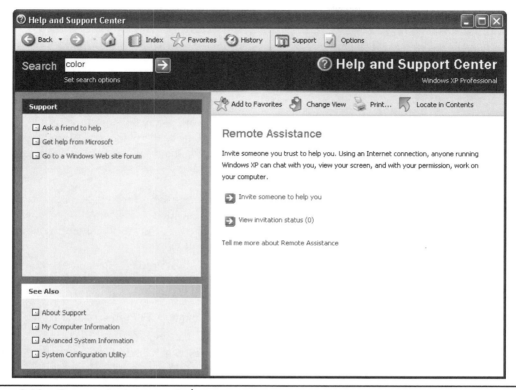

Figure 9-10   Remote Assistance window

extension and is the heart of each Remote Assistance connection. This file contains the specifics, in XML format, for establishing a connection with the requester's system. This file is not visible in Windows Messenger but is activated when the Remote Assistance link is clicked.

► *TIP*

If you receive an e-mail requesting help and cannot establish a link with the attached file, there may be a problem with the connection IP address in the file. Open the attached rcBuddy.msrcincident file in Notepad and check the value for the RCTICKET field. The ip_address parameter should point to the requestor's system. If it doesn't, correct the problem then save the file. Do not change any other parameter or field.

When both systems use public IP addresses, the Remote Assistance connection is easy. The computers connect directly on TCP port 3389. Routers within the network can recognize the system addresses and send the appropriate packets to their respective systems. Internet connection firewall in Windows XP automatically opens this port when a Remote Assistance connection is requested. In a workgroup environment, systems can communicate directly without having to pass through any routers.

▶ *TIP*

The preferred firewall workaround in a corporate environment is to establish a Virtual Private Network (VPN) connection. This solution enables traffic to pass through the firewall and eliminates possible security holes that can occur when opening ports.

If one or both systems obtain their IP address through Network Address Translation (NAT), a software- or hardware-based NAT device passes data between the single public IP address it uses to communicate with the Internet and the private IP addresses on the local network. The success or failure of this action depends on how the IP address is acquired.

- If Internet Connection Sharing (ICS) is used, the ICS server listens for Remote Assistance traffic on TCP port 5001 and forwards it to port 3389. This allows the connection to succeed, regardless of which computer requests the connection. If the ICS server is running Windows 98 Second Edition or Windows 2000, Remote Assistance will fail.

- If the IP address belongs to a residential gateway or a hardware router that supports the Universal Plug and Play standard (UPnP), the connection will be successful. If the router was manufactured before the year 2001, it may not support UPnP.

- If both systems reside behind NAT devices that do not support UPnP, the connection will fail.

- If only one system resides behind a NAT device that does not support UPnP, it is best to establish the Remote Assistance connection through Windows Messenger. In this scenario, a random port is used to establish the connection.

TRY IT   To request assistance remotely, use the following steps:

1. Open the Help and Support Center window. Under the Ask for Assistance section, click Invite a Friend to Connect to Your Computer with Remote Assistance.

2. From the right pane, select Invite Someone to Help You.

3. Choose to send the request through either Windows Messenger or e-mail.

4. Complete the request form, and then click OK or Continue, depending on which method you chose.

5. When the person who is going to help you receives the request, he or she will either click the link in Windows Messenger or open the attached request file in e-mail.

▶ *TIP*

If you are uncertain as to how the systems are connected, it is recommended that you use Windows Messenger to request the Remote Assistance connection.

Maintaining Security

Although Remote Assistance is a valuable tool, it is also a potential security risk. Anytime someone has access to your system, that person can install a Trojan application that could enable him or her to have unlimited access to sensitive files. Taking some simple precautions can help prevent these types of security breaches.

The following best practices are recommended when using the Remote Assistance feature:

- When sending a request using e-mail, set a short expiration time of one hour or less. Once the connection is established, the expiration time will not affect the connection. Expired RA tickets are useless to potential hackers.

- When sending a request using e-mail, use a sensible password. Do not include this password in the request; relay it to the person you are requesting help from in a separate e-mail or by phone.

- Expire invitations when they are no longer required. This is done by opening the Help and Support Center window and choosing Remote Assistance | View Invitation Status. When the status of requests displays, select the pending request and click Expire.

- Disable Remote Assistance on systems that contain sensitive information. To do this, open the Control Panel and select Performance and Maintenance | System. Click the Remote tab and uncheck the check box for Allow Remote Assistance Invitations to Be Sent from This Computer. This is shown in Figure 9-11.

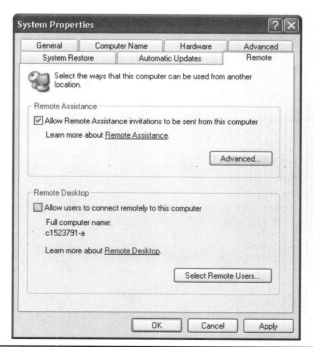

Figure 9-11   Disable Remote Assistance

TRY IT To disable Remote Assistance, use the following steps:

1. Open the Control Panel and select Performance and Maintenance | System.
2. Click the Remote tab and uncheck the check box for Allow Remote Assistance Invitations to Be Sent from This Computer.

Fine-Tuning Remote Assistance Performance

When using the Remote Assistance feature over a dial-up connection, the performance can be trying at best. To improve the performance, you can try a few tricks, including the following:

- Connect at 56Kbps or faster.
- Reduce the display resolution of the requester's screen to 800x600 with the fewest number of colors. Remote Assistance automatically disables any wallpaper or nonessential graphics the user has set.
- Avoid opening graphics-intensive windows, if possible, and disable desktop animations and other visual enhancements.
- Close any open applications that do not have anything to do with the problem you are trying to solve.
- When the person who is helping has control of the screen, instruct any other user who is receiving help not to move his or her mouse.

TRY IT To reduce the screen resolution, use the following steps:

1. Right-click a blank spot on the Desktop—*not* on an icon.
2. From the pop-up menu, select Properties.
3. Click the Settings tab, shown in Figure 9-12.
4. Reduce the resolution to 800x600 and the colors to 16, if possible.
5. Click OK.

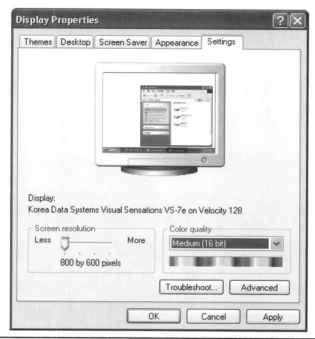

Figure 9-12   Display Properties Settings

Contacting Microsoft Support

If you have an active Internet connection, you can request help directly from the Microsoft Support Center. Depending on how you purchased your copy of Windows XP, you may or may not be required to pay a per-incident fee. Make certain you check this before requesting help or you may be unpleasantly surprised.

If you require support from Microsoft and do not have an active Internet connection, you can save the connection configuration to a file that can be submitted when your Internet connection is active.

Figure 9-13 shows the Microsoft Online Assisted Support window.

▶ *NOTE*

You must have an active .NET Passport account to use this feature.

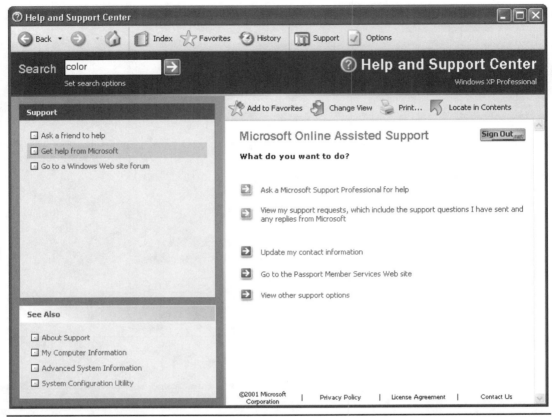

Figure 9-13   Getting help from Microsoft

TRY IT   To save connection information to a file, use the following steps:

1. Open the Help and Support Center window; then click the Get Support or Find Information in the Windows XP Newsgroups.
2. Click Get Help from Microsoft.
3. Sign on to your .NET Passport account.
4. In the Microsoft Online Assisted Support page, click the View Other Support Options link.
5. Click Save Information About This Computer to Submit to Microsoft Online Assisted Support.
6. Specify a location where you want to save the file.
7. When you are connected to the Internet, you can send the saved file to a support engineer.

CHAPTER 10

Logging On and Off and Shutting Down

TIPS IN THIS CHAPTER

Computer systems work best when you follow specific protocol during operation. You log in to let the system know who you are, so you can load personal settings and permissions and re-establish connections to shared resources. When you log off, any files you have open are "cleaned up," and allocated resources are released for other uses.

If only one user accesses a system—in a home network, for example—logging in is not a real issue. This security feature is a necessity mainly in corporate environments or for situations in which more than one user has access to a system. Windows XP makes sharing your system with multiple users a fairly painless ordeal. In the past, sharing your system might have meant putting up with having your desktop modified undesirably and perhaps discovering several new games or applications installed on your system without your knowledge. It also meant that everyone who used the system had access to your personal files.

Windows XP not only gives each user his or her own identity and personal settings, but it also enables users to switch from one particular configuration to another quickly, which avoids your having to close everything you are working on so that someone else can use the system momentarily. In Windows XP, you can quickly switch users even without closing the applications you have open. Later, when you switch back to your own configuration, you can continue working as if you had never logged off.

When multiple users access a computer in a Windows XP network or on a system, each user has his or her own user account. These accounts help to manage resources, permissions, and valuable information. Creating user accounts for each user enables each user to

- Customize the way items look on the screen when using an identity or user account
- See his or her own lists of Web Favorites and recently visited sites
- Protect personal settings
- Use a password to keep personal files private
- Log on faster
- Quickly switch between users without having to close programs

At the end of the day, shutting down your system properly, rather than just logging off, is an important practice that you should adopt, because doing so helps keep your system running smoothly. Behind the scenes, Windows XP has several processes open. If you were simply to power down the system without running the Shutdown application, these processes could be corrupted. Of course, in some situations, a system can power down at the most inopportune times, but such occurrences should be rare, and in most cases, your system can recover from these mishaps.

► *NOTE*

If your system operates in an area in which power outages are prominent, you might invest in an Uninterruptible Power Supply (UPS) unit. They cost about $99 and are well worth the cost. When the power goes off, the UPS unit will give you 15 minutes to shut down your system properly. More expensive units give you even more time.

Setting Up User Accounts

This is the heart of the login process in setting up user accounts. Several types of user accounts can be created:

- **Administrator**   Has permission to modify the system in any way and has access to other user accounts on the system. Each system must have at least one administrator. This account offers the ability to do the following:
  - Create and delete other user accounts on the system
  - Change user account names, identity pictures, passwords, and account permissions
  - Install and uninstall software
  - Change global settings
- **Standard**   On a system running Windows XP Professional in a domain environment, users of this type can
  - Install and uninstall software and hardware that does not alter computer settings established by the system administrator
  - Create, change, or remove personal account passwords
  - Change an identity picture
- **Limited**   Reserved for inexperienced users who use the system for specific tasks. Users of this type can
  - Create, change, or remove a personal account password
  - Change an identity picture
- **Guest**   Folks who do not use the system on a regular basis. They do not have a password and are restricted to the same limitations as a limited account user. These accounts make it convenient for visitors to perform the following:
  - Log in quickly
  - Check e-mail
  - Browse the Internet
  - Create and print documents and perform other, similar activities

Setting Up Accounts in a Workgroup

By default, the Administrator account is established when Windows XP is installed. The administrator is the only user who can create user accounts. The Windows XP Setup program requires that you also create at least one other account. If you are upgrading to Windows XP and already have user accounts established, those accounts are migrated over to Windows XP.

▶ **NOTE**

Accounts that are upgraded from Windows NT or Windows 2000 maintain their group membership and passwords. Accounts that are upgraded from Windows 95/98/Me become members of the Administrator group and do not have associated passwords.

Windows XP makes it easy to create and manage user accounts. If the system is not a member of a domain, the user account interface is simple and clean.

TRY IT To create a new user account in a workgroup environment, use the following steps:

1. Open the Control Panel and select User Accounts.
2. From the User Accounts window shown in Figure 10-1, click Create a New Account.
3. Enter a name for the user, and then click Next. Note that in the account name, spaces are permitted but are not recommended because they can cause problems in some applications and command-line tools. If you really want to use the user's full name, consider using underscores to separate the first and last names.
4. Select the type of account you want, and then click Create Account. The account will be created and you will be returned to the User Accounts window.
5. If you want to assign a password to the new account, click Change an Account, and then select the account name.

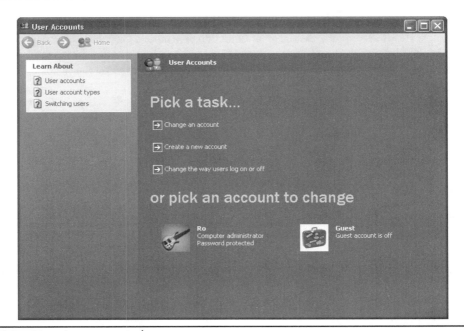

Figure 10-1 User Accounts window

Advanced Account Setup Options

In Windows XP, you can use four different interfaces to create and manage user accounts, depending on your environment and the version of Windows XP you have installed.

- **User Accounts**   If your system is not connected to a domain, this interface offers the simplest method for creating and managing user accounts.

- **Domain User Accounts**   If your system is connected to a domain, the User Account interface resembles the one in Windows 2000. This version offers some unique features that enable you to change an account's user name, configure automatic login, and eliminate the CTRL-ALT-DEL requirement if the Welcome screen is disabled.

- **Local Users and Groups Snap-In**   This Microsoft Management Console (MMC) snap-in offers more account-management features. This feature is described in greater detail later in this chapter in the "Using the Local Users and Groups Snap-In" section. This feature is available only in Windows XP Professional.

- **Command-Line Utilities**   This nonintuitive method of managing accounts offers the most direct and complete access to account tasks. It uses the Net User and Net Localgroup commands.

▶ *NOTE*

The Local Users and Groups snap-in is not available in the Windows XP Home Edition.

Each of these methods enables a system administrator to create and manage user accounts and security groups. How these interfaces appear and function depends on the way a system is configured. Whether you prefer a graphical interface or a command line, each tool offers particular functionality. Use the following table to determine the best interface to use for your particular needs.

Tasks	Workgroup Users	Domain Users	Local Users and Groups Snap-In	Command-line Utilities
Local User Accounts				
Creating, deleting, and grouping accounts	X*	X*	X	X
Change the user name		X	X	
Change the full name	X	X	X	X
Change the description		X	X	X
Change the identity picture	X			
Set passwords	X	X**	X	X
Set password hints	X			
Set password restrictions			X	X

Tasks	Workgroup Users	Domain Users	Local Users and Groups Snap-In	Command-line Utilities
Set logon hours				X
Enable/disable accounts	X***		X	X
Unlock accounts			X	X
Set account expiration dates				X
Specify a profile and logon script			X	X
Link accounts to .NET Passport	X	X		
Security Groups				
Create/Delete/Rename			X	X
Set group membership			X	X
Add a domain account to a group		X*	X	X

* Only one group per account is supported.
** Only for local accounts that were not used to log into the current session.
*** Only the guest account.

If the system is a member of a domain, the User Account interface resembles the one used in Windows 2000. If you still want to use this interface but are not connected to a domain, you can access it from the Start menu by selecting Run. In the text box, type **control userpasswords2**, and then press ENTER. The User Accounts window, shown in Figure 10-2, will open.

▶ *TIP*

If you use this account dialog often but do not want to have to access it from the Run command text box, you can place a shortcut into the Control Panel | Performance and Maintenance | Administrative Tools folder.

TRY IT   To add a user account on a domain, use the following steps:

1. Open the Control Panel and select User Accounts.
2. From the User Accounts window, click Create a New Account.
3. Click Add.
4. In the Add New User dialog, enter the user's information:
   - **User Name**   The name the user will use to log into his or her account.
   - **Full Name**   The user's full name.
   - **Description**   Use this field to describe the user. For example, you might want to enter the department the user works in, or his/her job title.

Figure 10-2   User Accounts window for domain members

5. Click Next.

6. Enter a password for the user, and then enter it again in the confirmation box. When you are done, click Next. This password should be generic and easy to remember. Later, the user can change the password to something more secure.

7. Select the level of access you want to grant the user, and then click Finish.

Changing Account Settings

Once you create an account, you may want to assign a password to that account or change the default picture. This is easily done from the User Accounts window, accessed by opening the Control Panel and choosing Change an Account. Select the account name you want to make changes for.

The following properties can be modified:

- **Change the name**   Click this option if you want to change the name of the user. This will not change the name of the user profile directory. Also, if you want to use more than one word in the user name, consider separating the words with an underscore. Spaces are allowed but could cause problems in other areas.

- **Create a password**   By default, no password is assigned when the account is created. For security reasons, it is recommended that a password is assigned to each account on the system.

- **Change the picture**   This picture, that identifies the user, can be any 96x96 pixel JPEG graphic.

- **Change the account type**   Click this option to either limit or expand the user's abilities.

- **Delete the account**   Click this option to remove the user account from the system. This process enables you to copy the user's personal files to a secure location before removing them from the local system.

   To change an account, use the following steps:

1. Open the Control Panel and choose User Accounts.
2. Click Change an Account.
3. Click the user name of the account you want to change.
4. Select the property you want to change.
5. Enter the information for that property.

Deleting an Account

As a system administrator, you can delete any account on the system, providing someone is not currently logged into the account you want to delete. When you choose to delete an account, you are given two choices regarding the user's files (Figure 10-3):

- **Keep Files**   Select this option to move files and folders stored on the user's Desktop and in the user's My Documents folder to a folder on your Desktop. The remainder of the user's profile, including e-mail folders, application data, Internet favorites, and registry settings, are deleted once you confirm that you want to delete the account.

- **Delete Files**   Select this option if you do not want to save any of the user's information.

When you delete a user's account, that user will no longer have access to his or her files, nor can the user log onto the system with the account you deleted. Every account on a network is issued a unique security ID (SID) when the account is created. Internal processes in Windows refer to an account's SID rather than the account's user or group name. This means that even though you re-create the user account, after it has been deleted, the following files that were associated with the deleted account will not be accessible by the user through his or her new account:

- Files the user had permission to access
- Encrypted files
- Personal certificates
- Stored passwords for Web sites
- Network resources

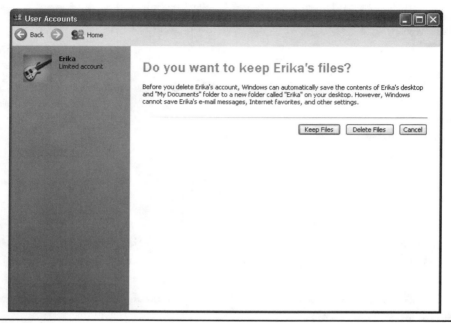

Figure 10-3   Deleting an account

If you delete an account using a tool other than User Accounts, the user's profile remains in the Documents and Settings folder. If you re-create the account using the same name, a new profile will be created, but it's a convoluted folder that contains the computer name appended to the user name. For example, the original folder may be named *C:\Documents and Settings\Erika*, while the new folder will be named *C:\Documents and Settings\Erika.DRAGON*. This can be confusing when trying to find the current profile for the user.

▶ *TIP*

If you deleted the user account with a tool other than User Accounts, do not remove the files or registry entries or you could affect other accounts on the system. Instead, right-click My Computer and select Properties from the pop-up menu. Click the Advanced tab, and then select Settings under User Profiles. Select Account Unknown; then click Delete. This will safely clean up any files that belonged to the user you had deleted.

TRY IT   To safely remove a user account, use the following steps:

1. From the Control Panel, select User Accounts.
2. Click the account you want to delete, and then select Delete the Account.
3. Answer the inquiry about the user's files, and then confirm your instructions.

Defining Logon Properties

If you are the primary user of the system and are connected to a workgroup, you are not prompted to log in unless you have created other user accounts. By default, the welcome screen (Figure 10-4) opens when the system boots and when it is awakened from sleep mode.

If the system is not part of a domain and more than one user account exists on the system, Windows XP offers two logon methods:

- **Welcome Screen**   This option is new in Windows XP. It offers a user-friendly way to access your personal login. This screen appears by default.

- **Classic Login**   This screen is familiar to users of Windows 2000 and Windows NT. When the Welcome screen is disabled or the system is part of a domain, users are presented with this screen. By default, the user must press CTRL-ALT-DEL to access this logon screen. This requirement can be disabled through the Advanced tab in the User Accounts window, if available.

Login options can be changed only by the system administrator through the User Accounts window, shown in Figure 10-5. This window is accessed from the Control Panel. Click User Accounts, and then choose Change the Way Users Log On or Off.

If you disable the Welcome screen, you automatically disable the ability to switch users quickly.

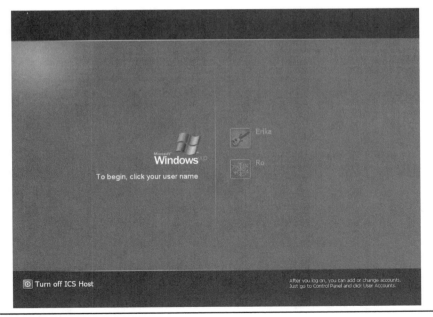

Figure 10-4   Welcome screen

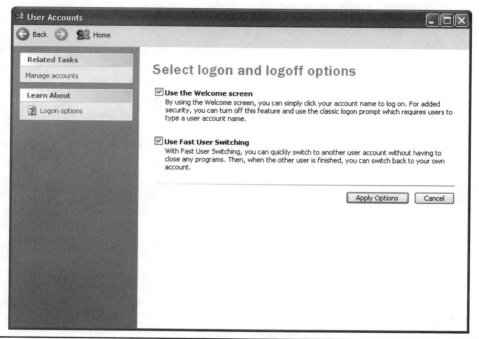

Figure 10-5   Login options

 To change the logon options, use the following steps:

1. Log on as an administrator.
2. Open the Control Panel and select User Accounts.
3. Click Change the Way Users Log On or Off.
4. Select the appropriate options, and then click Apply Options.

Bypassing the Logon Screen

Although bypassing the user logon screen compromises system security, it may become useful at some point in time—especially if you're the only one who uses the system. When you enable the bypass feature, you allow anyone to access your account information and files because no password or login information is required.

▶ **NOTE**

This option can be implemented only on systems that are not part of a domain.

TRY IT   To enable automatic login, use the following steps:

1. Open the Start menu and select Run.

2. In the text box, type **control userpasswords2**. Then press ENTER.

3. In the Users tab, clear the check mark for the Users Must Enter a User Name and Password to Use This Computer option.

4. Enter the user name and password you want to log on automatically each time the system boots.

Using the Local Users and Groups Snap-In

This MMC snap-in, available only in Windows XP Professional, offers more account-management features than the standard User Accounts window.

To access this feature, do one of the following:

- From the Control Panel, select Performance and Maintenance I Administrative Tools I Computer Management I System Tools I Local Users and Groups. Figure 10-6 shows the Local Users and Groups interface.

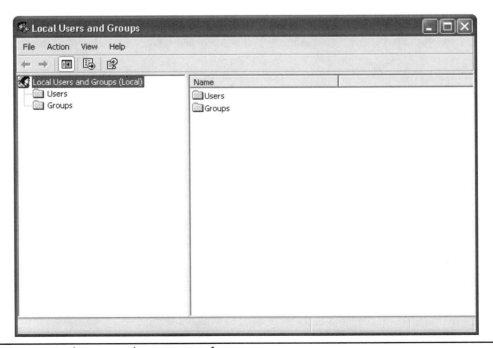

Figure 10-6   Local Users and Groups interface

- Click Start | Run, and then enter **lusrmgr.msc**.
- If the system is a domain member, click the Advanced tab in the User Accounts window, and then click the Advance button.

When you select the Users folder in the left pane, you can perform the following actions:

- **Create a new account** Right-click Users and select New User.
- **Delete an account** Right-click the account and select Delete.
- **Change the user name** Right-click the account and select Rename.
- **Change the full name or description** Double-click the account name and then click the General tab.
- **Set or change the password** Right-click the account and select Set Password.
- **Set password restrictions** Double-click the account name and then click the General tab.
- **Enable/disable an account** Double-click the account name and then click the General tab. Check or uncheck the Account Is Disabled check box.
- **Unlock an account** Double-click the account name and then click the General tab. Clear the Account Is Locked Out check box.
- **Set group membership** Double-click the account name and then click the Member Of tab.
- **Specify a profile and logon script** Double-click the account name and then click the Profile tab.

When you select the Groups folder in the left pane, you can perform the following actions:

- **Create a new group** Right-click Groups and select New Group.
- **Delete a group** Right-click the group name and select Delete.
- **Rename a group** Right-click the group name and select Rename.
- **Set group membership** Double-click the group name. In the Properties dialog, click Add. In the Select Users dialog box, click the Locations button to specify a computer name or a domain.

TRY IT   To add a domain user, use the following steps:

1. From the Control Panel, select Performance and Maintenance | Administrative Tools | Computer Management | System Tools | Local Users and Groups.
2. Right-click the User's folder and select New User.
3. Enter the user's information and then click the Locations button.
4. Specify the name of the domain for the user. Then click OK.

Setting Account Passwords

By default, user accounts are created without passwords. If the system contains sensitive information, or you simply want to secure your information, it is suggested that you create a password for each user account, especially the administrator account.

Even if you do not create an account password, remote users cannot log on to your system. This is a new feature in Windows XP. If you are running Windows XP Professional, you can ensure that this policy is in effect through Local Security Settings, which is accessed by running the secpol.msc command. Under Local Policies\Security Options, make certain that the Accounts: Limit Local Account Use of Blank Passwords to Console Logon Only policy is enabled. This policy cannot be disabled in Windows XP Home Edition.

▶ *TIP*

If you have auditing enabled, users may be prompted to enter a password even when one was not assigned. If this little glitch happens, nothing they do will satisfy the system's request and they will not be able to log on to the system. If you want to continue to use auditing, and want to avoid this problem, assign each user a simple password.

If you are going to go to the trouble of protecting your account, you should try to create a password that is not easily discovered. The following rules will help you choose a useful password:

- Choose a password that contains at least seven characters.
- Use a combination of uppercase and lowercase letters, numbers, and punctuation. For example, try something like, *MyDog7Spot13*.
- Separate words with numbers or random punctuation. For example, *Teen;Erika16Rae*.
- Try using the first letters of a familiar phrase, like *IwIwaOMw* (for "I wish I were an Oscar Meyer wiener").

Passwords are case-sensitive. You must enter your password exactly how you entered it when it was created, or your logon will fail. Passwords are created from the User Accounts window, as shown in Figure 10-7.

After you create your password, it is a good idea to create a password reset disk. If your system is not part of a domain, you can use the password reset disk to recover from the ever-dreaded forgotten-password syndrome.

TRY IT To set an account password, use the following steps:

1. From the Control Panel, select User Accounts.
2. Click the account for which you want to create a password.

3. When asked what you want to change for the selected user account, choose Create a Password.

4. Enter the password, using a combination of uppercase and lowercase letters, numbers, and punctuation. It is best to choose a password that is at least seven characters long, but this is not a requirement.

5. Confirm your password by entering it again.

6. Choose a phrase that will remind you of what your password is. Keep in mind that this phrase is viewable by other users.

7. Click Create Password.

8. If your system is not connected to a domain, continue with step 9.

9. Log off and then log on using the account and password you just created.

10. Open the Control Panel and select User Accounts.

11. Click the account name you are currently logged into.

12. In the Related Tasks pane, select Prevent a Forgotten Password.

13. Once the Forgotten Password Wizard launches (Figure 10-8), follow the instructions on the screen.

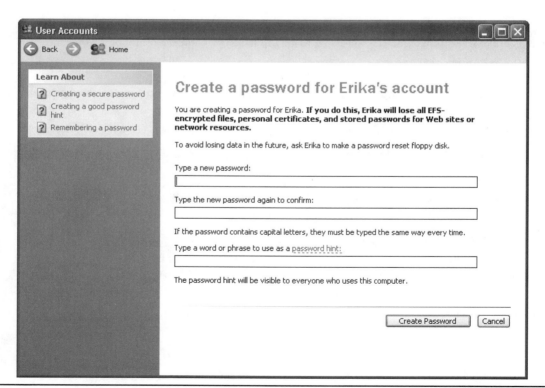

Figure 10-7 Create a password

Figure 10-8   Forgotten Password Wizard window

▶ **CAUTION**

If the system is not connected to a domain, do not remove or change a user's password unless the user has forgotten the password and no password reset disk is available. Doing so will prevent the user from being able to access his or her encrypted files and e-mail messages. If the system is connected to a domain, you can reset the account password without adverse affects.

Recovering from Forgotten Passwords

It happens to everyone; you go on vacation, have a great time, and then come back to work refreshed and ready to tackle anything. You sit at your desk and fire up the old system. It greets you with a friendly welcome screen. You click on your account and there it is; a blank password dialog. You stare at it for awhile, trying to remember what a password is, let alone the one you created. What is your password?

If you (or your account administrator) were proactive, a password reset disk was created and there is hope for you and your encrypted files and e-mail messages. If such a disk was not created, you will not be able to access your encrypted files and e-mail messages.

If a password is forgotten for an account that does not belong to a domain, the following two methods can help bail you out:

- **Password Hint**   This hint is established when a password is created. Its main purpose is to trigger your memory regarding the password. If you are using the Welcome screen, you can click the question mark icon in the password entry screen.
- **Password Reset Disk**   This recovery disk enables you to reset your password without having to remember your old password.

TRY IT   To use the password reset disk, use the following steps:

1. If you are using the Welcome screen and your logon fails, a link is displayed that enables you to use your password reset disk. Click this link to launch the Password Reset Wizard. If you are not using the Welcome screen, click the Reset button that appears when the logon fails.
2. Insert your password reset disk into the system's floppy drive.
3. Follow the wizard's instructions.
4. After you have successfully reset your password, remember to create a new password reset disk for future memory lapses.

Logging On

Depending on how your system is configured, you can log on to your system in several ways:

- If the Welcome screen is enabled, click your account name and then enter your password, if applicable.
- If the Welcome screen is disabled, you are presented with a logon screen that may or may not require you to press CTRL-ALT-DEL to access the account logon. Once the account logon dialog displays, enter your user name and password.
- If the system is configured to log you on automatically, you simply sit back and allow the system to log on for you.

TRY IT   To log on using the Welcome screen, use the following steps:

1. Click your account name.
2. If a password was created for you, enter the password and click OK.

Logging Off

When you step away from your system or are finished using it for awhile, it is good practice to log off so that others do not have access to your files. In all Windows XP versions, this is done easily from the Start menu.

 To log off, use the following steps:

1. Open the Start menu and click Log Off.
2. Depending on how your Welcome screen is configured, you are given one of two options:
   - Confirm your logoff request
   - Log Off or Switch User
3. Select Log Off.

Switching Users

One of the greatest new features of Windows XP is the ability to switch user accounts without having to exit from open applications. To use this feature, you must have the Welcome screen enabled and Use Fast User Switching option enabled. These settings are established through the User Accounts window, under Change the Way Users Log On or Off. Figure 10-9 shows this option.

 To switch users, use the following steps:

1. Open the Start menu and click Log Off.
2. Select the Switch User option.

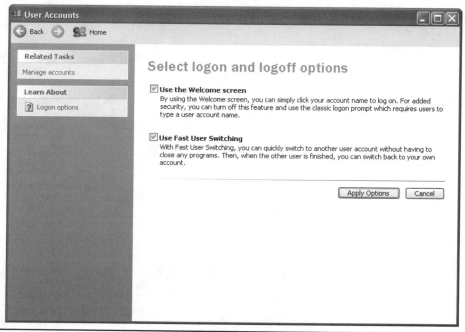

Figure 10-9   Welcome screen and Use Fast User Switching is enabled

Shutting Down

Shutting down your system before powering it off will help keep your system running without a glitch. This may be an overstatement, but it *is* important that you go through this process before powering down. The shutdown process closes files and processes and saves important system information.

TRY IT   To shut the system down, use the following steps:

1. Open the Start menu and select Turn Off Computer.
2. The following screen displays.

3. Choose one of the following options:

- **Hibernate**   Click this option to put the system in sleep mode. This mode saves your current system settings and open applications so that when you power the system back up, your system is restored to the condition it was in when you placed it in hibernation mode.

- **Turn Off**   Click this option if you want to power down the system.

- **Restart**   Click this option if you want to restart your system without having to power it off and on.

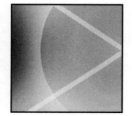

PART III
Networking

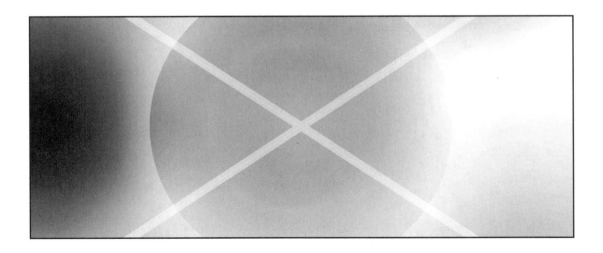

CHAPTER 11

Configuring and Managing Network Connections

TIPS IN THIS CHAPTER

A small network of two to ten systems all running Windows XP requires practically no setup configuration—that is, of course, if you have compatible hardware installed. Before you attempt to configure your network, you should ensure that you have compatible networking hardware.

When you run the Windows XP Network Wizard, it does the following for you:

- Configures the IP addresses
- Defines the workgroup name(s)
- Configures the Internet connection firewall
- Adds the required registry keys

You can configure three basic types of networks, each of which offers its own advantages and disadvantages:

- **Simple Peer-to-Peer**   This configuration is extremely easy to configure and requires little hardware. This type of network does not require a server, which means you don't have to manage users and shared resources. Each computer hosts its own database of user accounts and shared resources.

- **Workgroup**   This variation of a peer-to-peer network enables resources to be shared so that each system on the network can share folders and other resources installed on one system. A single Internet connection can also be shared. If you want additional security in this type of environment, you can configure a workgroup server running Windows XP Professional, which will allow you to control which users have access to particular resources.

- **Domain**   This type of configuration involves computers that share a single security database that is stored on one or more domain servers running either Windows .NET Server, Windows 2000 Server, or Windows NT Server. When you log onto a domain, your credentials are compared to those stored in the security database. A domain environment makes it easy to manage networks with more than ten systems in a network

Hardware Requirements

To set up a small home or office network, you need at least two systems with a network adapter installed. This type of adapter is also called a *Network Interface Card (NIC)*. These adapters can be installed internally using a Peripheral Component Interconnect (PCI) local bus slot or externally using a universal serial bus (USB) connection. In some systems, the network interface is part of the system motherboard.

To connect these two systems, you will also need one or more of the following:

- **Hub or Switch**   Using a central connection point such as a hub or a switch typically involves connecting to a residential gateway to add Network Address Translation (NAT) abilities and security features. Networks using the Home Phoneline Networking Alliance (HomePNA) standard do not require a hub.

- **Wireless** A wireless access point on networks using the 802.11b standards provide NAT abilities.

- **Cables** On an Ethernet network, each NIC connects to a hub with an eight-wire Category 5 patch cable using RJ-45 jacks. HomePNA networks connect to an existing phone jack using RJ-9 connectors.

- **Modem** This device is used to connect at least one system to the Internet. Various types of modems are available, ranging from the slower dial-up to the much faster cable modems.

▶ *TIP*

If you have only two systems in a network, you can connect them without using a hub. Instead of using a standard patch cable, use a crossover cable, in which two wires are crossed to simulate a hub connection.

Cables vs. Wireless

Although Ethernet has stood the test of time and has served us well, it is slowly being replaced by new wireless technology. Going wireless is a bit more costly than using the old Ethernet standby, but the convenience of wireless connectivity is well worth the additional cost. Ethernet will probably be around for quite some time, along with another good standby, HomePNA. The following table outlines some of the benefits and facts associated with each type of connection.

Connection Type	Speed	Requirements
Ethernet / Fast Ethernet Fast Ethernet Gigabit Ethernet	10BaseT (10Mbps) 100BaseT (100Mbps) 1Gbps	If the hardware supports auto-switching, the network can have networks that operate at different speeds. Ethernet adapters connect through a hub.
Wireless IEEE 802.11b	11Mbps	Uses base stations and network adapters with small antennas. Uses radio frequencies in the 2.4GHz range.
HomePNA	Approximately 10Mbps	Uses existing telephone jacks to connect each system in a daisy-chain topology. No hub is required.

▶ *TIP*

In the Help and Support Center, you can select Find Compatible Hardware and Software for Windows XP under the Pick a Task section. This utility will save you many headaches when trying to configure your network. Do not try using incompatible products; they are definitely not worth the effort.

Default Network Services

When you install networking hardware, Windows XP installs the following components:

- **Client for Microsoft Network**   Enables you to connect to systems running any 32-bit or 64-bit Windows operating system. At least one client is required on the local system to access resources on the network.

- **File and Printer Sharing for Microsoft Networks**   Required for sharing your files and printers with other systems running a Windows operating system.

- **QoS Packet Scheduler**   Installed on systems using Windows XP Professional. It enables Quality of Service (QoS) features provided by corporate networks and Internet Service Providers (ISPs). These features will be more evident and widely used once Internet Protocol version 6 (IPv6) becomes more popular.

- **TCP/IP Internet Protocol**   Provides connectivity across a variety of networks and to the Internet. In most circumstances, the default settings are acceptable without modification.

Using the Network Setup Wizard

Even if your network appears to be working normally, you can run this wizard to ensure that the system is set up correctly, including the permissions set on shared folders, registry keys, networking protocols, and the Internet Connection Firewall. When you first set up a network connection, you do so with the New Connection Wizard, shown in Figure 11-1. This screen is accessed from the Control Panel. Click Network and Internet Connections, and then choose Set Up or Change Your Home or Small Office Network.

During the process, you are given the option to create a Network Setup Wizard disk for other systems on the network. Even if you are a networking guru, you should run the Network Setup Wizard to establish a working base on all systems in the network. Then you can tweak and adjust the settings to suit your needs.

▶ **NOTE**

If you are using one computer to connect to the Internet and intend to share that connection with other systems on the network, you should first run this wizard on the system with the Internet connection before configuring the other systems.

When you configure Internet Connection Sharing (ICS) on a system that connects to the Internet, the other systems on the network are partially configured to use that system for Internet access. When you run the Network Setup Wizard on the other systems, you should see a dialog like the one shown in Figure 11-2.

Figure 11-1   New Connection Wizard

TRY IT   To run the Network Setup Wizard, use the following steps:

1. Open the Control Panel, and then click Network and Internet Connections.
2. Select Set Up a Home or Small Office Network.

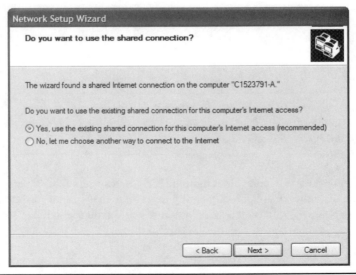

Figure 11-2   Network Setup Wizard with ICS configured

3. Click Next to advance through the first two screens. If you have already run this wizard once, your options will vary from those described in the following steps. See Figure 11-2.

4. In the Select A Connection Method screen, select one of the following options:

   • **This computer connects directly to the Internet. The other computers on my network connect to the Internet through this computer.**   Select this option if you have enabled ICS and want to use this system to connect other systems in the network to the Internet.

   • **This computer connects to the Internet through another computer on my network or through a residential gateway.**   Select this option if this system connects to the Internet through a residential *gateway*. If the system connects to the Internet through another system using ICS and this screen appears, something is amiss; check your network connection.

   • **Other**   Select this option if the system connects to the Internet directly or through a hub, or if the system does not connect to the Internet at all. If you select this option, you will be guided through a series of screens that further define the network connection.

5. After you have made your selection, click Next.

6. The option you selected in step 4 determines which series of screens will appear. Follow the simple instructions on each screen to complete the setup process.

7. Run this wizard on each system in the network. Once you run the wizard on the system through which you intend to share the Internet connection, the wizard becomes considerably easier to run on the other systems in the network. The wizard prompts you to enter or change the computer and workgroup names and then continues configuring the network and firewall.

8. When you complete the wizard, it is recommended that you adjust your security settings to ensure maximum security within your network.

▶ *TIP*

The name of the computer is generally established when the operating system is installed. Changing this name could have adverse effects, especially if the system is a database server. Unless changing the computer name cannot be avoided, it is best to leave the original name unchanged.

Configuring Wireless Connections

In a home network or a small office, wireless connections are less complicated than they are in large corporate environments or school campuses that have multiple access points. Fortunately, Windows XP automatically configures wireless adapters to work with one or more access points. An access point enables you to stay connected as you roam from one building to the next.

Along with these wireless access points come security issues. In a cabled environment, the system administrator can pinpoint what system is connected to what port. In a wireless environment, however, anyone who is in range of an access point can tap into the network. For this reason, each wireless network should be Wireless Equivalent Privacy (WEP) enabled. WEP uses encryption to protect data on the network. Typical network cards use a 40-bit key, consisting of five 8-bit ASCII characters to encrypt data. Other network cards support a 104-bit key that uses 13 characters—however, even with

13 characters of encryption, your wireless network is safe only from casual intruders. If security is a concern, you might consider using IP Security (IPSec). Details regarding IPSec can be found in the Microsoft Windows XP Professional Resource Kit documentation.

When you install a wireless adapter in a system, Windows XP recognizes the new hardware and launches the Connect to Wireless Network dialog. Windows XP detects access points that are in range and gives you the option to connect to one. Select an access point and then enter your encryption key in the Network Key text box.

▶ *TIP*

Make certain the Wireless Zero Configuration service is running. From Administrative Tools, select Services. If this service is not started, right-click the entry and choose Start.

If you don't see an access point listed in the Available Networks box, you may need to add it manually. This is common if the access point does not broadcast its network name. This and other advanced actions are accomplished through the Wireless Network Connection Properties dialog.

▶ *NOTE*

To set Wireless Connection Properties, you must be logged in with Administrator privileges.

If you do not want to use an access point, you can configure your wireless connection for ad-hoc mode instead of using the default infrastructure mode. By doing this, you are creating a simple point-to-point network. The option for this mode is enabled through the Wireless Network Connection Properties dialog. On the Wireless Networks tab, click the Advance button and enable the Computer-to-Computer (ad hoc) Networks Only option. Repeat this process on each wireless system in the network.

TRY IT   To configure wireless network properties, use the following steps:

1. Log onto the system as an Administrator.
2. Open the Control Panel and select Network and Internet Connections.
3. Select Network Connections, and then right-click the Wireless Network Connection icon.
4. Select Properties from the pop-up menu.
5. In the Properties dialog, click the Wireless Networks tab.
6. Set the following options as they apply to your network:
   - **Use Windows to Configure My Wireless Network Settings**   This option is enabled by default. When enabled, you can connect to an existing wireless network, change wireless network connection settings, configure a new wireless network connection, and specify preferred wireless networks. You are also notified when new access points are available. When you select a wireless network, your wireless network adapter is automatically

configured to match the settings of that network, and your system will attempt to connect to the network.

- **Available Networks**   If an access point does not broadcast its network name, it will not appear in this list until you add it manually by clicking the Add button. Specify the network name (Service Set Identifier) and, if applicable, the wireless network key settings. If you are not using an access point, enable the option This Is a Computer-to-Computer (ad hoc) Network; Wireless Access Points Are Not Used.

- **Preferred Networks**   This defines the networks you prefer to access when available. Their order of preference can be adjusted using the Move Up or Move Down buttons.

7. When you are done, click OK.

▶ *TIP*

If you are using third-party wireless software, disable the Use Windows to Configure My Wireless Network Settings option.

Configuring Dial-Up Connections

If you had existing dial-up connections prior to upgrading to Windows XP, those settings should be working fine. Just to warn you, though, there is no longer a Dial-Up Networking folder. Your dial-up connections are now stored with the other network connections in the Network Connections folder.

Before setting up a new dial-up connection, you need to gather the following information from the ISP or the party of the answering modem:

- Dial-up number for your area
- Logon name and password
- Configuration information, if any
- E-mail (POP3) server, if applicable

Once you have gathered this information, you are ready to set up a new dial-up connection. This is easily done using the New Connection Wizard, shown in Figure 11-3.

TRY IT   To configure a dial-up connection, use the following steps:

1. Open the Control Panel, and then click Network and Internet Connections.
2. Click Network Connections.
3. From the Network Tasks box, select Create a New Connection.
4. Click Next to begin the process.

Figure 11-3 New Connection Wizard

5. The following options are then available:

- **Connect to the Internet** Select this option if you are connecting to the Internet through an ISP.

- **Connect to the Network at My Workplace** Select this option if you are establishing a dial-up or Virtual Private Network (VPN) connection to your office.

- **Set Up a Home or Small Office Network** Select this option if you are connecting the system to an established home network or if you are creating a new home network.

- **Set Up an Advanced Connection** Select this option if you are connecting directly to another computer through a serial, parallel, or infrared port.

6. For a dial-up connection, you select the first option, Connect to the Internet. After making your selection, click Next.

7. Select the option that best describes your situation, and then click Next. The following options are available:

- **Choose from a List of Internet Service Providers** Select this option if you do not have an ISP and want to find one.

- **Set Up My Connection Manually** Select this option if you already have an ISP and have gathered the necessary information to complete the connection process.

- **Use the CD I Got from an ISP** Select this option if your ISP provided a CD that sets up the connection for you.

8. Select one of the following options, and then click Next:

- **Connect Using a Dial-up Modem**   This is the basic way for connecting to an ISP. It requires a modem and a phone line.

- **Connect Using a Broadband Connection That Requires a Username and Password**   Select this option if you connect to the ISP through a cable modem or digital subscriber line (DSL) link. This type of connection is also called a Point-to-Point Protocol over Ethernet (PPPoE) connection.

- **Connect Using a Broadband Connection That Is Always On**   Select this option if you do not have to sign onto the ISP each time you want to use it. This type of connection uses a DSL, local area network (LAN), or a cable modem.

9. The next screens will prompt you for the information obtained by your ISP. Provide the appropriate information to complete the process.

Internet Connection Sharing

It is common for home networks to have three or four computer systems scattered about the house. Teens are using the Internet for research, and the younger ones are learning the freedom of having information at their fingertips. If you are blessed with a teenager in the house, you will discover his or her endless chatting on the Internet is by far more palatable than listening to your phone bills mount and tying up phone lines. The problem is, however, that when they are using the system, you often take the back seat until the odd hours of the night, when everyone else goes to bed.

Several options can help solve this problem.

You can install a router or a residential gateway—a system that sits between the Internet connection and the network. If you are using a computer system to act as a gateway, you will need to install two network cards in the system. One connects to the Internet while the other connects to a hub. To make this system more secure, it is recommended that you do not have any sensitive information stored on it.

▶ *TIP*

If you opt between a router or a residential gateway, a router is a more secure choice. Routers provide built-in firewall protection and do not require ICS.

You can also use Internet Connection Sharing (ICS), which uses a central computer to route traffic between the ISP connection and the network. This configuration requires the system that is sharing the connection to have either two network cards or one network card and one modem, depending on how you connect to the Internet.

▶ *TIP*

If you are in the market for a residential gateway or router for your network, make certain that you purchase one that supports the Universal Plug and Play (UPnP) standard. This important standard enables certain applications to work seamlessly with Network Address Translation (NAT) features.

When ICS is enabled, the following occurs:

- The shared connection on the ICS host obtains an IP address from the ISP.
- When you run the Network Setup Wizard on the ICS host, an Internet Connection Firewall is placed on the shared connection—the network card connected to the hub.
- The shared connection on the ICS host uses a static IP address of 192.168.0.1 with a subnet mask of 255.255.255.0.
- ICS services automatically runs on the ICS host.
- A Dynamic Host Configuration Protocol (DHCP) allocator on the ICS host assigns IP addresses to other computers on the network. The default range is between 192.168.0.2 and 192.168.0.254 with a subnet mask of 255.255.255.0. Having a Domain Name System (DNS) proxy on the ICS host eliminates the need to specify DNS servers on other systems in the network.
- Auto-dial is enabled on the ICS host.

ICS is enabled through the Network Setup Wizard shown in Figure 11-4. Even if you are a network genius, it is recommended that you use this wizard to establish the basic settings. Later, you can go back and tweak the settings to fit your needs.

▶ **NOTE**

Always run the Network Setup Wizard on the ICS host first before running it on each system in the network.

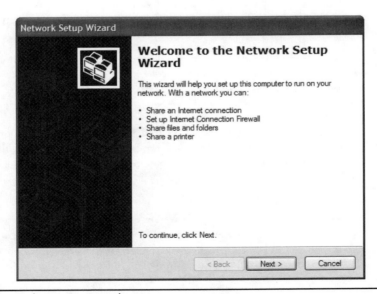

Figure 11-4 Network Setup Wizard

TRY IT   To set up the ICS host, use the following steps:

1. On the ICS host, log in as an Administrator.
2. Open the Control Panel and click Network and Internet Connections.
3. Click Set Up or Change Your Home or Small Office Network to launch the wizard.
4. Click Next twice to begin the process.
5. In the first setup screen, click the first option, as shown in Figure 11-5, This Computer Connects Directly to the Internet. Then click Next.
6. If your system has more than one type of network connection, select the one you want to use to connect to the Internet, and then click Next.
7. Confirm your selection, and then click Next.
8. Assign a name and a description for the system. Then click Next.
9. Either accept the default workgroup name or assign one of your own. Click Next.
10. Confirm your choices in the summary screen and then click Next to continue.
11. The last screen offers the following options:
    - **Create a Network Setup Disk**   Choose this option to create a setup disk that can be easily run on other systems in the network that intend to use this system to connect to the Internet.
    - **Use the Network Setup Disk I Already Have**   Choose this option if you have already created a setup disk.

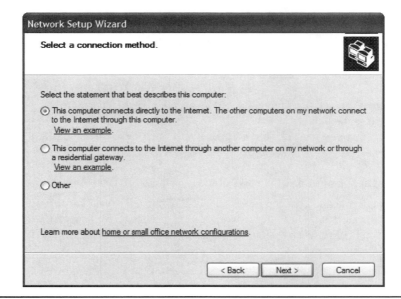

Figure 11-5   Enable ICS

- **Use My Windows XP CD**   Choose this option if you prefer to use the Windows XP CD to run the setup on the other systems.

- **Just Finish the Wizard. I Don't Need to Run the Wizard on Other Computers**   Choose this option if you do not intend to connect to the Internet through any other system.

  Select the first option if you have other systems in the network. Then click Next.

12. If you have other systems in the network to configure, insert the Network Setup Disk into the first system you want to configure. Open the Start menu and select Run. Enter **a:\netsetup**.

13. Follow the instructions in the wizard.

14. Repeat steps 11 and 12 for each system in the network.

▶ *NOTE*

If you are using this system as a database server, it is not recommended that you change the computer name, or you may have to reinstall the database software.

▶ *NOTE*

When the process completes, you may need to enter the DNS information manually. This varies from configuration to configuration. For example, your clients may need to point to the primary DNS server 192.168.0.1.

Securing a Peer-to-Peer Network

When you set up a peer-to-peer network without enabling ICS, you open your network to intruders who can access your shared resources. Using ICS helps to eliminate that problem by establishing a firewall between the Internet connection and the network.

Worse yet, if you are not using a NAT or router and are running Windows XP Home Edition, all your shared resources are at risk of being hacked, especially if you have a broadband connection that is always connected to the outside world.

If you determine that you must establish a peer-to-peer network, you can protect your resources in the following ways:

- You can purchase a third-party firewall product from ZoneAlarm or Symantec.

- You can disable file and print sharing on TCP/IP (Transmission Control Protocol/Internet Protocol) and enable it on the Internetwork Packet Exchange/Sequenced Packet Exchange (IPX/SPX) protocol for each system on the network.

- You can install a router that provides built-in firewall protection and does not require ICS. Also, other systems can still access the Internet even if the server is down.

TRY IT   To disable file and print sharing, use the following steps:

1. Open the Control Panel and choose Network and Internet Connections.
2. Choose Advanced | Advanced Settings.
3. Click the Adapters and Bindings tab (shown in Figure 11-6).
4. Under File and Printer Sharing for Microsoft Networks, click the network connection that connects to your hub. This box should contain a check mark.
5. Remove the check mark from the Internet connection.

Monitoring Network Performance

If your network is running slower than it should, you may need to consider upgrading your interface. One way to see how efficiently your network is running is to view a performance graph in the Networking monitor of Task Manager, shown in Figure 11-7. The next tip shows you how to access this information.

Because this system has two network connections, both are displayed in the screen in Figure 11-7, which also shows that neither network is in high use. This indicates that the 10Mbps Ethernet interfaces are working fine for this environment. If the bandwidth percentages averaged on the high end, it might be wise to upgrade to a 100Mbps Ethernet connection.

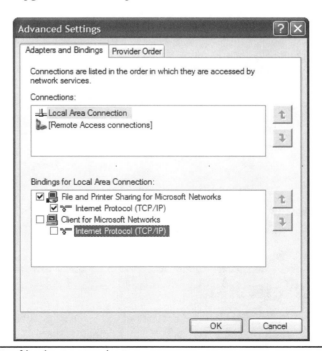

Figure 11-6   Disabling file sharing on the Internet

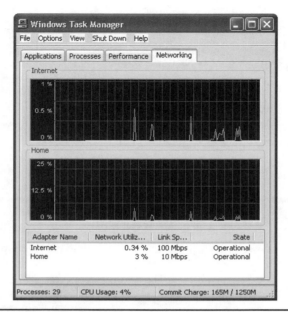

Figure 11-7 Networking performance graph

▶ *TIP*

If more than one network connection exists on your system, it is a good idea to rename each connection so each is distinguishable from the others. This can be done from the Network Connections folder in the Control Panel. If you get two compatible NIC cards, you can have different types of NIC cards for each connection as well.

 To monitor networking performance, use the following steps:

1. Press CTRL-SHIFT-ESC to open the Windows Task Manager.
2. Click the Networking tab.
3. Wait a few moments for the monitor to gather information.

Bridging Two Networks

The only reason you would need to bridge two networks together is if no physical way exists for you to connect the systems together as a single network. For example, two systems (system A and system B) can be connected, but only system A connects to the server. The server will not be able to see system B and system B will not be able to see the server unless you bridge the two networks together.

This feature is new to Windows XP and a handy one to use in a pinch. To connect these systems prior to the release of Windows XP, you would need to purchase a router and configure IP packet forwarding, which is easier said than done.

When bridging networks together, the following rules apply:

- You must be the system Administrator to create a network bridge.

- Bridges can be established between any two Ethernet, IEEE-1394, or Ethernet-compatible wireless adapters.

- Bridges cannot include a VPN, dial-up, Internet, or direct-cable connection.

- Adapters running ICS or Internet Connection Firewall cannot be added to a network bridge.

- Do not bridge an adapter using a public Internet address with an adapter that connects to a private network; use ICS instead.

- The system that connects the networks as a bridge must be turned on or the network bridge will not exist.

- Only one network bridge can exist on a given system. Each bridge, however, can contain up to 68 adapters.

To add or remove adapters to or from a bridge, right-click the bridge icon and select Add to Bridge or Remove from Bridge. To remove a bridge entirely, right-click the bridge icon and select Delete from the pop-up menu.

TRY IT   To create a network bridge, use the following steps:

1. Follow the same procedures for creating a standard network connection, using the Network Setup Wizard.

2. In the Select A Connection Method page, choose This Computer Connects to the Internet Through Another Computer on My Network or Through a Residential Gateway. Then click Next.

3. If at least two active network connections can be bridged, the Your Computer Has Multiple Connections screen will display. If less than two network connections are bridgeable, an error screen is displayed instead.

4. From the Your Computer Has Multiple Connections screen, select one of the following options, and then click Next.

   - **Determine the Appropriate Connections for Me**   Select this option if you want to bridge all the connections together.

   - **Let Me Choose the Connections to My Network**   Select this option if more than two connections are available and you want to exclude some from the bridge.

5. When the wizard completes its task, a new device called a Network Bridge appears in the Network Connections folder.

▶ *TIP*

To view the details of your network configuration, double-click the Network Bridge icon and then select the Support tab. To change the connection details, right-click the Network Bridge icon and select Properties from the pop-up menu.

Joining a Domain

If you are running Windows XP Professional and have an account on the domain server, you can join that domain and access its available resources. To join a domain, you must have Administrator privileges on the domain server.

▶ *CAUTION*

You will need to reboot the system after joining a domain.

TRY IT   To join a domain, use the following steps:

1. Log on as a local Administrator.
2. On the Desktop, right-click the My Computer icon and select Properties.
3. Open the Computer Name tab.
4. Check the Member of Domain option and then enter the name of the domain you want to join.
5. Click OK.
6. Enter the name and password of an Administrator for the domain you want to join and then click OK.
7. Follow the instructions. When the process completes, the system will reboot.

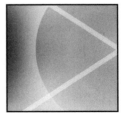

CHAPTER 12

Managing Users

TIPS IN THIS CHAPTER

anaging users is a simple task with Windows XP, whether you're in charge of a simple network running Windows XP Home Edition or a corporate environment running Windows XP Professional. Each user has his or her own custom environment that is loaded at each logon.

With Windows XP's new "quick switch" feature, discussed in Chapter 10, a user can quickly switch his or her computer configuration to allow another user to use the system, without having to close programs, so that when the first user logs on again, the active programs are still open.

User profiles and group policies make managing user accounts more tolerable. If a user is inexperienced, for example, a system administrator can customize the user's Desktop settings to make work easier and a bit more organized. These settings are stored in the user's *profile*. If the administrator wants to apply similar characteristics to multiple systems, a *group policy* can be created and applied to the appropriate user profiles.

▶ NOTE

Only a user with administrator privileges can add or remove user accounts. To learn more, see Chapter 10.

User Profiles

User profiles store user settings and personal files for a given environment. The type of information stored includes the following:

- Files stored in the My Documents folder
- Personal registry settings
- Microsoft application settings, such as views and other custom options the user has defined
- Cookies that are stored while the user accesses the Internet via Microsoft Explorer
- Shortcuts to Network Places

User profiles are created when a user logs onto the system for the first time. Any changes made to a personal environment are stored in the user's profile in the %SystemDrive%\Documents and Settings*username* directory. For example, if a user by the name of Erika logs on, and her operating system is stored on drive C:\\, her profile will be stored in C:\Documents and Settings\Erika.

If you updated the operating system from another version of Windows, the old user profiles are stored in %SystemRoot%\Profiles*username*. If the user had an existing user profile, the user's settings are copied to the new profile location.

The user profile directory is shown in Figure 12-1.

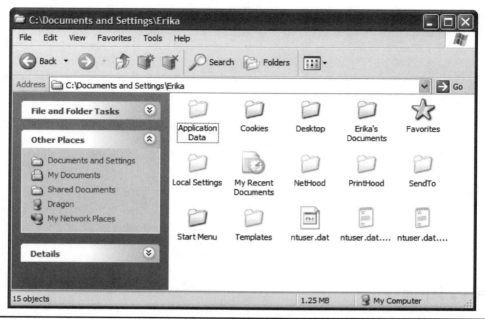

Figure 12-1   User profile directory

Each user's profile contains the following folders:

- **Application Data**   Contains a custom dictionary for word-processing applications, junk e-mail sender lists, a music CD database, and any other application data that application vendors decide to store here.

- **Cookies**   Contains Internet Explorer cookies, which often contain information regarding sites the user frequents. For example, if a user browses a site that asks for personal information, this type of information is stored in a cookie so that the site can display a user-specific screen.

- **Desktop**   Contains the files and shortcuts displayed on the user's Desktop.

- *Username's* **Documents**   Contains all the subfolders and personal files the user has created or saved in the My Documents folder.

- **Favorites**   Stores the Web addresses displayed in the user's Favorites list.

- **Local Settings**   Contains folders and files that are system-specific. If the user "roams" from system to system, these files are not included with the roaming profile. This folder contains the following subfolders:

  - **Application Data**   Contains system-specific application data.

  - **History**   Contains the browsing history of Web sites the user has visited on this system.

- **Temp**   Stores temporary application files.
- **Temporary Internet Files**   Stores the offline cache for Internet Explorer.
- **My Recent Documents**   Contains a list of documents the user has accessed recently. In some configurations, the 10 most recent documents are viewable from the Start menu.
- **NetHood**   Contains the shortcuts stored in the user's My Network Places folder.
- **PrintHood**   Contains shortcuts stored in the user's Printers and Faxes folder.
- **SendTo**   Contains a list of shortcuts used to send selected files to a specific location.
- **Start Menu**   Contains the items or shortcuts that appear under Start I All Programs.
- **Templates**   Contains shortcuts to document templates that the user uses to create new documents.

Windows XP supports the following profiles:

- **Local User**   This profile is automatically created when the user logs onto the system for the first time. It is stored in the %SystemDrive%\Documents and Settings*username* directory. Changes made to this profile affect only the local system.
- **Roaming User**   Roaming profiles are stored on a server and apply to any system the user logs onto, providing the system resides in the server's network. When the user logs onto the network, these settings are copied from the server to the local system. When changes are made to the user profile, they are stored on the local system and copied to the server when the user logs off of the network.
- **Mandatory User**   These profiles are similar to roaming profiles, except changes made to this profile are not copied to the server when the user logs off. When the user logs back onto the network, the local copy of his or her mandatory profile is replaced by the one on the server. This ensures that certain groups of users all have the same look and feel on their system, which can sometimes make it easier to support them when questions arise. If you do not want the user to change the local profile, you can define a policy setting to disable this ability.
- **All Users**   The settings stored in this profile affect all users on the system. For the most part, only users with administrator privileges can change this profile. Any user, however, can change the contents of the Shared Documents folder.
- **Default User**   This profile is used to establish new profiles for users who are logging on for the first time. Windows XP copies the contents of the default profile to the user's new profile. This profile can be changed by anyone with administrator privileges.

▶ *TIP*

To access the Start menu hierarchy quickly, right-click Start and select Explore to view the current user's settings, or click Explore All Users to view common settings.

Group Policy

Using the Group Policy feature, available only in Windows XP Professional, you can configure computers in the network, domain, or organization. System administrators commonly use Group policy to set standard desktop configurations and user restrictions, and to manage software installations.

Most of the Group Policy settings reside in the Administrative Templates extension of the Group Policy snap-in. The content for the Administrative Template folders is derived from the .adm files in the Group Policy object. When you enable, disable, or set a value for a policy in the Administrative Templates folder, Group Policy stores the information in a custom registry setting in a Registry.pol file. Group Policy uses the copy of Registry.pol in %SystemRoot%\System32\GroupPolicy\machine for settings you make in the Computer Configuration\Administrative Templates folder. It uses the copy in the User folder for settings made in User Configuration\Administrative Templates.

If the system is a member of a domain, it may be affected by other Group Policy settings that are not defined in your local Group Policy object. Group Policy settings are applied in the following order:

1. From those defined in the local Group Policy object.

2. From those defined in site Group Policy objects, in the order specified.

3. From those defined in domain Group Policy objects, in the order specified.

4. From those defined in organizational unit Group Policy Objects, from parent to child, and in the order specified for each unit.

The last policy applied overwrites any other applied policies when conflicting settings are encountered. Policy settings are *cumulative,* which means that all settings contribute to the resulting policy known as the Resultant Set of Policy (RSoP).

To view the settings on a Windows XP Professional system for a given user, enter **gpresult.exe** at the command prompt. The Help and Support Center also has a tool that displays Group Policy settings. You access the Help and Support Center home page by opening the Start Menu and choosing Help and Support. On the home page, select Use Tools to View Your Computer Information and Diagnose Problems. From the left pane, select Advanced System Information. From the right pane, select View Group Policy Settings Applied. The window shown in Figure 12-2 will show the results.

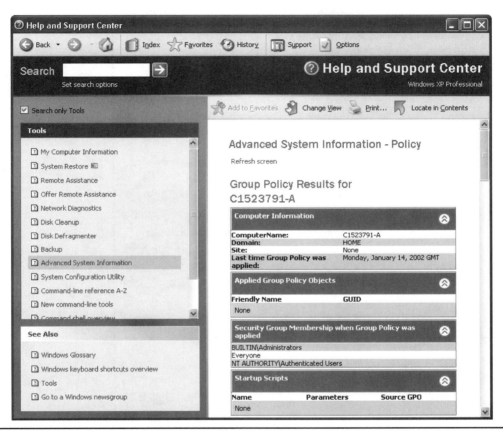

Figure 12-2 Viewing applied Group Policy settings

Modifying Profiles

When you modify your user profile, you change the way your system looks and responds to given actions. For example, if you are constantly copying files to a backup drive on another system, you might want to add a shortcut to the Send To folder. This shortcut is then available when you right-click a folder or file you want to send to the specified destination, as shown in Figure 12-3. By default, you can send selected files or folders to an e-mail recipient or to a floppy drive. Other options may be available, depending on the applications you have installed.

You can also personalize your Desktop and display attributes by choosing from among a variety of themes that can be customized. Right-click any blank spot on the Desktop, and then choose Properties from the pop-up menu. The Display Properties window is displayed, as shown in Figure 12-4.

Figure 12-3 The Send To option on the pop-up menu

Figure 12-4 The Display Properties window

Any folder in your profile can be modified by adding or removing items to or from their respective folders. If you are an administrator, you can change items in the Default User folder. Doing this will affect all new users on the system. When a new user logs on for the first time, the settings in the Default User folder are copied to the user's profile folder, where they can be further modified as needed.

Also, if you are an administrator, you can change the items in the All Users folder. Changes made to this folder affects all users on the system.

TRY IT   To add a shortcut to the SendTo folder, use the following steps:

1. Open Windows Explorer and navigate to your profile folder.
2. Double-click the SendTo folder to open it.
3. Right-click in a blank area in that folder and choose New | Shortcut from the pop-up menu. You'll see the Create Shortcut Wizard shown here:

4. In the text box, type the location of the item to which you want to provide a shortcut, or click Browse to choose a location.
5. Click Next, and then enter the name you want to appear in the Send To pop-up menu.
6. Click Finish.

To test the new menu item, use the following steps:

1. Open a folder, and then right-click a file.
2. From the pop-up menu, choose Send To.
3. The new item you added should appear in the pop-up menu. Choose that shortcut to send the selected file to the location specified.

Copying Profiles

When you copy a user's profile, it's not as simple as most copy operations. Right-clicking the profile folder in Windows Explorer and selecting Copy will get the job done, but it won't let you take care of some of the important user profile tasks, such as assigning the appropriate permissions to the new profile and creating the appropriate registry settings.

Instead, you should copy the profile from the User Profiles dialog box. Windows XP assigns the proper permissions to the profile copy so that the user can still modify the profile but other users cannot.

▶ *NOTE*

You cannot copy a profile when it is currently in use. The owner of that profile must log off first. Only system administrators can copy profiles.

 To copy a profile, use the following steps:

1. Open the Control Panel and select Performance and Maintenance.
2. Select System, and then open the Advanced tab.
3. Under User Profiles, click Settings.
4. From the Profiles stored on this computer list in the User Profiles dialog box, shown in Figure 12-5, select the user profile you want to copy, and then click Copy To.
5. In the Copy To dialog box, shown next, type the location for the new profile, or click Browse to select the path.

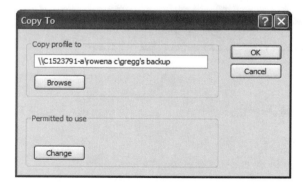

6. To assign a new user to the copied profile, click Change.

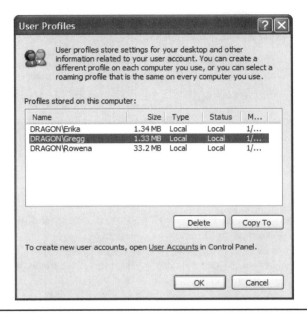

Figure 12-5   User Profiles dialog box

7. In the Select User or Group dialog box, type the user's name, group, or built-in security principle you are looking for in the Select this Object Type box, and then click OK. Or, as an alternative, click the Object Types button and then select the object you want from the list.

8. To specify a domain, click Look In, and then select the domain. You can click the Advanced button to narrow your search criteria.

Removing Profiles

As a system administrator, you can delete any account on the system, providing someone is not currently logged onto the account you want to delete. When you delete an account, you must choose between the following options regarding the user's files:

- **Keep Files** Select this option to move the user's files and folders that are stored on the Desktop and in the My Documents folder to a folder on your Desktop. The remainder of the user's profile, including e-mail folders, application data, Internet favorites, and registry settings, are deleted after you confirm that you want to delete the account.

- **Delete Files** Select this option if you do not want to save any of the user's information.

When you delete a user's account, that user will no longer have access to his or her files, nor can he or she log onto the system with the account you deleted.

Every account on a network is issued a unique security ID (SID) when the account is created. Internal processes in Windows refer to an account's SID rather than the account's user or group name. This means that even though you re-create the user account, after it has been deleted, the following files that were associated with the deleted account will not be accessible by the user through a new account:

- Files the user had permission to access

- Encrypted files

- Personal certificates

- Stored passwords for Web sites

- Network resources

If you delete an account using a tool other than User Accounts, the user's profile remains in the Documents and Settings folder. If you re-create the account using the same name, a new profile will be created but with a glitch: a "convoluted" folder that contains the computer name appended to the user name will be created. For example, the original folder may be named C:\Documents and Settings\Erika, while the new folder will be named C:\Documents and Settings\Erika.DRAGON. This naming can be confusing when you're trying to find the current profile for the user.

▶ *TIP*

If you deleted the user account with a tool other than User Accounts, do not remove the files or registry entries or you could affect other accounts on the system. Instead, right-click My Computer and select Properties from the pop-up menu. Click the Advanced tab, and then select Settings under User Profiles. Select the Account Unknown, and then click Delete. This will safely clean up any files that belonged to the user you deleted.

TRY IT   To safely remove a user account, use the following steps:

1. From the Control Panel, select User Accounts.
2. In the User Accounts dialog box, click the account you want to delete, and then click the Delete the Account option.
3. Answer the inquiry about the user's files, and then confirm your instructions.

Assigning Profiles

At times you may need to log onto another system as a different user, or you may want to join a domain and use the same profile you used for your local account. If you join a domain, the easiest way to transfer your local folders and files is to use the File and Settings Transfer Wizard. This wizard can be accessed through the command line by entering **migwiz**.

▶ *TIP*

This wizard can also be accessed from the Start menu by choosing All Programs | Accessories | System Tools | File and Settings Transfer Wizard.

If you haven't used your new domain account, you can also assign your local profile to your new domain account. You must be logged in as an administrator to accomplish this task.

To access the Local Users and Groups snap-in shown in Figure 12-6, enter **lusrmgr.msc** at the command prompt.

TRY IT   To assign a profile with the Local Users and Groups snap-in, use the following steps:

1. Open the Start menu and select Run.
2. Enter **lusrmgr.msc** to open the Local Users and Groups snap-in.
3. Open the Users folder, and double-click the name of the user to whom you are assigning the profile.
4. Choose Properties. The Windows XP Properties window opens, as shown in Figure 12-7.
5. In the Windows XP Properties window, click the Profile tab.
6. If you are storing the local profile in a roaming folder or in another folder that is different from the default folder, enter the location of the folder for the Profile Path text box.
7. If you want to run a logon script each time the user logs on, enter the name of the script in the Logon Script text box.

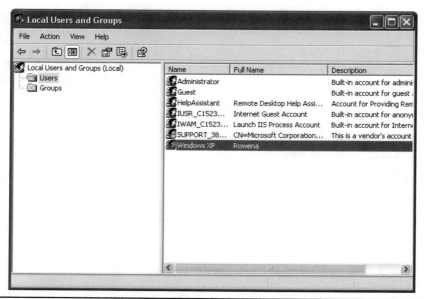

Figure 12-6   Local Users and Groups snap-in

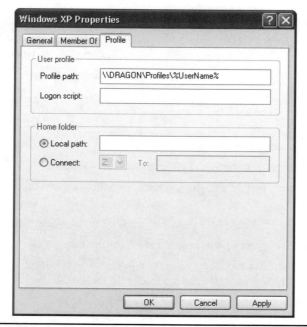

Figure 12-7   Windows XP Properties window

8. For the Home Folder section, either enter where the profile is to be stored in the Local Path text box or click Connect and select a remote location.

9. When you are done, click OK.

Changing Profile Folder Locations

You may want to change the location for the My Documents folder. This folder contains other folders that typically store large files, such as pictures, documents, and music. You may find it necessary to store these files in a better location where disk size is not an issue.

If you are using a roaming profile, moving the location of the My Documents folder could save you time when logging onto the system. When you move the My Documents files to another location, Windows XP does not have to save the files to and from your local disk each time you log on or off the system. Storing your data files in a central location can also make backing them up a much easier feat.

 To change your profile folder location, use the following steps:

1. Right-click the My Documents folder and choose Properties.

2. Open the Target tab, and click Move to open the Select a Destination dialog box shown here:

3. To select a new destination for the My Documents folder, click Make New Folder.

4. Then select the location to which you want to move the files.

5. Click OK to close the dialog, and then click OK to move the files.

6. Click Yes to move the existing documents to the new target location.

Using Roaming Profiles

You can use the same profile from any system within the network using this feature. When you log on, your profile is copied from the server to your local system. Any changes you make on the local system will be copied back to the server when you log off. If you often use several systems within a network, this handy tool can prove to be invaluable.

Although this feature can be incorporated into workgroup environments with quite a bit of work, it is designed to work in a domain environment. In a workgroup environment, each user with a roaming profile must have an account on each system he or she intends to use, and an account with the same user name and password must exist on the system where the roaming profile is stored. Even when all of this is done correctly, some features stored in the user's profile may not transfer over smoothly between systems.

▶ *NOTE*

The roaming profile must be stored on a system running Windows XP Professional with Simple File Sharing disabled.

TRY IT To set up a roaming profile, use the following steps:

1. Log onto the system as an administrator.
2. Create a folder called Profiles.
3. Right-click the Profiles folder you just created, and choose Sharing and Security from the pop-up menu.
4. Click the Sharing tab in the Profiles Properties window, as shown in Figure 12-8.
5. Select Share This Folder on the Network. The default sharing permissions that enable all users to have full control are appropriate for this application, because profiles can be accessed or changed only by the owner or a system administrator.
6. If you enable this feature on a system that is using an NT File System (NTFS) volume, click the Security tab and ensure that everyone has full control permissions.

To set up the user accounts to use the roaming profile, use the following steps:

1. On each system that will be using a roaming profile, including the server, log on as an administrator.
2. In the Run text box, enter the following command:
   net user *username* **/profilepath:***servername***\\profiles***username*
   For example, if you were entering this command for a user named Erika to access a shared profile on a server named DRAGON, you would enter the following command:
   net user Erika /profilepath:\\\\DRAGON\\profiles\\erika

Figure 12-8   Sharing tab on Profiles Properties

3. When you are done, use the procedures described earlier in this chapter in the section "Copying Profiles" to copy the local profile to the shared profile directory.

4. On the server hosting the shared profile, check the security settings for the profile folder, located in the folder's Properties window. If the name shows as an unknown user, add the correct user account and give it full control permission to the shared profile folder.

▶ *TIP*

*If all your systems are running Windows XP Professional, you don't need to enter the **net user** command from the command line. You can right-click the My Computer icon and select Manage. Navigate to System Tools\Local Users and Groups\Users, and then click the Profiles tab. For the Profile path, enter **servername**\\profiles\\%UserName%*.

Using Mandatory Profiles

Mandatory profiles work similar to roaming profiles with one exception: mandatory profiles cannot be modified on the shared folder, and therefore they cannot be changed. These types of profiles are used to keep user environments looking the same and to keep users from changing those settings.

TRY IT To set up mandatory profiles, use the following steps:

1. Follow the same procedure described in the preceding section, "Using Roaming Profiles" to set up roaming profiles.

2. In Windows Explorer, navigate to the shared mandatory profile folder you created.

3. Right-click the profile folder and select Properties from the pop-up menu to open the Properties window.

4. Open the Security tab.

5. Change the permissions for each user who is going to use this profile to the following:
   - Deny Full Control
   - Deny Modify
   - Allow Read & Execute
   - Allow List Folder Contents
   - Allow Read
   - Deny Write

6. Click OK to close the Properties window.

7. In the mandatory Profiles folder, change the name of the Ntuser.dat file to **Ntuser.man**. (Make certain you view hidden file extensions so that you don't accidentally change the name of the Ntuser.dat.log file instead. Doing this makes all of the profiles stored in this directory, mandatory.)

Accessing the Group Policy Snap-In

Group Policy settings are created with the Group Policy snap-in for the Microsoft Management Console. The Group Policy window, shown in Figure 12-9, can be accessed by entering the command **gpedit.msc** in the Run text box.

▶ *NOTE*

The Group Policy snap-in is available only in Windows XP Professional and can be accessed only by a system administrator.

TRY IT To access the Group Policy snap-in, use the following steps:

1. From the Start menu, select Run.

2. Enter **gpedit.msc**.

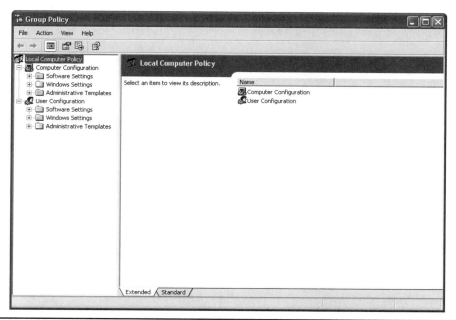

Figure 12-9   Group Policy window

▶ *TIP*

This extensive feature goes beyond the scope of this book. For details on how to implement Group Policy, consult Windows XP Help.

Remotely Accessing the Group Policy Snap-in

You may need to access the Group Policy console from another system. You can manage group policies from any system that supports the Group Policy snap-in.

TRY IT   To access Group Policy remotely, use the following steps:

1. From the Start menu, select Run.
2. Enter **gpedit.msc /gpcomputer:"*servername*"** to open the Group Policy dialog box. The *servername* can be one of two formats:
   - **NetBIOS**   For this style, enter the server's name. For example, if the server name is DRAGON, you would enter **"DRAGON"**.
   - **DNS**   For this style, enter the server name in the following format: **"*servername.domain*"**.

In either case, the *servername* must be surrounded by quotation marks.

Displaying Specific Policies

Another new feature in Windows XP is the ability to modify which policies are displayed in the Group Policy window. This can be useful if your configuration does not require most of the policies that Microsoft provides.

Hiding policies does not disable them, nor does it affect any underlying policy settings. If you want to filter the policies in the Computer Configuration or User Configuration folder, you must repeat the process described in the following steps for each folder.

▶ *NOTE*

This feature is available only in Windows XP Professional.

 To display specific policies, use the following steps:

1. From the Start menu, select Run.
2. Enter **gpedit.msc** to open the Group Policy dialog box.
3. Right-click Administrative Templates and choose View | Filtering to open the Filtering dialog box shown in Figure 12-10.
4. Uncheck the policies you want to hide, and then click OK.

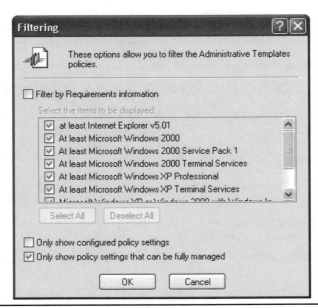

Figure 12-10   Filtering dialog box for Group Policy

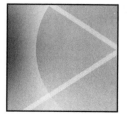

CHAPTER 13

Sharing Files, Printers, and Other Resources

TIPS IN THIS CHAPTER

Sharing folders and printers makes them available to other domain or workgroup members. Since Windows XP supports various networks and simultaneous use of multiple networking protocols, it is possible to share resources within a heterogeneous network environment. This enables systems running various operating systems to share resources with other computers on the network.

Windows XP introduces *Simple File Sharing,* a new concept that removes confusion from sharing resources over a network by providing a wrapper on the familiar, yet often confusing, security settings in Windows NT and Windows 2000. Simple File Sharing implements security settings that are appropriate for most computers shared by multiple users and small network groups.

The old familiar Windows 2000 sharing security is also available in Windows XP Professional. The main difference between Simple File Sharing and Classic Sharing is as follows:

- **Simple File Sharing**   Makes sharing your resources easy, but limits your ability to configure sharing options and permissions. When you select the share option, Windows XP uses the Guest account for all network logins, making the resources available to all users on the network.

- **Classic Sharing**   Similar to file sharing in Windows 2000, when a resource is shared, you can grant each user specific permissions for using the resource. You can also limit the number of simultaneous connections. This type of sharing requires more experience and effort to configure. Each networked system must be set up with the appropriate user accounts.

▶ **NOTE**

If a computer is joined to a domain, it always uses classic sharing. Windows XP Home Edition supports only Simple File Sharing. Windows XP Professional supports both sharing models.

By default, the Guest account is disabled, which in turn, disables sharing. If you have just installed Windows XP, you will be prompted to run the Network Wizard before sharing a resource. The Network Wizard ensures that computers on your network share the same workgroup name, sets up a shared firewall-protected Internet connection, and handles other details.

Although there is little reason to do so, you do have the option to bypass the Network Wizard by clicking the link that states: "If you understand the security risks but want to share files without running the wizard, click here." You are given the option to use the wizard or just enable file sharing.

If you just enable file sharing, two things happen:

- The Guest account is enabled. You can enable the Guest account manually from the command prompt, by entering **net user guest /activate:yes**. Doing this does not add the Guest account to the Welcome screen. To add the guest account to the Welcome screen, open User Accounts from the Control Panel and enable the Guest account. This also removes the Deny Logon Locally user for the Guest account.

- The Guest account is removed from the list of accounts that are denied access to the computer from the network.

Shared Resource and NTFS Permissions

Implementing shared resource permissions and NT File System (NTFS) permissions is accomplished in a similar way, but these two types of permissions provide two separate levels of access control. The only connections that are granted access to a network are those that successfully pass through both access controls. Shared resources and NTFS permissions are different and similar in the following ways:

- **Shared Resource Permissions** Control network access to a shared resource. These permissions do not affect local users. This type of permission control is defined in the Sharing tab of a folder's Properties window.

- **NTFS Permissions** Apply to folders and files on an NTFS-formatted drive. These permissions provide detailed control over an object. Users who are granted access can be given specific types of permissions, including the following:

  - Run programs

  - View folder contents

  - Create new files

  - Change existing files

  NTFS permissions are defined on the Sharing tab of a folder's Properties window.

  Both types of permission controls are combined in a restrictive manner. The appropriate user permission is first determined by the shared resource permissions. The NTFS permissions can "strip away" some of those permissions but cannot extend them. For example, if a user is granted full access through the shared resource permissions, and the NTFS grants read-only permissions, the user will only be able to read files from the shared resource. If the user has read permission on a network share, the user gets only read access when connecting over the network, regardless of how the user's NTFS permissions are configured.

▶ *CAUTION*

Files and folders created in a shared folder on an NTFS, while Simple File Sharing is enabled are owned by the local Guest account. This ownership does not change when you disable or enable Simple File Sharing. Even if you switch to Classic Sharing and implement tighter security, guest users continue to have full control over files that were created by any remote user while Simple File Sharing was enabled. It is highly recommended that the system administrator take ownership of these files and that the Everyone group is removed from the permissions list.

Command-Line Utilities

For those who prefer to use command-line options to manage resource sharing, Windows XP offers the Net.exe utility. The following examples show some of the most common commands and parameters used for managing network connections. To get more information on other commands and parameters, use the *net help* command. For example, if you need more information on using the *net share* command, you can type **net help share**.

Net Share Command

The *net share* command enables you to view, add, modify, and delete a shared resource. This command displays a list of the system's shared resources:

```
net share
```

The following command displays information regarding the shared resource, where *sharename* is the name of the shared device you want to view.

```
net share sharename
```

For example, if you are sharing a resource named Wookie, you would enter **net share wookie** to view the details of that resource.

This command creates a shared resource,

```
net share sharename = path /permissions /remark:"description"
```

where *sharename* is the name of the shared resource, *path* is the path to the shared resource, *permissions* is the permission level required to access this resource, and *description* is a description of the resource. For example, if you want to create a shared resource for a file folder called Wookie that requires unlimited access, you would use a command like the following:

```
net share wookie = c:\wookie /unlimited /remark:"wookie folder on drive c"
```

The following command adds a description to an existing shared resource, where *sharename* is the name of the resource and *description* is the description you want to assign to the resource.

```
net share sharename /remark:"description"
```

Finally, this command deletes the specified shared resource, where *sharename* is the name of the shared resource you want to delete.

```
net share sharename /delete
```

Net Use Command

This command lets you connect to shared resources over the network and displays the resources to which you are currently connected.

This command displays a list of resources to which you are currently connected:

```
net use
```

The next command maps a shared resource to a drive letter, where *mappedDrive* is the drive letter you want to map the connection to, *server* is the name of the server sharing the resource, and *sharename* is the name of the shared resource you want to connect to.

```
net use mappedDrive \\server\sharename
```

For example, if you wanted to map drive w to the shared wookie directory on the server called Chewy, you would enter **net use w: \\chewy\wookie**.

The following command deletes a mapped resource, where *mappedDrive* is the mapped drive you want to delete:

```
net use mappedDrive /delete
```

Net Session Command

This command enables you to view or disconnect sessions between your system and other clients that are accessing your shared resources.

This command displays a list of clients that are accessing your shared resources:

```
net session
```

This command disconnects one or all sessions that are currently connected to the system. If a *computerName* is not specified, all sessions are disconnected.

```
net session \\computerName /delete
```

Net File Command

This command enables you to view or close open files that are shared on the system.

This command displays a list of open shared files, including the file ID, which is used to close the file:

```
net file
```

This command closes the file specified by the *ID*:

```
net file ID /close
```

Enabling the Internet Connection Firewall

On a small network with only one Internet connection, you can share that Internet connection with other systems on the network by using the Internet Connection Sharing (ICS) feature. By default, if you enable ICS on a system running Windows XP, the Internet connection firewall is automatically enabled. This firewall protects your shared resources from unauthorized users. If your system is isolated from the Internet by a residential gateway, proxy server, or another firewall, you can disable the firewall feature.

The firewall monitors inbound and outbound communication between the computers it protects. Inbound traffic, originating from the Internet, is automatically blocked unless it is recognized as a response to outgoing traffic from a system on the local network. The firewall can be configured to allow specific forms of unsolicited traffic. For example, if you are hosting a Web site, you can configure the firewall to permit Hypertext Transfer Protocol (HTTP) Web Server service traffic to pass between the Internet and the Web server.

▶ *NOTE*

The Internet connection firewall should not be used with virtual private network connections and is not available in the Windows XP 64-bit edition.

 To enable the Internet connection firewall, use the following steps:

1. Open the Control Panel and select Network and Internet Connections.
2. Click Network Connections to open a list of network connections in the Network Connections window.
3. Right-click the network connection that directly connects to the Internet, and then choose Properties from the pop-up menu.
4. On the Connection Properties window, click the Advanced tab, as shown in Figure 13-1.
5. Make certain the "Protect my computer and network by limiting or preventing access to this computer from the Internet" option is checked.

▶ *NOTE*

Some options are available only when ICS is enabled.

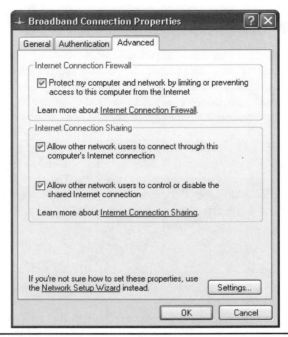

Figure 13-1 Enable Internet Connection Firewall

Enabling Simple File Sharing

By default, the Guest account is disabled. When you enable Simple File Sharing, the Guest account is automatically enabled. Simple File Sharing is by far the easiest way to share resources on your system.

▶ **CAUTION**

Unless a device is a SmartMedia, removable, or CD-ROM device, it should not be shared. It is highly recommended that you share only specific folders or files on a given drive.

TRY IT To enable Simple File Sharing, use the following steps:

1. Open Windows Explorer and right-click the file or folder you want to share.
2. From the pop-up menu, choose Sharing and Security.
3. On the file or folder's Properties window, click the Sharing tab, as shown in Figure 13-2.
4. Under Network Sharing and Security, check the Share This Folder on the Network check box.

Figure 13-2   Sharing tab for Simple File Sharing

5. Enter a share name in the Share Name text box.

6. If you want to enable users to view only the files on this share, uncheck the Allow Network Users to Change My Files check box. If you leave this check box checked, users will be able to read and write to the share, which means they can modify any files stored in that location.

▶ *TIP*

If you want to hide a shared folder from other Windows users, add a dollar sign to the end of the share name. The folder will be hidden, but users "in the know" can still access it if they include the dollar sign in the share name when establishing a connection. For example, if you want to hide a shared folder named wookie, you would enter the share name as **wookie$**. *When a user wants to connect to that share, the dollar sign must be included in the share name when the connection is established. Be warned, however, that these hidden shares are still visible to Apple Macintosh and Linux users.*

Sharing Folders with Classic Security

If you are logged on as an administrator or power user, you can share resources with others on the network. Using the classic security model enables you to set permissions for each share.

▶ *TIP*

If your system is using NTFS, make certain you set the NTFS permissions before sharing a folder or file. This ensures that security restrictions are enforced prior to you making the files accessible.

TRY IT ▶ To set file sharing with the classic security model, use the following steps:

1. Open Windows Explorer and right-click the file or folder you want to share.
2. Choose Sharing and Security from the pop-up menu.
3. Click the Sharing tab from the Properties window (Figure 13-3).
4. In the Network Sharing and Security pane, check the Share This Folder on the Network check box.
5. Enter a share name in the Share Name text box.
6. Type a description for the shared resource in the Comment text box.
7. If you need to limit the number of users who connect to the shared resource simultaneously, click the Allow This Number of Users option and enter the number of users who can connect to the resource—the maximum number of users allowed is 10. If you require that more than 10 users

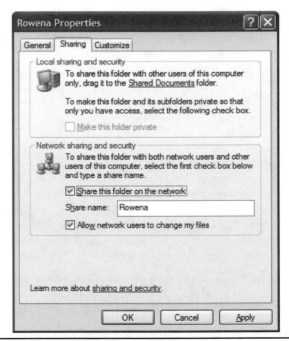

Figure 13-3   Sharing tab for the classic security model

be able to connect to the resource simultaneously, you must install a server version of Windows.

8. Click the Permissions button to open the Permissions window (Figure 13-4), where you can set the permissions required to access this resource.

9. In the Group or User Names list, select the name of the user or group you need to set permissions for when accessing this resource.

10. You can add a user or group to access the shared resource by clicking the Add button.

11. Select one or more of the following permissions:

   • **Full Control**   Lets users create, read, write, rename, and delete files in the shared resource. Users can also change permission settings and take ownership of files on NTFS volumes.

   • **Change**   Lets users read, write, rename, and delete files in the shared resource.

   • **Read**   Lets users read files in the shared resource. These users cannot change or delete files in this resource.

▶ *NOTE*

If you do not select Allow or Deny for a permission option, the user or group can inherit the permission through another group of which they are a member. If the user or group does not belong to another group, permission is denied.

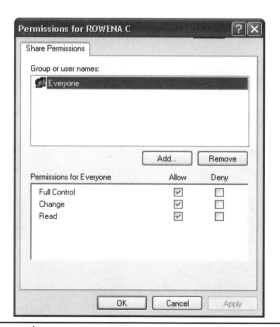

Figure 13-4   Permissions window

12. Click OK to return to the Sharing tab.

13. Click the Caching button to make the resource available offline. For more information regarding this feature, see Chapter 14.

14. When you are done assigning permissions, click OK.

▶ **NOTE**

A default administrative share name always ends with a dollar sign. This type of share is available only to administrators and is not visible with other shared resources. To create a new share that is visible and available to other users, click New Share in the Sharing tab, and then enter a share name.

▶ **TIP**

By default, the Everyone group is given access to shared resources. The Guest account is included in this group. If you do not want to give access to anyone who does not have an account, in step 10, add Authenticated Users to the list and delete the Everyone group. The Guest account is not included in the Authenticated Users group.

Using the Shared Folders Snap-In

If your system is running Windows XP Professional, the shared folders snap-in provides a centralized approach to managing shared folders. To use this snap-in, you must be logged in as an administrator and have Simple File Sharing disabled.

If you are running Windows XP Home Edition, you can still use this snap-in, but only to view shares on the system.

TRY IT To use the shared folders snap-in, use the following steps:

1. Right-click My Computer and choose Manage from the pop-up menu. The Computer Management window opens, as shown in Figure 13-5. (You can also access this snap-in by entering **fsmgmt.msc** at the command prompt. This technique loads the share snap-in without the full management capabilities.)

2. Navigate to the System Tools\Shared Folders directory.

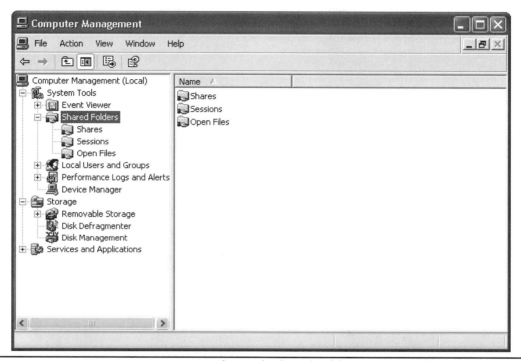

Figure 13-5   Computer Management window with Shared Folders snap-in highlighted

3. View or modify the permissions for a shared folder by right-clicking the folder and choosing Properties from the pop-up menu.

Warning Users in Active Sessions

When users are connected to shared resources on your system, you need to warn them before shutting down your system or some of their work may be lost or corrupted.

  To warn users of a system shutdown, use the following steps:

1. Right-click My Computer and choose Manage from the pop-up menu.
2. In the Computer Management window, navigate to the System Tools\Shared Folders directory.

3. Right-click the Shares folder, and then choose All Tasks | Send Console Message from the pop-up menu, as shown in the following illustration.

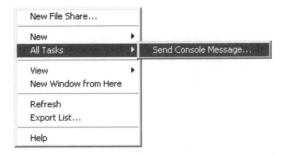

4. The Send Console Message dialog box, shown next, automatically inserts the names of users with active sessions and open files in the Recipients list. Type your warning message and then click Send.

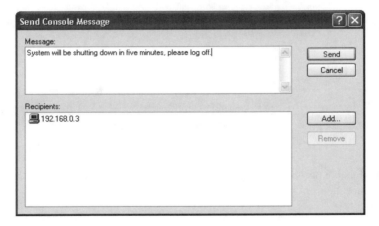

Disabling Automatic Discovery

The automatic discovery feature searches for available shares on the network. If you are working on a rather large network with several shares, you may not want this process to run each time you log onto your system. Windows XP offers a way to disable this feature.

 To disable automatic discovery, use the following steps:

1. Open Windows Explorer, and then select Tools | Folder Options.

2. Click the View tab of the Folder Options window.

3. In the Advanced settings list, uncheck the Automatically Search for Network Folders and Printers check box, as shown in Figure 13-6.

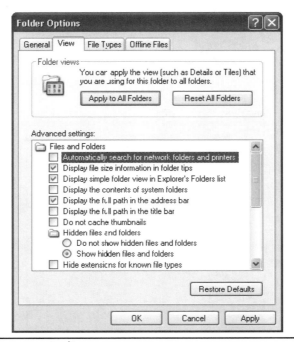

Figure 13-6   Disabling automatic discovery

Sharing Applications

This handy feature lets you share applications with another user. The program appears in a window on the other user's computer. Either you or the other user can control the program at any given time, so you can collaborate on a document, play a game, or develop a presentation together. Application sharing is accomplished through Windows Messenger.

TRY IT   To share an application, use the following steps:

1. Sign onto Microsoft Messenger.
2. Right-click the name of the person you want to share an application with, and then choose Start Application Sharing from the pop-up menu.
3. The person you invited will see the invitation dialog.
4. After that person accepts the invitation, another window appears on your screen prompting for the application to share. Select the application from the list, and then click Share, as shown in Figure 13-7.
5. If required, you can let the other user take control of the screen by clicking Allow Control.

Figure 13-7   Sharing an application

6. To take control of the application, double-click inside the application. Leave the Sharing dialog box open so you can unshare the application when you are done collaborating.

7. To end the sharing session, click Unshare in the Sharing dialog box. Then click Close.

▶ *NOTE*

This procedure may not work if one or both users' systems are behind a firewall or router. Also, both systems must be running the same version of Windows Messenger.

Mapping Shared Folders

When you map a network folder, the folder is available to you as an ordinary drive. For example, if you frequently access a shared folder on another system, you can map that share location to a drive letter. Each time you log on, this location is mapped to the assigned drive letter, and you can access it as you would a local drive on your system.

Although this is a great convenience, you don't want to "over-map" your network connections. Each mapped location takes time to connect. If you have several mapped locations, it could take your system some time to log onto the network.

This feature has basically been overruled by the convenience of My Network Places. In some instances, however, mapping is beneficial:

- When programs do not use the Windows common dialog boxes
- When you want to make a shared file or folder accessible from My Computer
- If you use a particular drive or folder on a regular basis

TRY IT   To map a shared file or folder, use the following steps:

1. Open Windows Explorer, and then choose Tools I Map Network Drive to open the window shown here:

2. Select an available drive letter from the Drive pull-down list.
3. Type the path and name of the folder or file you want to map, or click the Browse button to locate these items.
4. If you want this connection to be available each time you log onto the network, check the Reconnect at Logon option.
5. Click Finish.

Setting Up a WebDAV Directory

Web Distributed Authoring and Versioning (WebDAV) is an alternative to using the File Transfer Protocol (FTP) for transferring files from one system to another over the Internet. This method of transferring files is preferred over FTP because it employs the authentication methods supported by Internet Information Services (IIS).

Users running Windows 2000 or later with Internet Explorer 5 or later can use this extension of HTTP 1.1 to read and write files on a virtual directory managed by IIS. After the directory is set up, users can access it as they would any other shared folder on the network. When they open the directory, however, it resembles an FTP window.

TRY IT   To set up a WebDAV directory, use the following steps:

1. Open Windows Explorer and right-click the directory you want to share.
2. From the pop-up menu, choose Sharing and Security.
3. Click the Web Sharing tab, and then select Share This Folder.
4. Set the permissions for this directory, and then click OK.

Sharing Printers

Sharing printers is easy. You simply right-click the printer you want to share in the Printers and Faxes window and choose Sharing from the pop-up menu to open the Sharing tab on the Properties window, shown in Figure 13-8.

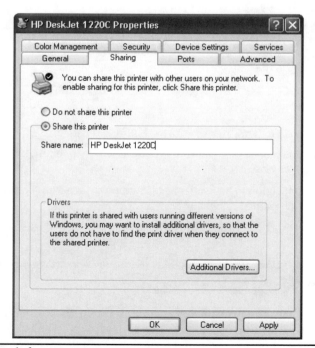

Figure 13-8   Sharing tab for printers

If the printer will be accessed by computers running other operating systems, you need to click the Additional Drivers button to install the required drivers before these computers can access the printer.

TRY IT   To share a printer, use the following steps:

1. Open the Control Panel, and then select Printers and Other Hardware.
2. Click View Installed Printers or Fax Printers.
3. Right-click the printer you want to share, and then select Sharing from the pop-up menu.
4. In the Sharing folder of the Properties window that opens by default, click the Share This Printer option.
5. Type a printer name in the Share Name text box. This is the name the users will see when connecting to the device, so you want it to be intuitive.
6. If some users are running other operating systems, click the Additional Drivers button and install the required drivers.
7. Click the Advanced tab, shown in Figure 13-9, to specify the times when the printer is available.
8. Click OK.

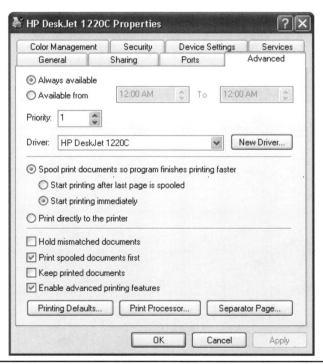

Figure 13-9   Advanced tab

CHAPTER 14

Working Remotely and Working Offline

TIPS IN THIS CHAPTER

W indows XP Professional offers some useful tools for those who do their work away from an office environment. With a remote connection, you can use the resources at the office as easily as if you were sitting at your office desk. At those times when a remote connection is not possible, you can choose to access files and Web sites offline.

The requirements for establishing a remote connection are relatively simple:

- **Remote System**   This is the system to which you connect. The system needs to be running Windows XP Professional and have a connection to the local area network (LAN) or the Internet. If you use a modem to connect to the network or Internet, you must configure the modem to answer incoming calls automatically. If you intend to connect to this system over the Internet, the system must be configured with a static IP address.

- **Client System**   This is the computer you are using at a "remote" location. This system can be running any version of Windows, and you must have installed the client software provided on the Windows XP Professional CD-ROM. You must have the ability to connect to the remote system through a dial-up connection, the Internet, a LAN, or through a Virtual Private Network (VPN) connection.

▶ *TIP*

*If you connect to the Internet using a cable modem or some other means that maintains a constant connection, you can enter **ipconfig** at the command-line prompt to learn the current IP address of the remote system. Unless the system loses its connection to the ISP, this IP address should not change often.*

When you connect to a system remotely, the screen resolution at your computer takes on the settings of the client system. These settings can be changed to improve performance over slower connections if necessary. They cannot, however, go beyond the settings of the client system. For example, if the client's screen resolution is set to 800x600, you cannot set the remote desktop to a higher resolution.

▶ *NOTE*

Although the remote desktop feature is not available in the Windows XP Home Edition, it is still possible to set up a remote connection through Remote Assistance or a third-party freeware application such as VNC from AT&T UK.

When you establish a remote desktop connection, your *local* resources also become available through that connection, which enables you to print to a local printer or store information to a local directory. The Clipboard can be used to copy and paste information between the client and the remote desktop. Drives are available in the remote desktop's My Computer area, as shown in Figure 14-1.

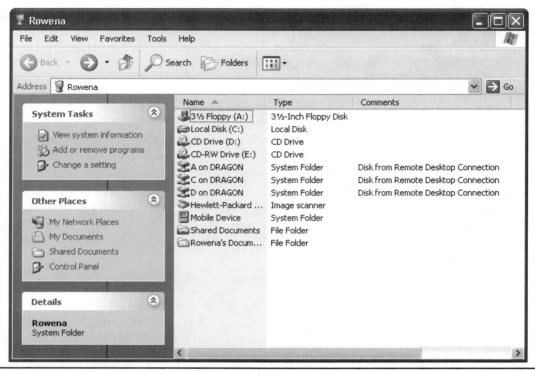

Figure 14-1   Rowena's remote desktop window

Printers are also accessible from the remote desktop. They appear in the Printers and Faxes window, as shown in Figure 14-2. The first printer on the list is the remote desktop printer.

Remote Access Through a Virtual Private Network

A VPN lets you connect through the Internet to access resources at the remote system. This type of connection requires more system resources, but the performance you receive as a result is often worth the cost. If you have a permanent connection to the Internet through a DSL connection or a cable modem, you can appreciate the full speed of that connection through a VPN—a clear advantage over a dial-up connection.

Tunneling protocols are at the core of VPNs. These protocols take advantage of the Internet infrastructure and its transmission protocols, working beneath the protocol of the intervening network to create a virtual path between the two networks. This type of networking provides a secure and cost-effective solution for connecting two systems through the Internet. Without tunneling protocols, you would have to pay phone companies to use their cables and to set up specific protocols on each end.

The connection path is created by encrypting each Internet Protocol (IP) packet or frame and wrapping it into another packet or frame that contains new header information that pertains to the

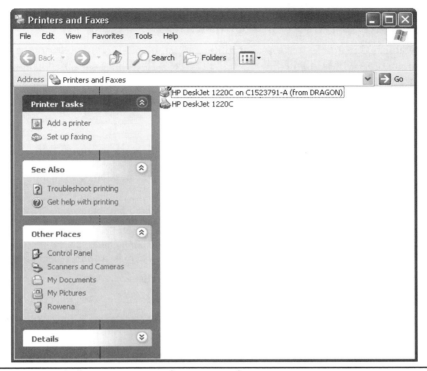

Figure 14-2   Remote desktop Printers and Faxes window

intervening network. When the frame is received at the remote system, the header is stripped and the frame is decrypted and forwarded to the appropriate router.

The three most common tunneling protocols in use today are as follows:

- **Point-to-Point Tunneling Protocol (PPTP)**   Enables IP, Internetwork Packet Exchange (IPX) or NetBEUI frames to be encrypted and wrapped in an IP header.

- **Layer 2 Tunneling Protocol (L2TP)**   Enables IP, IPX, or NetBEUI frames to be encrypted and sent over any IP, X.25, Frame Relay, or Asynchronous Transfer Mode (ATM) intervening network.

- **IP Security (IPSec) Tunnel Mode**   Enables IP packets to be encrypted and encapsulated in an IP header.

▶ *NOTE*

Windows XP uses PPTP or L2TP for VPN connections. Windows .NET Server or Windows 2000 Server can act as a VPN server using L2TP. Windows XP uses IPSec to enhance the security of network transactions.

Remote Desktop Keyboard Commands

If you have established a remote desktop connection and are in full-screen mode, the following keyboard combinations will be applied to either the remote or the client system, depending on how you have configured the remote desktop connection.

Client Keys	Remote Keys	Action
ALT-TAB	ALT-PAGE UP	Switch between programs
ALT-SHIFT-TAB	ALT-PAGE DOWN	Switch between programs in reverse order
N/A	CTRL-ALT-BREAK	Switch the remote desktop between a window and full screen
ALT-ESC	ALT-INSERT	Cycle through programs in the order they were started
CTRL-ALT-DELETE	CTRL-ALT-END	Display the Windows Security dialog if the remote system is a domain member; display the Task Manager if the remote system is not a member of a domain
CTRL-ESC	ALT-HOME	Open the Start menu
N/A	ALT-DELETE	Open the active window's control menu
SHIFT-PRINT SCREEN	CTRL-ALT-+ (plus) on numeric keypad	Copy a bitmap image of the remote desktop to the Clipboard
ALT-PRINT SCREEN	CTRL-ALT-– (minus) on numeric keypad	Copy a bitmap image of the active window to the Clipboard

Working Offline

Windows XP Professional offers a feature that is similar to the Briefcase in older Windows versions. Although the Briefcase feature is still available, the offline feature is easier to use. When you configure files or Web site favorites to be available offline, Windows XP caches copies of the files or sites on your local system. You can access and change the information on your local system, just as you would while working online. When you log onto the network, the cached files are automatically synchronized with the copies on your local system.

▶ *NOTE*

To use this caching feature, you must have Windows XP Professional installed on the system with which you intend to work offline. The systems that store the online copies of the files and favorites can run Windows XP Home Edition.

By default, offline files and folders are synchronized when you log off your account and are synchronized again when you log back on. This ensures that both systems contain the most current files or folders. This synchronization process involves the following operations:

- If you change a file offline and the online copy has not been modified, Windows XP updates the online copy with your offline changes.

- If you do not change the files in your offline cache but the online copies have been modified, Windows XP updates the offline copies in your cache.

- If both copies of a file have been modified, you can keep the cached version, the online version, or both.

Setting Up the Remote System

Before you can use the remote desktop feature, you must set up the remote system and the client system. To establish a remote desktop connection, you must have an assigned password.

TRY IT   To set up the remote system, use the following steps:

1. Log onto the remote system as an administrator.

2. Press WINDOWS LOGO KEY-BREAK to open the System Properties window. Then click the Remote tab, which is shown in Figure 14-3.

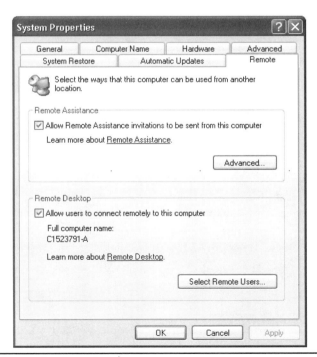

Figure 14-3   System Properties Remote tab

3. Under Remote Desktop, select the Allow Users to Connect Remotely to This Computer option. This allows the current user or members of the Administrator or Remote Desktop Users group that have an assigned password to connect to the system.

4. If you want to specify which users can connect to the system remotely, click the Select Remote Users button to open the Remote Desktop Users dialog box shown next. (If you do not want to select users, skip to step 6.)

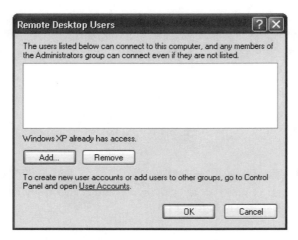

5. To add a user, click the Add button and enter the name of the user or group you want to add. To remove a user or group, select the name and then click the Remove button. Click OK when you're done to close this dialog box.

6. If you want to connect to this system through a dial-up connection, you need to install a modem and configure it to answer incoming calls automatically.

7. If you want to connect to this system through an Internet connection, and you're using Windows XP's firewall protection, you need to open the port used by the remote system. The next five steps show you how to do this.

8. From the Control Panel, choose Network and Internet Connections.

9. From the Network and Internet Connections screen, select Network Connections.

10. In the Network Connections window, right-click the Internet connection. From the pop-up menu, choose Properties.

11. In the Properties window, open the Advanced tab, and click the Settings button.

12. Select Remote Desktop. Click OK if you are using the Windows XP firewall.

▶ *NOTE*

If you are using a hardware firewall or a third-party firewall, configure the connection to use TCP port 3389.

▶ *NOTE*

If the remote system connects to the Internet through a router or residential gateway, you need to set up a VPN server. See "Configuring a VPN Server," shortly in this chapter.

Setting Up the Client System

If the client system is running Windows XP, the required software is installed automatically. If the client system is running Windows 95, Windows 98, Windows Me, Windows NT 4, or Windows 2000, you need to install Remote Desktop Connection from the Windows XP CD-ROM.

 TRY IT To install the Remote Desktop software, use the following steps:

1. Insert the Windows XP CD-ROM into the CD drive.
2. When the autostart menu appears, select Perform Additional Tasks | Set Up Remote Desktop Connection.

   Or, if you have autostart disabled, you can access this program from Windows Explorer. Double-click setup.exe from the CD drive.

▶ *TIP*

From the Start menu, you can click Run and then enter the following command to run the Remote Desktop program: **CDDriveLetter:\Support\Tools\msrdpcli.exe.** *(*CDDriveLetter *is the drive letter for your CD drive.) If you want to copy this program to a floppy disk, simply extract it from the CD and copy the files to the disk. The program takes approximately 800KB of space.*

Configuring a VPN Server

Windows XP supplies all the files you need for VPN server setup, providing you require only one incoming connection at any given time. If your remote system is not running Windows XP or you require more than one connection at a time, a number of third-party solutions are available for creating a VPN server.

When you create a VPN server, you allow others to connect to and access all of its resources. To set up a VPN server, you must be logged onto the remote system as an administrator.

 TRY IT To set up a VPN server, use the following steps:

1. Open the Control Panel and click Network and Internet Connections.

2. In the Network and Internet Connections screen, select Network Connections.

3. In the Network Connections window, under Network Tasks, select Create a New Connection. The New Connection Wizard opens, as shown here:

At this point, if the Location Information dialog box appears, you need to provide the required information, even if you do not intend to use a modem to make the connection. This dialog box is the result of a known Windows bug. If you close the window without providing the information, you may not be able to continue.

4. Click Next.

5. In the Network Connections Type window, choose Set Up an Advanced Connection, and then click Next.

6. If your system has a modem, serial port, parallel port, or an IrDA port, a Devices for Incoming Connections dialog box will open next. These options are used to set up an incoming dial-up, direct cable, or infrared connection. If this configuration does not apply to you, click Next.

7. In the Incoming Virtual Private Network (VPN) window, check Allow Virtual Private Connections. Then click Next.

8. In the Permissions window, select each type of user that can establish a VPN connection with this system. Then click Next.

9. In the Networking Software window, select each type of networking component you want to use for incoming connections. Then click Next.

   Note that for a connection to be successful, the remote and client systems must use the same networking protocol.

10. Click Finish.

Configuring a Remote Desktop Web Connection

If you are using a public Internet terminal, it will be impossible for you to install the Remote Desktop client software. You can, however, access your remote system through the Internet, providing the terminal is using Internet Explorer 4 or later.

The remote system must reside on a network that has a Web server using Internet Information Services (IIS). When the IIS was installed, the Remote Desktop Web component may or may not have been installed.

 TRY IT   To enable a remote desktop Web connection, use the following steps:

1. Log onto the Web server as an administrator.

2. Open the Control Panel and select Add or Remove Programs.

3. In the Add or Remove Programs window shown in Figure 14-4, click Add/Remove Windows Components.

4. In the Windows Components Wizard, select Internet Information Services (IIS), and then click the Details button to open the details window for Internet Information Services (IIS).

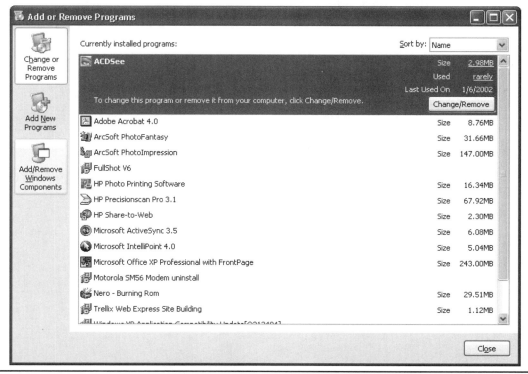

Figure 14-4   Add or Remove Programs window

5. Select World Wide Web Service, and then click the Details button to open the details window for World Wide Web Services.

6. Add a check mark to Remote Desktop Web Connection, as shown in the following illustration, and then click OK to close the World Wide Web Services details window. Click OK again to close the Internet Information Services (IIS) window.

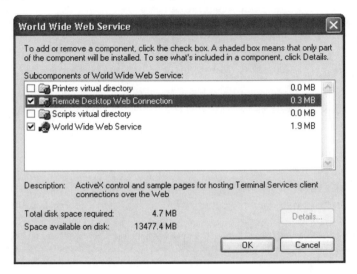

7. In the Windows Components Wizard, click Next to complete the installation. When the installation completes, you are returned to the Add or Remove Programs window.

8. Click the Close button to return to the Control Panel, and select Performance and Maintenance | Administrative Tools | Internet Information Services.

9. In the IIS window, click the system name in the Tree pane, and then navigate to Web Sites\Default Web Sites\Tsweb.

10. Right-click Tsweb and choose Properties from the pop-up menu.

11. In the Properties window, click the Directory Security tab to open it.

12. Under Anonymous Access and Authentication Control, click the Edit button.

13. In the Authentication Methods dialog, choose Anonymous Access, and then click OK in each dialog.

▶ *NOTE*

If you have not already done so, you need to set up the remote system to accept remote desktop connections. The next section shows you how to do this.

Initiating a Remote Desktop Connection

After you have configured the remote system to accept remote desktop connections and you have installed the client software, you are ready to make your connection.

Before you start the Remote Desktop application, you need to establish a connection to the remote system's network. This can be done through the Internet, a dial-up connection, or a VPN connection. Once that connection is established, you are ready to launch the Remote Desktop application.

 TRY IT   To establish a remote desktop connection, use the following steps:

1. Establish a link with the network on which the remote system resides.

2. Open the Start menu, and choose All Programs | Accessories | Communication | Remote Desktop Connection to open the Remote Desktop Connection dialog box shown in Figure 14-5.

3. In the Computer text box, type the name of the remote system or its IP address.

4. To specify the user name and the associated password required to log onto the remote system, click the Options button and follow the instructions on the dialog box that appears. Or simply click Connect.

Figure 14-5   Remote Desktop Connection dialog

5. If you click the Connect button without specifying the login information, a logon screen will appear, where you can enter the user name and password required to log onto the remote system. Then click OK.

6. If another person is logged on, you will be notified and prompted for further action. If Fast User Switching is enabled, the user who is currently logged on will be notified of your connection attempt and will have the opportunity to accept or reject the interruption. If Fast User Switching is disabled, the other user will be logged off without warning if you choose to kick him or her off the remote system.

▶ *NOTE*

Once the connection is established, the remote system displays either the Welcome screen, if enabled, or the Unlock Computer dialog. Whatever you do on the client system through remote desktop cannot be seen from the remote system's monitor.

Connecting Through the Internet

If you are connecting to a remote system through a Web server on the remote system's network, the remote desktop appears in a browser window. Before you can use this feature, you must set up the Web server to accept remote desktop connections. For details, see "Configuring a Remote Desktop Web Connection" earlier in this chapter.

▶ *NOTE*

Before you start, make certain your client system is connected to the Internet and that it is running Internet Explorer 4 or above.

TRY IT To connect to a remote system through a Web server, use the following steps:

1. Open Internet Explorer.

2. In the Address text box, type the URL for the Remote Desktop Web Connection home directory. By default, the URL follows this format: http://*serverName*/tsweb/, where *serverName* is the name or IP address of the Web server.

   If you are connected to the Intranet, meaning you are already connected to the network on which the remote system resides, all you need to do is enter the name of the remote system in the Address text box.

3. The Web browser displays a Remote Desktop Connection page. In the Server text box, enter the name of the remote server you want to connect to.

4. A warning is displayed regarding an ActiveX control that must be downloaded to the client system before the connection is made. Click Yes to accept the download.

5. When the logon screen displays, enter the user name and password required to log onto the remote system.

6. If another person is logged on, you will be notified and prompted for further action. If Fast User Switching is enabled, the user who is currently logged on will be notified of your connection attempt and can accept or reject the interruption. If Fast User Switching is disabled, the user will be logged off without warning if you choose to kick him or her off the remote system.

Customizing Remote Connections

When you launch the Remote Desktop application, the dialog box that is displayed enables you to enter the name of the system to which you want to connect. If you click the Options button, you can adjust the settings that determine how the remote desktop screen appears on the client system. If you are using a dial-up connection, you can improve performance by disabling many of the features and reducing the screen resolution. The settings that affect your connection performance are set in the Experience tab.

If you want to connect to several remote systems, you can define specific settings for each system and save those settings so they can be recalled when you make a connection to that system.

To access the remote connection options, click the Options button on the Remote Desktop Connection screen. You'll find the options you need on the various tabs, starting with the General tab shown in Figure 14-6.

On the General tab, you can define the following options:

- **Computer**   Defines the name or IP address of the remote system to which you want to connect. If you have entered this system at another time, its name or IP address is stored in the drop-down list.

- **User Name**   Defines the user name you want to use to log onto the remote system.

- **Password**   Defines the password associated with the user name.

- **Domain**   Defines the domain on which the remote system resides. If the remote system is not a member of a domain, the name of the remote system is reflected here.

- **Connection Settings**   Use the Save As and Open buttons to save and open the configuration settings. If more than one configuration has been saved, you can open the one you need to make a specific connection.

On the Display tab, shown in Figure 14-7, you can define the following options:

- **Remote Desktop Size**   Defines the size of the remote desktop screen as it appears on the client system. This setting does not affect the settings on the remote system. To view the remote desktop as a full-sized page, move the slider all the way to the right.

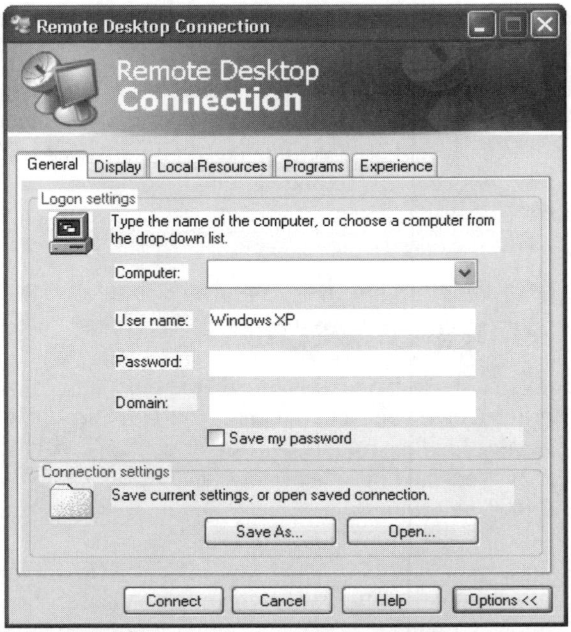

Figure 14-6   General tab

Figure 14-7   Display tab

- **Colors**   If you have a fast connection, you can view the desktop with True Color. If you have a slower, dial-up connection, you might consider reducing the number of colors to improve performance.

- **Display the Connection Bar When in Full Screen Mode**   Check this option if you want to display the connection bar at the top of the remote desktop screen. You can click the pushpin button on the Connection bar to hide the bar, and from this bar you can reduce the desktop to a Taskbar button on your client system, resize the window, or close the connection.

▶ **NOTE**

Closing the connection does not log you off the remote system.

Next is the Local Resources tab, shown in Figure 14-8.
On the Local Resources tab, you can define the following options:

- **Remote Computer Sound**   Choose one of the following options:
  - **Bring to This Computer**   Play event sounds on the client system.
  - **Do Not Play**   Do not play event sounds on the client system.
  - **Leave at Remote Computer**   Play the event sounds on the remote system.

Figure 14-8   Local Resources tab

- **Keyboard**   Specifies how you want the remote desktop key combinations to be applied. Choose from one of the following options:
  - **On the Local Computer**   Allow the key combinations to affect the client system.
  - **On the Remote Computer**   Allow the key combinations to affect the remote system.
  - **In Full Screen Mode Only**   Allow the key combinations to affect the remote system in full screen mode and the client system when not in full screen mode.
- **Local Devices**   Makes the client devices available in the remote desktop.

On the Programs tab, shown in Figure 14-9, you can specify a program you want to launch after the remote desktop connection is established.

On the Experience tab, shown in Figure 14-10, you can define the following options:

- **Connection Speed**   Lets you quickly change the options based on the type of connection you are using. For example, if you select Modem (28.8Kbps) from the connection list, all the check boxes will be cleared to improve performance. If you select LAN (10Mbps or higher) all the display options will be selected.
- **Allow the Following**   After you select the connection speed, you can clear or check these options if the recommended default does not meet your needs.

Figure 14-9   Programs tab

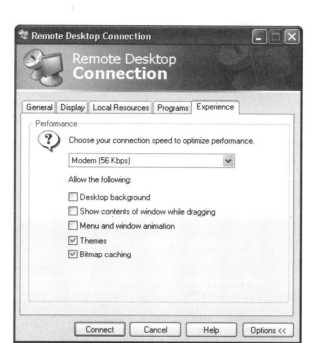

Figure 14-10   Experience tab

TRY IT   To customize remote connections, use the following steps:

1. Open the Start menu and choose All Programs I Accessories I Communication I Remote Desktop Connection.

2. In the Remote Desktop Connection screen, click the Options button to access the customization tabs.

3. Define the settings for the remote connection and click Save As to save those settings for future reference.

4. Click the Options button again to hide the customization tabs. Click Connect to establish the remote connection.

Connecting Remotely Using a VPN

You can establish a remote desktop connection through a VPN from any system running Windows. The following instructions are specific to Windows XP, but they are similar for other operating systems.

TRY IT To connect remotely using a VPN, use the following steps:

1. Open the Control Panel and select Network and Internet Connections.

2. In the Network and Internet Connections screen, select Network Connections.

3. In the Network Connections window, under Network Tasks, click Create a New Connection.

4. The New Connection Wizard opens. Click Next to begin the process.

5. In the Network Connection Type page, select Connect to the Network at my Workplace. Then click Next.

6. In the Network Connection page, click the Virtual Private Network connection option, and then click Next.

7. In the Connection Name page, type in the name for the connection. This name could be the location where the remote system resides or the name of the system you want to reach. Click Next.

8. In the VPN Server Selection page, type the IP address or the host name of the VPN server. Click Next.

9. If you want a shortcut to this connection to be placed on your Desktop, check the Add a Shortcut to This Connection to My Desktop option. Click Finish to complete the setup process.

10. The Connect Server dialog, shown next, opens automatically. Enter the user name and password required to log onto the VPN server, and then click Connect.

11. After the connection is established, you can initiate a remote desktop connection with a system on that network.

TIP

You can share your VPN connection with others on the network as a shared Internet connection.

 Setting Up an Offline Environment

To set up an offline environment, you must first disable Fast User Switching. When you do this, you must remember to close all open applications before logging off the system. This feature is available only in Windows XP Professional.

 To set up an offline environment, use the following steps:

1. Make certain that Fast User Switching is disabled. Open the Control Panel and select User Accounts.

2. In the User Accounts window, click Change the Way Users Log On or Off.

3. In the Select logon and logoff options window, shown in Figure 14-11, make sure that the Use Fast User Switching check box is cleared. Then click Apply Options.

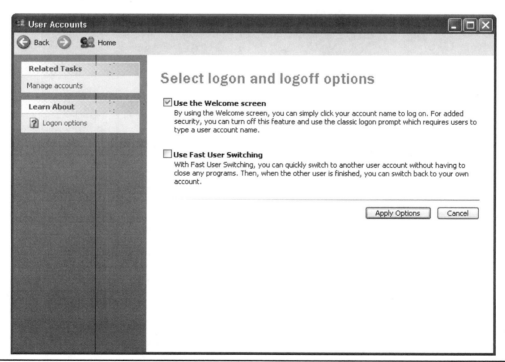

Figure 14-11   Disable Fast User Switching

4. Close the User Accounts window. Back in the Control Panel, select Appearance and Themes to open the Appearance and Themes window.

5. Choose Folder Options, and in the Folder Options dialog box, click the Offline Files tab to open it. The Offline Files tab is shown in Figure 14-12. Note that this dialog can also be accessed from the Windows Explorer Tools menu (choose Tools | Folder Options).

6. Check the Enable Offline Files option. If required, you can also check the following options:

   • **Synchronize All Offline Files When Logging On**   Performs a synchronization of your offline files when you log onto the system.

   • **Synchronize All Offline Files Before Logging Off**   Performs a synchronization of your offline files before you log off the system. If you check this option, make certain you log off and shut down the system or Windows XP will not have a chance to synchronize your files.

   • **Display a Reminder Every *nnn* Minutes**   Notifies you when the network connection is lost. If you are working offline, this notification can be a nuisance.

   • **Create an Offline Files Shortcut on the Desktop**   Creates a shortcut to your offline files. When this option is enabled, Windows XP creates a special system folder that contains the cache of your offline files. You can also view these files by clicking the View Files button.

   • **Encrypt Offline Files to Secure Data**   When enabled, only someone who logs onto the system with your user name and password can access your files. Keep in mind that temporary files created by some applications such as Microsoft Word are not encrypted.

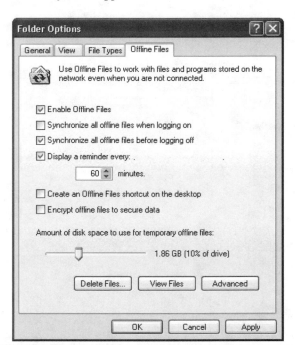

Figure 14-12   Offline Files tab

Either remove these temporary files when you are done or encrypt them manually through Windows Explorer.

- **Amount of Disk Space to Use for Temporary Offline Files**   By default, 10 percent of your disk space is allocated for temporary offline files. You can choose to increase or decrease this percentage if necessary.

7. When you are done, click OK.

8. To define how the system behaves in the event a connection is lost between the client and server, click the Advanced button to open the Advanced Settings dialog box shown here:

Synchronizing on Demand

If you are working on an offline file and want to synchronize it with the file on the server, you can perform synchronization on demand.

TRY IT   To synchronize files on demand, use the following steps:

1. In Windows Explorer, choose Tools | Synchronize. The Items to Synchronize dialog box opens, as shown in Figure 14-13.

2. Select the items you want to synchronize, and then click Synchronize.

3. If you want to customize the way your offline files are synchronized with the server, click the Setup button to open the dialog box shown in Figure 14-14.

4. Select the desired options, and then click OK.

Figure 14-13   Items to Synchronize dialog

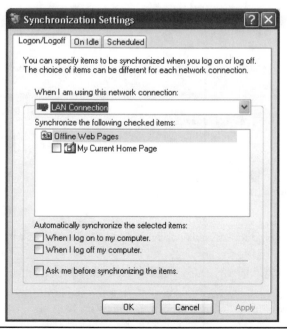

Figure 14-14   Synchronization Settings dialog

PART IV

Internet

CHAPTER 15

Getting Connected and Setting Internet Options

TIPS IN THIS CHAPTER

Windows XP makes it easy to get connected to the Internet, even if you don't know anything about it. When you double-click the Internet Explorer icon, Windows XP automatically checks for an existing connection. If one is not present, the New Connection Wizard automatically displays. In most cases, an Internet Service Provider (ISP) has already been obtained, but if not, the wizard lets you select from a list of ISPs.

ISPs offer various ways in which you can connect to the Internet. Some offer only dial-up services, while others offer broadband or digital subscriber line (DSL) services. When you determine how you want to connect to the Internet, your ISP is also determined, unless you choose to use a dial-up connection. Many ISPs offer dial-up connections, such as America Online (AOL) and Earthlink. Getting connected to either one of these ISPs is as easy as selecting them from the list.

Although, DSL and broadband connections are more desirable over standard dial-up, they are available in certain areas only. The following pros and cons should be considered when determining your Internet connection options:

- **Modem (Dial-Up)** These devices can be slow, and actually getting through to your ISP and maintaining your connection can pose a bit of a challenge during peak hours. Since dial-up modems operate with an analog signal, they tie up your phone line when you are connected to the Internet. The good thing about this type of connection is that it is relatively inexpensive to obtain an account with an ISP and you can connect to your ISP from any location that supplies a phone line. These types of modems can be internal or external. Internal modems plug into an expansion slot on the motherboard, or in some cases, they are a part of the motherboard. External modems connect to either a serial, parallel, or a universal serial bus (USB) port on your system.

- **DSL** These high-speed devices let you connect to the Internet through your existing phone lines. Because DSL uses a digital signal to communicate, this type of connection can be constant without tying up your phone line. Finding a DSL provider, especially in some remote areas, can be challenging. Some providers charge you for each hop (router) you go through to reach your ISP, so if several routers lie between you and your ISP, this type of connection can be expensive. When you sign up for a DSL connection, you are generally assigned an ISP as a package deal. In most instances, you can reach your ISP only from the machine connected to your DSL modem, which can make it difficult to retrieve e-mail messages from another system. DSL modems can be internal or external. Internal modems plug into an expansion slot on the motherboard. External modems connect to an Ethernet port on your system.

- **Broadband** This television infrastructure-based connection uses a cable modem to connect to the Internet. Cable modems use a special band of frequency that does not interfere with television signals. It provides a constant high-speed connection. Your broadband carrier will most likely be your ISP as well. This can make it difficult to retrieve e-mail messages from another location where your cable modem is not installed. Cable modems can be internal or external. Internal modems plug into an expansion slot on the motherboard. External modems connect to an Ethernet port on your system.

Depending on how your ISP operates, you may or may not be asked to log on before a connection to the Internet is established. If you are using a DSL or cable modem connection, your ISP may offer a constant connection, which means you do not have to log on. Your system is identified by a known computer name that the ISP assigns to you, or you may be given a static Internet Protocol (IP) address.

Thousands of ISPs are available around the world, so finding one is not much of a challenge. If you are not certain where to go or which ISP to use, here are a few suggestions:

- Ask friends and family members which ISP they use and why.

- Depending on where you purchased your computer, software may be available on the system that enables you to connect through a well-known ISP, such as MSN.

- Some systems are shipped with CD-ROMs that access common dial-up ISPs, such as America Online and Earthlink. Simply insert the CD-ROM and follow the directions that display as the software loads.

- If you are still uncertain, try one of the ISPs to which Windows XP refers when setting up your Internet connection.

If you already have an ISP and are upgrading to a new system, you can run the Files and Settings Transfer Wizard to transfer the settings on the old system to the new system.

For most applications, like small networks, the default Internet options are sufficient. On some occasions, however, you may need to tweak these settings to optimize your performance and increase system security.

Internet Security

An Internet connection requires a two-way communication between your system and the outside world. This means that uninvited intruders can access your system and leave unwanted gifts such as viruses on your file system. To protect your system and those that share the Internet connection, you need to take a few precautionary steps.

If you used the Windows XP Network Setup Wizard to configure your network, you should already have the most important security measures in place. By default, the Internet firewall is enabled on the system that connects to the Internet. This firewall protects you from intruders by blocking unsolicited messages and other hacker attempts.

If your systems connect through a hub, you should also disable File And Printer Sharing for Microsoft Networks on the Internet connection. If you have two network adapters in the system, those who are on your local network will still be able to share resources within the network.

If you have two or more systems with independent Internet access, they should be separated from the Internet connection by a router or residential gateway. This hardware device performs Network Address Translation (NAT), which hides the systems connected to it from the outside world. Only the gateway address is made available. The systems connected to this device are assigned private IP addresses that are known only by the internal network. If you are connected through a router or a residential gateway, there is no need to activate the Internet firewall or disable File And Printer Sharing.

Consider performing the following actions to ensure Internet security:

- Enable the Windows XP Internet connection firewall.
- Configure a Firewall Activity Log.
- Define which services can pass through the firewall.
- Disable File And Printer Sharing for Microsoft Networks.

Getting Connected

Before you can access the Internet, you need to set up an Internet connection. To do this, the following must be in place:

- A way to connect to the Internet—through a modem, DSL, or broadband connection
- Logon information, if required
- IP address, if required
- Access phone number for dial-up connections, if one is known
- DNS server address, if required

Most of this information can be obtained from your ISP, if you already have one. If you don't, and all you have is a way to connect to the outside world, you can still continue with the setup. Windows XP offers several ISP referrals through the wizard.

 To get connected, use the following steps:

1. If this is a clean install and no Internet connection is in place, open the Start menu and choose Internet Explorer. The New Connection Wizard launches automatically.

   If an Internet connection is in place and you want to add another one, open the Control Panel and select Network and Internet Connections. Then click Network Connections. Under Network Tasks, click Create a New Connection to launch the wizard.

2. Click Next to begin the setup process.

3. In the Network Connection Type screen, choose Connect to the Internet. Then click Next.

4. Depending on which option you choose, the instructions change slightly.

   - **Set Up My Connection Manually**   Choose this option if you already have an account with an ISP.

   - **Use the CD I Got from an ISP**   Choose this option if you want to use the CD provided by an ISP.

   - **Choose from a List of ISP Service Providers**   Choose this option if you want to select an ISP from the Windows XP referrals list.

5. Follow the directions on the screen to complete the process.

Enabling the Windows XP Internet Connection Firewall

If other systems on your local area network (LAN) use the Internet connection through your system, you need to activate the Windows XP Internet Connection Firewall (ICF). As an alternative, you can install a third-party firewall or a router or residential gateway between your network and the Internet.

TRY IT   To enable the Windows XP ICF, use the following steps:

1. Open the Control Panel and select Network and Internet Connections.
2. Select Network Connections to open the Network Connections window.
3. Right-click the connection to the Internet, and then choose Properties from the pop-up menu, as shown in Figure 15-1.
4. In the Properties window, click the Advanced tab shown in Figure 15-2.
5. Select Protect My Computer and Network by Limiting or Preventing Access to This Computer from the Internet.
6. Click OK.

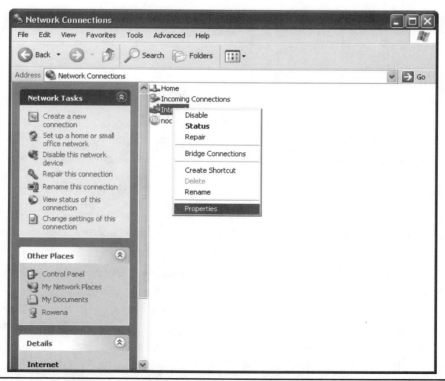

Figure 15-1   Network Connections window

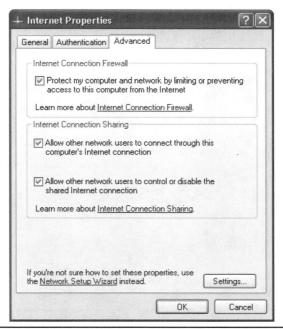

Figure 15-2   Internet Properties Advanced tab

Configuring a Firewall Activity Log

By default, the Windows XP ICF does not create an activity log. If you are curious about what the firewall is doing, you can enable and configure a firewall activity log that can be viewed in Notepad or some other text-editing application.

 TRY IT   To enable and configure a firewall activity log, use the following steps:

1. Open the Control Panel and select Network and Internet Connections.
2. Select Network Connections to open the Network Connections window.
3. Right-click the connection to the Internet, and then choose Properties from the pop-up menu.
4. In the Properties window, click the Advanced tab, and then click the Settings button.
5. Click the Security Logging tab to open it (Figure 15-3).
6. Check the options for the types of events you want to log.

   Unless you want to see who is accessing the Internet the most, you might want to simply log dropped packets. If you notice that several dropped packets are logged, this may indicate that someone may be trying to find a security hole in your system.

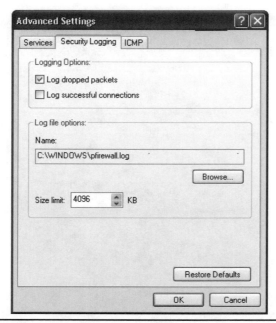

Figure 15-3   Advanced Settings Security Logging tab

7. In the Name text box, type the location and file name where you want the log to be stored.

8. To set a maximum size for the log file, enter the size in kilobytes in the Size Limit text box. This will prevent the file from becoming too large.

9. Click OK.

The activity log conforms to the Worldwide Web Consortium (W3C) extended log format, which enables you to analyze this data using third-party utilities. The first eight columns of information will probably be of the most interest to you. The log is shown here:

```
#Verson: 1.0
#Software: Microsoft Internet Connection Firewall
#Time Format: Local
#Fields: date time action protocol src-ip dst-ip src-port dst-port
2002-01-10  13:13:56  DROP  TCP  65.123.200.101  12.132.44.5  3619  80
```

As you can see from the report sample, the field headers do not align with the actual fields. The following table describes the first eight fields.

Item	Description
Date	Displays the year-month-day the event occurred.
Time	Displays the hour:minute:second the event occurred.

Item	Description
Action	Identifies the operation that was flagged by the firewall. These values can be either OPEN, CLOSE, DROP, and INFO-EVENTS-LOST.
Protocol	Identifies the protocol used for the communication. These values can be TCP, UDP, or ICMP.
Source IP	Identifies the IP address of the system that initiated the communication.
Destination IP	Identifies the IP address of your system or the one connected to the Internet.
Source Port	Identifies the port number through which the source system initiated the communication.
Destination Port	Identifies the port that the source system was trying to access on your system or the system connected to the Internet.

Defining Which Services Can Pass Through the Firewall

The Windows XP ICF automatically blocks all unsolicited incoming data packets. If you are running a Web, File Transfer Protocol (FTP), or Telnet site, you may want to allow incoming packets on a given Transmission Control Protocol (TCP) port.

When you enable a service on the system, incoming packets for that service are automatically accepted.

 To define services, use the following steps:

1. From the Control Panel, select Network and Internet Connections.
2. Select Network Connections.
3. In the Network Connections window, right-click the connection to the Internet, and then choose Properties from the pop-up menu.
4. In the Properties window, click the Advanced tab, and then click the Settings button to open the Advanced Settings window.
5. Click the Services tab (Figure 15-4).
6. Select the services you want to provide.
7. If a service you want to provide is not listed, click the Add button to add it. Be prepared to provide the following information:
   - A descriptive name for the service
   - The host system's IP address
   - The port number other systems will use to access the service
   - The port number the service uses for the network
   - The protocol the services uses (TCP or UDP)
8. Click OK.

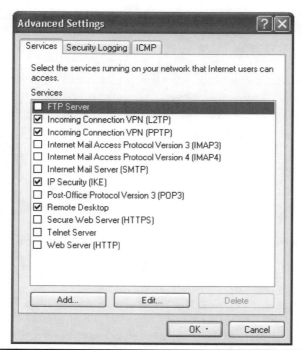

Figure 15-4   Services tab

Disabling File and Printer Sharing for Microsoft Networks

If you are not using a router or a residential gateway between your network and the Internet, it is highly recommended that you disable File And Printer Sharing on the Internet connection. Doing this does not prevent sharing over the LAN.

TRY IT   To disable File And Printer Sharing over the Internet, use the following steps:

1. Open the Control Panel and select Network and Internet Connections.
2. Select Network Connections.
3. In the Network Connections window, right-click the connection to the Internet, and then choose Properties from the pop-up menu.
4. In the Properties window, click the General tab (Figure 15-5).

Figure 15-5   General tab

5. Uncheck the File and Printer Sharing for Microsoft Networks option.

6. Click OK.

Configuring Internet Options

In most small networks, the default Internet configuration settings are sufficient to get you up and running. Depending on how you use the Internet, it might be beneficial to you to at least know what can be controlled during each Internet session.

TRY IT   To configure Internet options, use the following steps:

1. Open the Control Panel and select Network and Internet Connections.

2. In the Network and Internet Connections window, select the Internet Options link to open the Internet Properties window. Or, from Internet Explorer, choose Tools | Internet Options.

3. In the Internet Properties window, click the General tab (Figure 15-6).

4. On the General tab, you can configure the following options:

   • **Home Page**   Specify the first page you want to open each time Internet Explorer is launched.

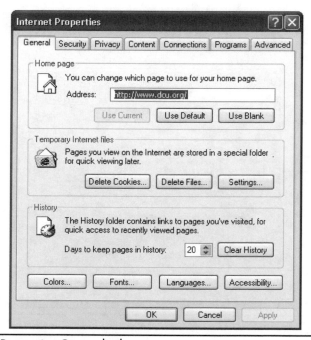

Figure 15-6 Internet Properties General tab

▶ *TIP*

In Internet Explorer, you can make the current page the new home page by choosing Tools | Internet Options. In the General tab, click the Use Current button to record the current URL in the Address text box. Click OK to save the change.

- **Temporary Internet Files**   Manage the files that are temporarily stored. Click Settings to view the temporary files folder and define how these files should be managed.

- **History**   Increase or decrease the number of links the history function stores for each session. The larger the number, the more cache is required. This cache is cleared when the session ends.

- **Colors button**   Define colors for specific types of links.

- **Fonts button**   Define a font for sites that do not have a font specified.

- **Languages button**   Specify the language you want the pages displayed in.

- **Accessibility button**   Override the way colors, fonts, and formatting are displayed. If you have a style sheet defined, you can assign that style sheet to each Web site you visit.

5. Click the Security tab (Figure 15-7).

Figure 15-7 Internet Properties Security tab

6. From this tab, you can configure the following options:

- **Select a Web Content Zone to Specify Its Security Settings**   Assign Web sites to various zones and define basic security settings. Each zone has its own security settings that can be modified on the Sites dialog box, accessed by clicking the zone icon and then clicking the Sites button. To add a site to a selected zone, click the Advanced button in the Sites dialog.

- **Security Level for this Zone**   Fine tune the security settings for the selected zone. The security options offered are the same as those in the Advanced tab of the Internet Properties window.

7. Click the Privacy tab (Figure 15-8).

8. On the Privacy tab, you can configure the following options:

- **Settings**   Set a privacy level that defines how your system handles cookies. If you do not want your information shared with other sites, you may want to block all cookies from being stored on your system.

▶ **NOTE**

These settings can affect certain sites that use a secure server, such as banking institutes.

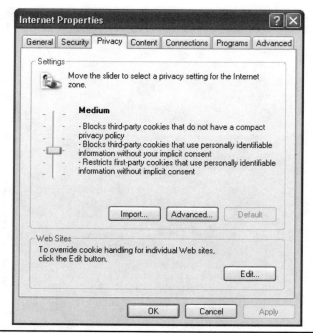

Figure 15-8   Internet Properties Privacy tab

- **Web Sites Edit button**   Block cookies from specific Web sites; click the Edit button to add the blocked Web site's Uniform Resource Locator (URL).

9. Click the Content tab (Figure 15-9).

10. On the Content tab, you can configure the following options:

- **Content Advisor**   Enable the Content Advisor to block sites with adult-related or inappropriate material.

- **Certificates**   Positively identify yourself to other Web sites.

- **Personal Information AutoComplete and My Profile buttons**   Automation features that complete forms in any site you visit by storing information you have entered previously.

11. Click the Connections tab (Figure 15-10).

12. On the Connections tab, you can configure the following options:

- **Setup button**   Establish a new Internet connection.

- **Dial-Up and Virtual Private Network Settings**   Add, remove, or modify a dial-up or VPN connection.

- **Set Default button**   Define one connection as the default if more than one connection is present.

Figure 15-9   Internet Properties Content tab

Figure 15-10   Internet Properties Connections tab

- **LAN Settings button**   Indicate that you're using a proxy server.

13. Click the Programs tab (Figure 15-11).

14. On the Programs tab, you can configure the following options:

    - **Internet Programs**   Specify which program to use for each Internet service.

    - **Reset Web Settings button**   Return the Internet options to the defaults.

    - **Internet Explorer Should Check to See Whether It Is the Default Browser** Make IE the default browser if more than one browser is installed.

15. Click the Advanced tab (Figure 15-12).

16. On the Advanced tab, you can configure the following options:

    - **Settings**   Define what is supported for all Web Sites that do not belong to a zone.

    - **Restore Defaults button**   Restore the Advanced tab options to their original defaults.

17. Click OK to accept your changes.

Figure 15-11   Internet Properties Programs tab

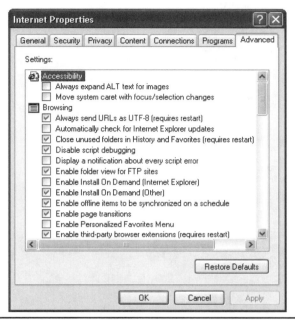

Figure 15-12   Internet Properties Advanced tab

Transferring Internet Settings from One System to Another

If you are upgrading to a new system and want it to use the same Internet settings as your old system, you can easily transfer these settings from one system to another with the Files and Settings Transfer Wizard.

TRY IT   To transfer your Internet settings from the old computer to the new one, use the following steps:

1. On the new system, open the Start menu and choose All Programs | Accessories | System Tools | Files and Settings Transfer Wizard.
2. Click the New Computer option, and then click Next.
3. In the next screen, shown in Figure 15-13, you are given the option of creating a Wizard Disk. If the old system is not running Windows XP, creating a Wizard Disk is recommended. Select the appropriate option and then click Next.

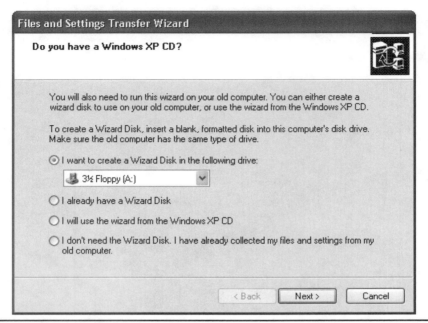

Figure 15-13   Create a Wizard Disk

4. Run the wizard on the old system by selecting Start | Run.

5. In the text box, enter *drive***:\setup**, where *drive* is the drive letter for the drive containing the Wizard Disk.

6. From the menu, select Perform Additional Tasks.

7. On the next menu, select Transfer Files and Settings.

8. If no cable connects the two systems, you need to gather the information from the old system before clicking Next on the new system. If you do have a cable connecting the two systems, go ahead and click Next now. You'll see the screen shown in Figure 15-14.

9. Choose the option that applies, and then click Next.

10. Follow the remaining instructions on the screen.

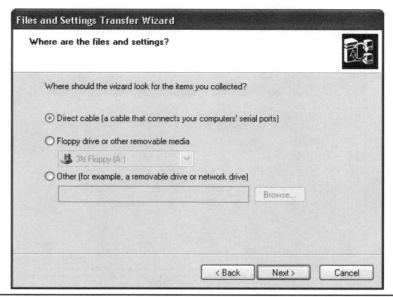

Figure 15-14 Where Are the Files and Settings screen

Hosting a Web Site

Using Windows XP Professional, your system can host one Web and one FTP site. However, the capabilities are limited—only 10 simultaneous TCP connections are permitted. If you require more connections, you need to upgrade to a server edition of Windows.

The Internet Information Services (IIS) capabilities on Windows XP Professional are basically designed for Web developers and not the general public. If the site is to be accessed by a small group of individuals outside the local network, the Web server must use a *static IP* address.

By default, the IIS components required to host a Web site are not installed.

TRY IT To install IIS, use the following steps:

1. From the Control Panel, choose Add or Remove Programs.
2. Click Add/Remove Windows Components to open the Windows Components window.

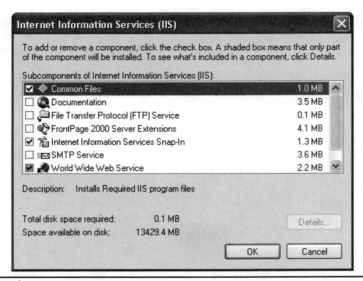

Figure 15-15 IIS subcomponents

3. Check the Internet Information Services (IIS) option, and then click the Details button to open Internet Information Services (IIS) details window, shown in Figure 15-15, that offer various subcomponents.

4. Select one or more of the following subcomponents, and then click OK.

- **Common Files** Installs a core group of files required by other components of IIS. Leave this option checked.

- **Documentation** Copies 9.15MB of help files in the *%SystemRoot%\Help\iishelp* directory. This documentation is helpful if you want to learn more about what IIS has to offer. This option is selected by default. If you already have a documentation set installed on another system, you may want to uncheck this item to save disk space.

- **File Transfer Protocol (FTP) Service** Installs the necessary components for an FTP site.

- **FrontPage 2000 Server Extensions** Installs the necessary server-side program extensions that enable you to use forms, discussion threads, hit counters, and full-text search ability on your Web site. If you use this Web-authoring tool, these extensions also make it easy to publish changes to your site.

- **Internet Information Services Snap-In** Installs this handy tool that lets you administer IIS through the Microsoft Management Console.

- **SMTP Service**   Installs the Simple Mail Transfer Protocol (SMTP) that supports an Internet mail system.

- **World Wide Web Service**   Installs the necessary components that enable you to transfer Web pages over the Internet.

5. Click Next to start the installation. You may be prompted to insert the Windows XP Professional CD-ROM.

6. Follow the instructions in the wizard to complete the installation.

CHAPTER 16

Browsing the Web with Internet Explorer

TIPS IN THIS CHAPTER

Internet Explorer 6.0 is the default Internet browser provided with Windows XP. Its easy-to-use interface and extensive features are intuitive enough for the beginner but advanced enough for those who need more from their everyday browser. For most applications, this browser works just fine as configured by default. To increase your browsing efficiency and security, however, you can modify these default settings.

Not all browsers are created equal. If you have used other browsers such as Netscape, you may have noticed a difference in the way some pages load. Depending on the content, some browsers can be faster than others. Content can also be displayed slightly different on one browser than on another. This is mainly due to a lack of standards when Web sites and browsers first came into being. Seeing a drastic need for a common protocol, the World Wide Web Consortium (W3C) was established in 1994. As most of us know, developing common standards that most developers can agree on is not a light challenge. Through the years, the W3C has made a significant impact in the way browsers and Web pages play together. If you are curious and want to know more about W3C, visit *http://www.w3.org*.

Before W3C, Web developers struggled to get their sites to work with common browsers. Now, most sites conform to the guidelines that W3C established. Once the browsers are designed to conform completely to the W3C standards, it won't be such a challenge to get the browsers to display conforming sites with more consistency. That's the theory, anyway.

Some of the most common browsers include Internet Explorer (IE) and Netscape, both of which can be downloaded and used for free. Other lightweight browsers, such as K-meleon and Netsponder, can also be downloaded for free. If you are into themes, check out NeoPlanet Dune, a simple browser that was inspired by Frank Herbert's *Dune*. Several add-ons can be added to your browser to make them faster or to give them greater functionality.

If you want to go with another browser and want to remove IE, its icons, and Start menu shortcuts, open the Control Panel and choose Add or Remove Programs. Click Add/Remove Windows Components. From the wizard, choose to remove Internet Explorer and then click Next.

Customizing the Interface

If you are a serious Internet surfer and efficiency is the name of the game, Internet Explorer's ability to modify toolbars and menus should peak your interest. You can customize the three optional toolbars in several ways: you can add or remove buttons, add or remove links, nix the Go button, or rearrange the toolbar elements to optimize space. When you are done, you can even lock your configuration to prevent it from becoming the victim of another person's fancy.

Before you can customize your browser window, you must first unlock the toolbar. Right-click any toolbar icon and deselect Lock the Toolbars.

 TIP

You can also click View | Toolbars to view this menu.

Once you unlock the toolbar, you'll notice that a dotted line appears along the left side of the toolbars and the menu bar, as shown in the following illustration. This dotted line is called a *handle*. If you position your cursor over the dotted line, you can drag that toolbar or menu bar to another location. For example, if you wanted to move your links just above your Address bar, you can drag the dotted line to place the links at the desired location.

► *TIP*

Some systems are touchier than others and will not allow you to insert a toolbar between other toolbars. If you have such a system, drag the toolbar to the bottom of the other toolbars, and then move down the toolbar you want to appear at the bottom.

Menu Bar · Toolbar

Handles · · · · · · Address Bar · Links Bar

If you do not want a toolbar to display, click View | Toolbar and deselect the toolbar you want to hide.

► *NOTE*

You can move the menu bar, but you cannot hide it.

Positioning the Toolbars

After you unlock the toolbars, each one displays a dotted-line handle to the left of the bar. Click and drag this handle to reposition the bar where you want it.

To conserve space, you can hide the links bar and place the toolbars beside the menu bar, as shown here:

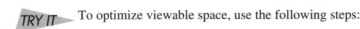 To optimize viewable space, use the following steps:

1. In Internet Explorer, choose View | Toolbars. Then deselect Lock the Toolbars.

2. To hide the Links bar, choose View | Toolbars | Links to remove the check mark.

3. To hide the Go button, right-click Address to the left of the Address bar, and then click Go Button to remove the check mark.

4. Grab the Address bar handle and drag it up next to the menu bar. If you slide it too far left over the menu bar, the menu bar will hide the rightmost menu and display a chevron, indicating that one or more items are hidden.

5. Grab the Toolbar handle and slide it up next to the Address bar. Depending on how many icons you have displayed in your toolbar, you may or may not see a chevron to the right of that toolbar, indicating that one or more items are hidden.

6. When you are happy with the arrangement, lock the toolbar to prevent it from being moved. To do this, choose View | Toolbars | Lock the Toolbars.

To view the hidden items, click the chevrons. This displays a vertical toolbar containing the hidden items. Click the item you want. The items in the toolbar can be repositioned, resized, and modified.

Modifying the Toolbar Buttons

The buttons that display in the toolbar can be added, removed, repositioned, and resized. You can even choose to remove the text that describes each button.

TRY IT   To modify the toolbar, use the following steps:

1. From Internet Explorer, choose View | Toolbars | Customize. The Customize Toolbar dialog box will be displayed:

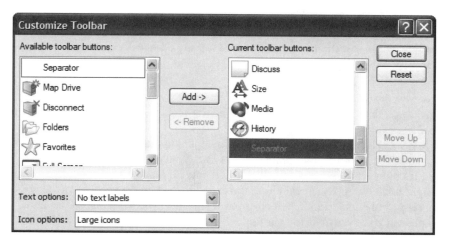

2. To add an icon to the toolbar, select it from the left pane and click the Add button. As a shortcut, you can just double-click the icon you want to add.

3. To remove an icon from the toolbar, select it from the right pane and click Remove. As a shortcut, you can double-click the icon you want to remove.

4. To change the order in which the icons appear in the toolbar, click the icon you want to move in the right pane and drag it to the desired location. You can also select the item and then click the Move Up or Move Down buttons.

▶ *TIP*

The buttons you use most often should be at the top of the list or in another convenient location.

5. Choose from one of the following Text options:
   - **Show Text Labels**   Select this option if you want the icon label to display below the icon.
   - **Selective Text on Right**   Select this option if you want the text to display to the right of the icon for nonintuitive icons only. (Unfortunately, it's not up to you to determine what *is* and what *is not* intuitive.)
   - **No Text Labels**   Select this option if you are an icon genius and can remember what each one does. This option lets you display more icons in a smaller area.

6. Choose from one of the following Icon options:
   - **Small Icons**   Select this option if your eyesight is still optimal and you want to fit more icons in the toolbar at one time.
   - **Large Icons**   Select this option if you do not enjoy squinting to see the icon image.

7. Click Close to save your changes.

Modifying the Links Bar

The Links bar was designed to hold the links of your favorite sites. By default, Microsoft populates this bar with several links. You can change this. The shortcuts in the Links bar are stored, by default, in %UserProfile%\Favorites\Links.

You can remove the default links from this bar by opening the folder in Windows Explorer. Then press CTRL-A to select all of the items, and press DELETE to delete them.

Of course, if you want to remove only one or two links, it may be easier to do it directly from the Links bar. Right-click the link you want to remove, and then choose Delete from the pop-up menu.

After you remove the undesirable links from the Links bar, you are ready to make this tool more useful. Not only can you store links to your favorite sites here, but you can also add links to documents and applications.

TRY IT   To modify the Links bar, use the following steps:

1. To see the Links bar (if it's not already viewable), choose View | Toolbars | Links.
2. Use one of the following techniques to remove any unwanted links from the Links bar:
   - Open the %UserProfile%\Favorites\Links directory and select the links you want to remove. Then press DELETE.
   - Right-click the link in the Links bar, and then choose Delete from the pop-up menu.
3. Use one of the following techniques to add a link to the Links bar:
   - Go to the site that you want to add to the Links bar. Then click the Internet Explorer icon to the left of the address in the Address bar, and drag it to the Links bar.
   - In your Favorites menu, click and drag the link to the Links bar.
   - Click and drag a file or application icon to the Links bar.
   - Copy a shortcut to the %UserProfile%\Favorites\Links directory.

Managing Cookies

Cookies are used by various Web sites to customize or target the information that is displayed as you visit Web sites. Basically, cookies are used to store information about your preferences as a Web user. By default, these cookies are stored in the %UserProfile%\Cookies directory.

You may have noticed how some sites seem to know that you are visiting their site. They may display something like, "Welcome back, Joe," or they may display advertisements for items that you might be interested in purchasing. These sites have saved a cookie in your personal directory that contains your name and links to sites you have visited or searches you have made in the past.

Now that you are frantically searching your memory for all the information you may have provided over the Internet, it is a good time to tell you that you can protect yourself from having this information available to sites that use cookies.

In versions of IE prior to 6.0, it was a major pain to control how cookies were used or controlled on your system. Windows XP has made some improvements in this area. By supporting the Platform for Privacy Preferences (P3P) standard, Windows XP enables IE to filter cookie transactions based on the content and purpose specified in your privacy preferences.

Sites that implement the P3P standard include a special HTML tag that identifies the type of cookies used and their intended purpose. When you access the site, IE compares the site's privacy statement with the preferences defined on your system. Based on the outcome, the cookie is either accepted or rejected. When IE accepts the cookie, it is good for only that session. Once you close the IE window, the cookie is removed.

When it comes to setting privacy preferences, it helps if you understand the lingo. Table 16-1 describes the terms used to identify certain privacy settings and their definitions.

Term	Definition
Compact Privacy Statement	Content in an HTTP header that identifies the content source, purpose, and lifetime of the cookies used by that site. Session cookies are removed when the IE window is closed.
Personally Identifiable Information	Contains your personal contact information including your name, e-mail address, home or work address, and site login credentials (user name and password).
Explicit Consent	Your permission has been granted to enable specific sites to use personally identifiable information.
Implicit Consent	You have not excluded a specific site from using personally identifiable information.
First-party Cookie	Cookies used by the site you are viewing. These cookies are generally used to personalize the site.
Third-party Cookie	Cookies commonly used by vendors that advertise on the site you are viewing. These cookies apply to sites other than the one you are viewing.

Table 16-1 Privacy Lingo

 To set cookie preferences, use the following steps:

1. From Internet Explorer, choose Tools | Internet Options.
2. In the Internet Options dialog box, click the Privacy tab. The options in Figure 16-1 will be displayed.
3. Use the slider to choose one of the following options:
   - **Block All Cookies** Disables the use of cookies.
   - **High** Blocks cookies that do not have a compact privacy policy or that do not identify information specified in your privacy settings.
   - **Medium High** Blocks third-party and first-party cookies that do not have a compact privacy policy or that do not identify information specified in your privacy settings.
   - **Medium** Blocks third-party cookies that do not have a compact privacy policy or that do not identify information specified in your privacy settings. Restricts first-party cookies that do not identify information in your privacy settings.
   - **Low** Blocks third-party cookies that do not have a compact privacy policy or that do not identify information specified in your privacy settings.
   - **Accept All Cookies** Accepts all cookies and allows all saved cookies on your system to be read.

Figure 16-1   Internet Options Privacy tab

4. If you have defined settings on another networked system, you can click the Import button to import those settings to your local system. If you want to modify the settings defined by your slider position, click the Advanced button. To return your privacy settings to the default values, click the Default button.

5. If some sites will not allow you to log on unless their cookies are accepted, you can change your privacy setting to a value other than Block All Cookies or Accept All Cookies and then click the Edit button. The Per Site Privacy Actions dialog box will be displayed, as shown in Figure 16-2.

6. In the Address of Web Site text box, enter the name of the site for which you want to allow or block cookies, and then click the Allow or Block button.

7. To remove a site from the list, select it and then click Remove.

8. Click OK.

9. Click OK again in the Internet Options dialog box to save your changes.

Figure 16-2   Per Site Privacy Actions dialog box

Managing Your Favorite Sites

Everybody has sites they visit on a frequent basis. Internet Explorer makes it easy to add a site to your Favorites list. Visit the site, and then choose Favorites | Add to Favorites. The following dialog box is displayed.

By default, the site title is used for the name of the favorite site you are adding. If necessary, you can change this name to something easier to recognize.

► *TIP*

If you want to add the site to the top of the Favorites list and not worry about the name, press CTRL-D.

IE stores your list of favorites in the %UserProfile%\Favorites directory. As your list of favorites grows, you may notice that IE may hide some of them to conserve space. If you want to see what is hidden, click the down arrow on the bar at the bottom of the menu. IE hides only those sites that have not been visited for awhile. If you want some sites displayed at the top of the list, click and drag those items to the appropriate location.

► *TIP*

If you do not want IE to hide any favorites, you can disable this feature by choosing Tools | Internet Options. Click the Advanced tab, and then uncheck the Enable Personalize Favorites Menu option.

If you want to make a site a little more conveniently available, you can click and drag that favorite to your Links bar. In addition, if you don't mind giving up some of your site display area, you can open the Explorer Bar by choosing View | Explorer Bar | Favorites. This action produces a list that appears to the left of your window, as shown in Figure 16-3.

Figure 16-3   Favorites Explorer Bar

▶ *TIP*

You can also press CTRL-I or click the Favorites button on the standard toolbar to display the Favorites Explorer Bar.

After you have added several sites, you can manage your favorites as you would files in a directory. You can create subfolders, rename shortcut links, move items, and delete items from one simple dialog box. From Internet Explorer, choose Favorites | Organize Favorites to access the Organize Favorites dialog box, shown next.

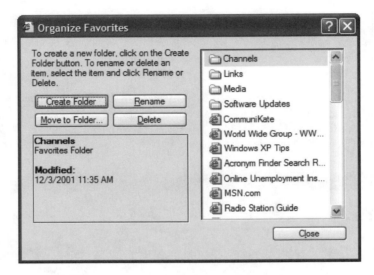

If you want to organize your favorites through Windows Explorer, you can easily access the Favorites folder in the following manner. Press and hold down SHIFT while choosing Favorites | Organize Favorites. This produces the Favorites directory, as shown in Figure 16-4.

Through Windows Explorer, you can manage your favorites just as you manage other files on your system.

TRY IT   To organize your favorites with the Organize Favorites dialog box, use the following steps:

1. From Internet Explorer, choose Favorites | Organize Favorites.

2. In the Favorites directory, click Create Folder to create a new folder.

3. If you want to reposition that folder, drag it to the new location.

4. To move links into a folder, drag the links to that folder. Or select the link and click the Move to Folder button.

5. To rename a link, select it and click the Rename button.

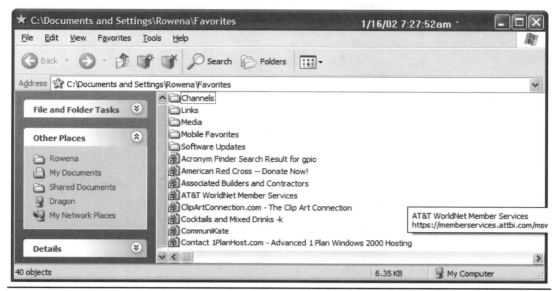

Figure 16-4   Favorites directory in Windows Explorer

6. To remove a link, select it and click the Delete button.

7. If you want to make a link available offline, select the Make Available Offline option. This feature is described later in this chapter.

8. When you are done, click Close.

Making a Favorite Site Available Offline

At times you may need to take your work with you where an Internet connection is unavailable. In these instances, it is convenient to make certain sites available offline. Also, if you are giving a presentation and speed and consistency is of the essence, it makes sense to make a site you intend to use for demonstration purposes available offline. This ensures that you get a quick response from each page you want to display, without having to rely on the speed of the Internet connection.

You can make a site available offline in the following ways:

- From the Add Favorite dialog box, click Make Available Offline. Click the Customize button to launch the Offline Favorite Wizard.

- From the Favorites list, right-click the link and choose Make Available Offline. The Offline Favorite Wizard is automatically launched.

- From the Organize Favorites dialog box, select a link and click Make Available Offline. Click Properties to configure the offline options.

The Offline Favorite Wizard walks you through the steps for defining the type of content you want to store on your local system for this site, as shown in the following illustration.

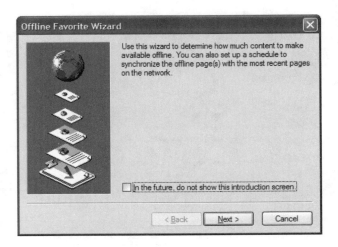

TRY IT   To make your favorite site available offline, use the following steps:

1. From Internet Explorer, add a link to your favorite site.

2. Open the Favorites menu and right-click the link you want to make available offline. From the pop-up menu, select Make Available Offline.

3. When the wizard launches, click Next to advance to the following screen:

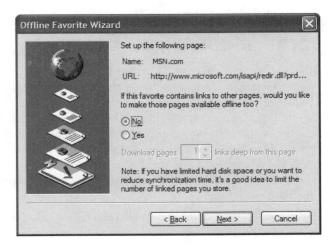

4. If the site you want to make available contains links to other pages in the same site, you may want to include those pages by selecting Yes. If the site connects to several other sites, you may want to specify how deep you want the links to go or you may end up with a large number of files to cache. Click Next.

5. Choose to either synchronize the site manually or on a scheduled basis, and then click Next.

6. If you chose to synchronize the site manually, skip to step 9.

7. If you chose to create a synchronization schedule, the following screen is displayed:

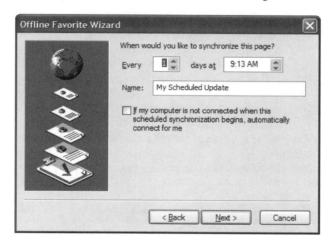

8. Specify how often you want this site synchronized, and then give the schedule a name. Click Next.

9. If the site requires a user name and password, check the Yes, My User Name and Password are... option, and then provide the necessary information.

10. Click Finish.

Searching the Internet

You can locate information about almost anything, providing you know what to search for and how to search for it. Internet Explorer provides the following ways to find the information you need:

- **Search Companion**   This search bar is designed to resemble the one used in Windows Explorer. It is configured by default.

- **Classic Internet Search**   This search bar resembles the classic style used in versions prior to Internet Explorer 6.0.

- **Address Bar**   When you type anything in the Address text box, IE tries converting your request to a URL. If that is unsuccessful, IE can send your request to a search provider.

To invoke the Search Companion, click the Search icon in the toolbar or press CTRL-E. The search bar shown here appears on the left side of your site display window.

In the large text box, type **Find** and then the string you want to search for. For example, if you need to find information about performing arts, you would type **Find performing arts**. Press ENTER to begin the search or click Search.

Once the search has been initiated, you are given the choice to send the search to other search engines, highlight the requested words on the resulting pages, or begin a new search.

If you prefer to use the classic-style search bar, click the Change Preferences link and then choose Change Internet Search Behavior. Click With Classic Internet Search and then select the default search engine you want to use for each initial search.

If the default search engine does not find the site you're interested in, you can click the Automatically Send Your Search to Other Search Engines link. This enables you to select another search engine from a list.

By far the easiest way to find what you are looking for is to enter your search phrase directly in the Address bar, as shown in Figure 16-5.

Internet Explorer will do its best to find a site that fits your entry. If it is unsuccessful, it will forward it to other search engines.

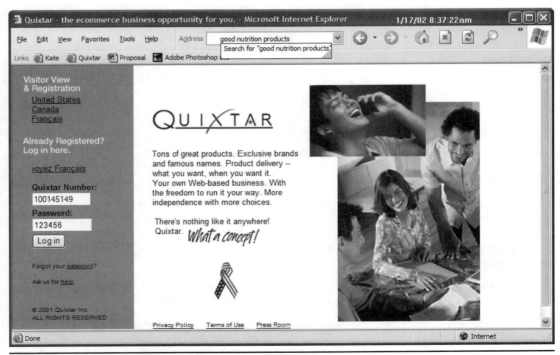

Figure 16-5 Searching from the Address bar

TRY IT   To search the Internet, use the following steps:

1. In the Address bar, type a phrase that describes the type of information you want to find. For example, if you want to find information on good nutrition, type **good nutrition**. If you want to find contractors that do kitchen and bathroom remodeling in Washington, type **kitchen and bath contractors in Washington**.

   IE looks at your phrase and adds the appropriate Boolean logic that most search engines recognize. For example, when you enter **kitchen and bath contractors in Washington**, IE asks the search engines to find sites that contain the following meta tags: *kitchen, bath, contractors*, and *Washington*.

2. Internet Explorer will display links to sites that match your criteria, as shown in Figure 16-6.

3. Click on a link to view its site.

4. If you do not find what you are looking for, you might try another search provider. By default, MSN is queried.

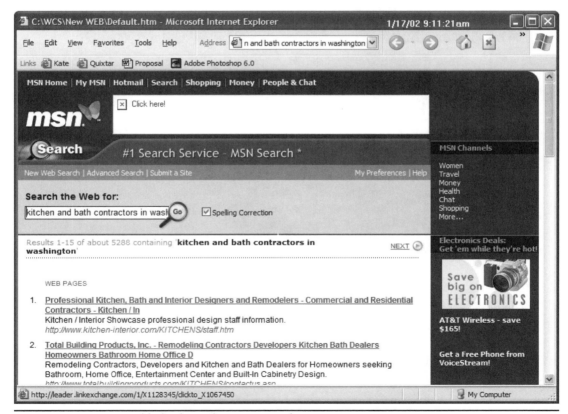

Figure 16-6   Suggested links through Internet Explorer

Changing the Search Assistant's Default Providers

Since not all sites are registered with all search providers, it is sometimes helpful for you to try other search engines to locate exactly what you need. By default, the MSN search engine is used. You can customize the search provider settings to select a different default engine, and to rearrange the order in which each search provider is queried.

TRY IT To modify the search provider settings, use the following steps:

1. Click the Search icon in the toolbar.

2. In the Search bar, click the Customize button. The dialog box shown in Figure 16-7 displays.

3. Choose one of the following options:

   • **Use Search Assistant**   Customize your search settings.

   • **Use One Search Service**   Choose a single search service.

   • **Use Search Companion**   Provides step-by-step instructions that help refine your search.

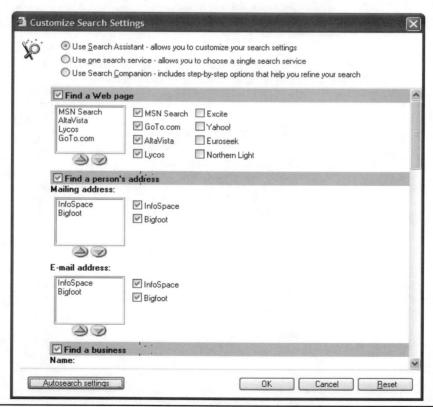

Figure 16-7   Customize Search Settings dialog box

4. The remaining options help you search categories that contain the specified search phrase. For each category, you can select a provider that you want to include in your search. The more providers you include, the slower your search results will be.

5. For each category, you can rearrange the order in which you want to query the selected providers. Choose the provider you want to move, and then click the up or down arrow below the list box.

6. If you use the Address bar more often than not, you can modify how it handles your request by clicking the Autosearch settings button. The Customize Autosearch Settings dialog box displays:

7. From the provider pull-down list, select the search provider you want to use for search phrases entered in the Address bar.

8. From the When searching pull-down list, choose one of the following actions:

   • **Do Not Search from the Address Bar**   Select this option if you do not want IE to translate phrases entered into the Address bar as search phrases.

   • **Just Display Results in the Main Window**   Choose this option if you want to see a list of links that meet your search criteria.

   • **Just Go to the Most Likely Site**   Select this option if you want IE to find the site that contains the most number of instances of words included in your search phrase.

   • **Display Results and Go to the Most Likely Site**   Choose this option if you want the Search bar to display other possible links while the main screen displays the most likely site.

9. Click OK.

 TIP

The Address bar search results option is set in Tools | Internet Options.

Managing the Web Cache

When you visit a site that contains static graphics, IE stores a cache of those site elements in a temporary cache. This cache is used for the current session. When you click the back button, you may notice that the page that took forever to load the first time does not take as long to load the second time. This is because IE will look in the cache for that page before requesting a load from the actual site. The larger your cache, the more information IE can store. This temporary cache is located in the %UserProfile%\Local Settings\Temporary Internet Files directory.

By default, IE reserves 3 percent of your available disk space to store Internet files for each session. If you have a large disk, this should provide more than enough space to store temporary files.

TRY IT To change your temporary cache size, use the following steps:

1. From Internet Explorer, choose Tools | Internet Options.

2. Click the General tab, and then click the Settings button under Temporary Internet Files. The following dialog box displays:

3. Adjust the amount of disk space to use by sliding the slider to the desired value.

4. If you are curious as to what files are in this folder, click the View Files button.

5. Click OK.

CHAPTER 17

Using E-mail and Newsgroups with Outlook Express

TIPS IN THIS CHAPTER

Outlook Express is the e-mail client that is automatically installed with Windows XP. Its snappy interface and user-friendly features make it a great choice for those who do not require a calendar feature or the ability to synchronize files with a mobile device. What it does offer is the ability to set up different identities on systems that have multiple users. Instead of having to switch users, all you need to do is switch identities to quickly view your e-mail messages. These identities can have their own personal address book and have access to a common address book shared by everyone.

Outlook Express also provides a Newsgroup client that lets you access the Internet's vast array of newsgroups from the same application you use to view e-mail messages. Newsgroups provide information on a particular subject. For example, if you're a wine connoisseur, you can receive information on upcoming wine-tasting events or winemaking secrets.

If you have a Hotmail account, Outlook Express conveniently stores your messages in a Hotmail folder. These Hotmail messages can even be worked with offline. When you reconnect to the Internet, the information stored in your Hotmail folder is synchronized with the Hotmail server.

Setting Up Mail Accounts

When you launch Outlook Express for the first time after installing Windows XP, the Internet Connection Wizard launches automatically. This wizard steps you through the process of setting up your first e-mail account. If you want to set up additional accounts, you need to launch the wizard manually. If you have more than one e-mail account, you can have Outlook Express check mail for all accounts or you can create a new identity for each account.

To set up an e-mail account, use the following steps:

1. From Outlook Express, open the Tools menu and select Accounts. The Internet Accounts dialog box will display:

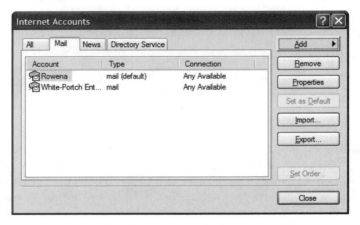

2. In the Internet Accounts dialog box, click the Add button, and choose Mail from the menu that appears. This action opens the Internet Connection Wizard.

3. In the Your Name window, you are given a chance to change the name that is displayed to your recipients. Enter a simple but intuitive name, and then click Next.

4. In the E-mail Internet Address window, enter the e-mail address you want your recipients to use when sending you e-mail, then click Next. The following E-mail Server Names window is displayed:

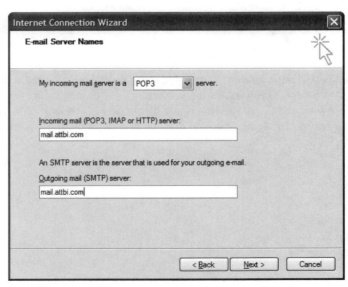

5. From the E-mail Server Names window, choose one of the following mail server options:

- **POP3**   Post Office Protocol 3 is popular with most ISPs. These servers offer access to a single inbox.
- **IMAP**   Internet Message Access Protocol offers access to multiple server-side folders.
- **HTTP**   Hypertext Transfer Protocol is popular with Internet mail servers such as Hotmail.

▶ *NOTE*

Currently, only Hotmail and Exchange Server support HTTP access.

6. Specify your incoming mail server. This field is required for all mail server options.

7. If your mail server uses POP3 or IMAP, you need to specify the outgoing mail server. In most cases, the incoming and outgoing server is the same. Click Next.

8. In the Internet Mail Logon window, enter the account name and password that your ISP gave you or that you have established with your ISP.

9. If you do not want to enter your password each time you open your mail program, check the Remember password option.

10. Click Next, then click Finish.

▶ *TIP*

If you want to change the Account name in the Mail tab of the Internet Accounts dialog box, select the name you want to change, and then click Properties. Enter the name you want to display, and then click OK.

Setting Up News Accounts

Setting up a news account is very similar to setting up a mail account. The only difference is the type of server you specify. Instead of using a POP3 and SMTP server, you specify a Network News Transport Protocol (NNTP) server.

 To set up a news account, use the following steps:

1. From Outlook Express, open the Tools menu and select Accounts.

2. Click the Add button, and choose News from the menu that appears. This will launch the Internet Connection Wizard.

3. In the Your Name window, enter a simple but intuitive name that will be displayed to other users when you post a message. Click Next.

4. In the Internet News E-mail Address window, enter the e-mail address you want newsgroup members to use when sending you e-mail. Click Next.

5. In the Internet News Server Name window, enter the name of your NNTP server.

6. If you need to log on to the NNTP server, check the My News Server Requires Me To Log On option.

7. Click Next, then click Finish.

Setting Up a Directory Service

If you are a domain member, this service provides information about available objects on a domain-based network. This service is not used in a workgroup environment or on standalone systems. This feature uses the Lightweight Directory Access Protocol (LDAP) to find information on other LDAP servers.

With a directory account, you can search for people or businesses on the Internet or in your active directory. Just press CTRL-E or click the Find button in the Outlook Express toolbar.

 To add a directory service, use the following steps:

1. From Outlook Express, open the Tools menu and select Accounts.

2. Click the Add button, and choose Directory Service from the menu that appears. This will launch the Internet Connection Wizard.

3. In the Internet Directory Server Name window, enter the name of the LDAP server you want to access.

4. If you need to log on to the LDAP server, check the My LDAP Server Requires Me To Log On option. Click Next.

5. In the Check E-mail Addresses window, click Yes only if your e-mail service does not check your address book for e-mail messages. Otherwise, this service will slow your performance.

6. Click Next, then click Finish.

Customizing Your Outlook Environment

Outlook Express lets you customize the layout of your Outlook Express environment through one simple dialog box.

 To customize the Outlook Express environment, use the following steps:

1. In Outlook Express, open the View menu and select Layout. The Window Layout Properties dialog box appears, as shown in Figure 17-1.

Figure 17-1   Window Layout Properties dialog box

2. In the Basic section, you can choose to show or hide the screen elements. These screen elements are identified in Figure 17-2.

3. Click the Customize Toolbar button to add, remove, or reposition the Toolbar icons. The Customize Toolbar dialog box displays:

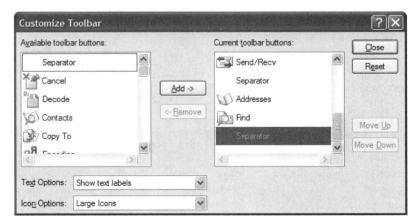

4. To add a button to the toolbar, select it from the left pane, and then click Add. As a shortcut, you can just double-click the button you want to add.

Folder List

Views
Bar →

Outlook
Bar →

Contacts →

Status
Bar →

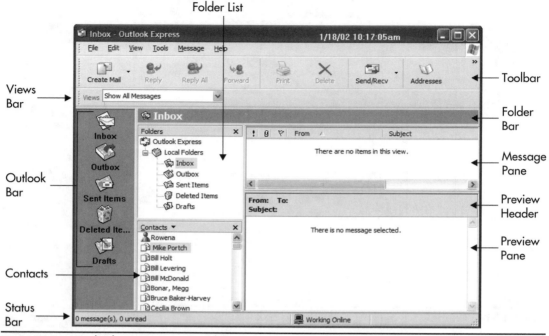

Toolbar

Folder
Bar

Message
Pane

Preview
Header

Preview
Pane

Figure 17-2 Outlook Express screen elements

5. To remove a button from the toolbar, select it from the right pane, then click Remove. As a shortcut, you can just double-click the button you want to remove.

6. To change the order in which the buttons appear in the toolbar, click the button you want to move in the right pane and drag it to the desired location. You can also select the item, and then click the Move Up or Move Down button.

▶ **TIP**

The buttons you use most often should be at the top of the list.

7. Choose from one of the following Text options:

- **Show Text Labels**   Select this option if you want the icon label to display below the icon.

- **Selective Text on Right**   Select this option if you want the text to display to the right of the icon for nonintuitive icons only. Unfortunately, you do not get to determine what is and is not intuitive.

- **No Text Labels**   Select this option if you are an icon genius and can remember what each one does. This option lets you display more icons in a smaller area.

8. Choose from one of the following Icon options:

   • **Small Icons**   Select this option if your eyesight is still optimal and you want to fit more icons in the toolbar at one time.

   • **Large Icons**   Select this option if you do not enjoy squinting to see the icon image.

9. Click Close to save your changes.

10. To view the results of your changes without closing the dialog box, click the Apply button. If you are satisfied with your choices, click OK.

Setting Outlook Options

The options available in the Options dialog box let you define how Outlook Express operates.

 To set common options in Outlook Express, use the following steps:

1. In Outlook Express, open the Tools menu and choose Options. The Options dialog box will appear, as shown in Figure 17-3.

Figure 17-3   Options dialog box

2. Click the General tab. By default, Outlook Express checks for new mail every 30 minutes. If you have a constant connection to the Internet, you may want to change this value to check more frequently, such as every 10 minutes.

3. If you have more than one e-mail program installed, you can make Outlook Express your default e-mail or news handler from the General tab.

▶ *TIP*

You can also check mail immediately by pressing CTRL-M.

4. To minimize dial-up connection time, you can change how Outlook Express behaves when using a phone line to connect to the Internet. By default, the connection setting for If My Computer Is Not Connected at This Time in the General tab is set to Do Not Connect. If you have a dedicated phone line, you may want to change this setting to Connect Only When Not Working Offline. If you are working offline, you don't want the system to waste time trying to establish a nonexistent connection.

5. If your ISP charges you for connection time, you have only one phone line, or the call is not local, you will want to click the Connection tab and choose Hang Up After Sending And Receiving.

6. By default, the formatting option in the Send tab is set to HTML. For most recipients, this format is acceptable. If you have a contact who must have only plain text in a message, you can open that person's record in the address book and configure that record to Send E-mail Using Plain Text Only.

▶ *TIP*

You can also compose new messages in plain text. In the New Message dialog box, choose Format | Plain Text.

7. In the Compose tab, you can choose how you want your message to look, including the font and color.

8. When you are done with your changes, click OK to close the Options dialog box.

Adding Signatures

You can create one or more signatures to include with each e-mail message you compose. These signatures can be created in Outlook Express or in another program such as Microsoft Word. If you create a signature in a separate application from Outlook Express, save the file with either a .txt or .html extension. HTML files give you more flexibility around being creative, but these signatures will only be accepted by recipients who accept HTML e-mail. In general, it's best to create your signature as a simple text file. You can still experiment with fonts and colors, just keep it simple.

Some common signatures include your name, position, and contact information. For example, you could have a signature that resembles the following:

Thank you,
~ Gregg Portch
Watchmen Construction Company, Inc.
(206) 555-3333
wcs@attbi.com
http://www.wcs-inc.net

Another popular addition is to include an inspirational quote. You can be very creative with signatures, but a good rule to follow is to keep them short and simple.

TRY IT   To create a signature, use the following steps:

1. In Outlook Express, open the Tools menu and choose Options.

2. In the Options dialog box that appears, click the Signature tab.

3. Click New to create a new signature in Outlook Express.

4. In the text box, enter the information you want to include in your signature.

5. Select the default signature name in the Signatures pane, then click Rename to give the signature an intuitive name.

6. By default, your signature is added to all outgoing messages. To add them to replies and forwarded messages, click the Advanced button. In the Advanced Signature Settings dialog box, choose the account type you want to add the signature to, then click OK. This will close the Advanced Signature Settings dialog box and return you to the Options dialog box.

7. To use a file for your signature, click the File option in the Edit Signature pane of the Signatures tab, and then click Browse to find the file you want to use.

8. The first signature you create is used by default. If you want to use another signature, select that signature in the Signatures pane, then click the Set As Default button.

9. When you are done, click OK to close the Options dialog box.

Managing Identities

With Outlook Express, multiple users can have separate lists of messages and contacts. If you have several e-mail accounts, you may want to keep the messages for each account in separate folders. This can be done by setting up an identity for each account you want to keep separate.

By default, Outlook Express creates a Main Identity. You can give this identity a more intuitive name and assign a password to an identity to prevent others from accessing it without permission.

Once an identity is created, you can change to that identity by opening the File menu and choosing Switch Identity. Select the Identity you want to open. Once that identity is open, you can set up the appropriate e-mail account for that identity and perform customizations.

 TIP

If you have more than one identity and would like to consolidate them, you can use the Import command to import the folder contents from one identity to another. Open the identity to which you want to import another identity's folders. Open the File menu and choose Import Messages | Microsoft Outlook Express 6. Select the identity for the files you want to import. When you are done, you can delete the identity you no longer need.

TRY IT   To manage identities, use the following steps:

1. In Outlook Express, open the File menu and choose Identities | Manage Identities. The Manage Identities dialog box appears, as shown in Figure 17-4. From this dialog box, you can add, delete, and modify identities.
2. Click New to add a new identity. In the New Identity dialog box that appears, type a name for the identity, and then click OK to return to the Manage Identities dialog box.

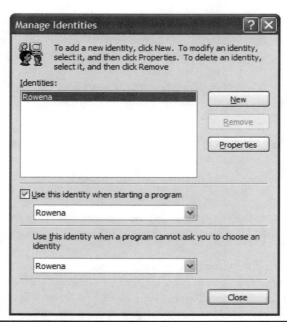

Figure 17-4   Manage Identities dialog box

3. To modify the name of an existing identity, select the identity name, and then click Properties. The Identity Properties dialog box appears. Make your changes, and then click OK to close this dialog box and return to the Manage Identities dialog box.

4. To remove an identity, select the identity name and then click Remove.

5. If you want to specify a default identity, check the Use This Identity When Starting a Program option, and then choose the identity you want to use from the pull-down list.

6. From the next pull-down list, choose the identity you want to use by default if an application cannot ask you to choose an identity.

7. When you have finished making your choices, click Close.

Managing Contacts

Outlook Express uses the Windows Address Book (WAB) to store, look up, and manage your contact information. The Windows Address Book is not really part of Outlook Express, it is just tightly integrated with it, along with other Windows applications such as fax clients, teleconferencing software, and Microsoft Office applications.

There are several ways to open the Windows Address Book:

- If Outlook Express is open, click on the Addresses icon in the toolbar or choose Tools I Address Book.
- Open the Start menu and choose All Programs I Accessories I Address Book.
- Open the Run command and enter **wab**.

▶ *TIP*

When you start the address book from the Run command, you are able to see the address books of other identities.

The Address Book window is displayed, as shown in Figure 17-5.

Choose View I Folders And Groups to display the folder bar on the left. If you want to categorize your contacts, you can create a folder for each category you want to store, such as Business, Family, Personal, and Leads. To create a folder, choose File I New Folder or click the New icon and choose New Folder. In the Properties dialog box, enter a name for the folder, and then click OK. Hold the CTRL key down while selecting the names you want to store in the folder you have created. When you are done selecting all of the names in a given category, click and drag one of the selected names to the desired folder; the other names you have selected will follow.

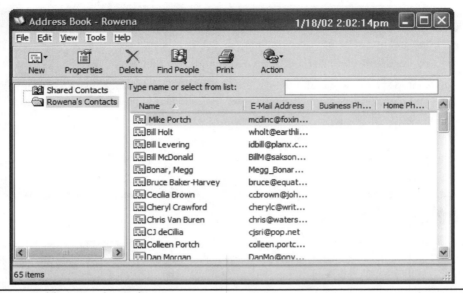

Figure 17-5 Address Book window

Groups enable you to store several contacts into a group. This is particularly useful when you e-mail the same group of people regarding an event. For example, you might be trying to plan a family reunion with more than 30 family members, all of whom have different e-mail addresses and who live all over the United States. You could create a group called Family and include the addresses of each family member. When you need to e-mail the family, just enter the group name "Family" in the address text box.

To create a group, click the New icon and choose New Group, or choose File | New Group. The Properties dialog box shown in Figure 17-6 is displayed.

Type a name for your new group, and then begin to add members. If the members you want to add are already in your address book, click Select Members. The Select Group Members dialog box will appear, where you can select the members you want to add. If you need to add a new contact to the group and to your address book, click New Contact. The Properties dialog box will appear, where you can add the new contact's information. When you are done, click OK to close the Properties dialog box, and then click OK in the Select Group Members dialog box to return to the Properties dialog box. If you want to add a contact to the group but not to your address book, enter the name in the Name text box, and then enter the e-mail address.

TRY IT To organize your contacts, use the following steps:

1. Open the Start menu and choose Run. In the text box, type **wab**, and then press ENTER. When you launch the address book in this manner, it enables you to see the address book of all identities.

2. If you do not see the Folders bar, click View | Folders And Groups. Select the name of the identity folder under which you want to create a new folder.

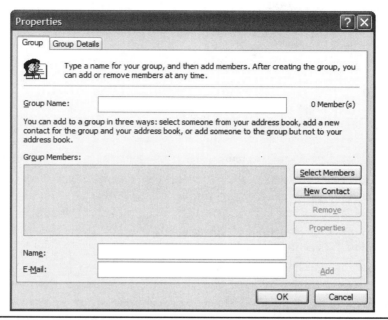

Figure 17-6   Properties dialog box

3. Click the New icon in the toolbar and choose New Folder.

4. Enter a name for the folder, and then click OK.

5. Hold down your CTRL key and select the contact names you want to move to the new folder. When you are done, click and drag those names to the folder you have created.

6. Click the New icon in the toolbar and choose New Group.

7. Enter a name for the group, and then add the members for that group.

8. When you are done, click OK.

Maintaining Your Mailbox

By default, Outlook Express is configured to compress your messages automatically. If you use your e-mail regularly, the folders in your mailbox can fill up rather quickly. It is highly recommended that you remove deleted messages on a regular basis. Outlook Express enables you to automate this task to some extent.

TRY IT To configure maintenance options, use the following steps:

1. In Outlook Express, click Tools | Options. The Options dialog box appears.

2. Click the Maintenance tab.

3. If necessary, you can specify how often Outlook Express compacts your folders by changing the *nnn* value in Compact Messages When There Is *nnn* Percent Wasted Space. Compacting your folders enables you to store more information in less space.

4. Click the Clean Up Now button to immediately apply the options you have defined.

5. To change the location of where Outlook Express stores your folder information, click the Store Folder button. This option is handy when you are running out of disk space and want to store your mail folders on another drive.

6. If you need to track mail transactions, you can build a log file for different account types. In the Troubleshooting pane, check mark the type of log file(s) you want to build.

7. When you are done, click OK.

Integrating the Address Book with Outlook

If you have been using Outlook Express and have recently loaded Outlook (an upgraded e-mail program that incorporates calendar scheduling and synchronization with mobile devices), there is an undocumented way in which you can integrate the address book with Outlook contacts. Implementing this feature was much easier in earlier versions. In Windows XP, however, you must edit the registry.

Once they are integrated, any changes made to one address book will be reflected in the other. This saves you from having to make the same change twice. The cost of this convenience, though, may not be worth it if you are using identities. When the address books are integrated, only your Outlook contacts will show in the folders list. Your shared and personal address books will not be displayed.

TRY IT To integrate your address book with Outlook contacts, use the following steps:

1. Open the Start menu and click Run. In the text box, enter **regedit**.

2. Navigate to HKEY_LOCAL_MACHINE\Software\Microsoft\WAB\WAB4.

3. Right-click in a blank area in the right pane, and then choose New | DWORD Value.

4. Name this value **UseOutlook**, and then double-click on it.

5. Set the value to 1, and then click OK. Setting this value to 1 enables this feature. To disable it and return to the standard address book mode, change this value to 0 or delete it.

Identifying Unknown Senders

Rude as it may seem, we have all received e-mail messages from unknown sources. If you receive mail from an address that is not included in your address book, you can use the Find People function to search an LDAP server for the registered owner of that address.

TRY IT To identify an unknown sender, use the following steps:

1. Copy the e-mail address to the Clipboard by selecting it and pressing CTRL-C.
2. Press CTRL-E to open the Find people dialog box.
3. From the Look In list, select an LDAP server, and then click inside the E-Mail text box.
4. Paste the address in the E-Mail box by pressing CTRL-V.
5. Click Find Now then wait patiently for the results.

Using Electronic Business Cards

This feature lets you exchange electronic business cards with other people through e-mail. You can also have this e-business card included in all outgoing messages. To store another person's e-business card, double-click the .vcf file attached to the e-mail message. It opens as an address book record.

TRY IT To create and send an electronic business card, use the following steps:

1. Open the address book and click the New icon, or choose File | New Contact. The Properties dialog box appears.
2. Enter the information you want to include in your business card, and then click OK.
3. In the Address Book dialog box, click File | Export | Business Card (vCard). The Export dialog box appears.
4. Give the file a name, then click Save. By default, the file is saved under %UserProfile%\My Documents.
5. Close the Address Book dialog box by pressing ESC.
6. You can either attach this file to an individual e-mail message or apply it to all outgoing messages. To apply it to all outgoing messages, Click Tools | Options, and then click the Compose tab. In the Business Cards pane, check the type of messages you want to include your business card file with, and then click the arrow to select the business card you want to include from the pull-down list.

Protecting Your System from Viruses

The quickest way to obtain a virus is by opening an e-mail attachment. If you receive an e-mail attachment from an unknown source, always save the attachment to your disk, then scan the saved file for viruses before opening it. As an alternative, you can protect yourself by enabling the attachment security option.

 To set up security for attached files, use the following steps:

1. In Outlook Express, open the Tools menu and choose Options.
2. In the Options dialog box, click the Security tab.
3. Check the option that reads "Do not allow attachments to be saved or opened that could potentially be a virus." Click OK.

Establishing Rules

Rules give you the ability to manage mail messages that meet specified criteria. For example, you might want to send all mail that comes from a particular source to a specific directory or forward it to a team of individuals. You can also choose to automatically reply to certain messages, or delete messages without ever having to see them. This is particularly useful when junk mail inundates your mailbox.

 To create a new rule, use the following steps:

1. From Outlook Express, open the Tools menu and choose Message Rules | Mail. The New Mail Rule dialog box is displayed, as shown in Figure 17-7.
2. Select one or more conditions for your rule.
3. Select one or more actions you want Outlook Express to take when one or more of the above conditions are met.
4. In the Rule Description area, click on the blue links to enter the specifics. By default, all of the conditions must apply. You can change the operators from "and" to "or" as needed.
5. Enter a name for the rule so that it is easily identifiable, then click OK.

 TIP

If you receive a message and want to create a new rule that applies to future messages that are similar, select the message and choose Message | Create Rule From Message.

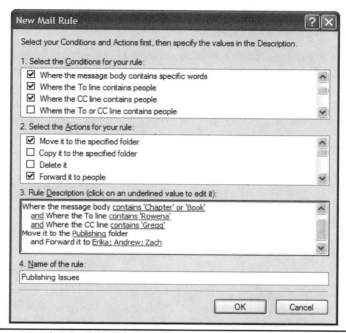

Figure 17-7   The New Mail Rule dialog box

Blocking Unwanted Mail

If you find your inbox being inundated with junk mail or messages from a person you would just prefer to ignore, Outlook Express offers a blocking feature. Once a sender is blocked, any messages they send to you will be placed directly into your Deleted folder.

TRY IT To block unwanted mail, use the following steps:

1. Select the message, and then choose Message | Block Sender.

2. In the confirmation box, click Yes to accept your decision.

3. If you later choose to allow the sender to send you messages, open the Tools menu and chose Message Rules | Blocked Senders List. Select the lucky sender, and then click Remove.

Setting Up a Newsgroup

Newsgroups function in much the same way as server-based mail systems in that they are accessible through the Internet. The messages reside on the server and, in most cases, you are given the choice as to what you want to download. Most people who subscribe to newsgroups do not want to view all of the articles that get posted for a given topic. Once you set your newsgroups up, you will want to change their properties to tailor how they manage news postings on your system.

   To set up a newsgroup, use the following steps:

1. In Outlook Express, open the Tools menu and choose Accounts. The Internet Accounts dialog box appears.

2. Click Add and choose News to launch the Internet Connection Wizard.

3. In the first wizard dialog box, enter the name you want others to see when you respond to a post. Click Next.

4. Enter your e-mail address you want others to use when sending you a post. Click Next.

5. Enter the name of your news server. If you do not have one, you can access Microsoft's news server by entering **msnews.microsoft.com**. This server does not require you to log on. If you entered another news server that does require a logon, check the My News Server Requires Me To Log On option. Click Next.

6. Click Finish to complete and close the wizard, and then click Close in the Internet Accounts dialog box to close that window.

7. When asked if you would like to download newsgroups from the news server you added, click Yes. The Newsgroup Subscriptions dialog box will display:

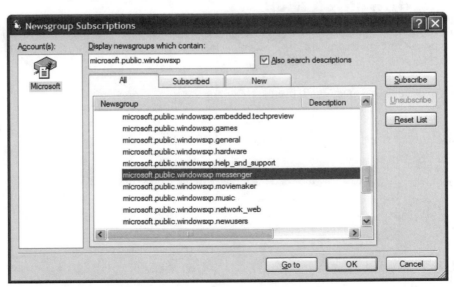

8. To view newsgroups that only pertain to Windows XP, enter **Microsoft.public.windowsxp** in the text box.

9. Select the newsgroups you want to subscribe to, and then click Subscribe. If you want to select more than one newsgroup, hold down your CTRL key while making your selections. The groups you have subscribed to will be marked with a subscription icon. If you later change your mind, you can select those newsgroups and click Unsubscribe.

10. From here, you can either select a newsgroup in the Subscribed tab and click Go To or you can click OK to exit the Newsgroup Subscriptions dialog box.

Downloading New Newsgroup Messages

There are several ways to read newsgroup messages, and some are more efficient than others. Unless you have an extremely fast connection and don't mind storing articles you may never read, it is recommended that you set your newsgroup server to only download the headers rather than the entire post.

If you set Outlook Express to download the entire message when viewed in the preview pane, you will be able to view the articles of interest very quickly. You can also choose to hide previously read messages and view any replies to a selected post.

 To read your newsgroup posts efficiently, use the following steps:

1. In Outlook Express, click on the newsgroup server. The window shown in Figure 17-8 will display.

2. Right-click a newsgroup, and choose Synchronization Settings | Headers Only. This setting affects all of the newsgroups under the selected server.

3. Double-click a newsgroup, and then choose View | Current View. In the menu, click Hide Read Messages.

4. Open the Tools menu and choose Options. In the Options dialog box that appears, click the Read tab and make certain the "Automatically download message when viewing in the Preview Pane" option is checked. Click OK to close the Options dialog box.

▶ *TIP*

To view the replies for a given post, click the plus sign beside the post.

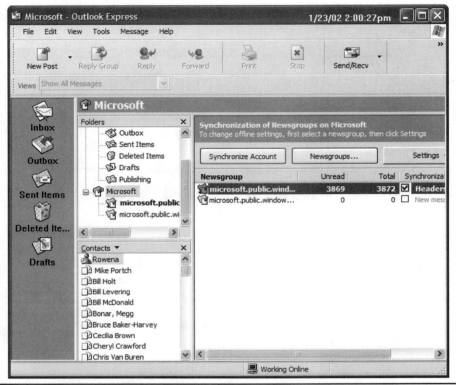

Figure 17-8 Synchronization of newsgroups

Preserving Newsgroup Posts

When you synchronize with the newsgroup server, any posts that have been deleted on that server will also be removed from your local system. If you want to save a particular post for future reading, you can save it as a file. To read the message later, double-click it from Windows Explorer.

TRY IT   To save newsgroup posts, use the following steps:

1. In the newsgroup folder list, select the post you want to save, and then click File | Save As.
2. Navigate to the desired location and give the .nws file an intuitive name, such as champagne-info.nws.
3. Click OK.

► *TIP*

You can also click and drag the message to a folder. Since these files are plain text files, you can change the file extension to .txt. This enables you to open the message in any text editor without having to open Outlook Express.

Viewing Posts and Replies

If you subscribe to a newsgroup, you will eventually want to create a post and reply to other posts. Outlook Express makes this very easy to do.

 To create a post and reply to posts, use the following steps:

1. Select the newsgroup you want to view posts for.
2. In the newsgroup preview pane, double-click on the newsgroup to view a list of posts.
3. When you submit a post, your name will appear in the From column. Click the plus sign to the left of the post to view replies.
4. To create a new post, click the New Post button.
5. To reply to a post, select the post from the right pane, then click Reply Group to post the reply to all members, or click Reply to reply only to the person who created the post.

CHAPTER 18

Using MSN Explorer and Windows Messenger

TIPS IN THIS CHAPTER

If you've ever signed up with Yahoo.com and liked the way they had made your e-mail, local weather, favorite links, and even some sharable Web directories easily accessible from one convenient location, you are going to love MSN Explorer. This new all-in-one software makes it easy to read your e-mail, talk to your online buddies, enjoy online music and video, and surf the Web. If you don't already have an Internet Service Provider (ISP), MSN Explorer offers that service as well.

MSN Explorer employs the following Microsoft Internet technologies:

- Hotmail
- Internet Explorer
- Windows Messenger
- Windows Media Player

MSN Explorer offers some smart features such as AutoComplete, a function that remembers your previous entries for Web addresses, e-mail names, and passwords. Advanced search tools correct mistyped words and provides other helpful features that help you find more information with a lot less searching.

The Automatic Update feature notifies you when there are updates that pertain to your system. These updates can be easily installed with a click of your mouse button.

MSN Explorer offers greater possibilities than Internet Explorer, including a new Web browser. When you sign into MSN Explorer, it will always open first when you launch Internet Explorer. Figure 18-1 shows the interface offered by MSN Explorer.

Windows Messenger was formerly known as MSN Messenger. This interesting chat program offers more than just the ability to hold multiple conversations with other users on the Internet, it offers tools that let you hold meetings online and request technical assistance from a support representative. If the person you are in session with is broadcasting a live video, you can view that video from within the Messenger window. Live audio is also supported.

If you have a Hotmail account, Windows Messenger alerts you when new messages arrive. You can even be notified about calendar events, stock price changes, and other events.

▶ *TIP*

Messenger Plus, available from http://www.patchou.com/msgplus/, *provides a variety of platform development tools that enable automatic logging of instant messages and some interface customizations. You can even play Internet games with other members without having to know their IP address.*

To use Windows Messenger, you need to have the following:

- Internet access with a 28.8Kbps or better connection
- A .NET Passport
- Optional sound card with a speaker, microphone, or headset, if you intend to use the audio features
- Optional Web camera, if you intend to use the video features

Figure 18-1 MSN Explorer browser window

▶ *NOTE*

In previous Passport accounts, you needed to have a Hotmail, MSN, or Passport e-mail address. The new version of Passport supports all e-mail addresses.

If you are using Windows XP's Internet firewall to protect your network, you will not have any troubles with Windows Messenger. These programs are designed to work with dynamic port assignments and both support Universal Plug and Play (UPnP).

Some routers purchased before the end of 2001 do not support UPnP. If you are using such a router, you will be unable to use the audio and video features in Windows Messenger. One of the advantages of using UPnP is it enables systems to detect devices on another network and work with them in a peer-to-peer fashion.

Windows Messenger uses the following ports:

- **Instant messaging** These TCP connections use port 1863 when it's available. If it is not available, Windows Messenger uses the same port as the Web browser. If it resorts to this, you will only be able to use Windows Messenger for instant messaging, not voice or video. If you are using a proxy server, open the Tools menu in Windows Messenger and choose Options. Click the Connection tab and provide the information for your specific proxy server.

- **File transfer** Up to ten simultaneous connections are supported on each port. These TCP connections use ports 6891 through 6900. If you are using an Internet connection firewall, you need to add rules to open these ports.

- **Whiteboard and application sharing** These applications use TCP connections to port 1503.

- **Voice and video** These features use ports that are dynamically assigned. They require UPnP support to get to an IP address on the local network.

Using MSN Explorer

MSN Explorer enables you to access your Hotmail accounts and other popular Microsoft Internet tools. When you click Start | All Programs | MSN Explorer for the first time, the MSN Installation Wizard will automatically launch. As you go through this wizard, you will be asked a series of questions which determine how the wizard will progress. If you simply want to use the MSN Explorer browser and not obtain a server-based e-mail account, the process is simple and fairly short.

This browser works in much the same way as Internet Explorer, only faster. Also, you are able to customize the home page to display your favorite topics, including games, news, shopping, and travel. If you don't like the layout, you can change that as well, even the colors. The interface for this browser is so simple and intuitive, even a beginner will be able to easily navigate through the customization options and browse the Web like a true expert.

TRY IT To install MSN Explorer, use the following steps:

1. Open the Start menu and choose All Programs | MSN Explorer.
2. The following confirmation dialog box will display:

3. Answer Yes if you want to use all of the features this browser interface has to offer. In many instances, it offers a faster response than Internet Explorer. If you prefer to use Internet Explorer over MSN Explorer, but still want to launch MSN Explorer when needed, answer No.
4. Read the Welcome dialog box, then click Continue.

5. In the Please Tell Us Your Location dialog box, click the DOWN ARROW to select the country or region where your system resides, then click Continue.

6. In the Do You Want MSN Internet Access dialog box, choose one of the following options, then click Continue:

    • Yes, I would like to sign up for MSN Internet Access and get a new MSN e-mail address.

    • Yes, I would like to sign up for MSN Internet Access but keep my existing e-mail address.

    • No, I already have Internet Access.

7. Depending on your choice in step 6, various dialog boxes will be displayed. Follow the instructions on the screen to continue.

8. When you are done entering your information, click Finish to complete the process. The MSN Explorer window opens with the default settings, most of which can be customized.

Using Windows Messenger with a VPN Connection

In some cases, you may have problems using Windows Messenger through a virtual private network (VPN) connection. This occurs when the VPN connection attempts to use the default gateway on the remote network for Internet connections while the VPN connection is active. This type of setup is common in corporate environments.

To fix this problem, you can disable the Use Default Gateway On Remote Network option in the TCP/IP Advanced Settings dialog box.

 To disable the Use Default Gateway On Remote Network option, use the following steps:

1. Log on to the system that is establishing the VPN connection. Open the Control Panel and click Network And Internet Connections.

2. Click Network Connections.

3. Right-click the VPN connection, then choose Properties from the pop-up menu.

4. Click the Networking tab. Select Internet Protocol (TCP/IP), then click the Properties button.

5. Click the Advanced tab in the Internet Protocol (TCP/IP) Properties dialog box.

6. In the General tab of the Advanced TCP/IP Settings dialog box, uncheck the Use Default Gateway On Remote Network option, then click OK.

Setting Up Windows Messenger

The first time you launch Windows Messenger, you will be prompted to create a Passport account. This account is required to use the Windows Messenger. Follow the prompts in the .NET Passport Wizard to create your account. Once you verify your e-mail address, you will be able to customize how your Windows Messenger operates.

▶ *NOTE*

You will not be able to customize your Windows Messenger interface until you verify your e-mail address. The verification e-mail may not be sent to you until the next day. Once you receive it, all you need to do is click the verification link in the body of the e-mail message.

By default, Windows Messenger is set to start up each time you log on to your system. The icon appears in the notification area of your status bar. If you do not have a .NET Passport account and do not intend to create one, you can stop Windows Messenger from trying to start each time you log on by changing the following options:

- In Outlook Express, choose Tools | Options. In the General tab, uncheck the Automatically Log On To Windows Messenger option. Click OK, then choose View | Layout. Make certain that Contacts is not checked.

- If you have a .NET Passport account, you can stop Windows Messenger from starting by opening the Windows Messenger window and choosing Tools | Options. Click the Preferences tab and uncheck the following options:

  - Run this program when Windows starts.

  - Allow this program to run in the background.

TRY IT   To set Windows Messenger options, use the following steps:

1. After you have verified your e-mail address, you can customize your Windows Messenger options. Open the Windows Messenger window and choose Tools | Options.

2. The Options dialog box opens. In the Personal tab, you can define the following options:

- **Type your name as you want other users to see it**   This name is what users will see when you sign on and when you engage in instant messaging sessions. By default, your e-mail user name is used.

- **My Message Text**   Click the Change Font button to change the font style, size, and color of the text you enter in the instant messaging window.

- **Show graphics (emoticons) in instant messages**   Check this option if you want to be able to include these emotion icons in your instant messages. If you deselect this option, the emoticons toolbar will not be displayed in your instant message windows.

3. In the Phone tab, you can define the following options:

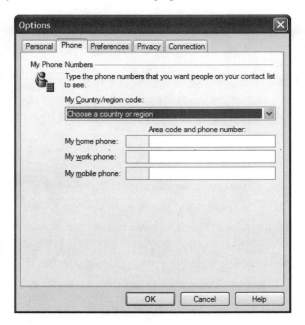

- **My Country/region code**   From this pull-down list, select the country or region in which your system resides.

- **My home phone**   If you want the people on your contacts list to see your home phone number, enter it in this text box.

- **My work phone**   If you want the people on your contacts list to see your work phone number, enter it in this text box.

- **My mobile phone**   If you want the people on your contacts list to see your mobile phone number, enter it in this text box.

4. In the Preferences tab, you can define the following options:

- **Run this program when Windows starts**   Check this option if you want Windows Messenger to automatically start when you start Windows and log on to the system. If you have this option checked and do not have a .NET Passport account, you will be prompted to create one each time you log on to your system.

- **Allow this program to run in the background**   Check this option if you want this program to run in the background. This option coincides with the one above it.

- **Show me as "Away" when I'm inactive for *nnn* minutes**   Check this option if you want your status to change to Away when your system has been idle for the specified amount of time.

- **Display alerts when contacts come online**   Check this option if you want to be alerted when one of the contacts in your contacts list becomes active.

- **Display alerts when an instant message is received**   Check this option if you want to be alerted when a person sends you an instant message.

- **Display alerts when e-mail is received**   Check this option if you have a Hotmail or MSN e-mail account and want to be alerted when a new message arrives.

- **Play sound when contacts sign in or send a message**   Check this option if you want to hear a sound each time one of your contacts signs in or sends you an instant message. This option can work with the alert system or independently. To change the default sounds, click the Sounds button.

- **Files received from other users will be put in this folder**   By default, all files sent by other users are stored in your %UserProfile%\My Documents folder. If this is unacceptable, you can change this location by entering a new one in the text box or clicking Browse to select a new location.

5. In the Privacy tab, you can define the following options:

- **My Allow List**   This list displays the names of the users who can see your online status and send you instant messages.

- **My Block List**   This list displays the names of the users who cannot see your online status or send you messages.

▶ *TIP*

If the listing All Other Users is placed in your block list, only the individuals in your allow list can contact you. If All Other Users is placed in your allow list, others can chat with you without you needing to add them to your allow list.

- **Which users have added me to their contact lists?**   Click the View button to see if the contacts you have added to your list have added you to their lists yet.

- **Alert me when other users add me to their contact lists**   Check this option if you want to be alerted when a contact you have added to your list adds you to their list.

- **Always ask me for my password when checking Hotmail or opening other .NET Passport-enabled Web pages**   Check this option if you want to maintain a level of security around your e-mail and other Passport-enabled Web sites. Checking this option could keep unauthorized users from viewing sensitive information.

- **This is a shared computer so don't display my tabs** Check this option if you do not want other users to be able to change your option settings.

6. In the Connection tab, you can define the following options:

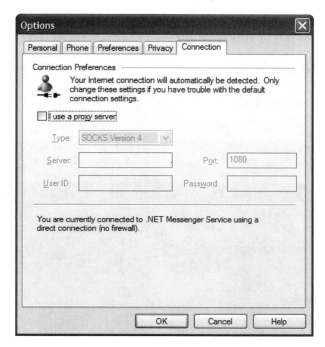

- **I use a proxy server** Check this option if you are using a proxy server to access the Internet.

- **Type** If you check the proxy server option, you need to select the type of proxy you are using. Choose one of the following:
  - HTTP Proxy
  - SOCKS Version 4
  - SOCKS Version 5

- **Server** Enter the name of the proxy server.

- **User ID** Enter the user ID required to log on to the proxy server.

- **Password** Enter the password required to log on to the proxy server.

- **Port** This value changes depending on the type of proxy server you are using. In most cases, this value should not have to be changed.

7. When you are done defining your options, click OK.

Adding Buddies to Your Contacts List

Unlike other instant messaging applications, Windows Messenger takes your privacy into account when it comes to who can and cannot contact you. When someone adds you to their contacts list, you are notified and given the option to allow this individual to contact you or block them from seeing your status or sending you future messages. Once you have added them to your contacts list, you can engage in an instant message session with that person. Buddies are shown in the Windows Messenger window, including their status, as shown in Figure 18-2.

   To add a new contact, use the following steps:

1. Open the Windows Messenger window. Click the Add A Contact link at the bottom of the window, under the I Want To... section. The Add A Contact dialog box will be displayed:

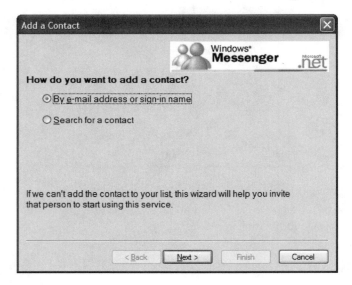

2. Choose one of the following options:

   - **By e-mail address or sign-in name**   Check this option if you know the person's e-mail address. If you choose this option, enter the person's e-mail address, then click Next.

   - **Search for a contact**   Check this option if you want to search for a contact who could have an e-mail address at Hotmail or in your address book. If you choose this option, enter the search criteria, then click Next.

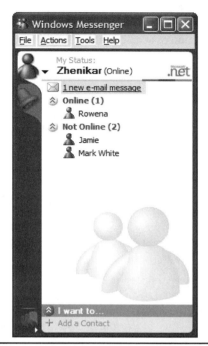

Figure 18-2 Windows Messenger window

3. If you have entered a correct e-mail address, the following dialog box will be displayed:

4. From this dialog box, you have a few options:

- Click the Send E-mail button to send the new contact a link that enables them to download Windows Messenger for free.
- Click Next to add another contact.
- Click Finish to close the Add A Contact dialog box.

Making Voice and Video Calls

In the not-so-distant past, voice over the Internet was not an attractive alternative to using the phone. Today, however, the following technology improvements make it possible to hold a decent conversation with little or no degradation in quality:

- Voice delays can be as short as 70 milliseconds, which is hardly noticeable. If you connect through a satellite, you could notice a bit more of a delay.
- Windows Messenger takes your connection into account when determining the best voice codecs to employ. Codecs are used to code and decode signals traversing the Internet. If you have a fast LAN or broadband connection, Windows Messenger uses codecs that provide telephone-like quality. The quality of the line decides the bit rate that Windows Messenger uses. This is all done automatically.
- The acoustic echo cancellation feature lets you use an ordinary microphone and speakers instead of a headset.

► **NOTE**

To place voice calls over the Internet, the firewall or router that protects your system must support UPnP.

Before you initiate your first voice or video call, you should run the Audio and Video Tuning Wizard from the Windows Messenger window. Choose Tools | Audio Tuning Wizard. This wizard, shown in Figure 18-3, should be run each time you install a new camera, microphone, speakers, or headset.

► **NOTE**

If you have a Web camera installed on your system, choose Tools | Audio and Video Tuning Wizard.

The procedure for placing a video call is similar to placing an audio call, only you choose to broadcast a video signal.

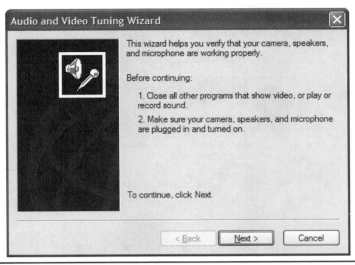

Figure 18-3   Audio and Video Tuning Wizard

TRY IT   To place a voice call, use the following steps:

1. From Windows Messenger, double-click the user you want to converse with. Click the Voice or Start Talking tab to send the invitation, as shown in the following illustration:

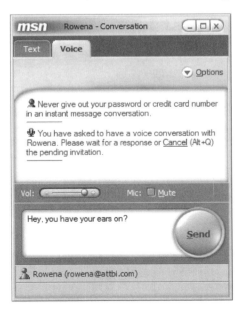

2. The following dialog box will display on the other person's screen, asking if they would like to accept your invitation. All they have to do at this point is click the Voice tab to accept the call.

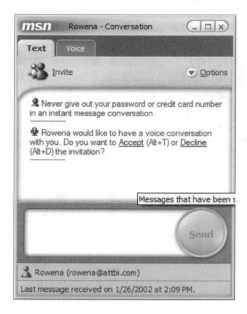

3. Begin your conversation. When you are done, close the window to disconnect.

Sending and Receiving Files

In many ways, sending and receiving files through Windows Messenger is better than sending e-mail attachments. Some of the advantages include:

- Some e-mail programs do not accept certain file types. Windows Messenger accepts all files.
- When you attach a file to an e-mail, a copy is stored in your Sent folder or on your mail server. When you send a file through Windows Messenger, the file that is stored on your local system is copied to the recipient's system. No copy is stored in your Sent folder or on the server.
- Some e-mail systems limit the size an attachment can be. Windows Messenger has no limitations for file size.

▶ *WARNING*

Windows Messenger does not check for possible viruses. Make certain you know the source of a file before accepting it.

▶ *NOTE*

You cannot send a file in a session that includes more than two people (counting yourself).

Up to ten files can be transferred at a time. If one system is behind a firewall, you can send files through Windows Messenger, but you must first configure your Internet connection firewall to open the right ports. If both systems are behind firewalls, you will need to configure both sides to open the appropriate ports or the file transfer will fail.

 To configure your Internet connection firewall to accept file transfers, use the following steps:

1. From the Control Panel, choose Network And Internet Connections.

2. From the Network and Internet Connections dialog box, choose Network Connections.

3. Right-click your Internet connection and choose Properties from the pop-up menu.

4. In the Internet Connection Properties dialog box, click the Advanced tab.

5. Click the Settings button. The Advanced Settings dialog box will open.

6. In the Services tab of the Advanced Settings dialog box, click Add. The Service Settings dialog box will appear.

7. In the Service Settings dialog box, enter a name for the service or the name of your system, and the port numbers you want to use, as shown here:

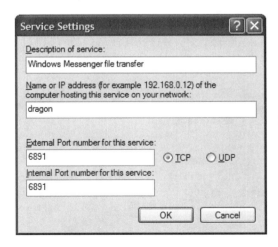

8. If you want to open additional ports for file transfer, repeat steps 6 and 7. You can use port values between 6891 and 6900.

To send a file, use the following steps:

1. Initiate a message session with the person you want to send the file to, then click Options and choose Send File, as shown here:

2. Choose the file you want to send, then click Open.

3. The recipient receives a notification regarding the file. They can either choose to accept or decline the transfer. If they accept, the file will be placed in their designated directory.

Holding Online Meetings

This feature lets you share applications and use a whiteboard that is viewable by all session members. This whiteboard resembles those used in conference rooms, only this one is electronic and easier to save and clean. You can even create multiple pages. With application sharing, you can all collaborate on a document that is open on one user's system. This can be very handy if you are preparing a presentation with a group of individuals in different parts of the country. Application sharing is discussed in Chapter 14.

The whiteboard functions like Microsoft Paint, except the whiteboard is designed to share drawings and other elements with another Passport member. All participants can take turns at contributing to the whiteboard image at any time. To use the whiteboard in a messaging session, open the Actions menu and choose Start Whiteboard. The Whiteboard window, shown in Figure 18-4, will be displayed on the systems of each session member.

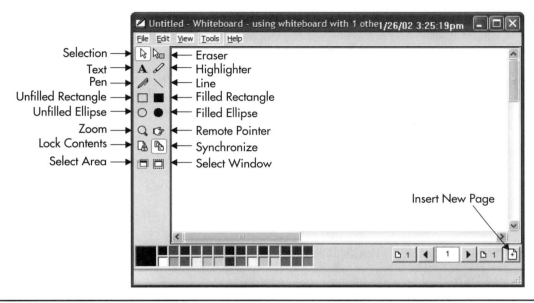

Selection → | ← Eraser
Text → | ← Highlighter
Pen → | ← Line
Unfilled Rectangle → | ← Filled Rectangle
Unfilled Ellipse → | ← Filled Ellipse
Zoom → | ← Remote Pointer
Lock Contents → | ← Synchronize
Select Area → | ← Select Window

Insert New Page

Figure 18-4   Whiteboard window

The tools in this window are used in the following ways:

- **Selector**   Use this tool to move, cut, copy, or recolor part of a drawing. To select more than one object, click and drag a rectangle around the objects you want to select.

- **Eraser**   Use this tool to erase all or parts of a drawing. When you click an object with this tool selected, that object is deleted. If you change your mind, open the Edit menu and choose Undelete. Only the last delete command can be undone.

- **Text**   Use this tool to add text to your drawing. Click this tool, then click where you want to place the text. Words are not wrapped, so to begin a new line, you must press ENTER. You can change the font and color if you wish.

- **Highlighter**   This tool is used to draw transparent lines over an object. You can use this tool to highlight an important fact or to bring attention to a particular element.

- **Pen**   This tool lets you add freehand elements to your drawing. Click and drag your mouse to draw the image you want. Release your mouse button to end the pen line.

- **Line**   Use this tool to draw straight lines. Unlike Paint's line tool, this tool does not enable you to draw perfectly straight lines by holding down your SHIFT key.

- **Unfilled rectangle**   Use this tool to draw a rectangle with an outline only.

- **Filled rectangle**   Use this tool to draw a filled rectangle of the currently selected color.

- **Unfilled ellipse**   Use this tool to draw an ellipse with an outline only.

- **Filled ellipse**   Use this tool to draw a filled ellipse of the currently selected color.

- **Select area**   Use this tool to paste a selected portion of any window into your drawing. This makes it convenient to show portions of a screen. When you click this tool, the whiteboard prompts you to select an area to paste, then gets out of the way so you can select an area of some other window.

- **Select window**   Use this tool to paste an entire window into your drawing. It works similarly to the Select Area tool.

- **Insert new page**   Click this icon to insert a new page. This is gives you the ability to create multiple pages of drawings.

- **Zoom**   Click this tool to enlarge your drawing. Click it again to return your drawing to its original size.

- **Remote pointer**   This tool displays a hand with an extended index finger. You can use this tool to draw attention to a certain area of the drawing. Click the tool again to hide the pointer. Each session member has a remote pointer that the other members cannot control.

- **Lock contents**   Use this tool to lock the whiteboard contents. This prevents others from changing the information.

- **Synchronize**   Use this tool to control the page that is currently being viewed. If the others are viewing one page and you want to view another, click this button to desynchronize your view. When you want others to view the same page as you, click Synchronize again.

   To start an online meeting session, use the following steps:

1. Select the first member you want to invite to your meeting.

2. In the conversation window, click the Invite Someone To This Conversation link.

3. From the Invite window, select the member you want to invite.

4. Repeat steps 2 and 3 to invite all of the necessary members.

5. Click the Start Whiteboard link to begin sharing a whiteboard drawing.

PART V

Having Fun

CHAPTER 19

Managing Photographs and Graphics

TIPS IN THIS CHAPTER

Windows XP works with several imaging devices to save and organize your favorite images and photos. The Scanner and Camera Wizard provide a quick and convenient way for getting images onto your system. Other wizards can be used to shrink your files so they can be shared over e-mail and public imaging Web sites, as well as printing and ordering pictures from online suppliers.

Enhancements made to Windows Explorer let you view thumbnail images of pictures stored in a directory. When you select an image, the thumbnail image is enlarged for better viewing. Double-click the image to view the image in full-scale and make simple modifications to it in Windows Picture and Fax Viewer.

To use Windows XP to its full extent with digital cameras and scanners, you do need the right hardware. Specifically, it must support the Windows Image Acquisition (WIA) standard and connect to your system through a universal serial bus (USB), SCSI, or IEEE 1394 cable. When you install one of these compliant devices, Windows recognizes them automatically and installs the appropriate drivers. An icon for the device is added to the Scanners and Cameras folder in the Control Panel. If you right-click the device icon, you can choose Properties and configure options that are specific to that device. If your device is not recognized, you will need to use the software that came with your device. In some instances, you may need to go to the manufacturer's Web site and download new drivers to work with Windows XP.

▶ *TIP*

If you own an older digital camera, there is still hope. If it is equipped with Compact Flash or SmartMedia memory cards, you can purchase an external memory card reader that connects to your system's USB port. These readers are the preferred choice for transferring images to your system because they don't require you to connect your camera and power it on. This not only saves time, it prolongs your camera's battery life. Make certain the reader you purchase is compatible with Windows XP. For laptops, you can purchase a Personal Computer Memory Card International Association (PCMCIA) card that reads digital camera memory cards.

Imaging applications like Microsoft Office XP, Microsoft Picture It! 2000 or later, and Adobe Photoshop are WIA-aware, which enables them to communicate directly with WIA-compliant devices. Some imaging applications are only compatible with TWAIN devices. Taking this fact into account, Windows XP provides a WIA compatibility layer that lets you capture and transfer images without additional software. This compatibility layer does not come without a few glitches, though. It only supports the Windows Bitmap (BMP) file format and does not allow you to use handy gadgets such as automatic document feeders. Some TWAIN devices let you save files in TIF or BMP format.

Older scanner devices use proprietary interfaces and will not be compatible with Windows XP's wizards. The device-specific drivers will still work, so long as they are Windows XP compatible.

If you are torn between installing the software and drivers that came with your device and using the WIA-based features of Windows XP, there is something to consider. If you install the device software and drivers, you will lose the ability to work with Windows XP's imaging wizards. On the other hand, if you use the software that came with your device, you may have more feature flexibility when it comes to choosing various options. If you are curious and don't really know which method will work best for your needs, set a System Restore checkpoint before installing the device drivers and software. If you later decide that the Windows XP image wizards best fit your needs, you can uninstall the device software and use the System Restore to restore the system to its previous configuration. For details on how to do this, see Chapter 26.

Once you get your favorite images on your system, Windows XP offers various methods for organizing them and making them available to share over the Internet. If you like the way the My Pictures feature displays your images in various types of views, you can customize other directories to show the same views as those available in My Pictures.

Using the Scanner and Camera Wizard

The easiest way to get a digital image on your system is by scanning it or copying it from a digital camera. Windows XP's Scanner and Camera Wizard makes it easy to copy your favorite images to your system's hard drive.

Depending on your device, the options in the Scanner and Camera Wizard can change slightly, but the core concepts remain the same. In some cases, this wizard will open automatically when you connect a camera or insert a memory card into a memory card reader. In other cases, you may have to open this wizard manually by opening the Start menu and choosing All Programs | Accessories | Scanner And Camera Wizard. The dialog box shown in Figure 19-1 will display.

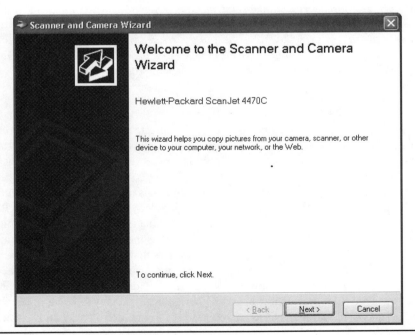

Figure 19-1   Scanner and Camera Wizard

This dialog box lists your WIA-compliant cameras or scanners that are connected to the system. If you have more than one device connected, you can click the device icon to target the wizard to that device. If you select a scanner, the dialog box will look like the one in Figure 19-2.

Click the Preview button to view the image on the scanner bed. By default, the image that is scanned is selected.

▶ **TIP**

If you have a small image you want to scan, place the image on a white sheet of paper before you place it in the scanner. Doing this causes the scanner to concentrate on only the image and not on the surrounding area.

Once the image is scanned in preview mode, you can make some adjustments. Click the Zoom button to enlarge the selected area to fit the size of the scanner bed. Click the Full Size button to view the image at the original size. If necessary, adjust the selection handles to fit around the image you want to include in your scan.

TRY IT To scan an image, use the following steps:

1. Place an image on your scanner bed.

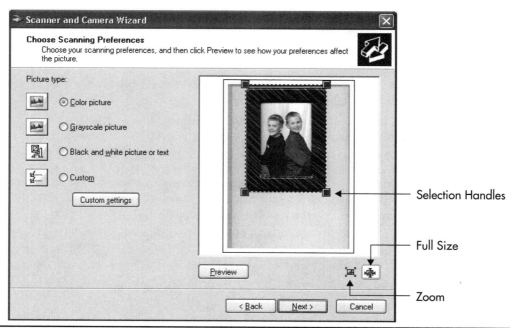

Figure 19-2 Choose scanning preferences

2. Open the Start menu and choose All Programs | Accessories | Scanner And Camera Wizard.

3. If you only have one device, click Next. If you have more than one device connected, select the scanner you want to use, and then click Next.

4. In the Choose Scanning Preferences dialog box, click the Preview button. This action scans the picture on the scanner bed and displays the image in the preview window.

5. Click the Custom Settings button. The Properties dialog box appears with the Advanced Properties tab showing. The following properties can be defined:

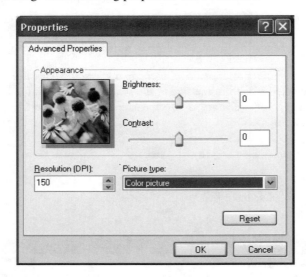

- **Brightness**   Adjust this value to add or subtract the amount of light in the image.

- **Contrast**   Adjust this value to add or subtract the amount of contrast or graininess in the image. The more contrast you have, the grainier it appears.

- **Resolution (dpi)**   In most instances, 150 dots per inch (dpi) is sufficient. If you intend to display the image onscreen only and don't ever intend to print it out, you can scan the image at 72 dpi. If you intend to print the image as is without enlarging it, 150 dpi is sufficient. If you intend to stretch the image, you need to use a higher resolution so you don't lose quality. If your scanner allows it, you might want to scan the image at the largest size you require. This will help to preserve the quality a little better. The resolution, size, and number of colors in an image determine the size of the image file.

- **Picture type**   Choose the type of picture you are scanning. Choosing the right type helps the scanner determine the optimal settings for the scan. If you are scanning a color photo but want to save it as black and white, it is best if you scan it as color and adjust the colors later.

6. When you are done making your choices, click OK to close the Properties dialog box. To test your settings, click Preview again.

7. If you are satisfied with the results, click Next. The following dialog box will be displayed:

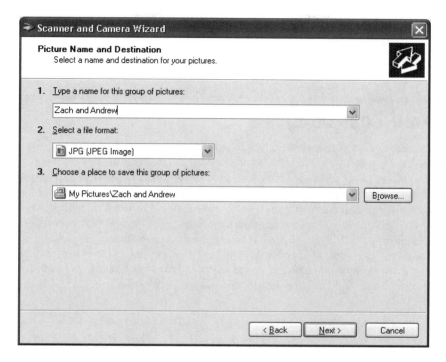

8. Enter a name for the group or folder you want to place this image in.

9. If you are using a WIA-compliant device, choose one of the following file formats. If you are using an older TWAIN device, you may only be able to choose BMP or TIF.

   - **BMP (Bitmap Image)**   Select this option if you want to use the image as wallpaper for your desktop.

   - **JPG (JPEG Image)**   Select this image if you are scanning a photograph or a very detailed picture with many color variations. This type of format is popular for images used on the Web.

   - **TIF (TIF Image)**   Choose this option if you are using the image in a document. This format condenses the image down nicely without degrading the quality.

   - **GIF (GIF Image)**   This is a good choice for Web graphics that do not require photo-realistic qualities.

   - **FXP (ACD See FXP Image)**   This format was developed by the Eastman Kodak Company for digital images. Use this format if you intend to make prints from your digital images.

   - **PNG (PNG Image)**   The Portable Network Graphics (PNG) file format was designed to replace GIF images in the Web world. Not all browsers support it yet. The latest versions of Netscape and Internet Explorer do support it.

10. Select a location where you want to store the image, and then click Next. This will begin the scanning process.

11. Once the image is scanned and saved to the location you specified, you can choose to send it to a photo shop to make prints, or you can format it to use on the Web. If you just want to save it to your disk, click the last option, and then click Next.

Optimizing Your Images

Digital images can be quite large, especially if a high resolution is used to capture them. In some cases, you need to have the highest quality to produce the desired results. For example, if you take a picture of your kids and want to enlarge it to three times its original size, you need to capture the image at about 1024 dpi. This lets you enlarge the image without losing too much detail. With today's multi-mega-pixel digital cameras and high-resolution scanners, this level of quality is not unusual.

Now that you have taken the image you want to enlarge, you discover that your relatives want to view it over the Internet. Well, placing a 5MB image on the Internet is insane, not to mention impractical. Before sharing this image with others over the Internet, you're going to want to optimize it.

Depending on how you want to use the image, choosing the right file format is imperative. The results of the compression can be quite drastic, as shown in Table 19-1.

▶ *TIP*

If quality is crucial, purchase a good imaging application like Paint Shop Pro or Adobe Photoshop. These applications offer a much better compression tool that can be fine-tuned to produce the best results.

The process of compressing files is basically the same for e-mail as for the Web. The only difference is that the Web Publishing Wizard, shown in Figure 19-3, lets you publish your images directly to a Web host. If your Web host is not supported by this wizard, you will not be able to publish your images in this way. MSN is a supported Web host. To access this wizard, select your image from Windows Explorer, then choose the Publish To The Web link in the File And Folder Tasks pane.

Original Image		Compression	
Description	**Size and Format**	**Small (640x480)**	**Large (1024x768)**
Scanned black and white 8.5x11" text document at 150 dpi	268KB (JPG)	36KB (JPG)	126KB (JPG)
Scanned grayscale 8.5x11" magazine page at 150 dpi	1.11MB (TIFF)	16KB (JPG) unreadable text	85KB (JPG) readable text
24-bit color photo from a digital camera at 192 dpi (1280x960)	556KB (JPG)	56KB (JPG)	235KB (JPG)
Scanned 3x5" 24-bit color photo at 300 dpi	6MB (BMP)	12KB (JPG)	66KB (JPG)

Table 19-1   Compression Results

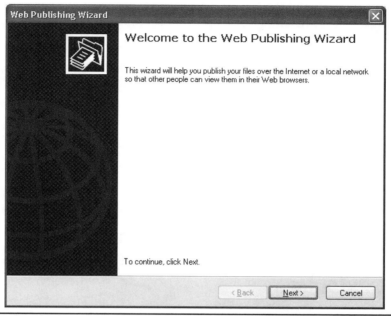

Figure 19-3   Web Publishing Wizard

TRY IT   To compress a file for e-mail, use the following steps:

1. From Windows Explorer, select the image you want to send with e-mail.
2. In the File And Folder Tasks pane, choose E-Mail This File. Alternatively, you can right-click the image file and choose Send To | Mail Recipient. The following Send Pictures Via E-Mail dialog box displays:

3. Click the Show More Options link to expand the options list. When the options list is expanded, the Show More Options link changes to Show Fewer Options, which enables you to hide the extended options list.

4. By default, BMP images are converted to TIF and TIF images are converted to JPG. If the file is already a JPG or a GIF, it is not converted at all. Select the file size you want to use, then click OK.

▶ *TIP*

If you have an imaging application installed, such as Adobe Photoshop or Paint Shop Pro, you can open this file and save it in any format that imaging application supports.

5. Your default mail program is opened and a new message is created with the compressed image already attached. Complete the Send To address and add your message. Click Send to complete the process.

Printing Digital Images

This new feature in Windows XP enables you to print your images in the most efficient manner. Using the Photo Printing Wizard, shown in Figure 19-4, you can size, crop, and rotate images to suit

Figure 19-4 Photo Printing Wizard

your needs. You can even lay out multiple photos on a single page, or create a single-page thumbnail index of an image folder. This wizard is accessed through Windows Explorer. Click the image you want to print, then choose Print This Picture from the Picture Tasks pane.

▶ *TIP*

To choose more than one image, hold down your CTRL *key and click the images you want to print. Right-click one of the selected images and choose Print from the pop-up menu.*

 To print images with the Photo Printing Wizard, use the following steps:

1. Open Windows Explorer and select an image to print.
2. From the Picture Tasks pane, click Print This Picture.
3. Click Next after reading the first page of the Photo Printing Wizard dialog box.
4. Select the printer you want to use and adjust Printing Preferences if necessary.
5. Click Next. The following dialog box displays:

6. From the Available Layouts, select the one that best fits your needs:

- **Full page fax print**   Choose this option if you want the entire image printed without any cropping. The image is centered on the page and rotated to fit nicely.
- **Full page photo print**   Choose this option if you want the entire image printed. The image is cropped slightly on two sides and centered.
- **Contact sheet prints**   Choose this option if you have selected multiple images and want to have a thumbnail index of each one on a single sheet of paper.
- **8 x 10 in. prints**   This layout removes approximately 6 percent of the shorter sides of the print.
- **5 x 7 in. prints**   This layout offers a very efficient way for printing two prints per letter-sized page. It removes approximately 5 percent of the longer sides of the print.
- **4 x 6 in. prints**   This layout removes more than 10 percent of the image. This can be quite drastic since the crops occur on the long edges of the print. For best results, choose the three-photo layout over the two-photo layout.
- **3.5 x 5 in. prints**   Choose this option to make the most of your page space with minimal cropping.
- **Wallet prints**   Choose this option to print nine images with virtually no cropping. If you have three separate images selected, this option lets you print three of each selected image.

▶ *TIP*

The automatic cropping that occurs may be acceptable for casual photos, but for carefully composed images, you may want to crop the images manually to fit your intended layout.

7. Click Next, then click Finish.

▶ *TIP*

If you want more control of how your image prints, open it in an imaging application like Adobe Photoshop or Paint Shop Pro to fine-tune the end result.

Organizing Your Images

By default, all WIA-compliant images are stored in your %UserProfile%\My Documents\My Pictures folder. When you use the Image Toolbar in Internet Explorer or any WIA-compliant image editing application, you jump to this folder. Under this folder, you should try to categorize your pictures into something intuitive. For example, if you have a series of photos shot on your vacation to Alaska in January of 2002, you could create a folder called Alaska_January_2002.

▶ *TIP*

You can change the name and location of the My Pictures directory without losing the automatic links to it from various applications. Go to the My Documents window and right-click My Pictures. From here, you can choose to move the folder location or simply rename it. Once you do, Windows XP automatically updates the Registry to reflect the change. If you have two or more partitions and one is used for storing system files, move the My Pictures folder to the other partition that is used for storing data.

The following enhancements made to Windows Explorer make it easy to manage your image files:

- **Filmstrip View** In this view, shown in Figure 19-5, you can click on a thumbnail image to see it in larger scale.

Figure 19-5 Filmstrip View

- **Thumbnail View**   This view, shown in Figure 19-6, displays each image in a thumbnail that is easily recognizable.
- **Picture Tasks**   This pane offers quick access to common image-related options.

▶ *TIP*

Try viewing your images in full-screen mode. Press F11 *to get rid of the window clutter. To return to normal view, press* F11 *again.*

 To categorize your images, use the following steps:

1. In Windows Explorer, create a new folder under the My Pictures directory by clicking File | New | Folder. Give the folder a name you want to use for a given category.
2. Click the Folders button in the toolbar to display the list of folders.

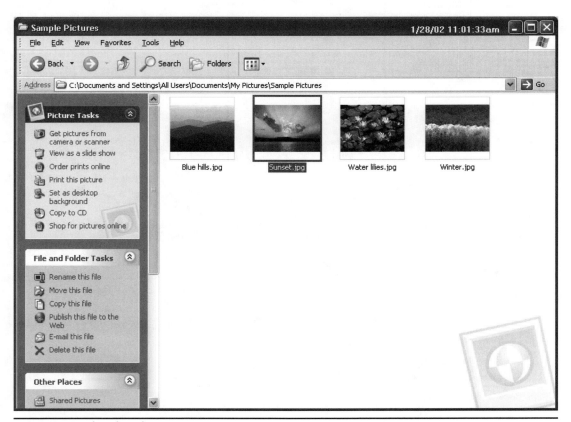

Figure 19-6   Thumbnail View

3. Go to the folder that contains the images you want to move to the new folder you just created. Hold down your CTRL key and select the images you want to move to the new folder.

4. Click on one of the selected images and drag the selected images to the new folder in the folders list.

5. Repeat these steps to create the categories for your images, until all of your images are stored in their respective locations.

Customizing Image Folders

When you create a new subfolder in the My Pictures directory, it automatically includes the Filmstrip and Thumbnail View options. If you want these same options to be available in other directories, you can customize them in the Properties dialog box.

TRY IT To customize image folders, use the following steps:

1. In Windows Explorer, right-click the folder you want to customize, then choose Properties from the pop-up menu.

2. Click the Customize tab.

3. From the Use This Folder Type As A Template list, choose Pictures (best for many files).

4. If you want the subfolders of this directory to use the same settings, check the Also Apply This Template To All Subfolders option.

5. For fun, you can select an image to display on this folder to make it easily identifiable. Click the Choose Picture button.

6. If you want to change the icon for folders, click the Change Icon button.

7. When you are done, click OK.

Put It to Work: Building a Photo Album

Using the information learned in this chapter, you can create a photo album of your favorite image files. The following steps will guide you through this process. Once you have created a photo album on your local drive, you can use a Web-authoring application to put your album on a Web site.

If you copy your picture files to a CD from the My Pictures directory, you are given the option of creating a slide-show presentation on the CD.

To begin, you need to have one of the following:

- Printed images that you can scan
- Photos taken with a digital camera

To get your images onto your system, use the following steps:

1. In Windows Explorer, click File | New | Folder to create a new folder for your images. If you do not create this folder under the My Pictures directory, you may want to customize that folder as described in "Customizing Image Folders."

2. If you are using a camera, connect it to your system or insert the memory card into an external reader. Using either the Scanner and Camera Wizard or the software that came with your camera, copy the images to the folder you created in step 1.

3. If you are using a scanner, use either the Scanner and Camera Wizard, as described in "Using the Scanner and Camera Wizard," or the software that came with your device to scan the images and save them to the new folder you created in step 1.

When you are done copying the images to your folder, you may want to change it to operate as a photo album. This lets you quickly access your album and display its contents efficiently:

1. Right-click the folder name and choose Properties from the pop-up menu.

2. Click the Customize tab.

3. From the Use This Folder Type As A Template list, choose Photo Album (best for fewer files), and then click OK.

Once you build your photo album, you can display it in a Web page, as shown here:

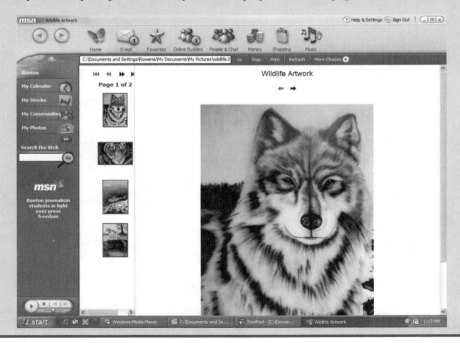

There are several ways in which you can build photo albums on a Web page. The following is just one way, using HTML. When the user clicks on a thumbnail in the left frame, the right frame displays a larger view of that thumbnail image.

When you copy the images into your photo album, they should be formatted for the largest size you intend to display.

This Web album is comprised of three HTML files:

- **Wildlife.html**   Used to build the frames
- **Wildlife1.html**   Used to display page 1
- **Wildlife2.html**   Used to display page 2

and three directories:

- **Images**   Contains the original image files (at their largest size).
- **Page**   Contains HTML files for each image displayed. These files contain the large images that are displayed in the right frame. These files are called Image1.html, Image2.html, and so on.
- **Thumbs**   Contains a smaller version of the original file.

Note, these files and directories must reside in the same directory. The following samples also contain navigational icons (GIFs).

Code for Wildlife.html

The following code is used to set up the frames in which the images are shown. The text in **_bold italic_** shows some of the variables you can change to fit your own page.

```
<html>
<head>
<title>Wildlife Artwork</title>
</head>

<FRAMESET COLS="130, *">
    <FRAMESET ROWS="100%">
        <FRAME NAME="thumbnail" SRC="wildlife1.html" MARGINHEIGHT=5
        MARGINWIDTH=7 SCROLLING=AUTO FRAMEBORDER="yes">
    <FRAMESET ROWS="100%">
        <FRAME NAME="image" SRC="page\image1.html" MARGINHEIGHT="10"
        MARGINWIDTH=0 SCROLLING=AUTO FRAMEBORDER="yes">
</FRAMESET>
</html>
```

Code for Wildlife1.html

This code is used to display page 1 of the images. The text in *bold italic* shows some of the variables you can change to fit your own page.

```
<html>
<head>
<title>Wildlife Artwork</title>
</head>
<body>
<basefont size="2" face="Verdana">
<table align="left">
<tr align="center" valign="top">
<td><table width="150"><tr><td align="center">
<center>
<a OnMouseOver="window.status='Home'; return true">
<img src="NavHomeD.gif" border=0></a>
<a OnMouseOver="window.status='Prev'; return true">
<img src="NavPrevD.gif" border=0></a>
<a href="wildlife2.html" OnMouseOver="window.status='Next'; return true">
<img src="NavNext.gif" alt="Next" border=0></a>
<a href="wildlife2.html" OnMouseOver="window.status='End'; return true">
<img src="NavEnd.gif" alt="End" border=0></a>
</center>
</td></tr>
<tr><td align="center">
<font face="Verdana" size="2"><b>Page 1 of 2</b></font><br>
</td></tr>
</table></td></tr>

<tr>
<td>
<div align="center"><center>

<table cellpadding="0" cellspacing="6">
<tr>
<td align="center" valign="top">
<table cellpadding="0" cellspacing="0">
<tr>
<td align="center" valign="top">
<table align="center" cellpadding="0" cellspacing="0">
<tr>
<td align="center" width="84" height="84">
<a href="page/image1.html" target="image">
<img src="Thumbs/tn_Wildlife0.jpg"
```

```
alt="Thumbs/tn_Wildlife0.jpg" align="top" width="55"
height="80"></a></td>
</tr>
</table>
</td>
</tr>
<tr>
<td valign="top">
<table align="center" cellpadding="0" cellspacing="0">
<tr>
<td align="center" valign="top">
<font face="Arial" size="2" color="#000000"><br>
</font></td>
</tr>
</table>
</td>
</tr>
</table>
</td>
</tr>
<tr>
<td align="center" valign="top">
<table cellpadding="0" cellspacing="0">
<tr>
<td align="center" valign="top">
<table align="center" cellpadding="0" cellspacing="0">
<tr>
<td align="center" width="84" height="84">
<a href="page/image2.html" target="image">
<img src="Thumbs/tn_Wildlife1.jpg" alt="Thumbs/tn_Wildlife1.jpg"
align="top" width="80" height="52"></a></td>
</tr>
</table>
</td>
</tr>
<tr>
<td valign="top">
<table align="center" cellpadding="0" cellspacing="0">
<tr>
<td align="center" valign="top">
<font face="Arial" size="2" color="#000000"><br>
</font></td>
</tr>
</table>
```

```
</td>
</tr>
</table>
</td>
</tr>
<tr>
<td align="center" valign="top">
<table cellpadding="0" cellspacing="0">
<tr>
<td align="center" valign="top">
<table align="center" cellpadding="0" cellspacing="0">
<tr>
<td align="center" width="84" height="84">
<a href="page/image3.html" target="image">
<img src="Thumbs/tn_Wildlife2.jpg" alt="Thumbs/tn_Wildlife2.jpg"
align="top" width="58" height="80"></a></td>
</tr>
</table>
</td>
</tr>
<tr>
<td valign="top">
<table align="center" cellpadding="0" cellspacing="0">
<tr>
<td align="center" valign="top">
<font face="Arial" size="2" color="#000000"><br>
</font></td>
</tr>
</table>
</td>
</tr>
</table>
</td>
</tr>
<tr>
<td align="center" valign="top">
<table cellpadding="0" cellspacing="0">
<tr>
<td align="center" valign="top">
<table align="center" cellpadding="0" cellspacing="0">
<tr>
<td align="center" width="84" height="84">
<a href="page/image4.html" target="image">
<img src="Thumbs/tn_Wildlife3.jpg" alt="Thumbs/tn_Wildlife3.jpg"
```

```
align="top" width="57" height="80"></a></td>
</tr>
</table>
</td>
</tr>
<tr>
<td valign="top">
<table align="center" cellpadding="0" cellspacing="0">
<tr>
<td align="center" valign="top">
<font face="Arial" size="2" color="#000000"><br>
</font></td>
</tr>
</table>
</td>
</tr>
</table>
</td>
</tr>
</table>
</center></div>

</td>

</tr>

</table>
</body>
</html>
```

Code for Wildlife2.html

This code is used to display page 2 of the images. The text in ***bold italic*** shows some of the variables you can change to fit your own page.

```
<html>
<head>
<title>Wildlife Artwork</title>
</head>
<body>
<basefont size="2" face="Verdana">
<table align="left">
<tr align="center" valign="top">
<td><table width="150"><tr><td align="center">
<center>
```

```
<a href="wildlife1.html" OnMouseOver="window.status='Home'; return true">
<img src="NavHome.gif" alt="Home" border=0></a>
<a href="wildlife1.html" OnMouseOver="window.status='Prev'; return true">
<img src="NavPrev.gif" alt="Prev" border=0></a>
<a OnMouseOver="window.status='Next'; return true">
<img src="NavNextD.gif" border=0></a>
<a OnMouseOver="window.status='End'; return true">
<img src="NavEndD.gif" border=0></a>
</center>
</td></tr>
<tr><td align="center">
<font face="Verdana" size="2"><b>Page 2 of 2</b></font><br>
</td></tr>
</table></td></tr>

<tr>
<td>
<div align="center"><center>

<table cellpadding="0" cellspacing="6">
<tr>
<td align="center" valign="top">
<table cellpadding="0" cellspacing="0">
<tr>
<td align="center" valign="top">
<table align="center" cellpadding="0" cellspacing="0">
<tr>
<td align="center" width="84" height="84">
<a href="page/image5.html" target="image">
<img src="Thumbs/tn_Wildlife4.jpg" alt="Thumbs/tn_Wildlife4.jpg"
align="top" width="80" height="80"></a></td>
</tr>
</table>
</td>
</tr>
<tr>
<td valign="top">
<table align="center" cellpadding="0" cellspacing="0">
<tr>
<td align="center" valign="top">
<font face="Arial" size="2" color="#000000"><br>
</font></td>
</tr>
</table>
```

```
</td>
</tr>
</table>
</td>
</tr>
<tr>
<td align="center" valign="top">
<table cellpadding="0" cellspacing="0">
<tr>
<td align="center" valign="top">
<table align="center" cellpadding="0" cellspacing="0">
<tr>
<td align="center" width="84" height="84">
<a href="page/image6.html" target="image">
<img src="Thumbs/tn_Wildlife5.jpg" alt="Thumbs/tn_Wildlife5.jpg"
align="top" width="80" height="58"></a></td>
</tr>
</table>
</td>
</tr>
<tr>
<td valign="top">
<table align="center" cellpadding="0" cellspacing="0">
<tr>
<td align="center" valign="top">
<font face="Arial" size="2" color="#000000"><br>
</font></td>
</tr>
</table>
</td>
</tr>
</table>
</td>
</tr>
</table>
</td>
</tr>
</table>
</center></div>

</td>

</tr>

</table>
</body>
</html>
```

Code for Page Files

This code is used to display the large image in the right frame. The text in ***bold italic*** shows some of the variables you can change to fit your own page.

```html
<html>
<head>
<title>Wildlife Artwork</title>
</head>
<body>
<div align="center"><font face="Arial" size="4"
color="#000000">Wildlife Artwork</font></div>
<basefont size="2" face="Verdana"><br>
<center>
<a OnMouseOver="window.status='Prev'; return true">
<img src="IndPrevD.gif" border=0></a>
<a href="image2.html" target="image" OnMouseOver="window.status='Next';
return true"><img src="IndNext.gif" alt="Next" border=0></a>
</center>
<p>
<div align="center"><center>

<table cellpadding="0" cellspacing="6">
<tr>
<td align="center" valign="top">
<table cellpadding="0" cellspacing="0">
<tr>
<td align="center" valign="top">
<table align="center" cellpadding="0" cellspacing="0">
<tr>
<td align="center" valign="middle">
<img src="../Images/Wildlife0.jpg" alt="../Images/Wildlife0.jpg"
align="top" width="412" height="599"></td>
</tr>
</table>
</td>
</tr>
</table>
</td>
</tr>
</table>
</center></div>
<p>
<center>
<b>Page 1 of 6</b><br>
```

```html
<div align="center"><font face="Arial" size="2" color="#000000">
<b>Copyright 2002 ~ Rowena White</b></font></div>
</center>
</body>
</html>
```

CHAPTER 20

Using Windows Media Player

TIPS IN THIS CHAPTER

Version 8 of Windows Media Player is an all-in-one client for rendering digital media. With it, you can listen to CDs or streaming audio files, play video content, listen to radio stations around the world, watch DVD movies, burn custom CDs, and create your own library of favorite songs.

With a click of a button, you can link to Web sites that provide information regarding the entertainment world. By default, Windows Media Player automatically links to the MSN Media Guide, a Web magazine dedicated to entertainment buffs who crave the latest information about their favorite artists. This site, shown in Figure 20-1, changes daily. To launch Windows Media Player, open the Start menu and choose All Programs | Accessories | Entertainment | Windows Media Player.

If you do not see the frame around your Windows Media Player window, it may be hidden. If this is the case, your Windows Media Player window will look like the one in Figure 20-2. If you like the standard frame, click the Show/Hide Menu Bar button.

Figure 20-1 MSN Media Guide

Show/Hide
Menu Bar

Figure 20-2 Windows Media Player window

► *TIP*

If you have a slow connection and don't want the MSN Media Guide to come up each time you open the Windows Media Player window, you can turn it off. In the Windows Media Player window, click Tools | Options. In the Media Player tab, uncheck the Start Player In Media Guide option.

If you don't like the traditional look of the Windows Media Player window, you can choose from a variety of skins, or download others if you can't find one that suits you. A skin is like a customized window frame. It can be traditionally square, or odd shaped. Just click the Skin Chooser button and make your choice from the skin selections shown in Figure 20-3. If you don't find one you like, click the More Skins button at the top of the screen.

To use the skin of your choice, press CTRL-2 or click View | Skin Mode. The Windows XP skin is shown in Figure 20-4. To return to full screen mode, press CTRL-1 or click View | Full Mode.

If you're into visual effects and you have a fast system, you might enjoy choosing one of the many light and color patterns that change with the beat of your music. Some of the patterns can be quite hypnotizing. To experiment, click View | Visualizations, and then choose from one of the many patterns.

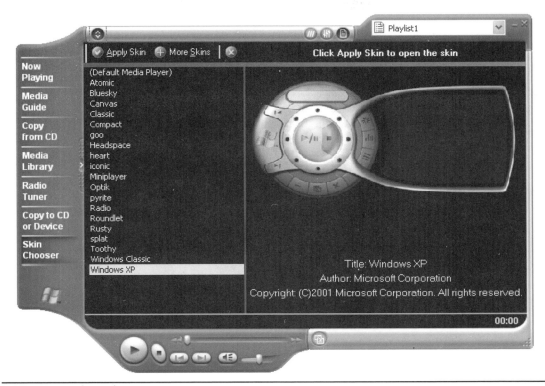

Figure 20-3   Skin selections

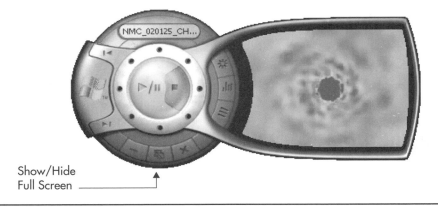

Figure 20-4   Windows XP skin

▶ *TIP*

If you have a slow system, this feature can slow things down a bit and cause your CDs or other music to skip now and then. To turn off Visualizations, click View | Now Playing Tools and uncheck Show Visualization.

There are a few nonintuitive buttons on the interface, as illustrated in Figure 20-5.

- **Show/Hide Menu Bar**   Click this button to show or hide the square frame around the Windows Media Player.
- **Turn Shuffle On**   Click this if you are playing a CD and want the songs to be shuffled.
- **Show Equalizer and Settings in Now Playing**   Click this button to view the equalizer tools.
- **Hide Playlist in Now Playing**   Click this button to hide the playlist.
- **Select Visualization or Album Art**   Click this button to view a list of available visualization patterns.
- **Previous Visualization**   Click this button to see the previous visualization pattern.
- **Next Visualization**   Click this button to see the next visualization pattern.
- **View Full Screen**   Click this button to view the Windows Media Player in full screen mode.

The MP3 files that you may be familiar with are still supported by Windows Media Player, but audio files that you create are saved in Windows Media Audio (WMA) format. This format achieves the same audio quality of the MP3, but at much higher compression. For example, one CD track encoded using WMA uses half the disk space as an equivalent MP3 file. If you need to create MP3 files from CD tracks, you can still do so. Just download an MP3 Creation Pack for Windows XP from Cyberlink Corporation (*http://www.cyberlink.com*), InterVideo, Inc. (*http://www.intervideo.com/jsp/Home.jsp*), or Ravisent Technologies, Inc. (*http://www.ravisent.com/products/index.html*).

▶ *TIP*

To find an MP3 Creation Pack for Windows XP, click Tools | Options. Select the Copy Music tab, and then click MP3 Information. This opens the Windows Media Technologies Web page.

Dealing with Corrupted Codecs

It's rare, but every once in a while you may come across a bad coder/decoder (codec) that causes your Windows Media Player to act up. If you suspect this is happening, you can disable the faulty codec.

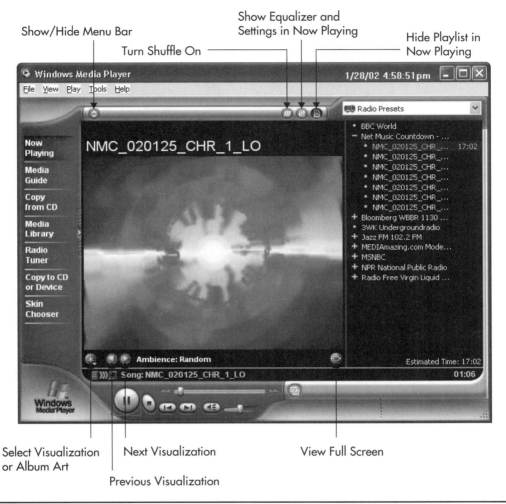

Show/Hide Menu Bar

Show Equalizer and
Settings in Now Playing

Turn Shuffle On

Hide Playlist in
Now Playing

Select Visualization
or Album Art

Next Visualization

View Full Screen

Previous Visualization

Figure 20-5   Windows   Media Player interface

TRY IT   To find and disable a bad codec, use the following steps:

1. Open the Start menu and click Control Panel.

2. From the Control Panel, choose Sounds, Speech, and Audio Devices.

3. From the Sounds, Speech, and Audio Devices dialog box that appears, click Sounds And Audio Devices, and then choose the Hardware tab.

4. Select the suspected type of codec (Audio or Video), and then click Properties.

5. Click the Properties tab.

6. Right-click the suspected codec, and then choose Properties from the pop-up menu. The following dialog box will display:

7. Try changing the codec's priority number. When two codecs are available to Windows Media Player for processing the same kind of media, Windows Media Player uses the one with the lower priority number.

8. If that doesn't do the trick, you can select the Do Not Use This (Audio or Video) Codec option. This will disable this codec until a new one can be obtained.

Working with AutoPlay

The AutoPlay feature is used to automatically respond to whatever type of CD is installed in your CD-ROM drive. For example, you may notice that when you install a program CD the startup program automatically launches. The same thing happens when you install a music CD. Windows Media Player recognizes the media type and immediately begins playing your music.

You can adjust the action that Windows XP takes when you insert specific types of CDs or DVDs.

 To customize how AutoPlay reacts, use the following steps:

1. Double-click My Computer.

2. Right-click the icon for your CD-ROM or DVD device, and then choose Properties.

3. Click the AutoPlay tab as shown in the following illustration:

4. From the pull-down list, choose a disc type.

5. In the Actions section, click one of the following options:

- **Select an action to perform**   Choose this option if you want one of the displayed actions to be performed for the selected disc type. If you choose this option, make a selection from the Actions list.

- **Prompt me each time to choose an action**   Choose this option if you want to make a choice each time the select disc type is detected.

6. Click OK.

Backing Up and Restoring Your Licenses

Some digital content is governed by a licensing agreement that protects the provider against illegal distribution of their media. This license is used to determine the period of time you are able to use the media, along with a few other details. When you download a file from the Internet, the content provider may or may not provide a license. If you play an unlicensed file that requires a license, Windows Media Player will prompt you to obtain the license before the file is played.

▶ *TIP*

If you want to avoid licensed media, open the Tools menu and choose Options. Click the Media Player tab and uncheck the Acquire Licenses Automatically option.

If you purchased a license for a given media file, you can move this file to another system. Once you do so, however, you cannot play that file on the system it was moved from. Before moving the media, you will want to back up your license information and restore it on the new system.

TRY IT   To back up and restore media licenses, use the following steps:

1. Open the Tools menu and choose License Management.
2. In the License Management dialog box, click Browse to specify a backup location. You might want to create your backup on removable media as well if the new system is not networked to the old system.
3. Click the Backup Now button.
4. If your new system is not on the same network as your old system, insert the removable backup into the new system.
5. Open Windows Media Player and click Tools | License Management.
6. In the License Management dialog box, click Restore Now.
7. Read the licensing information on the screen, and then click OK.

Viewing Media Information and Album Art

If your system connects to the Internet, you can use a service of the All Music Group (AMG) Web site at *http://www.allmusic.com/* to gain information regarding the CD or DVD you are currently playing. If the album art is found, it is cached on your system. The next time you play that CD, it will display the album cover in the visualization area.

TRY IT   To search for CD information, use the following steps:

1. Open the View menu and choose Now Playing Tools | Media Information. In the Now Playing pane, additional information is displayed at the bottom of the screen, including the album art.
2. If the information is found, click the album art. When you do this, the WindowsMedia.com Web page opens.
3. In the Buy Now page, you are given the option to view more information or buy the album you are currently viewing.

Using the Graphic Equalizer and the SRS WOW Effects

If your system is equipped with a good speaker system, you can take advantage of Windows Media Player's 10-band graphic equalizer that offers several preset equalizer settings. Click View | Now Playing Tools | Graphic Equalizer. The settings box shown in Figure 20-6 is displayed.

Click the Default button to choose from a variety of presets. Click the graphic to the left of the equalizer slides to choose how the buttons move on the slider. Click the Graphic Equalizer button to change views. Each view is preset for specific types of music. These settings can be modified to suit your individual tastes.

The SRS WOW effects offer a 3-D sound experience from only two speakers, providing your sound system can support it. To see if your system can support this feature, open the View menu and choose Now Playing Tools. Check SRS WOW Effects. This displays the controls at the bottom of the Now Playing pane. The controls shown in Figure 20-7 will display in the Now Playing area of your screen. If the On/Off button displays Off, click this button to enable this feature.

▶ *TIP*

Click the Select View button to quickly change between the graphic equalizer and the SRS controls.

TRY IT ▶ To use the equalizer and SRS WOW effects, use the following steps:

1. Click View | Now Playing Tools and check Graphic Equalizer.

▶ *TIP*

You can also click the Show Equalizer button at the top of the screen. This is the center button with the three vertical lines.

---

2. From the graphic to the left of the equalizer slide buttons, choose one of three possible ways in which the slide buttons can move:

   • **Top**   Sets the equalizer slides to move independently.

   • **Middle**   Sets the equalizer slides to move together in a loose group.

   • **Bottom**   Sets the equalizer slides to move together in a tight group.

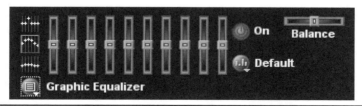

Figure 20-6   Graphic Equalizer

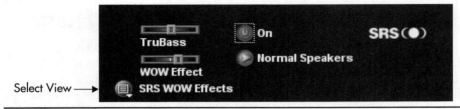

Figure 20-7   SRS WOW effects

3. Use the Select Preset button, just to the right of the equalizer slide buttons, to choose a preset pattern from which to start.

4. Adjust the sound to suit your needs by sliding the equalizer buttons up or down.

5. If your system can handle a lot of bass, click the View Select button and choose SRS WOW Effects.

6. Make certain the On/Off button reads On. For mega bass, slide the TruBass slider left or right until you obtain the right sound.

7. Select the type of speakers you have installed.

8. Slide the WOW Effect button left or right to obtain the right sound.

Copying CD Tracks to Your Hard Drive

With Windows Media Player, you can copy tracks from various CDs to your hard drive so you can burn your own custom CD with all of your favorite songs. You can listen to other music while the tracks are being copied. Your music library is stored in your %UserProfile%\My Documents\My Music directory.

TRY IT   To copy CD tracks to your hard drive, use the following steps:

1. Insert the CD into your CD-ROM drive.

2. In Windows Media Player, click the Copy From CD link in the Taskbar section.

3. In Figure 20-8, select the tracks you want to copy, and then click the Copy Music button.

4. The Copy Music Protection dialog box is displayed. If you want to be responsible for using the content in a nonethical fashion, check the Do Not Protect Content option, and then click OK.

Figure 20-8 Window Media Player

Editing Track Information

The AMG contains a library of more than 200,000 CD titles. If you do not see the title of your CD displayed in the title box, you can click the Get Names button to search for the CD by title or artist. Once that is done, you can edit the information before copying tracks to your hard drive. For example, if you don't like the information that AMG provides for a given track that you want to copy to your hard drive, you can edit this information prior to copying the track.

TRY IT To edit track information, use the following steps:

1. If the CD is recognized by AMG, you can right-click any field in the track area and choose Edit from the pop-up menu.

2. If your CD is not recognized by AMG, you can click the Get Names button and search for the CD by title or artist name.

3. If you created the CD yourself, you can click the Get Names button and choose the "This is a custom CD, I want to type the album information" option. A section is displayed at the bottom of the Now Playing pane. In this section, you can click a field you want to define. Your entries are automatically saved.

Managing Your Media Library

If you copy CD tracks to your hard drive, those tracks are automatically stored in the Audio directory. If you have been collecting music for some time and have files scattered about your disk, you can open the Tools menu and choose Search For Media Files, or simply press F3.

When you download media from the Internet, you can choose to add that media to your library, or you can configure Windows Media Player to automatically add each of the items you play. To do this, click Tools | Options, click the Media Player tab and check the Add Items To Media Library When Played option. You can also click and drag media files to the right pane of your Media Library. If an item is already playing, you can choose File | Add To Media Library.

Once you populate your Media Library, you can click the Media Library link in the Taskbar and click the Search button. This feature lets you search for media by various categories.

TRY IT To add items to your Media Library, use the following steps:

1. Search for the item you want to add, and then select it.

2. In Windows Media Player, click the Media Library link in the Taskbar.

3. Click and drag the selected item to the appropriate folder in your Media Library.

Creating a Custom Playlist

If you have several songs that you like to play together, you can create a custom playlist of those songs.

TRY IT To create a custom playlist, use the following steps:

1. In the Windows Media Player, click the Media Library link in the Taskbar.

2. Click the New Playlist button at the top of the screen. A new playlist dialog displays.

3. Enter a name for your playlist, and then click OK.

4. Select the Audio directory. The library automatically categorizes your audio files. If you want to view all of your audio files, click All Audio. If you want to view all songs by a specific artist, click Artists. If you want to view songs from a specific album, click Album.

5. Select the songs you want to add to your playlist and drag them into your playlist folder.

6. To rearrange the order in which the songs appear in the playlist, click on the playlist name, and then click and drag the songs to the desired location.

Adding Lyrics to Songs

Windows Media Player lets you add the lyrics to a song. These lyrics can then be displayed as the song plays.

TRY IT To add lyrics, use the following steps:

1. In Windows Media Player, click the Media Library link in the Taskbar.

2. Right-click the song you want to add lyrics for, and then choose Properties from the pop-up menu.

3. Click the Lyrics tab and enter the lyrics in the text box. Click OK when you are done.

Burning Custom CDs

Now that you have collected your favorite songs and have compiled them into a playlist, you are ready to burn them onto a CD so they can be enjoyed away from your computer. All you need is a CD recorder and a blank CD-R disk.

TRY IT To burn a custom CD, use the following steps:

1. In Windows Media Player, click the Media Library link in the Taskbar.

2. Select the playlist you want to copy to a CD, and then click the Copy To CD Or Device link in the Taskbar.

3. Your playlist displays in the left pane, with check marks. If there is a song you do not want to copy to the CD, remove the check mark.

4. When you make your selections, look at the total minutes for the selected songs at the bottom of the screen, and the total number of free minutes on the CD. Make certain you do not select too many songs for the CD. If a song will not fit on the CD, Windows Media Player will search for a song in your playlist that will fit. This could affect the order you had originally intended.

5. When you are satisfied with the selections, click the Copy Music button.

6. When the copy is complete, the CD is ejected automatically.

Watching DVD Movies

If you purchased your Windows XP system with a DVD drive installed, chances are it includes the required software decoder. If you place a DVD into your DVD drive and receive an error message, click the Troubleshooting link. The Troubleshooting page will offer a link that lists Windows XP-compatible DVD drives and software decoders. You may have to download a software decoder for your device.

 To play a DVD movie, use the following steps:

1. Insert the DVD movie into your DVD drive.
2. Open Windows Media Player and click Play | Play DVD.
3. You can jump to a particular chapter by double-clicking the chapter name in the right pane.
4. To view any features that are available on your DVD, click View | DVD Features. This list changes for each DVD.
5. If you want to watch the movie in full screen mode, press ALT-ENTER. This command toggles the view between full screen and normal mode.

Putting It to Work: Building a Playlist and Burning a CD

Okay, now that you have all the basics, let's put it all together and create a custom CD of your favorite songs.

To collect your favorite songs into your Media Library, use the following steps:

1. If you have several CDs that you want to copy songs from, follow the instructions in the "Copying CD Tracks to Your Hard Drive" section earlier in this chapter.
2. Search the Internet for music downloads. Some sites offer free music, while others require you to pay a membership fee or pay for each download.
3. Using one of the techniques discussed in "Managing Your Media Library," add your favorite songs.

Once you have collected your favorite songs and have added them to your Media Library, you are ready to create a playlist. A playlist should contain a set of songs you like to listen to together. For example, you may be in a playful mood and want to listen to very uplifting songs. In this case, you will want to create a playlist that contains only upbeat songs. A playlist can contain as many songs as you like, providing you have enough storage space to store them all.

To create a custom playlist, use the following steps:

1. In the Windows Media Player, click the Media Library link in the Taskbar.
2. Click the New Playlist button at the top of the screen.
3. Enter a name for your playlist, and then click OK.
4. Select the Audio directory. The library automatically categorizes your audio files. If you want to view all of your audio files, click All Audio. If you want to view all songs by a specific artist, click Artists. If you want to view songs from a specific album, click Album.
5. Select the songs you want to add to your playlist and drag them into your playlist folder.
6. To rearrange the order in which the songs appear in the playlist, click on the playlist name, and then click and drag the songs to the desired location.

After you have created your playlist, you are ready to copy them to a CD so you can listen to them when you are away from your system.

To burn a custom CD, use the following steps:

1. In Windows Media Player, click the Media Library link in the Taskbar.
2. Select the playlist you want to copy to a CD, and then click the Copy To CD Or Device link in the Taskbar.
3. Your playlist displays in the left pane, with check marks. If there is a song you do not want to copy to the CD, remove the check mark.
4. When you make your selections, look at the total minutes for the selected songs at the bottom of the screen, and the total number of free minutes on the CD. Make certain you do not select too many songs for the CD. If a song will not fit on the CD, Windows Media Player will search for a song in your playlist that will fit. This could affect the order you had originally intended.
5. When you are satisfied with the selections, click Copy Music.
6. When the copy is complete, the CD is ejected automatically.

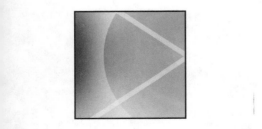

PART VI
Customizing Windows

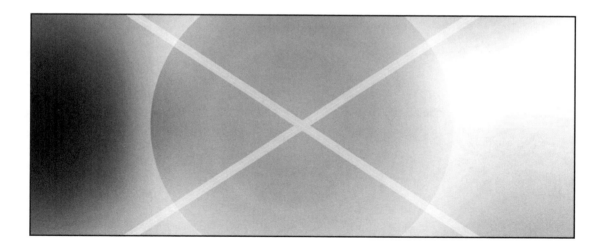

CHAPTER 21

Changing Desktop and Display Settings

TIPS IN THIS CHAPTER

E ven though the default Windows interface is clean, attractive, and well thought out, being able to personalize the appearance of the Desktop has always been important. After all, when the Desktop is organized the way you want and has looks that suit your needs and personality, it makes for a much nicer computing experience. This chapter presents techniques for organizing your Desktop, for customizing its appearance, and for altering your basic display settings.

Arranging Icons on the Desktop

Since the Desktop is really just a specialized folder, some of the tools for arranging the Desktop are the same as those used in regular folders. For example, you can choose to arrange the icons on the Desktop according to name, size, file type, or when the files were last modified. Since the Desktop is not a regular folder, though, some tools are missing. You cannot, for example, change the basic view of the Desktop—it is always in icon view.

All of the tools for arranging Desktop icons are available by right-clicking any open area on the Desktop. On the shortcut menu that opens, you'll find a submenu named Arrange Icons By that holds the following commands:

- **Name, Size, Type, and Modified**   Choosing any of these commands arranges the icons down the left edge of your Desktop according to the command you use. If there are more icons than fit in a single column, multiple columns are used.

- **Auto Arrange**   This command is actually a toggle, meaning that the Auto Arrange is turned either on or off (a check next to the command indicates it is on). When it is turned on, icons are automatically arranged down the left side of your Desktop, regardless of where you move or create them. Try moving an icon to another location and it will pop right back.

- **Align to Grid**   This command is also a toggle. When turned on, an invisible grid is enabled for your Desktop that is used to align icons. Whenever you move an icon, it snaps to the nearest location on the grid, presenting an easy way to keep an orderly Desktop.

- **Show Desktop Icons**   This is another toggle command; when it is turned off, Desktop icons are not displayed. This can be useful if you use Web content on your Desktop that is often obscured by icons and icon text. Instead of removing icons, you can turn their display on and off as needed.

- **Lock Web Items on Desktop**   Another toggle, this one prevents any of the Web items on your Desktop from being moved. For more on Web items, see "Adding Web Content to the Desktop," later in this chapter.

- **Run Desktop Cleanup Wizard**   This wizard is covered in the following section.

Running the Desktop Cleanup Wizard

The Desktop Cleanup Wizard is a new tool in Windows XP. You can run it manually by right-clicking any open area of the Desktop and choosing Arrange Icons By | Run Desktop Cleanup Wizard from the shortcut menu. The wizard works by creating a folder on your Desktop named Unused Desktop Shortcuts and helping you select unused shortcuts on your Desktop to move there. The wizard shows you the date that each shortcut was last used to help you make your decision.

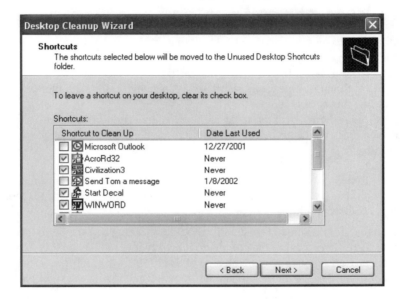

TRY IT   If you have just recently installed Windows XP, you will probably see a message pop up in your notification area after a few days offering to run the Desktop Cleanup Wizard for you. Once you close it a few times, it will not bug you again. If you have deactivated this automatic reminder and would like to activate it again, use the following steps:

1. Right-click anywhere on your Desktop and choose Properties.

2. Switch to the Desktop tab of the Display Properties dialog box that appears and click Customize Desktop. This opens the Desktop Items dialog box.

3. Select the Run Desktop Cleanup Wizard Every 60 Days option and click OK.

Managing Desktop Themes

A Desktop theme is a predefined set of Desktop customizations that you can apply all at once. There are two built-in themes in Windows XP: Windows XP and Windows Classic. Microsoft Plus! for Windows XP (a separate product) adds a few more, and there will no doubt be countless third-party themes available online over the years.

A Desktop theme includes the following information:

- The Desktop background, whether a picture or a color
- Desktop icons
- Screen saver
- Window and button styles, color scheme, and font size
- Advanced Desktop appearance options, including custom interface colors
- Mouse pointers
- Sounds associated with Windows events

Most of the settings on this list are covered in this chapter. Customizing mouse pointers and sounds are covered in Chapter 22.

Themes are managed using the Themes tab of the Display Properties dialog box, shown in Figure 21-1. To apply a new theme, make a selection from the Theme drop-down list. The selected theme is displayed in the Sample window so you can check it out before you actually apply it. Click OK to apply the theme. The Browse option on the Themes list lets you select a saved theme on your hard drive. The More Themes Online option takes you to the Microsoft Plus! For Windows XP Web site.

Figure 21-1   Use Desktop themes to manage collections of Desktop customizations.

> ► | **QUICK TIP**
> |
> | *In order for a Desktop theme to be displayed on the Theme drop-down list on the Themes tab,*
> | *it must be located in the C:\Windows\Resources\Themes folder (this is where new themes are*
> | *saved by default). Otherwise, you must use the Browse option to find the theme yourself.*

TRY IT To create a new Desktop theme, use the following steps:

1. Go to the Themes tab of the Display Properties dialog box and select an existing theme
   on which to base your new theme.
2. Go to the various locations in Windows to customize the appearance of your Desktop.
3. Return to the Themes tab and save your new theme under a different name.

Changing the Desktop Background

Choosing a Desktop background is a simple process. Right-click anywhere on your Desktop, choose
Properties, and then switch to the Desktop tab of the Display Properties dialog box. You can choose from
a long list of preinstalled background images or click Browse to locate your own. You can make a
background out of just about any kind of picture file (.bmp, .gif, and .jpg, to name a few) or out of
an HTML file. You can also use the Color menu to choose a plain color for your background.

If you choose a picture as your background, you can also specify its position on the Desktop. Options
include centered on the screen, tiled (the image is repeated over and over to fill the screen), and stretched
so that a single image fills the screen. If you choose to center a picture, the color specified on the Color
menu is used as a background.

If you choose to use an HTML file as your background, check out the section "Adding Web Content
to the Desktop" later in the chapter.

Customizing Desktop Icons

By default, Windows XP displays only one icon on your Desktop following installation: the Recycle
Bin. If you upgraded from a previous version of Windows, or if you have since added icons, you will
likely have more. You can change the basic icons that are displayed on the Desktop using the Desktop
Items dialog box, shown in Figure 21-2 (see the procedure in this section for details on how to get
there). Using the Desktop Items dialog box, you can specify which of the basic Windows icons
(My Documents, My Computer, My Network Places, and Internet Explorer) should appear on the
Desktop. You can also change the icons associated with each of these items. Finally, you can specify
whether the Desktop Cleanup Wizard runs automatically (see the earlier section "Running the Desktop
Cleanup Wizard" for more).

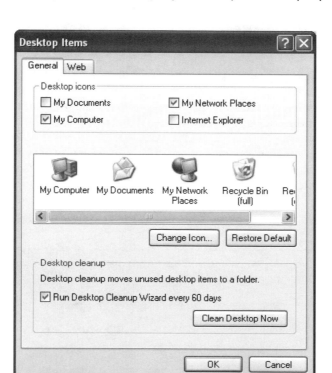

Figure 21-2   You can customize the appearance of Desktop icons.

▶ **QUICK TIP**

You can also toggle the display of Desktop icons by right-clicking their corresponding icons on the Start menu and choosing Show On Desktop.

TRY IT ▸ To modify the icons on your Desktop, use the following steps:

1. Right-click the Desktop, choosing Properties, and switch to the Desktop tab of the Display Properties dialog box.
2. Click Customize Desktop.
3. Specify which icons should show on the Desktop and change the icons for these items, if you want.
4. Click OK.

Adding Web Content to the Desktop

As you are probably aware, you can add Web-related content to your Windows XP Desktop. Actually, this feature started back in Windows 98, was named Active Desktop, and much fanfare was made over it. Since then, the name Active Desktop has been dropped and the feature has been pushed a little more to the background, but it is still there and can actually be useful and a little bit of fun.

The basic idea behind using Web content is that you can add Web pages or other Internet accessories (tickers and the like) that are always present on your Desktop and are continuously updated. Obviously, this feature is not very useful if you have a dial-up Internet account where you are connected only occasionally, but a persistent connection such as DSL or cable can make it worthwhile. Figure 21-3 shows a Desktop with an entire Web page and Figure 21-4 shows a Desktop with a couple of accessories.

> ### QUICK TIP
> *You can also use an image as Web content. The advantage of doing this is that you can drag the image around on your Desktop to a desired location.*

TRY IT   To add Web content to your Desktop, use the following steps:

1. Right-click the Desktop, choose Properties, and switch to the Desktop tab of the Display Properties dialog box.
2. Click Customize Desktop and switch to the Web tab on the Desktop Items dialog box that opens.

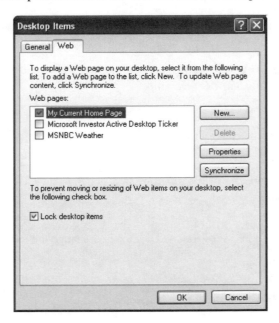

Figure 21-3   You can place your Internet home page or any other Web site directly on your Desktop.

3. A list of currently configured Web items is displayed. You can turn them on or off using the check boxes. To permanently delete an item, click Delete.

4. Click New to create a new Web item. A dialog box opens that lets you enter a Web address, browse for a local HTML file or image, or visit an online gallery of accessories you can install.

5. Web content is not synchronized with the Internet automatically. You can synchronize an item manually by clicking Synchronize. You can also set up an automatic synchronization schedule for an item by clicking Properties. The Properties dialog box that opens lets you set up a schedule and control how much disk space a downloaded item can use.

6. To prevent Web items from being moved around, select the Lock Desktop Items option. When the Desktop is unlocked, placing your pointer over a Web item on the Desktop makes a title bar appear that you can use to move and resize the item.

7. Click OK.

Figure 21-4   You can also decorate your Desktop with any number of Internet accessories.

▶ **QUICK TIP**

You can lock and unlock Desktop Web items quickly by right-clicking the Desktop and choosing Arrange Icons By | Lock Web Items On Desktop from the shortcut menu. When a Web item is unlocked, clicking the small down arrow at the left side of the title bar reveals a menu with many useful commands for controlling the item. You can synchronize the item, adjust its properties, and specify how much of the Desktop the item should consume.

Using Screen Savers

Since almost everyone is familiar with screen savers and since the basic interface for using them has not changed in years, there's very little to say about them you won't already know. However, there is one piece of advice this book can give. Don't use them unless you need to. For one thing, modern monitors do not suffer the same propensity for image burn-in as old monitors, so your screen isn't really being saved. For another thing, screen savers, especially third-party screen savers, are notorious for causing problems—crashes, freezes, and conflicts with other programs, to name a few. And finally, it's usually much better to have Windows just turn off your monitor after a period of inactivity if your video card and monitor support it. It's better for the environment and can save you some money on your utility bill.

In fact, there are only two good reasons for using screen savers. The first is that you just love them and simply can't do without them. The second is that you can have Windows require a password when the screen saver is deactivated before you can get back into your system. This offers the advantage of protecting your computer from prying eyes when you step away and forget to log off.

If you do choose to use a screen saver, keep it to the simpler ones that come with Windows. The three dimensional screen savers that come with Windows and many third-party screen savers usually consume a lot of system resources. In fact, some of these screen savers can keep your CPU running at near 100 percent capacity and have been known to cause overheating in the CPU.

Modifying Desktop Appearance

Windows XP makes it easy to customize the basic appearance of the Desktop, from modifying colors used for windows and menus to altering advanced display effects. All of this is done using the Appearance tab of the Display Properties dialog box, shown in Figure 21-5.

To begin with, there are three settings you can change on the Appearance tab itself:

- **Windows and buttons**   This menu lets you choose whether to use the new Windows XP style (rounded windows and buttons) or the classic Windows style. One advantage to using the classic style is that the Windows XP style can slow the performance of your computer a bit.

- **Color scheme**   This menu lets you choose a coordinated color scheme governing all the elements of windows, menus, and dialog boxes. If the Windows XP style is selected, only three color schemes are present: Blue (the default), Olive Green, and Silver. If the Windows Classic style is selected, a large number of color schemes are available, including some high contrast schemes for people who have difficulty seeing their display.

- **Font size**   Use this menu to specify the size used for fonts in menus, windows, and dialog boxes. Larger sizes are often easier to read, but can take some getting used to.

The Advanced button on the Appearance tab opens a separate dialog box, shown next, that lets you customize the colors for individual interface elements. Such elements include window backgrounds, menus, title bars, buttons, and many more. Pick an element from the Item drop-down list or by clicking the element in the sample display. For all elements, you will be able to change the basic color, listed as Color 1. For some items, you can change the size in pixels that the item takes up on the screen. For some items, you can also change the gradient color, listed as Color 2. Gradients are used in elements such as title bars where one color blends smoothly into another color.

Figure 21-5 Use the Appearance tab to modify the colors used in the Windows interface and to control advanced visual effects.

The Effects button on the Appearance tab opens a dialog box that lets you configure a number of advanced visual effects. You should know that most of these visual effects can affect Windows performance, but some of them are useful enough that it will probably be a willing sacrifice. Visual effects include:

- **Transition effect for menus and ToolTips**   Choose to have menus and ToolTips fade or scroll in and out of view. This option looks kind of nice, but ends up just making it take that much longer to get where you're going.

- **Smooth edges of screen fonts**   This option is quite nice, even if it does affect performance slightly. Select Standard font smoothing if you are using a conventional monitor (a CRT display) and Clear Type if you are using an LCD display. Either of these makes reading text onscreen much easier.

- **Use large icons**   This is useful if you have trouble seeing small icons. This option does not affect performance.

- **Show shadows under menus**   This is another purely cosmetic effect. Turn it off unless you really like it.

- **Show window contents while dragging**   This feature really slows down the dragging of windows and honestly isn't that useful. When disabled, dragging a window gives you an outline of the window to let you know where it will end up.

- **Hide underlined letters for keyboard navigation**   On menus throughout Windows (including the Start menu), you can select most commands by pressing a key letter, which is usually indicated in the menu command by an underlined character. You can also access a menu by holding down the ALT key while pressing the indicated letter for the menu. If this option is selected, the underlined characters are not revealed until you press the ALT key. This one is purely a matter of preference and does not affect performance.

Optimizing Display Settings

Display settings, such as screen resolution and the number of colors used, are configured using the Settings tab of the Display Properties dialog box, shown in Figure 21-6. The basic settings you can make are straightforward:

- Screen resolution governs the number of pixels used in displaying the Desktop. The available settings depend on your combination of video card and monitor, but typical settings include 800x600, 1024x768, and several higher resolutions. As you increase the resolution, each pixel on your display gets smaller and so do the interface elements on your Desktop. If you increase the resolution beyond a certain point, you may start to notice a flicker in your screen even if your setup supports the resolution. You'll have to experiment to find a setting that is right for you.

- Color quality represents the number of colors used in your display at one time. Higher numbers of colors generally mean a decrease in the graphics performance of your computer. The one exception to this rule is that 32-bit graphics perform just about as well as 16-bit

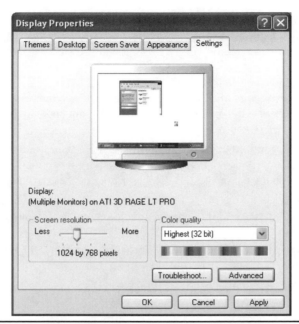

Figure 21-6 Adjust settings and troubleshoot video problems using the Settings tab of the Display Properties dialog box.

graphics. Interestingly, though, 24-bit graphics show a marked decrease in performance. Options typically include:

- **Medium (16-bit)**   This option displays 65,536 colors.
- **High (24-bit)**   This option displays 16 million colors.
- **Highest (32-bit)**   This option displays higher than 16 million colors, creating a near photo-realistic image.

Windows does a pretty good job of optimizing your display settings when it is first installed. It sets both the screen resolution and color quality to the highest setting supported by your display adapter, while making allowances for the basic speed of your computer. Nonetheless, you may want to play around with these settings to find the best combination for you.

▶ *NOTE*

You may notice that the old standby combination of 256 colors and 640x480 resolution is missing from the basic options. Windows XP doesn't include these on the Settings tab because most modern computers support at least 800x600 and 16-bit color. If you need to use a lower resolution, click Advanced on the Settings tab, switch to the Adapter tab of the dialog box that opens, click List All Modes, and choose a mode with the settings you need.

The Advanced button on the Settings tab opens a separate dialog box used to configure advanced options for your video card and monitor. Many video adapters create new tabs on this dialog box, but you can usually count on the following tabs being present:

- **General**   This tab lets you change the dots per inch (dpi) setting for your display to compensate for items too small to view at higher resolutions. You can also specify whether Windows should restart after changes are made to the display settings.

- **Adapter**   This tab lets you view the properties for your video adapter so that you can install new drivers and view resource settings. For more on using these properties, see Chapter 2. This tab also lets you view all display modes supported by your video adapter and monitor, providing more choices than on the basic Settings tab.

- **Monitor**   This tab lets you view the properties for your monitor and set a screen refresh rate, which is the rate at which your video adapter redraws the display on your monitor. Increasing the refresh rate can make your display more stable by reducing the visible flicker that occurs on some monitors. By default, rates that are not supported by your monitor are not displayed on the list and it's best to leave it this way; selecting too high a refresh rate can damage your monitor.

- **Troubleshoot**   This tab lets you adjust the hardware acceleration used by your graphics hardware and disable write combining, a feature that speeds up display of information to your screen. If you are experiencing video-related problems, try adjusting these values to see if you can locate the source of the trouble.

- **Color Management**   Many monitors support the use of color profiles that help ensure that the colors displayed on your monitor are as close to true as possible. If your monitor has a profile available, it is likely that Windows will detect it automatically. If you have a profile you have downloaded from your monitor's manufacturer, you can install it by clicking Add.

Using Multiple Monitors

Windows XP supports the use of up to four monitors on a computer. Each monitor requires its own video card and the video cards you use must be supported by Windows XP in order to do this. Once you get the hardware installed, setting up the displays in Windows is not difficult. Figure 21-7 shows the Settings tab of the Display Properties dialog box as it looks when two monitors are connected.

A representation of each monitor is shown in the display window. The primary monitor (the one on which the Start menu and Taskbar appear) is labeled with a one. When you first install an additional monitor, its icon is dimmed and the monitor itself displays nothing. To enable the monitor, select it by clicking its icon and then select the Extend My Windows Desktop Onto This Monitor option. Click Apply and the new monitor should come to life. Once your additional monitor is activated, you can choose your primary monitor by selecting it and using the Use This Device As The Primary Monitor option. That monitor will become number one and the rest will be renumbered.

When multiple monitors are connected, Windows extends the Desktop across all monitors. You can drag a window or icon straight from one monitor to the next. Using multiple monitors is a great way to organize your programs, especially if you spend a lot of time in front of the computer. If you

Figure 21-7   Using multiple monitors in Windows XP is a great way to increase your screen "real estate."

design Web sites, for example, you might keep your editor open on one monitor, a browser window open on another, and a graphics editor open on yet another.

You can orient Windows to the way your monitors are set up on your desk by dragging their icons around in the display window. The example in Figure 21-7 shows two monitors placed side by side, with their top edges aligned. You can drag monitors in all four directions; monitors can be beside one another, stacked vertically, or whatever else you can think of.

CHAPTER 22

Using the Control Panel

TIPS IN THIS CHAPTER

M ost customization and configuration in Windows XP is handled through a number of small utilities found in the Windows Control Panel folder, which is accessible from the Start menu. You will often hear these utilities referred to as applets, programs, or even as control panels themselves, but by and large these utilities take one of three forms: a tabbed dialog box for setting options, a specialized window, or a wizard. In this chapter, you will learn several general tips for working with the Control Panel window. Since most of the Control Panel utilities are straightforward and similar to the interface that's been used in previous versions of Windows, this chapter will not go over all of the utilities themselves. Instead, this chapter presents advice on getting the most out of certain utilities.

▶ **NOTE**

Many of the Control Panel utilities are discussed in other places in this book. For example, the Display utility is covered in Chapter 21, which discusses setting display and Desktop options. If you don't see a particular utility listed in this chapter, check the table of contents or index.

Switching to Classic View

Traditionally, the Control Panel window has been presented as a simple list of the utilities available inside. With Windows XP, the designers apparently decided that this was too confusing and introduced a new Category view. The idea is that the various tasks you can perform using the Control Panel are divided into broad categories such as Appearance and Themes or Performance and Maintenance, presumably to lead novice users more easily through their options. There are two problems with this approach. The first is that not all of the tasks and utilities fit neatly inside these categories, so you have to do a good bit of sifting around to find what you're looking for. The second problem is that simply choosing tasks from a list doesn't give you a good idea of where you are in the interface, what you are really changing, or what your other options may be.

Open the Control Panel window and choose the Switch To Classic View link from the tasks pane to see all of the available utilities. Spend some time playing around with the utilities and you'll find that the organization is much more efficient in Classic view.

Viewing the Control Panel as a Menu on the Start Menu

The Start menu is capable of displaying certain special Windows folders as menus instead of as simple links. The Control Panel is one of these and displaying it as a menu lets you choose and run any particular utility right from the Start menu instead of opening the Control Panel window first.

TRY IT   To view the Control Panel as a menu instead of a link on the Start menu, use the following steps:

1. Right-click any open space on the Taskbar, click Properties and switch to the Start Menu tab on the Taskbar And Start Menu Properties dialog box.

2. Click the active Customize button.

3. If you are using the Classic Start menu option, select the Expand Control Panel option on the Customize Classic Start Menu dialog box and click OK twice to apply your settings. You are now finished with the procedure.

4. If you are using the Start menu option (the default Windows XP option), switch to the Advanced tab on the Customize Start Menu dialog box.

5. From the Start menu items list, select the Display As A Menu option under the Control Panel category.

6. Click OK twice to apply your settings.

► **QUICK TIP**

Other special folders that you can display as a menu using the same steps include My Computer, My Documents, My Music, My Pictures, Network Connections, and System Administrative Tools.

Creating a Custom Toolbar Using the Control Panel Folder

The Windows Taskbar gives you the ability to create custom toolbars that work much like Windows XP's Quick Launch bar. Custom toolbars are created from folders and contain buttons for whatever is inside the folder. Since the Control Panel is just a specialized folder, you can create a custom toolbar from it. Figure 22-1 shows a Control Panel toolbar that has been detached from the main Windows Taskbar.

TRY IT To create a custom toolbar using the Control Panel folder, use the following steps:

1. Right-click any open space on the Taskbar and choose Toolbars | New Toolbar.
2. In the New Toolbar dialog box, expand the My Computer folder and select the Control Panel folder inside.
3. Click OK.

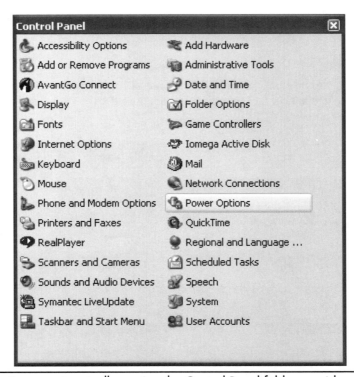

Figure 22-1   Creating a custom toolbar using the Control Panel folder provides quick access to the utilities inside.

Starting Control Panel Programs from the Command Prompt

You can launch most of the Control Panel utilities (and even open them to a particular tab) from the command prompt. This allows you to open the utilities from inside a batch file, program, or shortcut and to open utilities using the Command Prompt window, the Run dialog box, or an Address box in Windows Explorer. For example, if you often change the font size used in your display, you could create a shortcut to take you right to the appropriate tab of the Display Properties dialog box.

Most of the Control Panel utilities are stored as files with a .cpl extension in the \Windows\ System32 folder. You must use a program named control.exe to launch these files. The basic command for doing this looks something like the following:

```
control filename.cpl {utility_name} {,property_tab}
```

In practice, you usually don't need to include the *utility_name* parameter and you only need to include the *property_tab* parameter if you want to switch to a particular tab of the utility. Tabs are typically numbered starting with zero. To open to the default tab, you only need the actual file name.

As an example, the following command opens the Display utility and switches to the Screen Saver tab (the third tab):

```
control desk.cpl ,2
```

Table 22-1 shows the file names of the standard Control Panel utilities, whether the utility needs to have the utility name included in the command line, and whether the utility supports switching to a particular tab.

Utility	File Name	Applet Name	Supports Tabs
Accessibility Options	access.cpl	Not needed	Yes Numbering starts with 1
Add Hardware	hdwwiz.cpl	Not needed	No
Add or Remove Programs	appwiz.cpl	Not needed	No
Date and Time	timedate.cpl	Not Needed	Yes Numbering starts with 0, cannot access Internet Time tab with number
Display	desk.cpl	Not needed	Yes Numbering starts with 0
Folder Options	Type **control folders** at the command prompt	Not needed	No

Table 22-1   Minimum and Recommended Requirements for Installing Windows XP

Utility	File Name	Applet Name	Supports Tabs
Fonts	Type **control fonts** at the command prompt	Not needed	No
Game Controllers	joy.cpl	Not Needed	No
Internet Options	inetcpl.cpl	Not needed	Yes Numbering starts with 0
Keyboard	main.cpl	Keyboard	No
Mouse	main.cpl	Not needed	Yes Numbering starts with 0
Network Connections	ncpa.cpl	Not needed	No
Phone and Modem Options	telephon.cpl	Not Needed	Yes Numbering starts with 0
Power Options	powercfg.cpl	Not needed	No
Printers and Faxes	Type **control printers** at the command prompt	Not needed	No
Regional and Language Options	intl.cpl	Not needed	Yes Numbering starts with 0
Scheduled Tasks	Type **control schedtasks** at the command prompt	Not needed	No
SCSI Devices	Devapps.cpl	SCSI Devices	Yes Numbering starts with 0
Sounds and Audio Devices	mmsys.cpl	Not needed	Yes Numbering starts with 0
Speech	Type **control speech** at the command prompt	Not needed	No
System	sysdm.cpl	Not needed	Yes Numbering starts with 0
Tape Devices	Devapps.cpl	Tape Devices	Yes Numbering starts with 0
Taskbar and Start Menu	Not available		

Table 22-1   Minimum and Recommended Requirements for Installing Windows XP *(continued)*

TRY IT   To create a shortcut that opens the Pointer Options tab of the Mouse Properties dialog box, use the following steps:

1. Right-click any open space on the Desktop and choose New | Shortcut.
2. Enter **control main.cpl ,2** as the location of the item and click Next.

3. Enter **Adjust Pointer Options** as a name for the shortcut and click Next.

4. Double-click the new shortcut to jump to the Pointer Options tab.

Customizing Mouse Settings with Tweak UI

The Mouse utility in the Windows Control Panel should look pretty familiar. It provides you with several basic mouse settings to customize, including:

- Switching the left and right mouse buttons
- Adjusting the double-click speed
- Changing pointer graphics
- Changing pointer speed

While these settings are important, Microsoft has also made a separate utility available that you can use to further customize your mouse behavior. This utility, named Tweak UI, is part of a free add-on named Microsoft Powertoys for Windows XP, which is available for download at *http://www.microsoft.com/windowsxp/pro/downloads/powertoys.asp.*

Once installed, the Tweak UI utility, shown in Figure 22-2, lets you adjust a host of hidden Windows XP features. The mouse-related features that you can customize include:

- You can adjust how fast submenus appear when you point your mouse at them. The default delay in Windows XP is actually a little slow. Increasing this value to maximum speed makes submenus appear almost instantaneously.

- The double-click sensitivity adjusts the same value as the slider on the basic Mouse Control Panel utility, but the Tweak UI version gives you finer control.

- The drag sensitivity control adjusts how far you must move your mouse before Windows decides that you are dragging an object. Increase the value if you sometimes accidentally drag objects.

- The hover controls adjust how Windows determines when you are hovering your mouse over an object, so it will know when to pop up a ToolTip. The mouse must stay within a small region for a certain amount of time. You can set both the hover sensitivity (how big the region is) and the amount of time it takes to be considered a hover.

- The wheel controls allow you to adjust how many lines are scrolled when you turn the scroll wheel on a mouse that has one. You can also adjust it to scroll a page at a time.

- Turning on the X-Mouse behavior causes Windows to activate a window or dialog box whenever you move your mouse over it, instead of having to click the window.

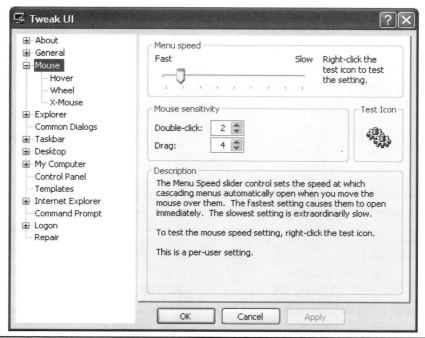

Figure 22-2   Tweak UI gives you access to a lot of hidden features, including some that affect mouse behavior.

Creating a Shortcut to Device Manager

Device Manager is a useful tool for managing the settings for the hardware on your computer. Normally, you must access it by opening the System Control Panel utility, switching to the Hardware tab, and then clicking Device Manager. If you use Device Manager often, you can save time by creating a shortcut. The executable file for Device Manager is devmgmt.msc (actually, it is a Microsoft Management Console file).

TRY IT   To create a shortcut that opens Device Manager, use the following steps:

1. Right-click any open space on the Desktop and choose New | Shortcut.
2. Enter **devmgmt.msc** as the location of the item and click Next.
3. Enter **Device Manager** as a name for the shortcut and click Next.
4. Double-click the new shortcut to open Device Manager.

Activating Advanced Power Options

All of the power management features in Windows XP are controlled through a single place—the Power Options Control Panel utility. This utility is used to perform a number of actions, including:

- **Setting power schemes**   This feature lets you control what happens to your computer after it is idle for a certain amount of time. You can have Windows turn off the monitor, turn off hard disks, or go into standby or hibernation modes. You can specify settings both for when the computer is plugged in and running on batteries (for notebooks or computers with battery backup).

- **Setting alarms**   This feature lets you set alarms to alert you when a low battery situation occurs. Alarms can display messages, make sounds, put the computer in standby or hibernation, and even run a custom program. You can set two separate alarms: a low battery alarm for when battery power reaches one state and a critical alarm for when it reaches an even lower state.

> **QUICK TIP**
>
> *If you want to test an alarm setting, just drag the alarm's threshold to 100% and unplug the AC power source for your computer. The alarm should trigger immediately.*

- **Checking power levels**   This feature lets you see exactly how much power is remaining in any batteries hooked up to the computer.

- **Set advanced options**   You can configure whether a power icon is shown in the notification area and whether a password is required when coming out of standby. You can also choose whether the computer goes into standby, hibernation, or simply shuts down when you press the power button.

- **Hibernate**   Configure whether hibernation is enabled on your computer and view the amount of disk space that hibernation will require.

Many of the settings discussed in this list require that your computer support certain power specifications. Two basic power specifications can be found in computers today:

- **Advanced Power Management (APM)**   Developed by Intel and Microsoft, APM is the technology that originally allowed a computer's BIOS to manage power. Windows XP can take advantage of many of the features of APM to power down certain components automatically in hopes of saving power.

- **Advanced Configuration and Power Interface (ACPI)**   Developed by Intel, Microsoft, and a few other companies, ACPI enables the operating system to control the amount of power provided to each piece of hardware on a system. If your computer supports ACPI, you'll have the option of sending your computer into a standby mode (where most of the hardware is powered down) and possibly of powering your computer up with a touch of your keyboard or mouse.

Your computer requires ACPI to be able to enter standby mode. It requires APM to be able to perform many functions, such as entering hibernation, displaying power levels for batteries, adjusting certain idle-time events, setting alarms, and controlling what happens when the power button is pressed. If your computer supports APM, an APM tab will be available on the Power Options utility. Enable APM on this tab to activate the advanced power features on all the other tabs of the utility.

Activating Speech Recognition Options

The Speech Control Panel utility is used to control two speech features that are new to Windows XP. Text-to-Speech is a feature that lets Windows interpret the written text in a document (e-mail, word processor, or whatever) and read it aloud to you in a very computer-sounding voice. Speech Recognition is the other new feature supported natively in Windows XP. Though the dictation function of speech recognition is of marginal value (mainly because its accuracy leaves a lot to be desired), you can also use it to give basic commands to Windows and many programs by voice—a pretty handy feature.

Of the two, only Text-to-Speech is activated when you first install Windows XP. The reason for this is that, while Windows XP supports speech recognition, it doesn't actually have a speech recognition engine built in. Once you purchase and install a supported engine, you can control much of its behavior using the Control Panel utility.

Popular speech recognition programs that should work with Windows XP include IBM's ViaVoice and Lernout and Haspie's Dragon Naturally Speaking.

► **QUICK TIP**

Microsoft Office XP does come with a speech recognition engine (actually a simplified version of the Lernout and Haspie engine), though it is not installed by default. To install it, choose the Speech command from the Tools menu of any Office application and have your installation files ready.

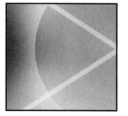

CHAPTER 23
Editing the Registry

TIPS IN THIS CHAPTER

ost Windows users never bother with the Windows Registry. After all, it's big and complicated, and one wrong move can mess up your system pretty badly. However, if you take the proper precautions (such as backing up the Registry before editing it), learn to use the proper tools, and perhaps most important, learn *when* editing the Registry is the proper choice, you'll find that the Windows Registry can be a pretty powerful tool.

What Is the Registry?

The Registry is essentially a database of operating system, hardware driver, and application configuration settings. The Registry is stored in a hierarchical database that often seems cryptic and can be modified directly only by using a special program named Windows Registry Editor—which you won't find on the Start menu.

Actually, you edit the Windows Registry all the time, without even realizing it. Every time you install or remove a program or set up new hardware, you are editing the Registry. Every time you customize your Desktop or change a program's settings, you are editing the Registry. In fact, the vast majority of changes that you can make in the Registry are available in the dialog boxes you find scattered throughout Windows. So why bother with editing the Registry? The simple answer is that a number of settings are available in the Registry that you just can't access in other ways.

Registry Structure

The Registry is structured using a number of components. To begin with, the Registry is stored in several different files on your computer. These files, or *hives,* are located in the \Windows\System32\ config and \Documents and Settings\username folders. However, when you use the Registry Editor, as shown in Figure 23-1, the Registry is presented to you as a seamless hierarchy that looks much like any folder tree you might see in Windows.

The Registry hierarchy is composed of the following elements:

- **Subtrees**   The entire Registry for a computer is shown as one tree that is divided into five subtrees. Each of these subtrees has a specific purpose and is further divided into *keys, subkeys,* and *entries.* The five subtrees are

  - **HKEY_CLASSES_ROOT (HKCR)**   HKCR contains information about file associations on the computer—what file types are opened with what applications. HKCR also holds definitions of every object that exists in the Windows XP environment. The keys that control these definitions control information about objects' shell interfaces, such as what commands are contained on the shortcut menu for an object.

  - **HKEY_CURRENT_USER (HKCU)**   HKCU contains the profile for the user who is currently logged on to Windows. A profile contains customized system, hardware, and application settings for a particular user. All this information is stored in a hive called USER.DAT, one copy of which exists for each user of a computer in the user's Documents and Settings folder.

Subtree

Key

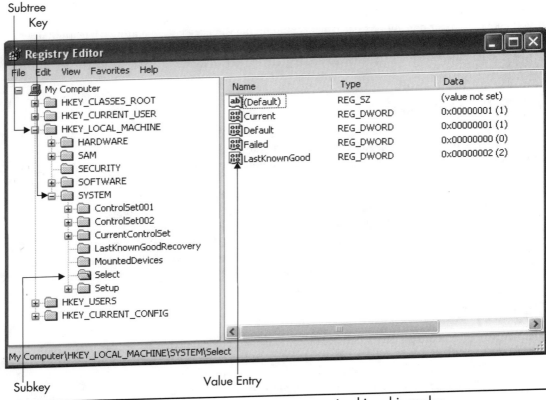

Figure 23-1 The various elements of the Registry are organized in a hierarchy.

- **HKEY_LOCAL_MACHINE (HKLM)**   HKLM contains entries that describe the CPU, system bus, and all other hardware configuration information collected by Windows during startup. HKLM also contains installed drivers, settings, and configuration data.

- **HKEY_USERS (HKU)**   HKU contains the profile information for all local users on the computer. At least two keys will appear in the HKU subtree. The first, .Default, contains a default group of settings that are applied whenever a user who does not already have a profile logs on to Windows. When a new user logs on, Windows creates a new key for that user and then copies all the information from the .Default key into the new key. The second key you will always see in the HKU subtree is for the built-in Administrator account.

- **HKEY_CURRENT_CONFIG (HKCC)**   HKCC holds information about the hardware profile currently being used and device information that is gathered during Windows startup.

- **Keys**   A key is something like a folder you would find in Windows Explorer. It can contain any number of subkeys and value entries.

- **Subkeys**   A subkey is a key that exists inside another key. Subkeys can hold additional subkeys and value entries.
- **Value Entries**   Value entries define the various properties of a key. Each entry has three parts: a name, a data type, and the value assigned to the entry. You edit these entries when working in the Registry.

The Registry Editor

While Windows NT and Windows 2000 allowed you to choose from two different programs, REGEDIT.EXE and REGEDT32.EXE, Windows XP includes only one editor—the Windows Registry Editor (Figure 23-1). If you type either command (**regedit** or **regedt32**) at the command prompt or in the Run dialog box, the same Windows Registry Editor program runs.

Backing Up the Registry

When you make a change to the Registry using the Windows Registry Editor, the change is made to your system immediately. You don't get the luxury of being able to review your changes and save the file, and there is no undo function. For this reason, it is extremely important that you back up your Registry before making any edits.

You can back up the Registry in three ways:

- *Include the Registry in a backup of your system.* If you are using the Windows Backup utility, you should use the System State option described in Chapter 25. If you are using a third-party backup program, make sure it is Registry-aware or make sure you include the various files that make up the Registry. These files are listed in Table 23-1. While this method takes the longest to perform, it offers the advantage of letting you restore your system should something serious go wrong that results in an inability to start Windows.

- *Make copies of the Registry files listed in Table 23-1.* Note that not all the files listed may be present on your computer. Use the search function to locate them all quickly

- *Use the Registry Editor's export feature to export the portion of the Registry you will be editing into a separate file.* You can then import this portion back should something go wrong. For details on this method, see the section "Creating a Registry Import File," later in this chapter.

Connecting to a Remote Registry

In addition to editing the Registry on the local computer, you can also edit a remote Registry for a computer on your network. From an open Registry Editor window, choose File | Connect Network Registry and from the dialog box that opens, choose the remote computer. When you are finished working on the remote Registry, choose File | Disconnect Network Registry.

You must have administrative permission on the computer containing the Registry to edit it. In addition, you can edit only values in the HKLM and HKU subkeys.

Registry Location	Files	File Locations
HKEY_LOCAL_MACHINE\SAM	Sam Sam.log SAM.sav	\Windows\System32\config
HKEY_LOCAL_MACHINE\Security	Security Security.log Security.sav	\Windows\System32\config
HKEY_LOCAL_MACHINE\Software	Software Software.log Software.sav	\Windows\System32\config
HKEY_LOCAL_MACHINE\System	System System.log System.sav System.alt	\Windows\System32\config
HKEY_CURRENT_CONFIG	System System.log System.sav System.alt	\Windows\System32\config
HKEY_CURRENT_USER	Ntuser.dat Ntuser.dat.log	\Documents and Settings*user*
HKEY_USERS\.DEFAULT	Default Default.log Default.sav	\Windows\System32\config

Table 23-1   Files Comprising the Windows XP Registry

Searching the Registry

The best way to make changes to the Registry is to have the instructions for a well-documented change sitting in front of you. That way, you can browse to the appropriate subkey, make the change, and be done with it. If you don't know the exact location of the subkey you're looking for, or if you just want to poke around looking for something interesting, regedit offers a pretty good search function. You can search for the key name itself, or even the data that is stored in keys. This can be a useful way to determine where important information is stored.

To begin a search, choose Edit | Find. The Find dialog box, shown in the following illustration, lets you specify the parameters of the search. You can enter a string (a sequence of characters), a numeric value, or the name of a key you want to find. Use the options labeled Keys, Values, Data, and Match Whole String Only to narrow down your search.

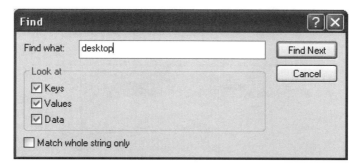

If the first instance found is not what you are looking for, press the F3 key to jump to the next instance that matches the search, without bothering to open the Find dialog box again.

Creating Registry Favorites

When you've found a key that you think you will be using in the future, save it as a favorite so that you can quickly access it again. Select the key, choose Favorites | Add to Favorites, and then name the favorite shortcut. To get back to this key in the future, just select it from the Favorites menu.

Changing Registry Values

Select any value entry in the right pane of the Registry Editor and then choose Edit | Modify. You can also right-click the value entry and select Modify, or you can just double-click the entry to open the Edit dialog box. Figure 23-2 shows two typical Edit dialog boxes used to change values for an entry. The top dialog box is used to change a string value and the bottom dialog box is used to change a DWORD value. Note that the data type for the value affects both the name of the dialog box and what kind of data you can enter. To change the value for the entry, just enter text into the Value Data box.

Adding a Registry Value or Key

To add an entry to the Registry, you first need to decide under what key you want to create your entry. After you've navigated to the key and selected it by clicking it once, you can create a new entry by choosing Edit | New, and then pointing to one of the listed data types that you can create.

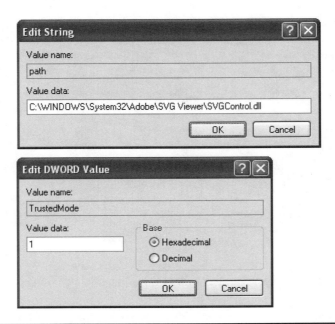

Figure 23-2   Use Edit dialog boxes to change values for a value entry.

Creating a Registry Import File

A Registry Import file is basically a special text file with a .reg extension that contains registry information. You create import files by selecting a portion of the Registry and choosing File | Export in the Registry Editor. Once you have an import file, you can import it back into a Registry either by double-clicking the file or by choosing File | Import in the Registry Editor. You can create Import files based on any branch of the Registry hierarchy. You cannot create Import files for a single Registry value.

Import files are particularly useful for two tasks:

- Creating a backup of a portion of the Registry that you are about to modify. Should something go wrong, it is easy to import the backup portion back into the Registry.

- Saving a particular Registry edit that you can take to another computer or send to someone else. You could, for example, save your favorite Registry hacks as import files so that you can give them to friends or apply them to future installations of Windows.

> **QUICK TIP**
>
> *If you need to make changes to several values in the Registry, you can export the keys containing those values, edit the exported file using a program like Notepad, and then import the changes back into the Registry. This method is quicker than using the Registry Editor Interface.*

TRY IT To create an Import file, use the following steps:

1. Click Start | Run.
2. Enter **regedit** into the Open box and click OK.
3. Select the key or subkey that you want to export.
4. Choose File| Export.
5. Enter a name for the Import file (.reg file) you will save, choose a location, and then click OK. If you want to export the entire Registry instead of just the selected branch (good for backing up the Registry), select the All option in the Export Registry File dialog box.

Trying a Sample Registry Hack

Windows Messenger starts automatically every time you start Windows XP, even if you don't use and have never configured the program. You can turn it off manually using the icon in the notification area, but you can also create a Registry edit that prevents it from loading at all.

TRY IT To edit the Registry so that Windows Messenger does not start with Windows XP, use the following steps:

1. Click Start | Run.
2. Enter **regedit** into the Open box and click OK.
3. Find and select the following subkey:
   HKEY_CURRENT_USER\Software\Microsoft\Windows\CurrentVersion\Run\MSMSGS.
4. Choose Edit | Delete.

Finding Other Good Registry Hacks

Registry edits are available all over the place—in books, Internet sites, and magazine articles. You should be careful about using edits that you find on less than reputable sites, however. While some may work, few have been thoroughly tested. Nonetheless, you can find reliable edits from a few Web sites, including these:

- **Microsoft TechNet**   TechNet's Knowledge Base contains literally thousands of technical articles on all versions of Windows. Many of the fixes and workarounds for common Windows problems on the site use Registry edits. Find the site at *http://www.microsoft.com/technet/*.

- **John Savill's Windows NT/2000 FAQ**   John Savill's site, in conjunction with *Windows* and *.NET* magazines, also has many Registry edits available. Find it at *http://ntfaq.com/*.

PART VII

Maintenance and Performance

CHAPTER 24

Managing Disks

TIPS IN THIS CHAPTER

Disk drives are among the most important resources on any computer. After all, there wouldn't be too much point to using a computer if you couldn't store what you created. Windows XP includes many advanced tools for managing and optimizing storage. This chapter examines disk partitions and file systems and then introduces you to several techniques used in Windows XP to manage disks.

Partitions

A partition is a logical section of a hard disk on which data may be written. Every hard disk must be partitioned before it can be used. Usually, a disk is set up as one big partition, but you may also divide a disk into several partitions. When you partition a disk, you decide how much disk space to allocate to each partition.

Some people create separate partitions so that they can install more than one operating system for use with the same computer. Others use multiple partitions simply as a way of organizing files. For example, you might use one partition to hold system and application files, another for documents you create for business, and still another for personal documents.

Partitions come in three forms:

- **Primary**   A primary partition can be set as the bootable partition. A computer running a Windows operating system can use up to four primary drives (three if you also use an extended partition), any one of which may be set as the active, or bootable, drive.

- **Extended**   An extended partition provides a way to get around the four primary partition limit. Extended partitions cannot be formatted and used, but they serve rather as a shell in which you can create logical partitions.

- **Logical**   Any number of logical partitions may be created inside an extended partition. Logical partitions may not be set as the active partition, and thus cannot be used to hold most operating systems. Instead, logical partitions are normally used for organizing files. All logical partitions are visible, no matter what operating system is booted.

File Systems

A *file system* is the system used to keep track of information stored on a partition. It tracks specifically where all the files and folders are stored on the disk and tracks the amount of free space on the disk. Windows XP supports three file systems:

- **File Allocation Table (FAT)**   FAT was first introduced in DOS. Partitions formatted using FAT are limited to 4GB and are readable by all versions of Windows. FAT is a relatively slow file system that does not do a very good job of handling the way files are stored on disk, resulting in a good bit of wasted disk space.

- **FAT32**   FAT32, a 32-bit version of FAT, was introduced with the second release of Windows 95. Partitions using FAT32 may be up to 2 terabytes in size and are recognized by all versions of Windows after Windows 95 (Service Release 2) and after Windows NT 4.0. Neither FAT nor FAT32 provides any intrinsic file-level security.
- **NT File System (NTFS)**   NTFS was introduced with Windows NT. Partitions using NTFS may be up to 2 terabytes and are recognized by all versions of Windows NT, Windows 2000, and Windows XP. NTFS provides such features as file-level security, compression, and encryption. NTFS also makes more efficient use of disk space than FAT or FAT32.

If you are using Windows XP as your only operating system on a computer, you should definitely format your partitions using NTFS. You should consider using FAT32 only if you are dual-booting with Windows 98 or Me, as those operating systems will not recognize partitions formatted with NTFS. While Windows XP can read partitions formatted using FAT, it cannot format partitions using this older file system. Note that any of the Windows operating systems can read shared information over a network regardless of the format; formatting limitations apply to operating systems installed on the same computer.

Drive Letters

Every partition and removable disk in Windows is assigned a drive letter. Assignments normally go as follows:

- A: is reserved for your first floppy drive.
- B: is reserved for a second floppy drive, even if you don't have one.
- C: is normally used for the primary partition on your first hard disk. Typically, this is the partition onto which Windows is installed.
- D: through Z: are used for other partitions, CD-ROM drives, other removable disks, and mapped network drives.

While Windows does not always assign drive letters in an order that makes the most sense to you, drive letters are easy enough to reassign. You'll learn how in the section "Changing Drive Letters," later in this chapter.

Creating and Deleting Partitions

Working with partitions and drive letters in Windows XP is accomplished with the Computer Management tool, which is available in the Administrative Tools folder in the Windows Control Panel. You use the Computer Management tool to access several different system tools and to manage the storage devices on your computer. To work with partitions, you must open the Storage container and select Disk Management. This view is shown in Figure 24-1.

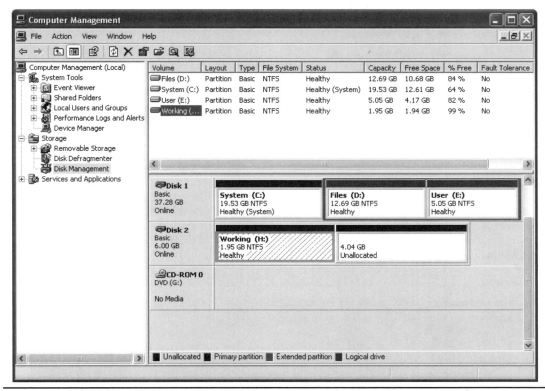

Figure 24-1   The Computer Management tool provides quick access to a number of system utilities.

The right pane displays current disk information. The top half shows all formatted partitions on your computer. The bottom half shows each disk drive on the computer (including removable disks) and the allotment of partitions on those disks. The computer represented in Figure 24-1 is set up as follows:

- Disk 1 is a 40GB drive (a couple of gigabytes are eaten up by disk formatting, so it has 37.28GB available) with three partitions. These partitions have the drive letters C:, D:, and E:. The C: partition is a primary partition, indicated in dark blue. D: and E: are logical partitions indicated in light blue and surrounded by a green frame that represents the extended partition that contains them.

- Disk 2 is a 6GB drive that has one 2GB partition and 4GB of unallocated space that may be partitioned.

TRY IT   To create a new partition in unallocated space, use the following steps:

1. Right-click the unallocated space (represented by a brown bar) and choose New Partition from the shortcut menu. This starts the New Partition Wizard. Click next to go past the Welcome page.

2. Choose whether you want to create a primary partition or an extended partition or a logical drive, and then click Next.

3. The Wizard presents minimum and maximum sizes for the new partition. Specify the size for the new partition and click Next.

4. Choose the drive letter for the new partition from the drop-down menu. Alternatively, you can mount the partition inside an empty NTFS folder so that folder actually becomes the new partition for users and applications. Windows addresses the partition by a path rather than by a drive letter. You can also choose not to assign a drive letter or path if you want to do so later. Click Next when you've made your choice.

▶ **QUICK TIP**

Mounting a partition in an NTFS folder provides several advantages: Mounted drives are not subject to the 26-drive limit, as are lettered drives. You could also establish disk quotas on the folder without establishing quotas for the entire drive containing the folder (since the folder would actually be a reference to the separate partition).

---

5. Choose whether or not you want to format the partition. If you format the partition, you can also specify the following information:

- **File System**   Choose NTFS or FAT32.

- **Allocation Unit Size**   The size of sectors used in the partition. Any individual file will consume this amount of space, even if the actual file is smaller than the specified size. For this reason, it is almost always better to leave this at the default or choose the lowest setting. The one advantage to choosing a larger size is that larger files can be written more quickly to disk, as an entire sector is written at once.

- **Volume Label**   The name of the drive as it appears in Windows Explorer.

- **Perform a Quick Format**   If a partition has already been formatted with this file system, you may be able to perform a quick format that rewrites the master file table and skips disk testing. It's usually best not to use this option.

- **Enable File and Folder Compression**   Allow compression to be used at the individual file and folder level.

6. Click Finish to create the new partition and begin formatting if you chose to format the disk. Note that while the partition is being formatted, you cannot perform other activities that involve the new partition, but you can continue to work with other partitions.

Formatting Partitions

Unformatted partitions are represented in the Disk Management window as a normal partition, but they are not labeled with a particular file system (You can see in Figure 24-1 that formatted partitions are all labeled NTFS.) You can format any partition, whether it is already formatted or not, from the Disk Management window. Note that all data on a partition is lost when it is formatted. To format a partition, right-click a partition and choose Format. A dialog box opens where you can specify the volume label, file system, allocation unit size, and other options. Choose your options and click OK to begin formatting. Windows warns you that all data on the drive will be overwritten.

Changing Drive Letters

Windows does its best to assign drive letters intelligently. Drives A: and B: are always reserved for floppy drives. After that, letters are normally assigned on a first-come, first-served basis with disk partitions given priority over removable storage. This can cause problems, however. Assume, for example, that you have a single disk partition with the drive letter C: and a CD-ROM with the drive letter D:. If you install a new disk or create a new partition, the new partition will likely be assigned the letter D: and the CD-ROM will be bumped up to E:.

This may sound logical, but there's a problem. Any applications you have installed using the CD-ROM drive may expect to find a CD on the old drive letter if you need to install new features or if the application requires the presence of the CD to run. Also, shortcuts to files on drives whose letters are reassigned may be rendered nonfunctional after a letter change.

Fortunately, you can reassign drive letters easily from the Disk Management window.

TRY IT   To reassign the drive letter for a drive or partition, use the following steps:

1. Right-click the partition you want to reassign. To reassign a drive, such as a CD-ROM drive, right-click the disk label. Choose Change Drive Letter and Paths from the shortcut menu.

2. In the dialog box that opens, click Change.

3. Choose a new drive letter from the drop-down list and click OK.

4. Click OK again to change the drive letter. Reassigning drive letters normally does not require you to restart Windows.

Converting a Partition from FAT32 to NTFS

Windows XP provides a way for you to convert a disk partition from FAT32 to NTFS. This is a one-way conversion; Windows XP has no built-in way to convert in the other direction. Conversion is done using the CONVERT command at the command prompt using the following syntax:

```
Convert volume /FS:NTFS [/V] [/CvtArea:filename] [/NoSecurity] [/X]
```

- *volume*   Refers to the drive letter or volume name of the partition to be converted. If you use a drive letter, be sure to include the colon after the letter (C:).

- **/FS:NTFS**   Specifies the conversion to NTFS.

- **/V**   Switches the conversion to verbose mode, where more detailed information is displayed during the process. This switch is optional.

- **/CvtArea:*filename***   Specifies a contiguous file in the root directory of the drive that will be used as a placeholder for the system files. This switch is optional.

- **/NoSecurity**   Configures security settings on all files and folders on the converted partition at the default level. This makes all files available to the Everyone group. This switch is optional.

- **/X**   Forces the volume to dismount if any files are currently opened. This switch is optional.

Running the Disk Cleanup Wizard

The Disk Cleanup Wizard scans your hard drive for unnecessary files (such as temporary files, Internet cache files, and old program files) and then deletes them. Disk Cleanup is a simple and effective way to help make sure that the free space on a hard drive is maximized.

> ### QUICK TIP
>
> *You can start the Disk Cleanup Wizard by clicking the Disk Cleanup button on the General tab of a drive's Properties page.*

 To run the Disk Cleanup Wizard, use the following steps:

1. Choose Start | All Programs | Accessories | System Tools, and then click Disk Cleanup.

2. On the Select Drive dialog box that opens, choose the drive you want Disk Cleanup to examine and then click OK.

3. After scanning the drive, Disk Cleanup shows you how much disk space it can free up by eliminating the most common forms of unneeded files. These include the following:

   - Downloaded Program Files, which are all files contained in the \Windows\Downloaded Program Files folder

- Temporary Internet Files, which are contained in the \Documents and Settings*username*\ Local Settings\Temporary Internet Files folder

- Temporary Offline Files, which are contained in a hidden folder on your Desktop

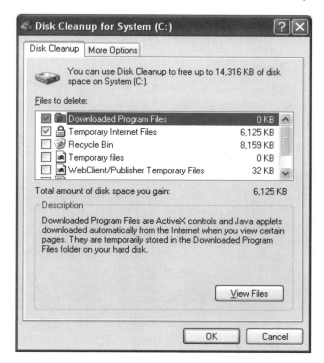

4. You can customize the kinds of files that will be removed by selecting or deselecting items from the Files to Delete list. Highlight any category of files and click the View Files button to see a list of the actual files that will be removed in a separate dialog box. From this dialog box, you can specify individual files to remove or keep. Click OK when you are done.

5. Disk Cleanup asks whether you are sure you want to perform the actions you have selected. Click Yes, and Disk Cleanup will begin deleting the selected files.

Compressing a Drive

Many of the tools for managing a drive or partition are available on the property pages accessible by right-clicking the drive in Windows Explorer and choosing Properties from the shortcut menu. Figure 24-2 shows an example of a drive's properties.

Assuming compression is turned on for an NTFS partition, you can compress any file or folder on a disk using that item's Properties dialog box (see Chapter 5 for more details). To compress the root

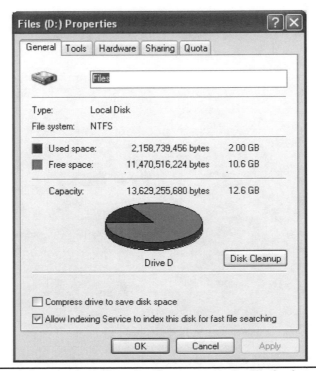

Figure 24-2   A drive's properties reveal much information and provide shortcuts to disk management tools.

folder of a drive, or to compress an entire drive at once, you must use the drive's Properties dialog box. On the General tab, select the Compress Drive to Save Disk Space option and click OK. Windows opens a dialog box asking whether you want to compress just the root folder or all subfolders and files on the drive as well. Make your selection and click OK.

Scanning a Disk for Errors

During the course of normal operation, files on a disk can become corrupted, blocks on a hard drive can become unusable, and file allocation tables can become inaccurate. To help repair all this, Windows XP includes a utility for checking drives for errors. This utility is available on the Tools tab of a drive's Properties dialog box. Click Check Now to open the Check Disk Files dialog box. Click Start to have Windows run a basic scan of the drive that looks for file and directory structure errors. You also have two advanced options:

- **Automatically Fix File System Errors**   Normally, Windows will stop scanning when it detects an error and ask you whether to fix it or not. Select this option to have Windows go ahead and do what it thinks best.

- **Scan for and Attempt Recovery of Bad Sectors**   Selecting this option makes the scan take much longer, as Windows performs an exhaustive examination of your hard drive. This option is a must if you suspect disk errors or if you just haven't performed a full scan in a while. Bad sectors on a disk can cause any number of strange problems, from crashing applications to corrupted documents to freezing Windows.

► **QUICK TIP**

You can also run an error check from the command line using the chkdsk *command, which offers you even finer control over the process. Type* **chkdsk /?** *at the command prompt for help on using this command.*

Defragmenting a Partition

When you delete a file on your computer, Windows doesn't really remove it—it just marks that space as available for new information to be written. When a new file is written to disk, part of the file might be written to one available section of disk space, part might be written to another, and part to yet another. This piecemeal writing of a file is called *fragmentation*. It is a normal process and Windows keeps track of files just fine. The problem is that when a drive has a lot of fragmentation, it can take Windows longer to find information. You can speed up drive access significantly by periodically defragmenting your drive.

Windows XP includes a utility called Disk Defragmenter that you can use to defragment a drive. You can access Disk Defragmenter through the Computer Management window (as shown in Figure 24-3), by clicking Defragment Now on the Tools tab of a drive's Properties dialog box, or by running Disk Defragmenter from the System Tools folder on the Start menu.

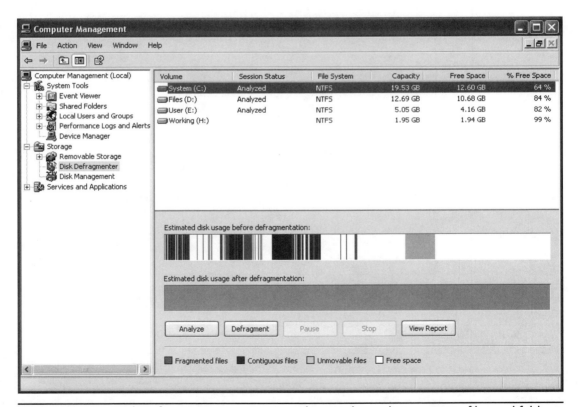

Figure 24-3   Use Disk Defragmenter to optimize a drive and speed up access to files and folders.

The top part of Disk Defragmenter shows all partitions available on your computer. The Session Status column indicates whether a partition has been analyzed for fragmentation. To analyze a partition, select it and click Analyze. When the analysis is done, Windows will let you know whether it thinks the partition should be defragmented. A graphical representation (just below the disk partitions) shows the estimated disk usage before defragmentation, indicating fragmented, contiguous, and unmovable files. A second graphical representation is added to show estimated disk usage after defragmenting a partition. Click View Report to see a detailed analysis of disk space and a list of many of the fragmented files on the disk.

To defragment a partition, click Defragment. You can pause or stop a defragmentation at any time and restart it later without damaging the data on your disk.

QUICK TIP

Running programs can affect the performance of or impede Disk Defragmenter. This applies especially to programs that access the disk in the background and that monitor disk access (such as virus checkers). Close all programs before defragmenting a disk.

CHAPTER 25

Backing Up and Restoring Windows

TIPS IN THIS CHAPTER

Computers fail, and people make mistakes—simple facts that make having a good backup plan essential, whether you are backing up only your own computer or a network of computers. Windows XP includes an update of a tool that has been around through several versions of Windows— a program named Backup. This chapter shows you some techniques involved in using this program and how to use some other backup methods.

Choosing Backup Hardware

Some of the previous versions of Backup allowed you to back up only to a supported tape drive. This changed with Windows 2000. In Windows 2000, and now in Windows XP, backups can be written to tape or created as a single file that can be stored on any drive accessible by Windows. This includes CD-R and CD-RW drives, ZIP drives, hard drives, floppy drives, a shared folder on a network, and even a folder on the Internet.

For the most part, backing up to all of these devices works the same way (although Backup does have some special features for working with tape drives): you select the drive as the place to store your backup file when you run the backup. Nonetheless, each type of device has its advantages and disadvantages. Here are a few tips for using different types of backup media:

- Backing up directly to a CD-R or CD-RW drive can be a bit slow. It is best to do this when you will not need to use your computer for a while. Alternatively, you could back up to a file on your hard disk and then copy that file to a CD later. The advantage of backing up to CDs is that they hold a lot of information and they have a long shelf life.

- Backing up to tape drives can also take a while (though modern tape drives are pretty fast). Unfortunately, you usually don't have the option of backing up to the hard disk and then transferring the file to tape later, the way you can with a CD. Try to schedule tape backups when you won't need your computer for a while.

- Tape is a *linear* medium, meaning that files are stored in a long string on the tape. To find a single file or a group of files can take a considerably longer time than with other backup media. If you need to be able to retrieve individual files quickly out of your backups, tape is not the ideal choice.

- If two identical tape drives are installed on your computer, Backup can recognize only the first drive. If, for some reason, you need two tape drives on your computer and need Backup to recognize both, you'll have to make sure the drives are different models.

- Versions of Windows previous to Windows 2000 supported Quarter Inch Cartridge (QIC) and other floppy interface-based tape drives. Starting with Windows 2000, this support was dropped. Integrated Development Environment (IDE), Small Computer System Interface (SCSI), parallel, and PC Memory Card International Association (PCMCIA) tape drives are still supported.

- Backing up to floppy disk is pretty much a bad idea, unless you're backing up a few very small files and you just don't have any other choice. Even then, it would be better just to copy the files to a floppy disk.

- If you have a small network, it's very inexpensive to build a computer that is used just for storing everyone's backups or to add a large hard drive to an existing computer. You just need a computer that's able to run Windows and has a hard drive big enough for the job.

Backing Up with Windows Backup

Unless you have never used a backup program, Windows Backup will seem pretty simple and familiar. Basically, you choose what files you want to back up, specify where to back them up, and maybe set a few advanced backup options along the way. A backup wizard walks you through the various choices, but it is really just as easy to do it manually—plus you get a little better control that way.

TRY IT To use the Backup utility, use the following steps:

1. The first time you start Backup (choose Start | System Tools), the Backup or Restore Wizard starts.

2. Unselect the Always Start in Wizard Mode option on the first page of the wizard and click the Advanced Mode link to do away with the wizard.

3. Click the Backup tab on the main screen of Windows Backup to get started. Figure 25-1 shows the Backup tab of Windows Backup.

4. Use the two Explorer-like panes to select the files you want to back up. Checking the box next to an item includes it in the backup. A folder with a gray check mark indicates that only some of the items in the folder are included. The System State option backs up the Windows Registry and a number of important configuration files.

5. Next, choose the destination for the backup. If a tape drive is available, you can choose whether to back up to tape or to a file. If no tape drive is available, File is your only option.

6. Use the Backup Media or File Name box to enter the exact location to save the backup file (or click the Browse button to find a location).

7. When you're ready, click Start Backup.

8. A Backup Job Information dialog box appears, where you can configure some additional settings and information. Enter a description to help identify the backup and choose whether to append the backup to existing media or overwrite existing media.

9. When saving a backup to a file, you can think of the file you create as the media. A single file can hold multiple backup jobs. You can also configure a number of advanced options or set up

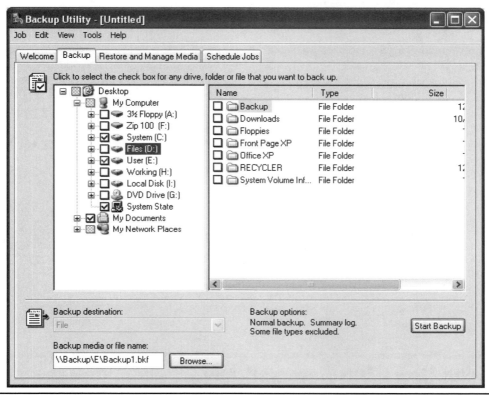

Figure 25-1   Use the Backup tab to set up a backup job.

a schedule for performing the job using a simple calendar-based scheduling tool. When you are done, click Start Backup. Windows will let you know when it's finished.

Backing Up over a Small Network

Setting up Windows Backup to back up over a small network is almost as easy as setting it up to back up a single computer. The first decision you need to make is in what direction to perform the backups. Assuming you are backing up to a shared network location, you can configure each computer on the network to run Windows Backup and store the backup file to the shared location. Or you could schedule the computer that hosts the shared location to run Windows Backup and simply pull files over the network for the backup.

Both methods have advantages and disadvantages. Overall, it is best if you can dedicate a computer that is not used much as the backup computer. Configure all the backup jobs on that computer to pull files over the network and back them up to a local drive. This provides a number of advantages:

- You don't have to go to each computer to set up or change the backup jobs or to view backup reports.

- Other computers do not have to spend time and resources running the backup software.

- Other computers do not need to be given permissions to access the shared backup location. Note that the backup computer operator may need to be given permissions on all the other computers, however.

- After all the backups are done, you can also configure the backup computer to back up to additional media, such as CD-R or tape.

Logging Users Out Automatically Before Scheduled Backups

After you have configured an automatic backup of a group of networked computers, you might run across an interesting dilemma. Windows Backup is not very good at backing up files that are in use, especially if some of the computers running those files do not run Windows XP or use NTFS (both of which the new Volume Shadow Copy technology in Windows XP Professional require). Even if you have scheduled backups to occur during nighttime hours and have instructed people to log out of Windows when they leave for the day, people often forget to do this, and important files can be left out of the backup as a result. Add to this the fact that, even when some applications are shut down, Windows often still thinks files are open. This can obviously ruin a backup procedure. Fortunately, a relatively easy fix to this problem is at hand.

 To create a shortcut and modify it always to run the program in a maximized window, use the following steps:

1. Open Notepad and type the following command: **rundll32.exe shell32.dll,SHExitWindowsEx 0**. This command forces a logoff sequence in Windows, abandoning all open programs (any saved documents are lost).

2. Save the file and name it **logoff.bat**. Sometimes, Notepad will append a *.txt* extension to the file. If it does, find the file in Explorer and remove the extra extension. A good way to prevent Notepad from appending the extension in the first place is to enclose the file name using quotation marks when naming the file; this forces the file name to be created exactly as you type it.

3. Copy the file to each computer that you need to log off.

4. On each computer, use the Scheduled Tasks tool to have the batch file run automatically just before the automated backups are scheduled to begin.

5. Once a user is logged off, Windows Backup should not encounter any files that are in use.

Restoring a Backup

Windows XP makes restoring files from a backup just as easy as backing them up in the first place. Before you get started with a restoration, though, you may need to take a few other actions—this depends on what you are restoring and why.

The first action you'll need to take is determining what you intend to restore. If you are going to restore a few files or a folder, you have a few choices: You can just restore them to their original location on your computer, or you can restore them to an alternative location (a new folder, for example), so that you can compare the restored files to any originals and decide what to keep. Finally, you can restore them to a different computer altogether. This option can be useful if you don't want to disturb your computer with a restore job, or if you want to move files to another computer using the Backup utility.

TRY IT   To restore your entire system (say, after a crash), use the following steps:

1. Fix whatever caused the computer to crash.

2. Reinstall the same version of Windows you were using before and use the same volume, hardware, and configuration options used on the previous system. This step is necessary because Windows XP will need to be installed before you can run the Backup utility.

3. Finally, restore the backup with System State information.

4. To perform a restore, open the Restore and Manage Media tab in Windows Backup, shown in Figure 25-2.

5. In the left pane, expand the media holding the backup you want, and check the box next to the items you want to back up.

6. From the Restore Files To drop-down list, choose whether you want to restore files to their original location, to an alternative location (using the same folder structure as the original location), or to a single folder (using no folder structure—all files are dumped to a single folder).

7. When you're ready, click Start Restore.

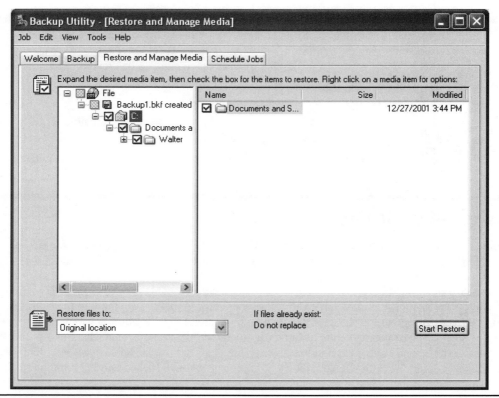

Figure 25-2   Windows Backup makes it easy to restore files.

Running Backup from the Command Line

You can also run Windows Backup from the command line, which allows you to run a backup as part of a batch file of script. You can find details for running Backup from the command line by typing **ntbackup /?** in any command prompt window or by using the Run dialog box.

Finding Important Backup Locations

The easiest kind of backup to configure is a full system backup—in which you back up your entire hard drive in one shot. This kind of backup takes the longest, but it ensures that you'll be able to return your system to pretty much the state it was in before a catastrophe.

Another option is to back up only your personal files—e-mail folders, favorite Web pages, documents, and so on. If your computer fails, you have to reinstall Windows, reinstall your programs, and then restore your personal files from backup.

Although reinstalling Windows and then restoring personal files takes more work than restoring a full system backup, people use this type of backup for a couple of reasons. The first is that some people just like reinstalling Windows once in a while because it provides a good chance to reconfigure and clean things out. The other reason is that backing up only your personal files takes considerably less space and less time when performing the backup. Many people can get away with backing up everything to a couple of 100MB ZIP disks or to a single CD, something you can't do so well when you are backing up gigabytes of Windows and application files.

If you choose to do a full system backup, you won't need to think about which files to back up, and so on. If you choose to back up only select files, it may be helpful to know where Windows XP keeps important files that need to be included in the backup. Table 25-1 details the common default file locations in Windows XP that you'll want to consider when backing up.

Location	Description
C:\Documents and Settings*username*\Application Data	Holds saved program files and information for many programs. Outlook Express e-mail and news folders are saved in this folder in a subfolder named Identities.
C:\Documents and Settings*username*\cookies	Holds small files saved by Internet Explorer that contain personal settings (username, password, etc.) for some Web sites.
C:\Documents and Settings*username*\Desktop	Holds all items placed on a user's Desktop.
C:\Documents and Settings*username*\Favorites	Holds all Web pages added to the Favorites menu in Internet Explorer.
C:\Documents and Settings*username*\Local Settings	Holds settings and files for many programs. For example, Outlook stores its personal folders (which hold locally stored e-mail, etc.) and settings in this folder by default.
C:\Documents and Settings*username*\My Documents	The default location that many programs (such as Microsoft Office) stores documents the user has created.
C:\Documents and Settings*username*\Start Menu	Holds customized shortcuts, etc.
C:\Inetpub	Holds the Web site and FTP site created by Internet Information Server.
C:\Program Files	Holds folders for each installed program on your computer. While many programs now store their settings and saved files in the Documents and Settings folder, many others (like games and some graphic editing programs) still save files in their own folders within the Program Files folder.
C:\Windows	While some programs may save settings in the Windows folder, most now use the Documents and Settings folder instead, making backups easier.
C:\Windows\Fonts	Holds all fonts installed on Windows. If you have installed fonts, you should back them up from this folder.

Table 25-1   Common File Locations in Windows XP

Location	Description
C:\Windows\Offline Web Pages	Holds offline Web pages synchronized using Synchronization Manager.
C:\Windows\Resources\Themes	May hold custom Desktop themes you have downloaded and installed.
C:\Windows\Security\Logs	Holds any security logs created on your computer.
C:\Windows\Tasks	Holds any tasks you have created using Task Scheduler.

Table 25-1   Common File Locations in Windows XP *(continued)*

Backing Up with XCOPY

The XCOPY command is a holdover from the early DOS days, but it is still quite a useful utility, especially when you need to create fairly simple automated backup routines. You can use XCOPY to copy all the files and subfolders in a folder to another location, including to a network share. XCOPY has a number of optional switches that allow you to do things like create new folders during the copy, specify whether to overwrite duplicate files, verify new files, and much more. Since it is a command, XCOPY can also be included as part of a script or batch file. For complete details on using XCOPY, type **xcopy /?** at the command prompt.

Backing Up with Send To

If your backup device is permanently available, such as a separate hard drive or a CD-R drive, you can use the Send To menu to create a quick and fairly efficient backup system. If you are using a CD-R drive, you'll find that a shortcut to your drive is already on your Send To menu. Whenever you send a file to your drive, the file is actually copied to a temporary folder. You can view the files waiting to be copied to CD by opening the My Computer window. When you are ready to copy the files, choose the Write These Files to CD command in the task pane of the My Computer window.

If you want to set up a separate location on the Send To menu (such as a hard drive or network location), create a shortcut to that location and copy the shortcut to the \Documents and Settings\ *username*\Send To folder or to the \Documents and Settings\All Users\Send To folder.

This method also works well if you are configuring backup for a small network and don't mind making users responsible for their own backups. Install a hard disk or create a partition on one computer large enough to hold all the files that users might back up, share the drive, and then create a shortcut to it on each user's Send To menu.

 NOTE

Keep in mind that using the Send To feature is just like copying a file in Windows Explorer. You must have permission to access the file, and the file must not be open by an application. For this reason, Send To is best when used as a simple way to back up user documents.

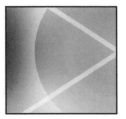

CHAPTER 26

Using Windows XP Troubleshooting Tools

TIPS IN THIS CHAPTER

Computers are complicated, so it should come as no surprise that there are all kinds of things that can go wrong with a computer running Windows XP. The computer itself is comprised of sometimes dozens of pieces of hardware, any of which can fail or conflict with other hardware or software. Windows files can become corrupted, system settings can be improperly configured, and applications can conflict with one another or with Windows.

Since there are so many potential points of failure, it is impossible for a single chapter in a book like this to go in depth on troubleshooting particular systems. Instead, this chapter presents some general troubleshooting techniques, such as how to isolate the cause of a problem and how to go about troubleshooting. It also presents tips on using many of the troubleshooting tools that come with Windows XP, some of which you may never have heard of.

Preventing Problems in the First Place

Obviously, it is best if you can avoid having any problems at all. While it's unlikely that you can prevent all problems, keeping your computer in good shape can help stop many common failures before they occur. Following are some tips for keeping your computer running smoothly:

- *Buy reliable hardware and software.* The old adage is true—you do get what you pay for. Buying cheap, off-brand hardware and software can lead to headaches. Quality-testing is not all it can be, products that claim to work with Windows XP often do not, and hardware drivers are usually sub par. When you can, buy recognized name brand products and check out what other users are saying about them.

- *Don't use beta or unsigned drivers.* It's tempting to download the newest beta drivers with all the great new features for a piece of hardware, but resist. Driver problems are one of the main causes of hardware failure and conflict. Also, use only signed drivers whenever possible.

- *Keep your disk clean.* Remove applications that are no longer being used and run the Disk Cleanup tool (discussed in Chapter 24) often. This not only helps to maximize your available free space (which helps prevent problems and improve performance), but can help clean out unused Registry entries.

- *Scan your disk for errors and defragment it often.* These tools, also discussed in Chapter 24, help identify and fix problems before they grow too big.

- *Keep Windows updated using the Windows Update site.* Covered in Chapter 2, Windows Update makes the latest patches and updates for Windows XP available online.

- *Back up your computer regularly.* When major problems do occur, you can still recover.

Isolating a Problem

Often, the most difficult part of solving a problem with Windows is figuring out exactly what the problem is. Sometimes what appears to be a problem with one thing (such as a particular application that keeps crashing) can turn out to be a problem with something else entirely (such as bad blocks on your hard drive). Ask yourself the following questions to help narrow the scope of your problem until you can identify the culprit:

- *Have you documented the error?* If you get an error message, write it down (or at least the pertinent information). Also write down what you were doing when the problem happened. If a problem is intermittent, you may not be able to isolate it until it has happened enough times that you can spot trends.

- *Have you tried just restarting the computer?* Often, turning your computer completely off and back on can clear out any gremlins that may be causing a problem. If you are lucky, the problem just won't happen again.

- *Did it ever work?* If the problem continues, and particularly if it is a problem with something not working, ask yourself if it ever worked. Did a particular program or document ever load correctly or did the hardware device ever work? If so, when was the last time you remember using it?

- *How isolated is the problem?* If a document won't open, will other documents open in the same program? Are other programs experiencing the same problem? If something won't print, will other documents print in the same program? Will other programs print? Asking yourself these questions can narrow the scope of the problem considerably.

- *Did you make any changes before you noticed the problem?* If you know something worked at one point and then stopped, the next step is to figure out anything you might have done to cause the problem. Did you make any configuration changes (not necessarily to the item itself, but any changes)? Have you installed any new hardware or software? If so, write down any changes that you remember so you can address them one by one.

- *Does anyone else use your computer?* If so, you need to ask them all of these questions as well.

- *Can you reproduce the problem reliably?* If you can cause the problem whenever you want by following the same steps, it's usually easier to identify the problem.

Testing Solutions to a Problem

Once you think you have isolated the cause of your problem, or at least narrowed it down to a few problems, it's time to list the possible fixes. Listing and testing potential fixes to a problem is also part of the troubleshooting process. After all, until the problem is fixed, you are still not certain whether you have correctly identified it. Write each fix down and use the following tips to test them:

- *Test fixes one at a time.* Never try to apply several fixes together and see if they work. Although it takes a bit longer, testing one fix at a time helps you more clearly identify the problem and will help you avoid it or fix it more easily in the future.

- *Start with the least invasive fixes.* This usually means fixes that you can undo easily, such as a simple configuration change. Reinstalling, removing, or updating items such as drivers or programs is more invasive because they are difficult actions to undo.

- *Try to undo a fix before you try another fix.* This goes along with testing fixes one at a time. If you try something and it doesn't work, undo it if possible. Otherwise, you run the risk of compounding the existing problem.

- *Document as you go.* Write down the fixes that don't work along with the fixes that do. You'll be surprised at how much you can learn about Windows along the way. Plus, it's frustrating to have a friend ask you for advice on fixing a problem and only being able to say, "You know, I fixed that same problem once, but I just can't remember what I did."

Using the Windows Troubleshooters

Windows XP includes a number of built-in troubleshooters that can help you identify the cause of common problems. A troubleshooter is available for most problem types, including Windows startup, hardware, networking, and many more. Each troubleshooter walks you through a series of questions aimed at narrowing down your problem and then suggesting a fix. Most of the problems and fixes included in the troubleshooters are fairly basic configuration changes, but they are an excellent place to start and can help you think about the problem in the right way even if they can't help you solve it directly.

> ### QUICK TIP
>
> *Troubleshooters are also good for something else. If you often have other people who come to you for help fixing problems, sending them off to run the troubleshooters first can help make sure that at least they've already tried all the easy stuff before you get involved.*

TRY IT To start one of the Windows troubleshooters, use the following steps:

1. Click Start and then click Help And Support.
2. Click the Fixing A Problem link.
3. Click the Troubleshooting Problems link at the left of the window.
4. From the list of Overviews, Articles, and Tutorials, click the List Of Troubleshooters link.
5. Click the link for the troubleshooter appropriate to your problem and follow the directions for the Troubleshooter Wizard.

Using the Microsoft TechNet Knowledge Base

One of the most valuable resources in troubleshooting Windows problems is available for free online—the Microsoft Knowledge Base, part of Microsoft Support. Go to *http://support.microsoft.com/* and click the link that takes you to the Knowledge Base. Enter the product you need help with and type in keywords for your problem. Try making your searches as specific as possible to start and then make them broader if you don't find what you are looking for. If you are getting a specific error message or have an event code from Event Viewer (see the next section), enter that information. The Knowledge Base has literally thousands of articles on fixing very specific problems with all Microsoft software, including Windows XP.

Using Event Viewer

As you may know, Windows records many events in logs. You can view the logs of both local and remote computers using the Event Viewer utility, shown in Figure 26-1. You'll find Event Viewer in the System Tools folder on the All Programs menu. You should use Event Viewer regularly to check up on the status of your computer.

Type	Date	Time	Source	Category	Ev
Information	1/14/2002	2:34:17 PM	Application Popup	None	26
Information	1/14/2002	2:34:17 PM	Application Popup	None	26
Information	1/14/2002	2:34:17 PM	Application Popup	None	26
Information	1/14/2002	2:34:17 PM	Application Popup	None	26
Error	1/14/2002	2:34:01 PM	acpi	None	4
Error	1/14/2002	2:34:01 PM	acpi	None	5
Information	1/14/2002	2:34:22 PM	eventlog	None	60l
Information	1/14/2002	2:34:22 PM	eventlog	None	60l
Information	1/14/2002	2:33:00 PM	eventlog	None	60l
Error	1/14/2002	2:32:57 PM	disk	None	11
Error	1/14/2002	2:32:57 PM	hpt3xx	None	15
Error	1/14/2002	2:32:37 PM	disk	None	11
Error	1/14/2002	2:32:37 PM	hpt3xx	None	15
Error	1/14/2002	2:32:17 PM	disk	None	11
Error	1/14/2002	2:32:17 PM	hpt3xx	None	15
Error	1/14/2002	2:31:57 PM	disk	None	11
Error	1/14/2002	2:31:57 PM	hpt3xx	None	15
Error	1/14/2002	2:31:37 PM	disk	None	11
Error	1/14/2002	2:31:37 PM	hpt3xx	None	15
Error	1/14/2002	2:31:17 PM	disk	None	11

Figure 26-1 Event Viewer displays logs of events recorded by Windows and other applications.

Windows XP maintains three distinct logs:

- The Application log is a record of events generated by applications. All Windows services write their status information to this log. This is the most valuable log for monitoring the general health of a computer.

- The Security log is a record of events based on any auditing settings you have configured.

- The System log is a record of events that concern components of the system itself, including such events as device driver and network failures. This is the most valuable log for finding information on specific errors.

You will encounter three types of events in the Application and System logs, and a unique icon identifies each event type so you can easily distinguish between the information entries and the error entries. These event types include errors (a stop sign icon), warnings (an exclamation point), and information (a lowercase *i*).

Double-click any event to open it and view detailed information, such as when the event occurred, an event ID, a description of the event, and suggestions for fixing any problems.

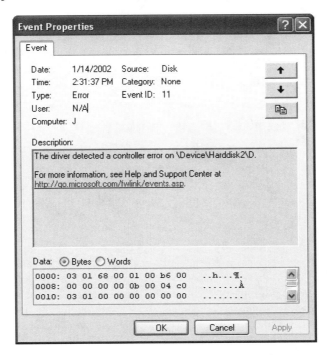

Using System File Checker

Windows XP can usually detect when a system file is missing and replace it for you without any intervention (or even knowledge of the fact) on your part. You can test this by going into your Windows directory and simply deleting (or, safer, renaming) a Windows file. For example, go to your \Windows folder and rename the file taskman.exe (the executable for Task Manager) to taskman.test. Refresh the window and you'll see that Windows almost instantly re-creates the taskman.exe file for you.

Even with this ability, system files can become corrupted or the wrong versions of system files can be installed by errant applications, and these types of problems often slip by Windows unnoticed. Windows includes a command-line utility named System File Checker that scans several thousand basic Windows files, comparing them against the original versions that shipped with Windows. If it finds a mismatch, it replaces the original file.

To run the tool, just type **SFC** at the command prompt followed by any of the following common options:

- **/scannow**   Performs an immediate scan of your system.

- **/scanonce**   Performs a scan the next time your system boots up.

- **/scanboot**   Performs a scan every time your system boots up.

- **Revert**   Returns the System File Checker to its default settings. Use this to turn off the /scanboot option, for example.

Using Windows XP Startup Modes

There is a very useful menu lurking behind the scenes of the Windows startup process. If you have a problem booting Windows XP, the Advanced Options menu can be a lifesaver. You can display it by pressing the F8 key once just after the hardware startup routine (hard drive detection and so on) finishes to display the boot menu and then press F8 again to get to the Advanced Options menu.

There are number of alternative boot options you can use to the normal boot process, including:

- **Safe Mode**   This mode loads only the basic files and drivers needed to get Windows running and allow access to your disks. It is designed for when you configure something in Windows (such as installing a new driver) that causes Windows not to start properly. You can boot into Safe Mode, restore the original settings or make other changes, and then hopefully restart Windows in normal mode again. You can also boot a safe mode with networking enabled and a safe mode that does not load the Windows GUI, but leaves you at the command prompt instead.

- **Enable Boot Logging**   This option causes Windows XP to start normally, but create a log file that displays all the drivers loaded when Windows starts. This log file is found at \Windows\ntbtlog.txt.

- **Enable VGA Mode**   This option starts Windows XP normally, but uses a standard VGA driver. This is particularly useful if you have installed a video adapter driver that doesn't display correctly. This driver is also used when starting Windows XP in Safe Mode.

- **Last Known Good Configuration** This option starts Windows XP using the hardware configuration that was saved the last time Windows XP successfully shut down. If you have installed a new device and driver only to find out that Windows can no longer start, you can shut down your computer, remove the device, and then restart using the last known good configuration.
- **Debugging Mode** This option starts Windows normally, but sends debugging information to another computer through a serial cable. This option is primarily useful when developing software for Windows XP.

Using the System Information Tool

The System Information tool displays detailed information about all aspects of your system, including hardware resources, driver and application details, Internet settings, and more (see Figure 26-2). You can open it by going to All Programs I Accessories I System Tools on the Start menu and clicking System Information.

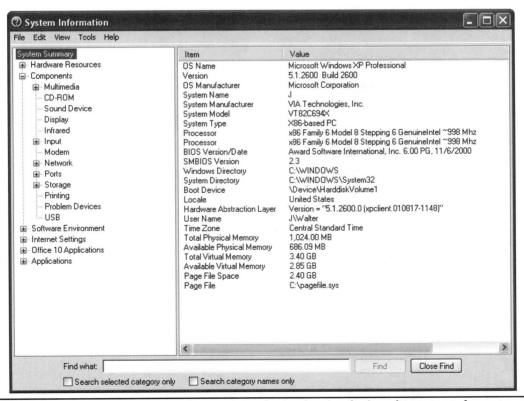

Figure 26-2 You can use System Information to display hard to find configuration information.

Use the System Summary tree in the left pane to select information to view. The details are shown in the right pane. Note that you cannot change information using System Information; the tool is for display purposes only. Tools on the System Information menus also let you print a report, export system information to a text file, or connect to a remote computer on a network to view its system information.

Using Dr. Watson

Dr. Watson is a tool that waits in the background and takes a snapshot of your system's state whenever it detects a program or system crash. The information it captures includes memory usage, tasks that were active, and any system modules loaded at the time of the crash. While much of the information in a Dr. Watson log file is very technical and won't be of much use to anyone but Microsoft Technical Support, there is some information that may be of use to you.

You don't need to do anything to have Dr. Watson monitor your system; it is always watching. Start the Dr. Watson utility by typing drwtsn32 in the Run dialog box or command prompt. The main Dr. Watson window shows a number of advanced options you can set for controlling the monitoring of crashes. Right-click any option and choose the What's This command to see more information about it.

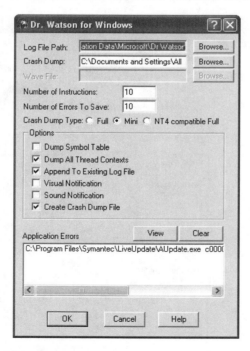

A list of recent crashes is shown in the window at the bottom. Select an event and click View to open the log file for that event. You can view a snapshot of system information at the time of the crash and view all the tasks that were open. This can often help you determine whether a particular piece of hardware or software is causing a problem you may be having.

Restoring to a Previous State with System Restore

It is almost always a specific change that causes problems in Windows—installing a new application, adding new hardware, installing an update, or making a configuration change. Windows includes a handy program named System Restore that runs in the background and monitors changes to your system. System Restore takes snapshots of your system configuration and saves backups of pertinent files (such as the Registry and Windows system files). You can use System Restore to return to any saved configuration, essentially wiping out any configuration changes you have made since then.

By default, System Restore creates a system checkpoint snapshot once per day and also creates a snapshot when it detects that you are about to install a new application or hardware driver. Because System Restore is not always perfect in detecting these activities, you can also manually create a snapshot whenever you want.

When you restore a particular snapshot, the backed-up files are copied back to their original locations, returning your computer pretty much to its original state. There are, of course, a few caveats:

- System Restore does not remove application files. If you install an application and find it causes a problem, use System Restore to return your system to its previous state. This wipes all references to the application from the Registry and restores any system files overwritten during the application's installation. However, it does not remove application files. For this reason, you should either uninstall the program before using System Restore or delete the program files manually afterward.

- System Restore cannot resurrect missing documents. If you delete a document by mistake or a file becomes corrupted, System Restore cannot bring it back.

- If you need to undo a hardware addition, remove the hardware from your system first and uninstall any software that may have been installed. Then use System Restore to return your system to its previous state.

- Returning a system to a previous state undoes all changes made to the system back to that point in time. If you have installed three applications and then discover that it is the first application causing problems, returning the system to its state prior to the installation will wipe out changes made by all three installations. You will have to reinstall the other two applications.

- Since System Restore does not always detect installations, always create a manual restore point before any new system change.

▶ | *QUICK TIP*

You can change System Restore's automatic monitoring of your system by right-clicking My Computer and choosing Properties. In the Properties dialog box, choose the System Restore tab. You can turn off System Restore for all drives or for any individual drive. You can also configure the amount of disk space System Restore is allowed to use on a drive. Even if you turn System Restore off, you can still create manual restore points.

TRY IT To manually add a System Restore restore point, use the following steps:

1. Click Start, then select All Programs I Accessories I System Tools I System Restore.
2. On the opening page of the System Restore Wizard, select Create A Restore Point and click Next.
3. Enter a description for the restore point that describes the change you are about to make to your system and click Create.
4. System Restore displays information about the restore point. Click Close.

TRY IT To return your system to a previous restore point, use the following steps:

1. Click Start, then select All Programs I Accessories I System Tools I System Restore.
2. On the opening page of the System Restore Wizard, select Restore My Computer To An Earlier Time and click Next.
3. On the calendar, click the date that contains the restore point to which you want to return (see Figure 26-3). You may have to look around a bit to find the right one. When you find the right date, click the restore point you want and click Next.

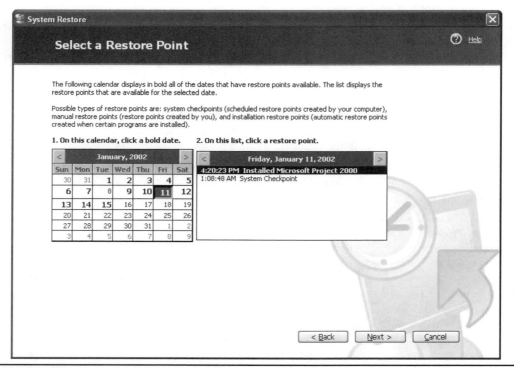

Figure 26-3 Use the calendar in the System Restore Wizard to locate a desired restore point.

4. System Restore displays information about the restore point. Click Next to begin the restore process. You may be prompted to restart Windows when the restoration is complete.

▶ **QUICK TIP**

If you perform a restoration and it does not solve your problem, you can undo the restoration. Start System Restore again and choose Undo My Last Restoration on the opening page of the wizard. You should do this before making any other changes to your system, as those changes will be lost when you undo the restoration.

CHAPTER 27

Monitoring and Improving Performance

TIPS IN THIS CHAPTER

Windows XP is one of the best performing versions of Windows, outperforming Windows Me and Windows 2000 on similarly configured computers. Windows starts faster and resumes from standby and hibernation more quickly. In addition, applications start faster, and disk and video handling is better than ever before. When Windows XP is first installed, it should be pretty well configured for optimum performance. Over time, however, clutter can build up and performance can begin to suffer.

This chapter shows you a number of ways that you can improve the performance of various aspects of Windows. It also introduces you to some of the tools used to monitor Windows and hardware performance.

Optimizing Windows Startup

When Windows XP is first installed, it starts to monitor your system's behavior and optimizes system settings to speed up subsequent boots. Similarly, Windows optimizes program files and memory uses so that they launch more quickly as you use them. It is important to recognize that this optimization is taking place and allow a sufficient number of reboots and launches to train the system before deciding whether you need to optimize the performance of your system.

Windows startup is fairly complicated, and there are a number of ways that you can optimize that process for a quicker startup time. These include:

- Check the BIOS settings for your computer to see whether there are unnecessary actions you can eliminate from the startup process. For example, on many computers, you can skip the memory check that occurs when you turn on your computer—something that can take quite some time when you have a lot of memory.

- If you have your system configured for dual-booting, you can reduce the amount of time Windows displays a menu of operating system choices at startup. Configure this setting by opening the System Control Panel, switching to the Advanced tab, and clicking the Settings button in the Startup and Recovery section.

- Remove any unnecessary applications that start automatically with Windows. This is covered in the next section of this chapter.

- When you remove a hardware device from your computer, make sure that any drivers and software installed with the device are also removed.

Stop Unnecessary Background Applications

Many applications install bits and pieces that run in the background as you use Windows. Normally, these are useful pieces of the application, such as the monitor that lets your anti-virus software check files for viruses as they are downloaded. Often, these are programs that you could easily live without.

When this is the case, it is best to prevent them from loading with Windows so that they do not consume valuable resources.

You can sometimes tell what background programs are running because they are represented by icons in the notification area, but this is not always the case. Even if there is an icon present, turning the program off usually requires different steps depending on the program.

To prevent unnecessary background applications from running, try the following:

- If there is an icon in the notification area, try right-clicking or clicking it to see if you get a shortcut menu. Often there is a command for setting preferences that you can use to figure out how to prevent the program from loading when Windows starts.

- If there is no menu for the icon, try checking the Startup folder on your Start menu. Often programs place shortcuts here to load components with Windows. You can also try running the program associated with the icon and seeing if there are instructions for preventing the program from loading.

- You should also check the Startup folder for applications that load, but do not place an icon in the notification area.

If all else fails, Windows includes a program named the System Configuration Utility that you can use to fine tune Windows startup. Run the program by typing **msconfig** at the Run dialog box or command prompt. The System Configuration Utility contains a number of tabs that you can use to configure different aspect of the startup process. These tabs include:

- **General**   Use this tab to select a type of startup to use the next time Windows boots. A diagnostic startup is the same thing as starting in Safe Mode. A selective startup lets you choose what types of components should be loaded (represented by the other tabs on the utility).

- **SYSTEM.INI, WIN.INI, BOOT.INI**   These tabs represent system files that Windows XP uses primarily for compatibility with previous versions of Windows. In earlier versions, these files were used instead of a centralized system Registry. Turning items on and off using these tabs is generally safer than editing these files directly, should you ever need to do so.

- **Services**   This tab presents a list of services that load with Windows. While you can use this tab to prevent services from loading, it is much safer (and just as easy) to use the Services element of the Computer Management utility.

- **Startup**   This is probably the most important tab used in optimizing Windows startup. It presents a list of all program components that load with Windows, whether they are represented in the notification area or not. Turn off the programs you do not want to load and restart Windows. You can return and reselect the applications whenever you want.

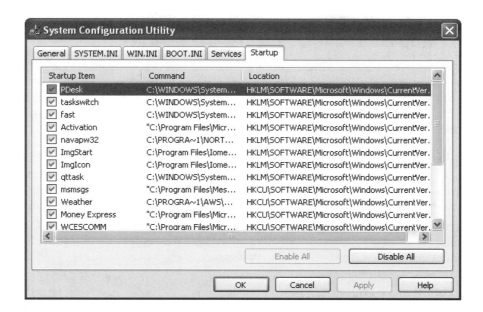

▶ *NOTE*

You must be logged on with an account of the Computer Administrator type in order to use the System Configuration Utility.

Keep Your Hard Disk in Top Shape

Many of the functions in Windows rely on having enough disk space free to operate, including Windows' virtual memory system and programs that need to create temporary files, to name just two of the most important. Add to this that just about every function in Windows relies on speedy hard disk access, and you can see why keeping your hard disk optimized is important. Windows includes a number of utilities that can help you with this job, including:

- **Disk Cleanup Wizard**   This application scans your hard disk looking for files that can be safely removed, helping you to free up disk space.
- **Disk Defragmenter**   This program rearranges the data on your hard drive so that files are written to disk contiguously. During the defragmentation, it also places more frequently used files toward the front of the disk so that they load faster.
- **Chkdsk**   This utility scans the files and directory structure of your disk to make sure they are free of errors.

You can learn more about using all these utilities in Chapter 24.

Keep Windows from Using Up Disk Space

Many of Windows XP's features require a certain amount of disk space to perform their functions. For example, Internet Explorer claims a percentage of disk space for storing temporary Web files so that they don't have to be downloaded every time you visit a Web page. Put together, the space these features use can be considerable. Fortunately, you can tame these programs' disk use fairly easily. Some of these programs include:

- **Recycle Bin**   By default, the Recycle Bin can use up to 10 percent of your disk space to store deleted files. More space provides a better safety net against accidentally deleted files, but 10 percent is a bit excessive given the size of modern hard drives. Right-click the Recycle Bin and use the slider to bring this value down.

- **Internet Explorer**   Internet Explorer also uses up to about 10 percent of your disk space. If you'd rather it use less, select the Internet Options from the Tools menu of Internet Explorer. Click Settings and use the slider to set the amount of space that can be used.

- **System Restore**   System Restore (covered in detail in Chapter 26) creates automatic restore points by backing up vital system files at regular intervals and before new software and hardware is installed. These restore points take up space. You can turn off System Restore, control the disk space used, and delete old restore points by opening the System Control Panel dialog box, switching to the System Restore tab, and using the settings found there.

Remove Unnecessary Services

Another type of program that loads during Windows startup is a service. A service is usually a small piece of code that provides support to Windows or another application and services work closer to the hardware level than the other types of programs that start with Windows. For this reason, you need to be a little more careful working with them than with other programs. Many provide functions vital to Windows. That said, it is fairly easy to control the services that load during Windows startup.

   To view and control the installed services on your system, use the following steps:

1. Click Start and then click Control Panel.
2. Double-click the Administrative Tools icon.
3. Double-click the Services icon. This opens the Services dialog box (Figure 27-1), which shows all the local services on your computer, along with their status (whether they are started or not) and their startup type (automatic or manual).
4. Select a service to display a description that not only tells you what the service is for, but usually what will happen if the service is disabled, as well.

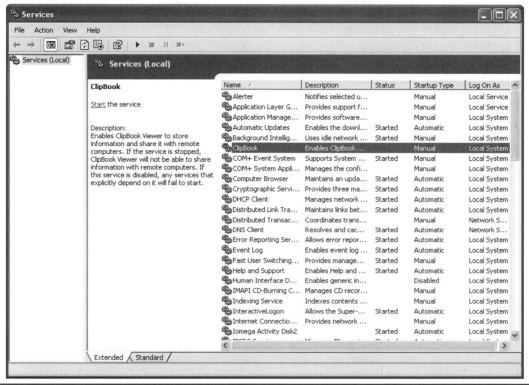

Figure 27-1   The Services dialog box provides a good description of any selected service.

5. Use the VCR-like controls on the toolbar or the commands on the action menu to control the service. Commands include starting, stopping, pausing, and restarting (which stops and then starts) the service.

6. Right-click a service to open its Properties. From the Properties dialog box, you can configure whether the service starts automatically with Windows or not, as well as a host of other options.

Turn Off Fast User Switching

Windows XP's fast user switching feature lets you switch between different user accounts without logging off. Each user can even have their own applications running while another user uses the computer. While this feature presents obvious advantages, it also comes with an equally obvious disadvantage. The more applications your computer is running at the same time, the slower it will perform, whether those applications are run by one or multiple users. If you frequently have problems with other users leaving applications running and if this tends to slow you down, try turning off the fast user switching feature. This actually requires one user to quit all applications and log off before another user can access their account, but the performance improvement may be worth the tradeoff.

 To disable fast user switching, use the following steps:

1. Click Start and then click Control Panel.
2. In the Control Panel window, double-click User Accounts.
3. Click the Change the way users log on or off link.
4. Disable the Use Fast User Switching option and click Apply Options.

Remove Unnecessary Network Protocols

If you installed Windows XP from scratch or bought a new computer with Windows XP preinstalled, only the TCP/IP networking protocol is likely to be installed on your computer. This is fine, as it is the protocol used on the Internet and on most modern local networks. If you upgraded to Windows XP from a previous version of Windows, it is possible that you will have additional networking protocols installed, such as NetBEUI or NWLink (sometimes called IPX/SPX). If these protocols are not used on your network, or if you don't have a network, these extra protocols can slow your system down.

 To remove unnecessary network protocols, use the following steps:

1. Click Start and then click Control Panel.
2. Double-click Network Connections.
3. Right-click a network connection and choose Properties from the shortcut menu.
4. Select the protocol that you want to remove (they are normally labeled as protocols and have an icon that looks like a network cable) and click Uninstall.
5. Once you have removed the protocols, click OK.

Managing Paging Files

Like most modern operating systems, Windows XP uses virtual memory. Virtual memory is created by extending the physical memory assigned to an application to the computer's hard drive. Windows may assign some memory to an application, but not necessarily enough to satisfy all that application's needs. Instead, access is monitored by Windows, which continuously reorganizes the memory structure to meet applications' needs. By correctly anticipating applications' needs and sending pages of memory off to disk as necessary, this process allows a computer to operate with far less physical memory.

When Windows stores memory to hard disk, it uses a special file called a paging file. You can configure some aspects relating to how Windows uses the paging file using the Virtual Memory dialog box. Open it by switching to the Advanced tab of the System Control Panel applet, clicking Settings in the Performance section, switching to the Advanced tab of the Performance Options dialog box that opens, and clicking Change.

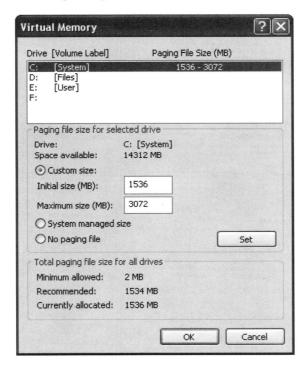

The Virtual Memory dialog box shows the size of the paging file for each disk on your computer and the total paging file size for all drives combined. The files on all disks are combined and treated as a single area for paging memory to disk. Breaking the file up across multiple disks (especially disks on different disk controllers) can decrease the time it takes to write memory information to the paging file. Note, however, that breaking up a file across multiple partitions on the same disk can actually decrease the performance of the paging file.

For the most part, Windows does a good job of managing the size of the file itself. Unless you have a good reason for changing it, you should probably just leave it alone. However, if possible, you want to avoid having your paging file on the same disk as your system files. If you want to change the size of the file, first select the drive and then choose the Custom size option. Enter an initial size, which is the minimum size that the page file cannot shrink below, and a maximum size. When you're done, click Set.

Setting Advanced Performance Options

The Advanced tab of the Performance Options dialog box (open it using the Advanced tab of the System Properties dialog box) also contains two other performance options for configuring your computer to run under special circumstances. These options are:

- **Processor Scheduling**   Use of the processor is normally optimized for running programs. You can set this option to be optimized for running background services. This option is best if the computer you are configuring is acting mainly as a file, print, or Web server.

- **Memory Usage**   Memory is also optimized for running programs by default. If the computer you are configuring is running mainly services instead, select the System cache option.

Minimizing Visual Effects

Many of the new visual effects in Windows XP can slow the perceived performance of your computer by making dialog boxes, windows, and menus take longer to open and work with. Windows tries to match the visual effects used to the capabilities of your computer, but it doesn't always choose the best settings for you. In practice, while many of the effects look nice, there are few that you can't live without, and turning them off can give you a nice performance boost.

You could poke around the various dialog boxes in Windows looking for all these settings, but the designers of Windows were kind enough to provide access to all of the visual effects in a single location just so that users could tweak performance. Open the System Control Panel applet, switch to the Advanced tab, and click the Settings button in the Performance section.

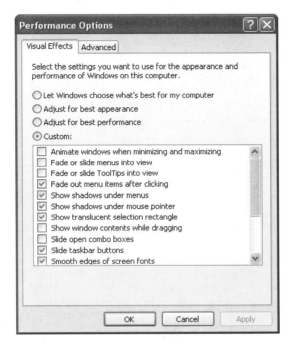

You can choose from four options:

- Let Windows manage the visual effects based on your system resources.
- Adjust the effects for best appearance, which actually just selects all the effects.
- Adjust the effects for best performance, which disables all the effects.
- Manage your own effects using the Custom option.

Table 27-1 lists the visual effects along with descriptions of those that are not self-explanatory.

Monitoring Performance with Task Manager

Task Manager provides information about applications and processes currently running on your system, and real time (though somewhat limited) system and networking performance levels. You can start Task Manager by right-clicking the Windows Taskbar and clicking Task Manager or by pressing CTRL-ALT-DEL. Two tabs of the Windows Task Manager dialog box are used in measuring performance: Performance and Networking.

Visual Effect	Description
Animate windows when minimizing and maximizing	Causes a zoom effect when you minimize or maximize a window.
Fade or slide menus into view	This setting not only uses up some resources, but makes you wait a bit longer to access menu items.
Fade or slide ToolTips into view	ToolTips are the pop-up descriptions that appear beside certain items when you hold your pointer over them.
Fade out menu items after clicking	
Show shadows under menus	
Show shadows under mouse pointer	
Show translucent selection rectangle	Draws a filled-in rectangle when selecting multiple items on the Desktop instead of just a rectangle outline.
Show window contents while dragging	This setting really hogs the resources, because Windows must redraw the window multiple times while it is being moved.
Slide open combo boxes	A combo box is a drop-down list of items that you open from within a dialog box.
Slide Taskbar buttons	This causes Taskbar buttons to slide to the left when other programs are closed or to the right when new programs are opened.
Smooth edges of screen fonts	This setting does consume some resources, but is probably one of the more useful visual effects, making screen fonts easier to read, especially at higher resolutions.
Smooth-scroll list boxes	This causes the contents of a list box to scroll smoothly when you click the scroll bar rather than just jump down a few items in the list.
Use a background image for each folder type	Different types of folders in Windows XP can use different background images. Many of the special Windows folders, such as Control Panel, make use of this effect.
Use common tasks in folders	This setting causes folders in Windows to show the list of available tasks related to the files in the folder to the left of the actual file list.
Use drop shadows for icon labels on the Desktop	This setting creates a transparency effect on text labels for icons, but this transparency really only allows you to see any other icons obscured by an icon on top. The transparency does not allow you to "see through" the Web layer of the Desktop.
Use visual styles on windows and buttons	This setting is an important one in that it controls the new look of Windows XP. If you disable it, your Desktop will look like the old Windows 2000 Desktop.

Table 27-1   Visual Effects in Windows XP that Can Affect Performance

The Performance tab has four gauges indicating various aspects of system performance:

- **CPU Usage**   Indicates the percentage of processor cycles that are not idle at the moment. If this graph displays a high percentage continuously (and not when there is an obvious reason, such as a big application), your processor may be overloaded. If your computer has two processors, two graphs are shown.

- **PF Usage**   This is the percentage of the paging file that is currently being used. If this value runs near 100% continuously, you may need to increase the size of the paging file or decide whether you need more memory.

- **CPU Usage History**   This graph shows how busy the processor has been recently, although it only shows values since Task Manager was opened. You can use the Update Speed command on the View menu to specify how often the values are refreshed. The High value updates about twice per second, Normal once every two seconds, Low once every four seconds. You can also pause the updates and update the view manually by pressing F5. This is a useful method if you want to monitor some specific activity.

- **Page File Usage History**   This graph shows how full the page file has been over time, although it also only shows values since Task Manager was opened. Values set using the Update Speed command affect this history as well.

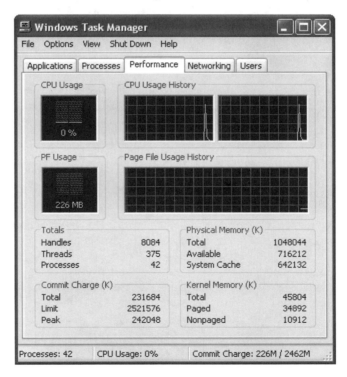

The Networking tab indicates the current network traffic over various network connections on your computer. If you do not have any networking connections configured, this tab is not shown. If you have more than one connection, a separate line is shown on the graph for each connection.

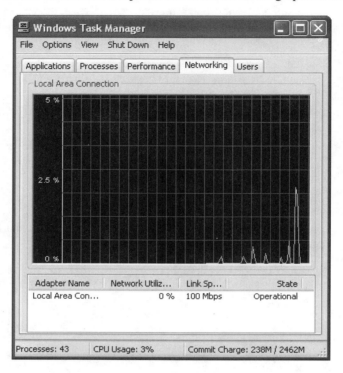

Monitoring Performance with System Monitor

While Task Manager is good for getting a quick overview of the current performance of your system, another tool, named System Monitor, provides much more sophisticated performance monitoring. System Monitor is used to measure the statistical data generated by various components of your computer. System Monitor breaks down that data into three distinct pieces:

- An *object* represents a major system resource that is either physical or logical in nature. Examples of physical objects are physical disks, processors, and memory. An example of a logical object is TCP, which represents one of the major networking protocols of the TCP/IP suite.

- A separate *instance* of an object exists for every component of the type the object represents on your computer. For example, if you have three hard disks attached to your computer, there would be three instances of the physical disk object.

- Each instance of an object is further broken down into *counters,* which are the actual aspects of the object that can be measured. For example, the physical disk object includes a number of counters such as %Disk Time, %Idle Time, and Average Disk Bytes per Read.

Start System Monitor by opening the Administrative Tools folder in the Windows Control Panel and double-clicking Performance.

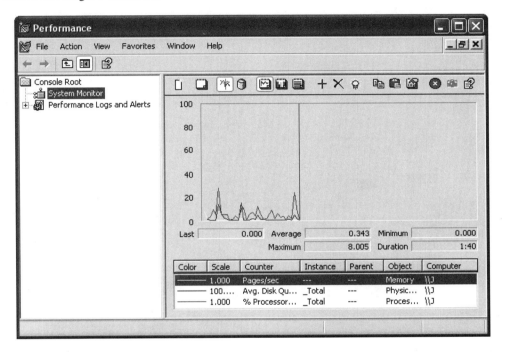

Three performance counters are added to the Performance graph by default when you first open System Monitor:

- **Pages/sec**   This represents the rate at which pages are read from or written to disk during virtual memory operations. Consistently high values can indicate that not enough memory is present on a system.

- **Avg. Disk Queue Length**   This represents the average number of read and write requests queued for the selected disk. Consistent values above zero means requests are backing up, which may indicate not enough memory or a slow disk system.

- **%Processor Time**   This represents the percentage of elapsed time that the processor spends executing nonidle tasks. Consistently high values (over 80%) may indicate that your processor is slowing down your system.

These counters give a good overall indication of your computer's performance, and you can monitor them over time by leaving the System Monitor running in the background. If you want to measure other aspects of your system performance, check out the System Monitor help files. They actually do a pretty good job of explaining System Monitor use and describing many of the available counters.

Index

INTERNATIONAL CONTACT INFORMATION

AUSTRALIA
McGraw-Hill Book Company Australia Pty. Ltd.
TEL +61-2-9417-9899
FAX +61-2-9417-5687
http://www.mcgraw-hill.com.au
books-it_sydney@mcgraw-hill.com

CANADA
McGraw-Hill Ryerson Ltd.
TEL +905-430-5000
FAX +905-430-5020
http://www.mcgrawhill.ca

**GREECE, MIDDLE EAST,
NORTHERN AFRICA**
McGraw-Hill Hellas
TEL +30-1-656-0990-3-4
FAX +30-1-654-5525

MEXICO (Also serving Latin America)
McGraw-Hill Interamericana Editores S.A. de C.V.
TEL +525-117-1583
FAX +525-117-1589
http://www.mcgraw-hill.com.mx
fernando_castellanos@mcgraw-hill.com

SINGAPORE (Serving Asia)
McGraw-Hill Book Company
TEL +65-863-1580
FAX +65-862-3354
http://www.mcgraw-hill.com.sg
mghasia@mcgraw-hill.com

SOUTH AFRICA
McGraw-Hill South Africa
TEL +27-11-622-7512
FAX +27-11-622-9045
robyn_swanepoel@mcgraw-hill.com

**UNITED KINGDOM & EUROPE
(Excluding Southern Europe)**
McGraw-Hill Education Europe
TEL +44-1-628-502500
FAX +44-1-628-770224
http://www.mcgraw-hill.co.uk
computing_neurope@mcgraw-hill.com

ALL OTHER INQUIRIES Contact:
Osborne/McGraw-Hill
TEL +1-510-549-6600
FAX +1-510-883-7600
http://www.osborne.com
omg_international@mcgraw-hill.com